P9-DXR-478

Table of Contents

Prelude

Like most preludes, this one serves as an introduction. It precedes an extensive compilation of strategies, views, and tips on innovation, gathered from interviews with over 45 senior leaders, authors, consultants, specialists, and educators. A prelude can also be an introductory piece of music that comes before a more significant work. So why reference music in a work about innovation? Musical metaphors can aptly illustrate how successful innovators initiate and sustain innovation.

For example, symphony orchestra leaders achieve mastery, by building on traditions and past successes. Jazz musicians produce new music or taking existing music in new directions. And some musicians skillfully blend classical and contemporary music by both "orchestrating" and "improvising." Although we might associate innovation with musicians, visual artists, and brilliant inventors, it's useful to see how it can happen almost anywhere, when people open their minds to its many manifestations. With that, let's see what a highly innovative architect learned by tapping into an unlikely source.

Biomimicry: Nature-Inspired Design

When Mick Pearce was tasked with designing a green building in Africa, he studied 30-foot high termite mounds in Zimbabwe. Why? Their sophisticated buttressing makes them so durable they can only be removed with dynamite. What had even greater significance for his green project, however, is the way these mounds maintain a constant internal temperature. We can appreciate how this would be important for buildings without conventional heating and cooling systems, but why would termites need a constant internal temperature inside their mounds? Amazing but true is that a termite's primary food supply is a fungus that can only survive at 87 degrees Fahrenheit.

So how are these simple organisms able to maintain this exact temperature when those outside their dwellings typically fluctuate between 35 and 104 degrees? Pearce wasn't able to fully comprehend this, but he did know that, in part, it was enabled by the termites' collaborative teamwork. Through close observation, he saw them add wet mud to facilitate an evaporative effect. He also saw them build complex convection systems through a series of heating and cooling vents that opened during the day and closed at night. Fascinated, Pearce watched as the termites systematically worked 24/7 to open vents by digging new tunnels and close them by plugging up old ones.

When Pearce was also asked to design a green building in Australia, he learned how the shape—and the north-south positioning for which its "compass mounds" are named—enable the termites to either optimize or minimize the effect of the sun's energy. By incorporating what he had discovered, Pearce was able to design two signature green buildings: the Eastgate Building in Harare, Zimbabwe and the Council House 2 Building in Melbourne, Australia. (For details of his green designs, see the *Greenbiz.com* article, "How Termites Inspired Mick Pearce's Green Buildings," by Tom McKeag, an instructor at the California College of the Arts and the University of California, Berkeley.) To learn about other examples of nature's genius, see the book *Biomimicry: Innovation Inspired by Nature*, by Janine Benyus.

Innovation Enablers and Drivers

What else can the Mick Pearce story tell us about innovation? First, the natural mud used for the termite mounds helps to dispel the notion that innovation must be expensive. Second, like the sophisticated buttressing that sustains these mounds, innovation requires strong infrastructures. Third, innovation is dependent on robust processes such as the termites' convection systems. And fourth, like the termite's' collaborative efforts, the best innovations are most often facilitated by teams and partnerships.

Although Pearce's designs mimicked nature, the inspiration that fueled his innovations manifests in a variety of ways for other innovators. Writers, visual artists, musicians, and composers often tell how their inspiration arrives in dreams. Others describe it as a response to complex problems or challenges. Inspiration can also manifest as a strong desire to give something back to the world from years of accumulated wisdom and hard-earned life lessons.

When envisioning this book, I wanted to share the innovation strategies of the multinational companies and not-for-profit and public organizations for which I'd provided senior leadership or leadership consulting services. Drawing from best practices in industries that included high tech, healthcare, financial services, communications, and consumer products, I had identified 30 universal drivers and enablers that I viewed as essential. Wanting to tap into others' expertise as well, I sought out key leaders and practitioners from organizations known for innovation in addition to best-selling authors, leading educators, and consultants. Knowing that different ideas and approaches would come from a team effort, I also responded affirmatively when two consultants who specialize in leadership and innovation offered to help produce this book.

A Valuable Resource

Andrea Zintz's leadership consulting expertise, extensive knowledge base, advanced studies in leadership and organizational development, and her corporate experience made her a perfect choice for the chapter that introduces the *Leading Innovation* subsection. Before starting her own consulting and coaching business in 2000, Andrea had held several senior leadership positions at Johnson & Johnson (J&J), which included leading a global leadership program from the company's corporate headquarters. While serving on the management board of a highly successful J&J start-up, and functioning as Vice President of Human Resources, she also focused on how the most successful organizations create the kind of environments that favor innovation.

In addition to her experience and expertise, Andrea brought to this effort many of the personal qualities that support innovation. Among them were her "can-do" approach, unbelievably high energy level, contagious enthusiasm, and strong character. I especially want to express thanks for the countless hours that she spent on multiple rounds of edits, making her a living example of Thomas Edison's famous quote, "Innovation is 1% inspiration and 99% perspiration."

Described in two of this book's chapters is yet another strength that Andrea Zintz consistently applied to this effort. I could only put a name to it after discovering the parallels between music and leadership. "Yes, and" means, "*Yes*, I like your idea *and* here's how I'd like to build on it." The "Yes, and" concept illustrates the kind of collaboration that occurs among accomplished jazz musicians yet also has applications in other environments. Andrea's willingness to say "Yes" to others' ideas and approaches, in combination with her ability to build on them, surely made her a valuable team player and friend.

A Powerful Team

My highest praise also goes to Megan Mitchell, who made my innovation journey a rich experience, both personally and professionally. Exceptionally bright, open-minded, and willing to challenge the status quo, Megan is also one of those rare "old souls" who, in this case, served as a highly empathetic "shock absorber" when we encountered many seemingly impenetrable obstacles and delays.

Megan drew on functional expertise that came from a variety of disciplines including corporate innovation, learning and development, human resources, marketing, and sales. Subsequent to her former role as Director of Leadership and Innovation at J&J and Pfizer Consumer Health (PCH) in Canada, she had been consulting with a variety of client organizations on creativity and innovation. She had also been teaching executives about leadership and innovation in classes at the Centre of Excellence for Innovation Management at the Schulich Executive Education Centre at York University in Toronto, Canada. And she had been serving as the Centre's Program Director.

Megan expanded my views on innovation when she showed me what it can achieve if it's broadly defined. In this respect, she helped me see how, when people shift old paradigms, innovation can improve the quality of life for people in developing countries as business innovation does in the developed world. Megan's insights about social innovation, combined with her skill at leading large-scale projects, and her knowledge of the frameworks needed to drive innovation, uniquely qualified her to write the introduction to the *Inspiring and Enabling Innovation* subsection.

In that chapter, Megan brings a deep understanding of how virtual and physical environments can both inhibit, and create, the best conditions for innovation. She also shares her knowledge of the different creativity styles required at each stage of the innovation process as well as the vital role that creativity plays in jump starting innovation and taking ideas beyond initial launch. A lifelong learner with an insatiable appetite, Megan ensured that this book would bring the fresh approaches and new thinking that would make it a valuable resource for leaders, practitioners, educators, and students.

From Ideas to Innovations

Proving that innovation is best facilitated by teams, both Megan and Andrea's experience, knowledge of leadership and innovation, and their ability to skillfully connect many concepts and ideas, was reinforced by their patience during the many years that it took to get this book published. To conclude, innovation must begin with ideas—such as my 30 innovation enablers—but ideas don't constitute innovation until they bring value. With that in mind, it's our distinct pleasure to share the success stories, game-changing strategies, lessons learned, and many tips described by the leaders and experts featured in this book. We hope that you'll embrace what you learn and pass it on so that we can collectively meet the needs of many in today's ever-changing global environment.

Marilyn Blocker
Principal, Innovation Outcomes
info@innovationoutcomes.com
www.innovationoutcomes.com
www.linkedin.com/in/marilynjblocker

Introduction: Sustainable and Meaningful Innovation

Frans van Houten, Chief Executive Officer and Chairman of the Board of Management and Executive Committee at Royal Philips N.V.

■ ■ ■

Ask people to define "innovation" and you will see how many associate it with the latest products and technologies. However, new inventions are only a part of Philips' success story. Even back in 1891, our company's visionary leaders believed that success extended far beyond product innovation. Their goal was to build a prosperous enterprise while also improving the well-being of society and individuals. Now, more than 127 years after the company's inception, that goal remains the same—even as Philips has evolved from a manufacturer of products as varied as light bulbs, televisions and home appliances to a focused leader in health technology for use in hospitals and homes.

By continually increasing our capacity for innovation, we have set ourselves an ambitious, challenging goal: to improve the lives of three billion people per year by 2025.

What are some of the global challenges that we're seeking to address? Today people are living longer, with almost 900 million people worldwide over 60 years of age. By 2050, that figure will have increased to some 2.4 billion. Indeed, the Economist Intelligence Unit estimates that global health spending is rising an average of 5.2% per year as a consequence—and is set to bust $9 trillion by 2018.

For some time, we have also been responding to the world's growing and rapidly aging population by delivering solutions that help increase access to healthcare and improve outcomes. Through a number of innovations, we have been able to reduce costs through greater efficiencies in healthcare delivery systems. Moreover, by teaming up with healthcare professionals in hospitals and health systems, we are driving improvements in patient outcomes, quality of care delivery and productivity.

However, there is another global challenge that Philips is addressing. The worldwide consumption of food and the inexorable need for fresh water, energy, and other resources are already putting a huge strain on our resources and social systems. By 2050, demands will increase as the world's population grows to a projected nine billion. One way in which Philips is meeting the demands of scarce resources is through the transition from a 'linear' economic model to a circular one. Instead of relying on the world's current "make, take, and dispose" model, we are continually reusing, remanufacturing and recycling. This is essential if we are to deliver quality, sustainable healthcare solutions day after day, year after year.

It is clear that no one organization can solve all the challenges it faces by going it alone, and Philips is no exception. Our company's pioneering role in "open innovation" decades ago has enabled us to capitalize on critical partnerships in innovation eco-systems, large and small, around the world. Today we continue to join hands with non-profit and government organizations, academia, and institutions of many kinds to leverage our unique and complementary capabilities and expertise.

So what are some other time-tested strategies that have enabled Philips' meaningful innovations and staying power? We have demonstrated that research and development is a vital investment that brings significant and sustainable value to customers in all parts of the world. Since the introduction of the very first Philips product, we have also epitomized the need to reinvent continuously, in response to the changing demands of customers and society as a whole.

We continue to attract and retain talent who share our ambitions and values. I remain convinced that success in dealing with today's challenges is determined by individuals who exhibit the courage to take ownership and make bold decisions; who team with others to excel; and who are determined to make a meaningful difference in the world.

As the many contributors to this book ably illustrate, organizations must keep innovating. Regardless of how you might apply what you learn from these experts, be assured that they are inviting you to join the ever-growing group of people who are working to make our world a better place—now and in the future—through meaningful and sustainable innovation.

Frans van Houten
CEO and Chairman, Royal Philips

■ ■ ■

Frans van Houten is CEO and Chairman of the Executive Committee and the Board of Management of Royal Philips, a position he has held since April 2011. He first joined the company in 1986 and has held multiple senior global leadership positions across the company, including co-CEO of the Consumer Electronics division and CEO of Philips Semiconductors. Frans is passionate about business transformation and performance management and is a long-time champion of the company's strategic approach to innovating sustainably. He leads the company in its goal to make the world healthier and more sustainable and to deliver on the company's stated goal of improving three billion lives per year by 2025. Frans holds a Master's degree in Economics and Business Management from the Erasmus University in Rotterdam and is a member of the European Round Table of Industrialists.

Why This Book?

Why another book on innovation? And once again, why an innovation book with musical metaphors? Can leaders in the world of business possibly learn anything of value from the world of musicians and musician leaders? You might be surprised by the parallels.

The 40+ organizational leaders, prominent educators, best-selling authors, and subject matter experts who were interviewed for this book address what happens between the beginnings and endings of most organizations' lifecycles. They describe how start-up companies can evolve from exciting entrepreneurial enterprises into boring bureaucracies and how even long-established companies can fail if they don't innovate. However, there is also much to be learned from jazz musicians and symphony orchestra leaders about creative talent and opposing forces that can inhibit innovation.

What can leaders almost everywhere learn from music leaders?

In an industry that isn't subsidized in the United States, symphony orchestra leaders face significant challenges. JoAnn Falletta, Music Director for both the Buffalo Philharmonic Orchestra and the Virginia Symphony Orchestra, and one of our featured leaders, says, "Often the very survival of the institution will hinge on the skill of the maestro." (See joannfalletta.com.) Music directors like Falletta have been battling obsolescence for years. Those who have kept their organizations afloat have typically been early adopters of innovation. By necessity, they've also developed innovation leadership competencies—and leaders almost everywhere can replicate them.

Another area in which leaders in other venues can learn from music leaders is how to inspire today's multi-generation workforce. Those in business environments often grapple with the challenge of managing knowledge workers, particularly Millennials. Given the similarities between these professionals and creative talent in the world of music, symphony orchestra leaders have much to teach about motivating and managing today's brand of talent. They've been doing it for hundreds of years.

Symphony orchestra leaders also represent the full set of competencies needed to inspire and sustain innovation. Knowing this, it shouldn't come as a surprise that successful business leaders possess many of the same skills and abilities of successful symphony orchestra leaders and accomplished jazz musicians. However, there's still another area in which leaders in other environments can learn from music leaders, and it's about balance.

Why is the concept of balance so necessary for successful innovation?

Jazz musicians are known for continually exploring, experimenting, and co-creating—while also putting a high priority on balance. These musicians—as well as symphony orchestra leaders—have gained considerable expertise in recognizing the invisible forces that drive creativity. They also have a special kind of knowledge regarding how to balance these forces. Successful innovators, like musicians and musician leaders, know they must manage many invisible forces if they're to successfully initiate and manage change or adapt to ongoing shifts in their environments.

Many business leaders are unaware of these invisible forces, and even if they are, they sometimes ignore them, which can compromise innovation. Later in this chapter, I write about the need to explore new territory while simultaneously employing business-as-usual approaches. This is the first of ten pairs of opposing forces that leaders must balance if they're to successfully innovate. Summarized here, and described in greater detail in the *Managing and Leveraging Innovation* chapter, the second pair of opposing forces is manifest in orchestration and improvisation.

What other opposing forces require balance?

Today there's still too great a tendency for organizations to *produce* ideas rather than *execute* them, so the third pair of opposing forces consists of idea generation and execution. The fourth pair of opposites regards the degree to which organizations innovate. For example, some respond to changing needs gradually, with incremental innovations such as new or enhanced products or services, adjacencies, or expanded distribution channels. Other organizations rely on disruptive innovations that can significantly change markets' or even entire industries. If innovations are only of the incremental type, an organization's growth can be limited and its sustainability compromised. However, disruptive innovation usually translates to increased risk, so when assessing risk versus opportunity, successful leaders consider both incremental and disruptive innovation.

The fifth area that demands balance regards the forces of action and strategy. When action precedes strategy, execution will inevitably be unfocused and chaotic, so leaders must ensure the right focus. The sixth area in which balance needs to be achieved is between value creation and value preservation. Leaders usually respond to this pair of opposing forces by innovating—and by also creating risk management strategies such as stage-gating. This and other processes encourage new ideas and approaches while also preventing or mitigating catastrophic mistakes or misallocated funds. To balance this pair of opposing forces, leaders need to know when it's best to take small (incremental) risks and when to employ more radical (or disruptive) approaches.

When leaders lack the skills to achieve a good balance between the seventh pair—people and processes—they can focus too intently on the "process side" of innovation and underestimate the "people side." They can also put too much focus on people and not enough on processes. In a similar vein, balance must be achieved in the eighth area of opposing forces, between individual freedom and organizational alignment. Leaders must be skilled at aligning individual and organizational agendas.

How might a jazz metaphor help to balance opposing forces?

In the last chapter of this book, you'll learn more about the many parallels between jazz and successful innovation, but for now, let's look at how the ninth and tenth areas can be balanced by what jazz tells us. Leaders must have appropriate risk management structures in place to ensure that too much experimentation—or improvisation—doesn't invite failure. However, they must also redefine "failure" as a fundamental step in the innovation process that enables aspiring innovators to rule out certain options or strategies through a process of elimination.

The tenth area in which balance needs to be achieved regards the opposing forces of structure and flexibility. Since jazz musicians don't follow a designated leader, they must improvise by performing extemporaneously, as individuals and teams. Improvisation enables jazz musicians to achieve success by finding the "sweet spot"—the point at which individual freedom is successfully balanced with structure and discipline. Successful business leaders do this by aligning personal and organizational agendas and by also determining whether their organizational structures are able to flex with changes in their internal and external environments.

Most people would agree that it's easy for leaders to fall behind their competition if they don't improvise, or don't do it quickly enough. There's a particular need for improvisation in start-up operations, which typically operate with small margins for error, few refined processes, and little or no organizational memory from which to draw. However, mature organizations also need to be expert at improvisation if they're to survive and thrive in today's hyper-competitive environments.

What can be learned from this book?

In one section, you'll learn about 36 innovation enablers and in another, from 6 innovation success stories, 2 from each major sector. Through quotes from many leaders, subject matter experts, best-selling authors, symphony orchestra leaders, jazz musicians, and jazz soloists, you'll discover universal principles that facilitate successful and sustainable innovation. And by reading the success stories of the music leaders featured in this book, you'll witness how their organizations have survived, and thrived, in an industry where obsolescence has become the norm.

Does this book contain a magic formula for innovation? Many books claim to have one. This does not, but there is a differentiating success factor that you'll see throughout. It's the ability of successful innovators to push beyond traditional ways of operating to embrace and execute new ideas and strategies. However, as important as it is to learn how leaders accomplish this, it's also useful to explore the ways in which they've succeeded in the past.

Why are orchestration and improvisation critical for successful innovation?

Today, symphony orchestra leaders deliver music that's hundreds of years old to audiences who never seem to tire of it. Like these maestros, many leaders in today's mature organizations have achieved mastery and excellence through enduring structures. These factors don't fully support changing times, however, and concert halls bear little resemblance to today's fast-paced, highly distributed, and tech-enabled workplaces. So although a symphony orchestra metaphor underscores the need to build on past successes, it can also symbolize obsolescence. Despite that, it's a valuable tool for understanding at least one important element of sustainable innovation that's described next.

Aspiring innovators often believe that it's necessary to challenge the status quo in its entirety and start innovation from scratch. Sometimes this is necessary, but most often sustainable innovation begins with assessments of what's made an organization successful in the past. These are typically its assets, core strengths, and institutional memory, which includes lessons learned about what has and hasn't worked in the past, as well as what should be discarded and what can be built on.

Clearly there's a benefit in continuing some of the best practices of the past, yet "next practices" are also essential. The famous violinist, Joshua Bell once said, "Being in music, you need this youthful sense of discovery and wonder for what you're doing and [for] keep[ing] your imagination open." Today, organizations in almost any industry can quickly fall behind fierce competitors and disruptive innovators if they fail to adopt new ways. In this respect, jazz is a useful metaphor for the constant and courageous exploration of new territory. It's also symbolic of the calculated risks that people take when they build on other's ideas to produce "new music" or take existing music in different directions through improvisation.

Jazz is also a helpful metaphor for innovation because of its basic element: change. Few would dispute that innovation brings with it change, but unlike jazz musicians—who are excited and energized by it—most people in work environments fear change. Consequently, leaders must skillfully improvise in order to manage it. From these examples, we can see how aspiring innovators must be skilled at both orchestration and improvisation.

How does organizational change contribute to innovation failure?

Bob Dylan once said—"There is nothing so stable as change." It might be obvious that initiating change in almost any environment is risky, but innovation failure is inevitable if leaders try to preserve outdated or irrelevant elements in their organization's missions, business models, or cultures. Nick Donofrio, one of the senior leaders who endorsed this book, would enthusiastically agree. As the IBM Fellow Emeritus and former EVP Innovation and Technology, he once said, "Successful leaders in today's world know that change is always coming, so they don't wait for it. They look for it and capitalize on it."

Leaders like Donofrio know this is often easier said than done. When the change that comes with innovation isn't managed skillfully, it can significantly disrupt day-to-day operations. That's because change doesn't come about simply by enhancing the efficient, repeatable, and predictable processes that ensured value in the past. It comes about when leaders initiate as well as respond to change—and when they actively transform their organizations' cultures. Today, these are vital leadership competencies.

Why does innovation continue to be more challenging?

Decades ago, when our world began to grow continually more complex, leaders in the industrial economy needed to expand their previous focus on tangible (hard) assets to include intangible (soft) assets. With this, speed and efficiency became increasingly essential for maintaining a competitive advantage—and in some cases, even basic survival. When companies expanded globally and moved out of their regional or national niches into unfamiliar territory, they needed to draw more heavily on the knowledge, skills, and abilities that resided within their human resources—the employees and leaders who make innovation happen.

Shorter product cycles, increasingly scarce resources, global competition, and lower entry barriers are only a few of the challenges that have continued to demand new and diverse ways of thinking and operating. All of this has made it more difficult for leaders to be present and available to employees— particularly if they're also expected to assess whether processes are keeping pace. Today, a continuing stream of new technologies and innovations is even more essential than in the past. Leaders of organizations that own disruptive innovations leverage them as powerful weapons, while competitors experience them as serious threats. This is particularly the case when innovations have the potential to substantially change market conditions and disrupt entire industries.

Successful leaders are fully aware that any disruptive strategies they might employ today will soon be countered by other ideas or inventions that are equally impactful. That's because innovation is like a demanding race without a finish line. With that in mind, are there other contributing factors to the challenge of this never-ending race? Of course. Our consulting work has given us many opportunities to witness how leaders at even the most well-intentioned organizations often retreat to familiar and comfortable territory when presented with challenges that require new thinking and approaches.

What maximizes organization and innovation success?

We've also seen organizations resist the temptation to coast on past successes—and how, in more digital and highly distributed work environments, their leaders are communicating and collaborating differently. We also witness their efforts to employ better ways to delegate and develop people so they can continually build on their organizations' intellectual capital. In the chapter *Leading Innovation*, there are many examples of the kind of leadership that innovation requires.

One of this book's endorsers, Dr. Robin Karol, views effective innovation leadership as a delicate balancing act between people and processes. As a former CEO of the Product Development Marketing Association, retired senior R&D leader at DuPont, and author of *Product Development for Dummies*, Dr. Karol possesses great knowledge of what makes innovation happen. She also believes that successful "orchestration" is a key driver of effective innovation, and she suggested the symphony orchestra metaphor and the concept of orchestrating innovation that appear throughout this book.

Now I must admit that, at first, I wasn't keen on the orchestra metaphor because of the limitations previously mentioned. I didn't see it as being representative of today's changing demographics or diverse workforces. And with orchestra leaders traditionally operating out of a single location, I didn't feel that it addressed the need to manage people in geographically distributed and often remote locations. However, I found something even more disturbing about this metaphor: I didn't want the world-renowned autocratic conductors of the past to be examples of the leadership that's needed for innovation.

In fact, what immediately came to mind when Dr. Karol first suggested the orchestra metaphor was how the Italian conductor Arturo Toscanini had once told his musicians, "God speaks to me, and you get in the way." I could only imagine how people today, particularly Millennials, would respond to that message. Of course, Toscanini's leadership style needs to be considered in context. In his time, leaders in almost all venues were expected to create a certain mystique and aura. They needed to command respect through control. Contrast that with the collegial and co-creative styles of today's leaders and see if you agree with one of our featured music leaders, Eric Whitacre, who says, "The very best conductors let the players make the music."

How do leaders empower people to innovate?

For the most part, the command-and-control styles of highly acclaimed maestros—in the world of music and business alike—are now gone. Today the leadership style that seems best for both knowledge workers and creative staff is exemplified by Michael Tilson Thomas, Music Director of the San Francisco Symphony and Artistic Director of the New World Symphony Orchestra in Miami Beach, Florida. Tilson Thomas once said about leading, "Being a conductor is kind of a hybrid profession because most fundamentally, it is being someone who is a coach, a trainer, an editor, a director."

Clearly, the nature of today's workforce has contributed to changes in leadership styles. In his book *Inside Conducting*, Christopher Seaman, Conductor Laureate for Life of the Rochester Philharmonic Orchestra, writes, "You are dealing with professional people with skills." Consequently, leaders today communicate standards of performance in very different ways than in years past. Rather than telling people how to do their jobs, they recognize people's skills, express desired outcomes, and guide people only when necessary. In this way, they provide the freedom to innovate, but not in the form of a blank check. Effective leaders today encourage autonomy while also ensuring personal responsibility.

How do today's leaders inspire?

To optimize an organization's innovation potential, leaders and employees alike must actively support the creative process. Leaders in most environments today distribute power through a democratic approach that stimulates and rewards creativity and innovation. Symphony orchestra leaders achieve it by involving musicians in the selection of musical scores as well as decisions about *how* the music will be played. Business leaders invite employees to participate in a broad range of problem-solving and decision-making activities that most often include task forces and project teams.

These activities inspire trust, and trust is the basis for the implied contract between employees and highly innovative organizations. The jazz metaphor, one of two in this book, effectively illustrates how trust can enable innovation. In jazz, all players have an equal role, and all must have confidence that no one player will monopolize. By contrast, most symphony orchestras (and other organizations) aren't leaderless. At the top, there's usually a single "conductor." So how do successful leaders maintain control while still inspiring innovation through democratic relationships?

When interviewing Dominic Alldis, a symphony orchestra conductor, jazz musician, and Honorary Associate of the Royal Academy of Music in London, I asked him to answer this question and to also comment on the specific leadership competencies required in today's environments. Responding as an educator who works with leading business schools and companies, Alldis said, "Conductors have special privileges and responsibilities that parallel those of business leaders. They must create a dialogue that goes beyond words, with a good deal of their communication conveyed nonverbally as well as intellectually and emotionally." Trust is paramount, but leaders must also do more.

How do leaders sustain innovation after the initial spark has been ignited?

When I also asked Alldis for his thoughts about how leaders initially inspire and how they continue to motivate, he responded with another musical metaphor: "First, there is the joy of execution. Second is the journey and immersive experience in which team members engage. And third is the beauty of the 'sound' when people synchronize with one another." He then added, "All this, however, is incumbent on people's desire to follow. That must come from a place of humility—not in a way that's subservient—but of a desire to give generously. When this happens, there's an irresistible energy, and that's what excites, inspires, and keeps people engaged." (To learn more about Dominic Alldis, go to musicandmanagement.com.)

Successful leaders keep people engaged by building and maintaining relationships with a variety of internal and external stakeholders. The section *Managing and Leveraging Innovation* describes the types of partnerships that are essential for innovation. Today, leaders need to be skilled at building partnerships with employees, consumers, communities, and even competitors. However, partnerships tend to also make innovation more complex and challenging. The leaders who are most effective at partnering with employees create safe environments for their ideas. When ideas aren't actionable, they communicate why. And when they're viable, they ensure that they're executed—with the necessary resources and ongoing support. These leaders also celebrate milestones and reward people equitably for their accomplishments.

How does the "Yes, and" approach facilitate innovation?

When considering the need for an ongoing stream of new ideas and approaches, we can appreciate how the same skillful improvisation that powers jazz is imperative for business success. When further comparing successful innovators to members of jazz ensembles, we see that both skillfully "play" with new ideas by engaging in ongoing trial-and-error experimentation. This, in contrast to leaders who rely on improvisation as simply a means by which daily fires are extinguished.

If you're finding these comparisons helpful, there's another element of jazz that relates to innovation. In the *Prelude*, and in more detail in the *Managing and Leveraging Innovation* chapter of this book, I describe the concept of the "Yes-and" approach. That's when people build on one another's ideas in various ways by essentially saying, "Yes, I agree with you, and here's where I'm going to take your idea next." Why is this an important innovation driver?

"Yes, and" is an acknowledgement of the need to co-create and engage in disciplined experimentation while also building on the time-tested strategies, norms, structure, discipline, and standardized approaches that characterize successful organizations. Today's successful innovators continually work to replace "Either/or" thinking with "Yes, and" approaches.

When is innovation not the answer?

Manifest in classical music (and also in classical literature) is the concept of "denouement," a piece that signals an ending. The denouement acknowledges that certain parts or segments must be finished before something new can be introduced. Even if you're not a classical literature or music enthusiast, you might be aware of the need to sometimes make an ending to create a beginning. This is evident in many aspects of our lives, and it's fundamental to the concept of "creative destruction" put forth by the late Harvard economist Joseph Schumpeter.

Creative destruction holds that organizations need to replace old ways with new ways if they're to continually increase their efficiency and dynamism. Does that always mean innovation? University of Michigan professor and innovation consultant Jeff de Graff put forth three provocative questions in a presentation at the 2012 conference of the League of American Orchestras entitled "Driving Innovation: A Roadmap for Practical Implementation." He said, "What if the key to tremendous innovation is not about *starting* something?" "What if [it's about] *stopping* something?" and "What if the real ability … isn't about starting new … but about stopping something that you took to be *sacred*?"

Leaders at organizations with staying power seem to instinctively know when to discontinue a product, service, or process that has become too expensive or that no longer meets current or anticipated future needs. Besides being skilled at combining both old and new "music," leaders at these organizations also know when and how to bring about positive endings. Whether endings are of a temporary or permanent nature, these leaders honor them, so here are some other provocative questions: What might you be holding onto that's so sacred it should be maintained at all costs? If you're a student, how might that interfere with learning? If you're an educator, how might it inhibit your teaching? And if you're a leader or a consultant, what might it extract in terms of missed opportunities?

What is regarded by many as the most powerful innovation enabler of all?

The answer to this question might surprise you. Leaders in not-for-profit organizations, particularly those in the social sector, know that there's a certain kind of magic that incentivizes people to do their best. It occurs when they're working toward a common and powerful mission. To them, there's nothing like this high-octane mix to provide the fuel for innovation. Leaders who create compelling missions, and know how to secure buy-in, can ignite a passion that's sometimes unstoppable. That's because when people believe that their work is making the world a better place, they're driven to greater heights than if they're simply "doing their jobs."

When leaders define innovation broadly, as "anything new that brings value," they can leverage its potential to not only enhance internal and external processes, but also improve customer relationships, create more expansive distribution systems, and produce win-win strategic partnerships. A broad definition of innovation also enables leaders to catalyze paradigm shifts and bring about positive social impact in the same ways that innovation can increase profitability. In a 2012 BBC News article, "Can a Company Live Forever?" author Kim Gittleson cites the work of Professor Makoto Kanda, of Meiji Gakuin University. Kanda sees a common denominator in organizations that have staying power: It's their "focus on a central belief or credo that's not exclusively tied to making a profit." In this book's introduction, Philips' CEO and Chairman Frans van Houten validates this and views "meaningful innovation" as one of his company's most enduring forces.

So why the almost monomaniacal focus on innovation these days?

All organizations, successful or not, have something in common: Like people, they aren't immortal, and they function best when they're able to face their mortality and accept it. I don't mean this in a morbid sense, but rather that organizations, like certain people, can often enhance their lives—and even extend them—by continually innovating and reinventing. So why then is it so important for people and organizations to accept their mortality? Because to live well is to remember that even the most compelling visions, missions, and goals are time bound.

How does this truth play out for organizations? Those who view themselves as immortal—and coast on past successes—sometimes end up as victims of hostile takeovers. Before going down, they often generate considerable press. Other endings receive little fanfare—sometimes only a quietly descending curtain that signals the termination of a lengthy life-and-death struggle. Surprisingly, many organizations with shortened lifespans have done almost all the right things. They've responded well to the changing needs of consumers, clients, or patrons—they simply didn't do it *quickly* enough.

All this said, the endings of some very special organizations—well-known or otherwise—are dramatically different from the previous scenarios. Their deaths, usually a result of natural aging, mark an end to lives that were well-lived. Some even defied mortality with enduring and meaningful legacies—but sadly, for most organizations today, the "music" ends prematurely—and unnecessarily.

What are some organizations that have exceeded average life expectancy?

What secret might the few enduring organizations have for exceeding normal life expectancy? Author Ariel de Geus, in his book, *The Living Company*, describes a study conducted by the Shell Oil Company many years ago. He writes, "Human beings have learned to survive, on average, for 75 years or more, but there are very few companies that are that old *and flourishing*." Mark J. Perry, Professor of Economics and Finance at the University of Michigan, echoes these findings. In an August 18, 2014

American Enterprise Institute article in *AEIdeas*, he states that 88% of the Fortune 500 companies listed in 1955 had disappeared by 2014.

In her 2012 BBC News article, Gittleson also cites the research of Yale University Professor Richard Foster. Noting that the average lifespan of leading U.S. companies on the S&P 500 index decreased by over 50 years in the last century, Foster says it went from a 67-year lifespan in the 1920s to a mere 15 years. Looking at total casualties in the United States, we see very few notable exceptions to average life expectancy, but we can learn from them and others.

Gittleson cites statistics from Tokyo Shoko Research, which indicates there are more than 20,000 organizations in Japan that are over 100 years old and a "handful" that are even more than 1,000 years of age. And once again, Gittleson references the work of Professor Makoto Kanda, who studies "shinise," a Japanese word for his country's longest-living companies. Have *shinise* discovered an ancient long-life elixir? If so, might leaders everywhere be able to learn from them as well as from the strategies of enduring organizations in other parts of the world?

What separates long-lived organizations from those that don't reach average life expectancy?

As you might guess, leading innovators maximize average life expectancy by employing many strategies. Because today's economies are less stable and more difficult to influence than in the past, successful leaders proactively buffer their organizations by continually anticipating market changes and preparing for them. They do this by setting aside reserves for difficult times and by positioning themselves for worst-case scenarios. In these ways, they ensure that their organizations will survive recessions and depressions—and possibly even optimize their ability to *thrive* in down times.

Today's volatile market conditions, fluctuating interest rates, and disruptive technologies often create challenges that go beyond the scope of even the most sophisticated scenario planning. That's why so many leaders attribute innovation failure to the unforeseen external forces that they believe to be beyond their control. However, several of the experts interviewed for this book assert that rather than *causing* problems, unanticipated forces often reveal threats that have been lying dormant for years, right beneath the surface.

Leaders at enduring organizations tend to be proactive and calculating risk takers who know how to maximize opportunities in various scenarios. In the same space where others struggle or fail, these leaders are often able to increase market share, expand distribution channels, and eliminate competition through acquisition. Despite that, leaders of enduring organizations don't play roulette. No matter how cash rich their organizations might be, they don't take on excessive debt or roll the dice aggressively on "big ideas" unless those actions are well considered or required as last-resort strategies. With an overriding goal to optimize their organizations' potential for long life, these leaders wouldn't dream of operating without safety nets, contingency plans, and leadership succession plans. Above all, they know how to ensure viability and sustainability by willingly carving out the necessary time, effort, and resources to ensure long life.

How else can leaders maximize their organizations' potential for long life?

In a Harvard Business Review Article, "The Living Company," author Ariel de Geus says, "If you look at [commercial corporations] in light of what they could be … most … are underachievers [who] develop and exploit only a small fraction of their potential… Consider their high mortality rate." De Geus then asks "How do we know that many of the deaths are premature?" He responds to this question by saying, "Because we have evidence of much greater corporate longevity," and he cites a few long-lived organizations in the private sector. Paulo Carmini, one of the contributors to this book, has served in senior leadership roles at two "centenarian companies"—previously as a vice president at Steelcase and currently as CEO of Herman Miller, Canada.

Before you conclude that organizations with staying power exist only in the private sector, however, be aware that not-for-profit organizations such as the International Red Cross, the American Red Cross, and the Girl Scouts of America U.S.A. (an organization featured in this book) have all achieved centenarian status. And many public organizations, such as the U.S. Coast Guard (also featured in this book), have survived for over 100 years. In part, these organizations have achieved long life through operational excellence, but that can accomplish only so much. Kim Gittleson says, "Although there are exceptions to every rule, the most important factor for survival is an emphasis on innovation and reinvention."

As experienced consultants and former leaders, Andrea Zintz, Megan Mitchell, and I have repeatedly witnessed how internal, as well as external, forces can also cause organizations to fail. That's why leaders at long-lived organizations ensure that people's ideas and efforts are adequately supported through efficient and effective processes. In the same way that symphony orchestra maestros have passed on musical compositions to succeeding generations, leaders at enduring organizations know that future leaders will be needed to sustain their organizations' values, institutional memory, and innovation capability. Consequently, to ensure continuity, they often commit substantial resources to formal processes that develop these leaders.

What expertise can I expect to access in this book?

To provide a broad perspective of the many approaches by which organizations expand their life expectancy, Andrea, Megan, and I interviewed over 40 experts and senior leaders at well-known companies such as 3M, Amazon, GE, The Hershey Company, IBM, P&G, Toyota, and many more for this book. Captured in our interviews are also the successes of leaders from lesser-known organizations that are highly innovative in their own right. Also included are the perspectives of senior leaders, best-selling authors, educators, and practitioners from a wide range of disciplines. In this book, you'll see contributors from Dartmouth's Tuck School, INSEAD, the University of Pennsylvania's Wharton School of Business, Yale University, and York University's Schulich School of Business.

Our "team" of experts also consists of several highly innovative symphony orchestra leaders, a choral conductor, and previously cited Dominic Alldis, symphony orchestra leader, jazz musician, and Honorary Associate and educator at the Royal Academy of Music in London. By reading about the challenges of our featured leaders and subject matter experts, you'll become acquainted with the many ways in which leading innovators in all major sectors ensure sustainability.

In the subsection *Inspiring and Encouraging Innovation*, you'll see the important role that creativity plays in jumpstarting innovation, and how creativity, culture, and collaboration help to sustain innovation. In *Leading Innovation*, you'll learn about how successful leaders motivate people to perform at their full potential and how they shape, stimulate, and support innovation. And in the *Managing and Leveraging Innovation* subsection, you'll learn about the processes and organizational infrastructures that are needed to support people's ideas and game-changing strategies. You'll also see how successful innovators leverage the complex interplay of people, partnerships, and processes.

What are the credentials, goals, objectives of this book's authors?

What makes us uniquely qualified to write this book? Our backgrounds are mentioned briefly in the *Prelude* and in greater detail in the *Author Biographies* section, but here's a quick snapshot. Before starting an independent consulting practice, Andrea Zintz functioned as Vice President of Human Resources at a highly successful start-up at J&J (Johnson & Johnson) and served on this start-up's management board. She also led a global leadership program from J&J corporate headquarters. As the president of Strategic Leadership Resources, she currently provides executive coaching and leadership development services to clients and also shares her expertise by volunteering on numerous not-for-profit boards. Andrea's practical experience is supported by an MA and Ph.D. in Human and Organization Systems from Fielding Graduate University.

As an innovation consultant and educator, Megan Mitchell draws from experience in her former corporate role as Director of Leadership Development and Innovation at Pfizer Consumer Healthcare, Canada. Her broad background also includes functional experience in sales, marketing, and human resources management. Additionally, Megan serves as Program Director for the Centre of Excellence for Innovation Management at the Schulich Executive Education Centre at York University in Toronto,

Canada. There she also teaches innovation, strategy, and leadership, helping program participants and clients achieve competitive advantage by tapping into their organizations' creative potential.

As Managing Principal of Innovation Outcomes, I draw from over 30 years of senior leadership experience at The Coca-Cola Company, GTE (now Verizon), Providence Health and Services, a subsidiary of John Hancock Financial Services (now Manulife), and most recently as a vice president at the Philips Silicon Valley Center, a high-tech incubator site of Royal Philips (previously known as Philips Electronics). I hold an MBA and a Master of Science in Management from the University of Maryland and have served on numerous boards. I've been assisting clients in building innovation capability through coaching, team development, and culture transformation for decades. I've also been a guest lecturer, graduate school advisor, and adjunct professor at New York University (NYU), where I taught an undergraduate course in creativity and innovation.

As former active members of senior leadership teams at prominent and well-respected organizations, the three of us have met challenges at all stages of our organizations' development, from start-up to maturity. As consultants, we're able to share many best and next practices from our former employers as well as those of our clients. Consistent with the experts who we've featured in this book, our goals and objectives are simple: We want to guide you in formulating a sustainable innovation strategy and securing the necessary buy-in and commitment to effectively execute it. Based on the premise that a team of dedicated people typically exceeds the results of most individuals, I believe you'll benefit greatly from our collective viewpoints and expertise as well as that of the many subject matter experts and others featured in this book.

How has this book been designed for easy reading?

Knowing that most people today have little time to read, this work is essentially a "just-in-time" reference that can be easily accessed as needed. As previously mentioned, our 6 success stories and 36 innovation enabling chapters will undoubtedly help leaders inspire, lead, and leverage innovation. The "sound-bite" innovation enabling chapters contain detailed descriptions of innovation drivers and enablers that have been distilled to their very essence in question-and-answer formats. From these and other chapters, you'll quickly learn how successful start-ups and mature organizations alike leverage a broad range of "people" and "process" enablers to achieve and sustain innovation.

Since all our innovation enabling chapters stand alone and are cross-referenced to similar topics, you can read this book in whatever way you'd like. If you want to skip to the ends of chapters in the *Innovation Enablers* section, you'll see assessment questions as well as bulleted tips and strategies that summarize learnings. If you're an educator or student, you'll find it easy to match your syllabus to this flexible format. And if you're a leader, practitioner, or consultant, our menu of options can help you replicate what's worked well for others. This book can also assist you in constructing a customized portfolio of potential innovation strategies for your organization or client organizations.

Closing Thoughts

I hope that our symphony orchestra and jazz metaphors will be as helpful as the collective experience and many tips shared by this book's contributors. Most likely we have similar goals—to produce beautiful "music" by continually learning, arriving at new insights, introducing new ideas, and reframing yesterday's reality with new information. With that, I encourage you to share your experiences by contacting Megan Mitchell, Andrea Zintz, and me, at our respective e-mail addresses listed at the end of our chapters.

In concluding, I want to extend my deepest appreciation to Frans van Houten for his introduction and to the many other contributors who so generously shared their knowledge and experience. I'm also fully appreciative of the time that Nick Donofrio, Jim Amos, and Dr. Robin Karol took to review and endorse this book, and I want to extend a special "thank you" once again to Dr. Karol for suggesting the orchestral metaphor. My deepest "thanks" also go to Megan and Andrea for their brilliant insights, patience, and friendship during this sometimes daunting project. I'll now close by wishing everyone who made this book possible the very best in their never-ending journeys to successful innovation.

Marilyn Blocker
Managing Principal, Innovation Outcomes
info@innovationoutcomes.com
www.innovationoutcomes.com
www.linkedin.com/in/marilynjblocker

I. Innovation Success Stories

Section I Introduction

Leadership That Transforms

An interview with James H. Amos, Jr., President and CEO of the National Center for Policy Analysis; Chairman of Procter & Gamble's Agile Pursuits (franchising board); former Chairman of Tasti D-lite/Planet Smoothie; Chairman Emeritus/former CEO of Mail Boxes Etc./The UPS Store; and Author

As chair of Proctor & Gamble's Agile Pursuits Franchising Inc. and former CEO of the world's largest pack and ship retail business and non-food franchise, Jim was instrumental in introducing two of the biggest global companies to business format franchising. While functioning as the Chairman and CEO of Mail Boxes Etc./The UPS Store, he led a highly effective business transformation effort that enhanced the company's technology platform, substantially improved communication and morale, and utilized a more inclusive strategic planning process—all of which increased accountability and significantly improved financials. Under Jim's leadership, the company doubled revenues and tripled net income and gross sales. As past Chairman of the International Franchise Association (IFA) and a franchising thought leader, Jim provided direction and assistance to over 10,000 franchisees and earned the IFA Hall of Fame Award, the highest recognition in franchising. Jim has authored four critically acclaimed books and serves on—or has served on—the following boards: Ken Blanchard's Faith Walk Leadership Foundation, Meinecke Car Care Systems, Oreck Corporation, SkinPhD, The HealthStore Foundation, The Marine Corps Heritage Foundation, The Marine Corps Military Academy, The National Veteran's Administration, the University of Missouri, WSI of Canada, Zig Ziglar Corporation, and numerous others.

■ ■ ■

If people aren't innovating and reinventing, they're not thriving. Today, leaders, organizations—and even entire countries—risk obsolescence, and even future collapse, if they fail to reinvent and innovate. Some leaders have good intentions for reinventing but lose their way because they rely on formulas that worked in the past or on compasses that show "magnetic north" as opposed to "true north." The gap between them can sometimes be significant. If we define true north literally, it describes our position with respect to the North Pole. Figuratively, it means getting on the right course and proceeding in the right direction. Some people find true north instinctively, and others are fortunate enough to be guided by leaders who help them find it. I always tell people, "You have to want to go up higher, to find your true north."

A Matter of Attitude

When I returned from serving in Vietnam, I had my own experience with feeling off course. Fortunately, I had a recurring and powerful dream about self-empowerment that served as a catalyst for change. Since that time, I've felt compelled to provide guidance and direction to others—through my writing and responsible leadership. As a way of describing leadership that transforms, I'd like to share a few thoughts about how individuals and leaders—by acting collectively—can chart a course and stay on track. Let me first start with the concept that our attitude is our single greatest asset—or liability—because it forms the foundation from which we all build. We know that it's often not *what we are*—but *what we think we are*—that prevents us from realizing our full potential and from re-inventing ourselves. Others can shape our attitudes by providing bridges that enable us to move from where we are to where we'd like to be.

Volunteers, Not Hostages

Enriching and compassionate relationships can change attitudes, and that's something that we, as leaders, must keep foremost in our minds. We must embrace the mandate for constant innovation by facilitating transformation through individuals. Napoleon once said that the way to lead people is to show them the future through a dream that can inspire hope and be pursued by faith. Breathing life into a dream—or a vision—is a necessary leadership skill because dreams can be harbingers of hope and powerful incentives that help people push through fear and other barriers to go up higher and find their true north.

Personal responsibility and accountability are other fundamental aspects of transformative leadership. Leaders must insist on these qualities in themselves and others—and continually model them. They must also help people—individually and collectively—through relationships that can make them stronger and better able to deal with adversity. Synergy and solidarity are necessary for innovatively solving today's complex problems. Relationships are essential for achieving both individual and organizational goals, and for helping to determine direction and reinforce our foundations. When relationships fail, we all fail—countries, systems, organizations, and leaders—yet many leaders don't think of their employees as people with whom they have relationships. They think of them more as "hostages" or simply as "workers" who are paid to do certain jobs. However, the most innovative and highest-performing employees are propelled by a higher purpose that goes beyond pay, and so viewing employees as "volunteers" is more accurate. That's because, no matter how much we might pay them, employees—and leaders—are free to leave at any time. And many do—when organizations function poorly, and leaders fail to inspire and connect.

Charting and Staying the Course

Whenever I've had the opportunity to bring social values to a business entity, the results have intensified drive, enthusiasm, and communication; brought meaning and purpose to work; and gained buy-in and commitment immeasurably. Goals are a key factor in finding true north because they propel the human heart to soar while protecting it from wishful thinking. And because our goals require accurate assessments of our strengths and weaknesses they compel us to see who or what we're becoming in pursuit of them. Goals can also inspire courage when we're faced with daunting obstacles or when we need to reexamine our values. Few would argue that core values constitute the heart and soul of any organization or country—and values begin with individuals in that the right goals enable us individually and collectively to go up higher.

Today's complex problems also require individuals capable of teamwork. Teamwork often requires leaders to personally transform—and attain superior results by modeling excellence and helping others reach their full potential—instead of employing old command-and-control approaches. When leaders seek to inspire people to new levels of creativity and innovation, they need to be willing to experiment with and change almost everything—except their organizations' values. Those may include caring, honesty, integrity, fairness, trust, respect, commitment, and accountability. Although innovating usually means charting a new course, effective leaders must also "stay the course"—with core values.

In closing, transformational leaders are keenly aware of their priorities. They're also realists who know that their journeys through life have only the illusion of permanence. Wanting most to make a difference—yet knowing that they might have limited time—their focus is on the legacies that they'll leave behind. If recipients of their legacies believe they can go higher to achieve true north, they'll be able to employ their best gift, namely the moral compass that will live on in their minds and hearts long after their leaders have passed. Going forward, people who have worked for transformational leaders might occasionally lose their way, but they'll still have the tools, attitude, and confidence to find true north again. We must also remember that transformation leaders are also guided by true north on their moral compasses. This is one of the many ways in which these leaders truly innovate and transform. It's also how they can achieve immortality in the process of empowering others.

■ ■ ■

To learn more about leadership, see our chapters entitled *A Business Case for Coaching, Employee Engagement, Leadership Assessment, Leadership Development, Meaning and Purpose,* and *Shared Vision and Values.* To learn more about James Amos, go to jimamosblog.com.

Global Prosperity: Pushing the Price-Performance Paradigm

An interview with Vijay Govindarajan, Ph.D., Professor of International Business; Founding Director of the Tuck Center for Global Leadership, Tuck School of Business at Dartmouth College; former Chief Innovation Consultant at G.E.; and Best-selling Author

After receiving his Chartered Accountancy degree, Vijay Govindarajan (known as "VG") was awarded the President's Gold Medal for obtaining the first rank nationwide. He subsequently earned an MBA with distinction and a doctoral degree from Harvard Business School. Before joining the faculty at the Tuck School, VG served on the faculties of Harvard Business School, INSEAD (Fontainebleau) and the Indian Institute of Management (Ahmedabad, India). VG consults with CEOs and top management teams in more than 25% of the Fortune 500, including companies such as Boeing, Coca-Cola, Colgate, Deere & Company, FedEx, GE, Hewlett-Packard, IBM, J.P. Morgan Chase, J&J, New York Times, P&G, Sony, and Wal-Mart. VG has received numerous awards for his research and is a frequent keynote speaker at CEO Forums and conferences including the BusinessWeek CEO Forum, HSM World Business Forum, and World Economic Forum at Davos. In 2012, he was ranked #3 of the Top 50 Management Thinkers by The London Times. The Economist described VG as a Rising Super-Star. Business Week ranked him among the Top Ten Business School Professors in Corporate Executive Education and Outstanding Faculty. VG also ranked among the Top Five Most Respected Executive Coaches on Strategy by Forbes. His most recent book is *Three Box Solution: A Strategy For Leading Innovation*, HBR Press, April 2016.

■ ■ ■

Growing up in a small town in southern India, I witnessed many problems with few solutions. Therefore, it should come as no surprise to you that I have always focused my research on real problems. In the first 25 years of my career, I tried to learn everything that I could about innovation. In the last 10 years, my focus has expanded to learning about how innovation can solve large problems in developing countries. In the *Why This Book?* chapter, we learn that innovation can catalyze paradigm shifts and bring about positive social impact in the same ways that it can help organizations increase profitability. We also learn how the need for innovation is most evident in resource-constrained economies, where innovation can have its greatest impact, both financially and socially.

A Solution for Big Problems

When referring to problems in developing countries, economists often use terms such as "economic inequality," "the rich-poor gap," "the divide between poor people and rich people," and "the divide between poor nations and rich nations." They also use terms such as "poor countries," "rich countries," and "poor" and "rich" economies. Years ago, when doing research on developing countries, I was faced with as many questions as answers. From what I had continued to observe—even with the passage of time—was that the majority of people conveniently divided the world into two camps. The first consisted of the estimated one to two billion people who were rich enough to be "consumers." And the second was comprised of the estimated five or six billion "non-consuming" poor who could not purchase even essential products and services. The poor were often left to be taken care of by charity, and I regret to say that not much has changed today.

In 2010, I decided to address this problem in my own way by raising consciousness through a Harvard Business Review article and post (along with Christian Sarkar). I asked why people in the developed world couldn't provide ultra-low-cost housing for people in the developing world. Using social media, I also put forth an innovation challenge—a contest that was somewhat of an experiment. I invited people to produce ideas for how to build a $300 house in a poor country. (See www.300house.com.) My challenge was based on the assumption that today's technology, combined with our increased capacity for innovation, might be able to produce solutions for people in poor economies as well as rich economies.

My innovation challenge was deceptively simple. However, the purpose of an innovation challenge is to explore possibilities, not certainties. Even knowing that, I was pleasantly surprised to see many submissions, and all showed great ingenuity. Six prizes went to people who were able to produce the most viable options for something that might seem to have been totally out of reach.

Seeing that people who are non-consumers have the same problems and many of the same needs, desires, and ambitions as consumers, I am faced with a persistent question: Why should poor people not have the same access to essential products and solutions as rich people? Surely there could never be enough money in the world to "donate people out of poverty," but sustainable businesses are in an excellent position to attack it. With that, two more questions persist for me: What if people—and companies—were to innovate for both the rich *and* the poor? Certainly it is possible to do both, and I will illustrate this next with several examples.

Meanwhile, my second question is, "Why would companies in the rich world want to do that?" I will tell you that many companies in developed nations are making a great deal of money in developing countries, but not necessarily *for* the people who reside in them. However, I will share two examples of organizations in India that are making even greater profits than similar organizations in the U.S., and in the same line of business. And the organizations in India are innovating for the poor. First, however, I will tell you a story that most clearly demonstrates the tremendous impact that innovation can have in a poor country.

A Lot More for a Lot Less

Non-consumers often do not get needed medical care. Consequently, their infections and untreated diabetes can result in amputation. These problems are exacerbated near the borders of Thailand and Burma, Cambodia, Laos, and Myanmar. Buried on approximately 796 kilometers of land are non-visible land mines that have affected the lives of over 400,000 residents who have lost limbs. For people in these countries, losing an arm or leg is akin to losing a life because it often means losing one's livelihood.

When a physician named Dr. Therdchai Jivacate (better known as "Dr. J") completed a residency in rehabilitative medicine in the U.S., and returned to his native Thailand, he dreamed of a solution for the many people there who had lost limbs. Knowing that artificial limbs in the U.S. typically sold for $20,000 USD at that time, Dr. J wondered how he might invent one for less money. With that, he accomplished what many might deem impossible: He developed a prosthetic limb for a cost of only $30 USD, and he provided it to over 25,000 amputees in Thailand at a low cost or for free.

Little Cost for a Lot of Value?

By now, you must certainly be asking how Dr. J accomplished this. I will tell you that he did it through three disruptive innovations. Dr. J's first innovation was to lower the cost of materials by substituting titanium, a very expensive element in traditional prosthetic limbs. By replacing titanium with recycled plastic yogurt containers, Dr. J was able to provide universal access to a product for an ultra-low cost. In addition, he achieved timely delivery of his artificial limbs. For example, in the U.S., back then, delivery time on an artificial limb was approximately seven to ten days, whereas Dr. J's limb took only one to three days. And because his limbs were considerably more lightweight, they were more comfortable for amputees. Even more amazing is that Dr. J's limbs were as durable, or more so, as artificial limbs in the U.S. He proved this by creating a prosthetic leg that was strong enough to support the weight of a 2,500-pound baby elephant that had lost its leg to one of the many landmines in the area.

Dr. J's second disruptive innovation was in response to the shortage of technicians qualified to fit prosthetic legs. He trained local people to fit prosthetic limbs. You might ask whether practitioners without formal training could effectively accomplish this, and I will tell you that these technicians are more skilled than most professionals in the U.S. Keep in mind that Thai amputees put far more stress on their legs than do most people living a Western lifestyle. To make a living in Thailand, amputees must be able to walk or run on uneven payment, work in watery rice paddies, and even climb trees to harvest coconuts. With that, how can Dr. J's technicians possibly fit people with artificial legs that meet these requirements? They can because they're amputees themselves.

If this isn't amazing enough, there is still another benefit that Dr. J's amputee technicians bring: With their practical and first-hand experience with the prosthesis, they almost always—and very quickly—inspire trust and hope in new patients. Because Dr. J's amputee technicians were unable to make a living before getting their artificial limbs, they are passionate about their work. Now able to help thousands of other amputees, these practitioners do not view the work that they are doing as mere "jobs." They believe they are doing "God's work." And I can tell you that when people approach their jobs as if they're doing God's work, their results are outstanding!

However, there is still more to Dr. J's story. In 1992, after observing that the least likely people to obtain prosthetic limbs in Thailand were those living in the country's remote borderlands, Dr. J founded the Prosthesis Foundation. With that, he launched his third disruptive innovation: He organized teams of volunteers and specialized personnel to provide low cost or free prosthetic limbs—and did it in only six days—from over 200 mobile workshops. And with the benefit of Thai royal sponsorship, Dr. J was also able to expand his operation to Malaysia, Laos, and Myanmar.

The Innovation Challenge

What can we learn from these disruptive and frugal innovations? And what important questions might Dr. J's story raise? If companies were to innovate for the poor as well as the rich, the world's current consumers, and non-consumers alike, could afford their products and services. As long as these products and services were of good quality and sold at affordable prices, people everywhere would likely want them. And if innovations for the five or six billion poor were to migrate to rich countries, these products and services could also enhance the lives of the one or two billion rich.

Although this kind of innovation would call for different ways of doing business, the basic business models of companies in the rich world would remain the same. Leaders could make money regardless of *where* their business might be done. What is more, this kind of innovation would not mean sacrificing a company's mission to make money nor would it require an increased focus on corporate responsibility or charity. However, converting the non-consuming poor into consumers would be no simple task. It would mean changing an outmoded way of thinking and a long-standing paradigm in rich countries. Instead of spending a considerable amount of money to innovate, companies would need to spend less and create new business models in the same way that people in poor economies have been doing out of necessity. Would learning how to do more with less be so difficult?

Value for Money vs. Value for Many

I am a firm believer in capitalism; however, I also believe there is far too much emphasis on maximizing short-term shareholder value. So given that innovation is fundamentally about changing the rules of the game, we might ask what happens when organizations like Dr. J's change the game itself. And what happens when some organizations shift their "value for money" to "value for many"? Do their efforts yield worthwhile profits? Companies that are successfully innovating in under-developed countries are doing so because they have shifted their values as well as their mindsets. Instead of focusing exclusively on "making more money," they have identified ways to "do a lot more with a lot less for a lot of people." How have they accomplished this?

Clearly it costs less to innovate in countries like India and China, even if the materials used are the same as those in the developed world. And there is no lack of examples of organizations that are doing more with less through disruptive innovations. G.E., John Deere, and PepsiCo are a few U.S. companies cited in the book that I co-authored with Chris Trimble entitled *Reverse Innovation: Create Far From Home; Win Everywhere*. However, other organizations are competing with disruptive innovations as well. A good example is Narayana Hrudayalay Heart Hospital (also known as NH Hospital) in Bangalore, India.

In 2012, when *Reverse Innovation* was published, NH Heart Hospital was doing open-heart surgery with much of the same equipment as that used by the Mayo Clinic—but for a cost of approximately $3,000 USD in India, compared to tens of thousands of dollars in the U.S. And Aravind Eye Hospital, also in India, was doing cataract surgery for $200 USD, compared to several thousand for the same operation in the United States. In some cases, surgery at these two hospitals was even being done on a zero cost basis because leaders in these organizations believed (and still do) that no one should be turned away because of an inability to pay. "How can they do this?" you ask. They operate on a 60/40 ratio where people in the 60th percentile (who can afford their services) subsidize the costs of the 40% who cannot afford them. Yes, I can imagine you think that not all companies would want to adopt the 60/40 model, but this is not the only way that organizations like Aravind and NH Heart Hospital have achieved profitability. They have also discovered how to "do more with less."

Assembly-line Healthcare?

Although I have used examples here that show significant disparities in cost, I do not want to imply that frugal innovation is only about reducing cost. The defining quality of this kind of innovation is its ability to push the envelope of the price-performance paradigm. With that in mind, you are probably still asking how surgery in India can be 25 times less than the same surgery done in the U.S., but if I teach you about "Manufacturing 101," you will understand how. The business models of the organizations performing these operations parallel those of Henry Ford, who achieved efficiencies through concepts such as specialization, economies of scale, and the assembly line. Knowing that, would you want to have heart surgery "assembly-line style"? Probably not, unless you're familiar with fixed cost analysis, and unless you know that the cost of use (in this case, the cost of the surgical equipment) decreases when a fixed cost item is used more frequently.

Here is a simple example of how organizations can leverage their fixed costs: A hospital in the U.S. might use expensive equipment ten times a month, whereas hospitals in India use that equipment over 100 times a month. Put another way, the revenues from one patient in the U.S. who might pay $20,000 for this surgery are the same as ten patients in India who might each pay $2,000. By now, you might be thinking that the services offered by these organizations must be of lesser quality than in developed countries, yet this is not true. Surprisingly, people in poor economies demand much higher levels of quality than people in rich economies because they believe they work very hard for their money. Consequently, they are astute observers of customer value, and they consider very carefully anything that could affect their livelihoods.

Knowing that people in these countries have few options from which to choose—and that companies with a dominant position sometimes cut corners—you might still have concerns about quality. If so, prepare to be surprised when I tell you that the quality of services provided by both hospitals just mentioned *exceeds* that in the U.S. For example, the mortality rate for open heart surgery in the U.S. is 2%, as compared to 1.2% in India. In part, this is because doctors in India gain a great deal of expertise from doing many surgeries—and from many different *types* of operations. And so hospitals in India have not only achieved economies of scale with the quantity of operations performed; they have also improved their quality of service through the *amount* of service provided. And surprisingly, the average profit margin of Indian hospitals is 15%, compared with an average profit margin of 12% in U.S. hospitals.

Applied Innovation

By now you should also be asking how the hospitals that I've mentioned are achieving cost efficiencies through innovation, rather than through simple fixed cost utilization and subsidy-type delivery models. I will tell you that they do it through applied innovation. Let me explain further. One of the reasons why doctors in India can perform open heart surgery for less money is that they don't need to invest in costly heart-lung machines such as those used in the US, which stop peoples' hearts before surgery and restart them afterward. What? Doctors in India operate on "beating hearts?" Yes, and what is equally surprising about this are the numbers of doctors from the U.S. who sit at the feet of India's cardiac surgeons, to learn how this is done so they might replicate it.

The implications of performing surgery at a low cost while still achieving higher profits are not to be underestimated—particularly when cost-saving innovations can be multiplied by high numbers to yield greater profits in other industries as well. I like to think of it in this way: There are a few people in the developed world who are capable of spending a lot, and there are a lot of people in developing countries who are capable of paying a little. If you do the math, you can see why the large numbers of micro-consumers in China and India are now important considerations for many companies. Today there are mega-markets in these countries, and many companies are leveraging these markets because they see how "a little for a lot" can play out in profits. You can also see, from my examples, that by innovating to create new businesses or to expand existing businesses, companies operating in under-developed countries can improve economic conditions significantly. When that happens, people gain better access to health care and quality education, and their standard of living improves dramatically.

As you know, developing economies today are continuing to grow at fantastic rates. With increased globalization and further advances in technology, there is no longer a question of whether the gap between poor markets and rich markets will close—only about *how quickly* it will close. With this, you might still wonder how companies can expect to make a reasonable profit, given what people in poor markets might want and what they can reasonably afford. I can tell you that innovating for the poor as well as the rich is only possible with new, low-cost solutions that are similar to Dr. J's innovations—and those at the hospitals I've cited. They have enabled universal access and world-class quality at an ultra-low cost. So I am once again back at my most enduring question: "Why don't we innovate in these markets as well as exporting to them or setting up manufacturing facilities in them?"

A Magic Formula?

Even though I have been studying innovation for over 35 years, I continue to think of it as an emergent field. By that I mean innovation is a *next practice*, rather than a *best-practice* endeavor. And this concept of next-practice matters, in part, because we live in a world that is constantly changing, for better or for worse. A good example of this was how the 2008/2009 recession fundamentally "reset" the world economy when growth began shifting from rich countries to poor countries. In the aftermath of the recession, I could easily envision how businesses might profit by bringing people in weak econo-mies into their consuming base.

Then in 2008, I was offered a two-year assignment at GE, as the company's Chief Innovation Consultant. My primary task was to work with executives in GE's healthcare division to explore how the company might leverage markets in India and China. This assignment was close to my heart because it took me back to my roots in Southern India. Excited about how GE's efforts might also encourage other companies to explore opportunities in these markets, I co-authored a Harvard Business Review article in October of 2009 with my colleague Chris Trimble and with GE's CEO, Jeff Immelt. In the article, entitled "How GE is Disrupting Itself," we introduced the term "reverse innovation." Our intent was to describe how innovation that is typically done in rich markets could be "reversed" by doing it in poor markets. And by calling this method "reverse innovation," we also suggested that some innovations could have the potential to migrate "in reverse," from poor countries to rich countries.

Even at the time we wrote this article, reverse innovation had enormous potential. The International Monetary Fund (IMF) had estimated that GDP in the developing world was roughly the equivalent of 35 trillion USD—nearly half of the world's GMP. According to IMF projections at the time, developing countries would soon account for two-thirds of the world's GDP growth. Knowing that growth rates for China and India were more than double those of developed countries at that time, one could readily understand why GE wanted to expand markets in poor countries—and why other companies did as well. So could reverse innovation contain the magic formula for converting the five or six billion non-consuming poor into consumers?

The Center of Gravity

To realize the full potential of reverse innovation, company leaders must imagine how one person with ten dollars has an entirely different set of wants and needs than ten people who each have one dollar to spend. Leaders also need to ensure that their businesses are fully aligned with the interests of people in developing countries. That does not mean simply asking, "Where is the market for my transplanted global strategy?" It means asking, "How can I use my global resources and global competencies to solve the problems of non-consumers?"

Leaders in rich countries also need to accept that the organizational architecture that facilitated their success in established markets can become the villain in new markets. Unfortunately, many leaders believe that successful reverse innovation can be accomplished through a simple change to their sales strategies or by ramped up production and distribution. They often predicate business models on these simplistic approaches and are then disappointed with the results. If leaders want to meet increasing demands in high-growth areas, they must compete in ways that include far more than mere geographic expansion. However, this type of competition is not easy. Reverse innovation almost always requires companies to reshape the entire way that they do business, and that typically means shifting the center of gravity. By that, I mean securing and utilizing local talent and delegating power to that talent. If leaders don't facilitate this shift, they sow the seeds of failure.

Obstacles

I can make a strong case for reverse innovation. Even after taking into consideration the great strides that countries such as India and China have made, many of these countries' poor are still underserved.

On the up side, this means there is still tremendous potential for meeting the needs of many and making a profit in doing so. But then how might companies unlock the potential for non-consumers to become consumers?

Few people would argue with the logic of untapped buying power in emerging markets such as China and India—and also in South Asia, Africa, Latin America, and Eastern Europe. And to them, I would still say, "Proceed with caution." Why? Because the concept of reverse innovation might sound simple, but making it happen is not. First, reverse innovation is not always a quick process. It typically occurs in three major stages: Stage One is innovating in a developing country. Stage Two is taking the innovations to other under-developed countries. And Stage Three is bringing these innovations to rich countries. Even though some companies have experienced success with reverse innovation, they have only started to tap its full potential because they are still in its early stages. That's because most of these companies do not yet have the mindset for reverse innovation. What does that require?

Years ago, a University of Michigan professor named C.K. Prahalad and his colleague, Richard Bettis, a professor at the University of North Carolina's Kenan-Flagler Business School, invented the term "dominant logic." It refers to the business models, strategies, and processes that ensure commercial success in established markets. Prahalad and Bettis believed that, to eradicate "poverty through profits," companies would need to overcome their dominant logic and "forget" about what had defined their success to date. The concept of dominant logic aptly applies now to businesses that want to reverse innovate because it means that their leaders must first overcome their dominant logic. That typically means taking a clean slate approach by creating new designs and performance scorecards that are consistent with the local values, tastes, and cultural attitudes of people in other markets.

Winning Strategies

I am sometimes asked if reverse innovation is simply a new way of looking at the "bottom of the pyramid," another concept put forth by C.K. Prahalad. This concept holds that companies operating in weak economies could "do well by doing good." Although reverse innovation can produce some of the same results as bottom-of-the-pyramid initiatives and other types of innovation, it originates from a different source: It comes from a formal business strategy that is based on a profitability model. That's why my answer is "no" when people have asked if reverse innovation might be simply another term for "inclusive innovation," "inclusive growth," or "social innovation."

To further clarify, reverse innovation is also not the same as "glocalization" or outsourcing. Glocalization, a strategy still employed by some companies that export to developing countries, is about selling lower-end products or those with scaled down features to poor people. Additionally, although reverse innovation can include outsourcing, it goes far beyond simply transferring tasks from one part of the world to another or directing local people to carry out prescribed activities. Put into the simplest terms, reverse innovation is about innovating *for* emerging markets, as opposed to merely exporting *to* them. And as previously mentioned, it is also about innovations in developing economies that have the potential to eventually move to developed economies.

I continue to witness how winning strategies and disruptive innovations can create opportunities by changing entire industries and markets. Regardless of where these opportunities might emerge, reverse innovation can enable organizations to expand their markets, create jobs, and make profits. Considering the tremendous business impact that this kind of innovation can have on the developing world, it matters little what we call it as long as it takes "business as usual" to "business at its *best.*"

Final Thoughts

Are there any negative implications to closing the rich-poor gap? I will admit that at least one effort to narrow the rich-poor gap created some problems years ago, but it was not related to reverse innovation. When many organizations began outsourcing, economic and purchasing power increased in developing countries, and with that, poor people experienced a narrowing of the gap. Conversely, people in developed countries also felt the gap narrowing—but not in their favor. This perception was particularly true if they had lost jobs due to their work migrating to operations in under-developed countries. I assert that it is not appropriate to close the rich-poor gap by causing people in rich countries to give up something when there are solutions by which everyone can win.

Not everyone agrees with me on this point. Although some leaders view developing economies as opportunities to do successful business in a space that is still relatively uncontested, others continue to view them as "disruptive innovators" and major threats. Most interesting, however, are the views of some social scientists, who believe that income inequality is a *positive* thing. They assert that it fosters aspirational consumption and healthy competition, and they believe that inequality incentivizes poor people to seek wealth-generating opportunities.

These same social scientists warn, however, that when opportunities in developing countries initially involve taking on debt, they can eventually lead to even greater inequality and potential economic instability. Another of their arguments against economic equality is the social inequality that can sometimes come with it. They assert that income gaps can reduce social cohesion. They also believe that when gaps continue to widen within communities, there can be potential for social unrest and even an overall weakening of society. Of course, innovating for everyone removes many, if not all, of these concerns.

A Look Ahead

I predict that, in the next 20 years or so, reverse innovation will bring the greatest potential for mega opportunities. I believe it will transform just about every industry and will become the largest growth vector. In fact, I'm also convinced that reverse innovation is not optional. Although it has already taken hold in the consumer goods and healthcare areas, it brings enormous potential in other industries as well, such as education, transportation, and energy.

In closing, someone recently asked me to describe what I believe to be the number one problem in the world today. As I have said in many presentations over the years, companies in the rich world have world-class capabilities, yet they still innovate primarily for consumers in the rich world. Although there is nothing wrong with that, innovation does not need to be an either-or scenario. With that, why not also innovate for non-consumers? My observations over the years tell me that few business leaders surpass their goals, and few exceed expectations of themselves. Those that do tend to view themselves as having a higher purpose than to simply make money. By attempting to solve both business and social problems, they're driven to innovate beyond their previous limitations.

Surely eliminating income inequality would represent the highest form of human achievement. However, because performance is ultimately a function of purpose and expectations, we would need people from a broad range of disciplines to raise ambitions and keep them high. Narrowing the rich-poor gap would also require a *business mind* and a *social heart* working together. Today's expanded capacity for innovation can easily catalyze this powerful combination, so why not take up the call and make the world a livable place for *everyone* versus only a select few?

■ ■ ■

To learn more about Vijay Govindarajan, his awards, and his many books on innovation, go to www.vg-tuck.com. To visit VG's blog, go to www.vijaygovindarajan.com. To learn more about related topics in this book, see *A Business Case for Strategic Partnerships and Alliances*, *A Design Mindset*, *Business Model Innovation*, and *Consumer Insights* in this book.

Health Awareness and Attitudes: Catalyzing Health Education

An interview with Donna T. Pepe, President, Communications Strategies, Inc. and former Vice President of Public Affairs, Johnson & Johnson, Pharmaceutical Sector

Donna T. Pepe's lifelong passion for women's healthcare has been the focus of her career for more than 30 years and has led to being a part of some of the most revolutionary product launches and public relations campaigns in the field. While functioning as Johnson & Johnson's (J&J's) first female vice president with worldwide marketing communications responsibility for companies in the pharmaceutical sector, Donna changed the way that J&J marketed prescription products to consumers. Through her many powerful initiatives—and by creating a strategy of going directly to end users, rather than selling exclusively to physicians—she elevated women's health awareness and effectively changed how all pharmaceutical companies marketed to women. Donna's TRUTHRUMOR campaign, the first-ever direct-to-consumer advertising campaign for birth control pills, won her the American Advertising Federation's ADDY award. Then, after heading the public affairs and marketing communications group for all J&J companies in the Pharmaceutical Sector, Donna founded her own marketing communications and public relations agency, Communication Strategies. In 2011, she received the Outstanding Entrepreneur award from the National Association of Female Executives, Woman of Excellence from the National Association of Professional Women, and Leading Woman Entrepreneur from Own It Venture and New Jersey Monthly.

■ ■ ■

How did a creative branding effort powerfully educate healthcare providers and consumers about the severity of allergies and the cost of not treating them? When we think about health awareness initiatives, we often associate them with organizations in the not-for-profit or public sectors, whose primary missions are to raise awareness and educate. Yet some companies raise awareness and bring social value at the same time that they create profitable products and services. This is a story about how Schering Plough (now Merck & Co), in partnership with Communication Strategies, Inc., contributed to the knowledge base about allergies and made a lasting impact on how the public understands them. It aptly demonstrates how companies can create a win-win impact for the public good while also enhancing their bottom lines.

In the late 1990s, neither physicians nor consumers truly understood the relationship between allergies and asthma, a potentially life-threatening condition. Amazing as it might seem today, even physicians viewed allergies as trivial, so people often weren't treated or were treated ineffectively. However, all that changed in January of 1997, when consciousness was raised by a seemingly unrelated event: the recall by the U.S. Food and Drug Administration (FDA) of the first prescription allergy drug, Seldane, due to its serious side effects, including deaths. For reasons still unknown today, the FDA announced that only Allegra (Claritin's competitor for prescription allergy medication) was approved to "replace" Seldane as a safe and effective alternative. Since Allegra and Claritin had similar profiles, and neither drug had the fatal and serious cardiac side effects of Seldane, it was unclear why the FDA hadn't also mentioned Claritin. Especially perplexing was that Claritin's sales at that time had been exceeding Allegra's and it had also been on the market longer. What is clear, in retrospect, is that the inequity created by the FDA's endorsement of Allegra had served as a powerful catalyst for a brand-enhancing marketing campaign as well as a favorable outcome for allergy sufferers and for the prevention of asthma.

The Innovation Challenge

What efforts did Schering-Plough make to counteract the FDA's implied endorsement of Allegra and its associated challenges? At that time, patients needed prescriptions to obtain Claritin or Allegra, which usually also required doctor and prescription co-pays. The greatest challenge in converting an over-the-counter (OTC) market to a prescription-based market were the many practitioners who were telling patients to buy OTC allergy medications despite their side effects. Schering needed to exploit disadvantages of over-the-counter medications and their side effects, which ranged from mild drowsiness to an inability to work or drive a car. That called for new ways of thinking about allergies and communicating that thinking to the general public. It also required an innovative approach that would shift the paradigm to go beyond traditional sales and marketing strategies.

Schering-Plough's senior leaders decided they needed outside assistance to solve a problem of this magnitude so they brought in Donna Pepe, the President of Communication Strategies, Inc., who had a long-standing record of bringing about paradigm shifts in the market. In addition to defining and overcoming obstacles that were preventing Claritin's market-share growth, Donna would need to create a plan to spur growth. This would mean expanding the allergy marketplace by educating consumers and health care practitioners about the seriousness of allergies. It would also require reframing how the general public viewed allergies and drawing a parallel between allergies and other health issues, including asthma.

Winning Strategies

In addition to showing how Schering-Plough and CSI provided powerful education to healthcare providers and consumers, this story describes how they were able to shift the mindset that had previously trivialized allergies. Donna's team and their partners at Schering accomplished this while achieving brand and marketing success for Claritin that permanently and indelibly impacted the allergy category and defined how allergies are viewed today.

From Breakdown to Breakthrough

Working together, Donna and Schering formulated a number of strategies that began with a public awareness campaign to educate people about the different types of allergies, their causes, and the best way to treat them. Since the incidence of asthma is much higher in low-income communities, Schering partnered with The Children's Health Fund (CHF), a non-profit group whose mission was to educate and treat allergies and asthma in these communities. Schering had a mobile unit built, and through a grant, provided CHF the financing required to build an additional mobile unit. These units traveled throughout low-income areas, providing free medication and treatment for allergies and asthma.

Schering-Plough and CSI then engaged a recognizable and sympathetic public figure to speak about allergies and become the "face" of Claritin. Although today, public figures commonly endorse pharmaceutical products, Schering-Plough was the first to hire a celebrity in an integrated marketing campaign for a prescription drug. The Good Morning America show anchor, Joan Lunden, had suffered from allergies and was successfully using Claritin. CSI and Schering's consumer marketing team tied Lunden to all elements of the education campaign—from TV, radio, and print advertising to direct marketing and to appearances at medical meetings and on Capitol Hill.

Knowing that women were the main consumers of healthcare products for their families, Schering then applied for pediatric indications. After receiving approval, Schering and Donna educated consumers and health care providers about the finding that if mothers have allergies, their children will likely have allergies as well. By featuring Joan and her daughters, who also suffered from allergies, they catapulted the brand's name recognition and deepened consumers' understanding of allergies. In fact, one of the very first product placements for Claritin was in ABC's television series, "All My Children," when one of the soap opera stars appeared to be suffering from seasonal allergies.

Ongoing Challenges

Together, Schering and CSI were making significant headway in their campaign but were still facing challenges with prescribers. First, they needed to broaden the base of prescribers from allergists to family practitioners. They also needed to influence family practitioners to stop treating allergies as trivial. Additionally, Schering and CSI wanted to obtain consensus among medical associations and consumer advocacy groups about the seriousness of allergies. They also wanted these groups to underscore the importance of treating allergies properly in order to avoid asthma and other comorbidities. Scientific evidence was required to support this position.

As a first step toward building evidence, the company formed alliances with the AAAAI (American Academy of Allergy, Asthma and Immunology) and the Allergy and Asthma Foundation of America (AAFA). After spearheading an educational campaign entitled "Allergy Action," CSI and Schering formed the "Coalition Against Allergies"—a multi-disciplinary group of physicians and other healthcare advocates who could serve as advisors for their various specialties and as educators/spokespeople for the campaign. Spearheaded by the AAAAI, 25 major medical associations and patient advocacy groups came together for a year to develop the first—and to this day—only medical treatment guidelines for allergies. CSI then helped to facilitate sessions with these groups to reach agreement on guidelines and to finalize outcomes.

By clearly communicating messages about the different types of allergies, Schering and CSI provided the message platform to healthcare providers that could facilitate a better understanding of how to identify and treat allergies. The next challenge for Schering and CSI was to disseminate these new guidelines to those treating allergies in a clear and concise way, underscoring the role of Claritin and its strengths. Donna says, "We decided to develop pocket-sized guides that were well received and viewed as valuable references to both family practitioners and pediatricians who were treating patients with allergies. We took the message straight to physicians via the sales force."

Before completing the campaign, Donna and her counterparts at Schering realized that during allergy season, it would be important to raise awareness of pollen counts. However, at that time, these counts weren't part of weather forecasts on TV or radio, so Donna approached the American Broadcasting Company (ABC) to develop the pollen and allergy advisory forecast. She also ensured that it was broadcasted at the conclusion of weather reports and just prior to Claritin commercials.

Final Thoughts

Today, pollen counts are a standard category in weather reports and part of people's daily conversations. More importantly, allergies are no longer trivialized. Many people now know that if untreated, allergies can result in asthma and other medical problems. This is a prime example of how an innovative branding effort can solve an innovation challenge, while simultaneously creating success for companies and adding value for consumers. Additionally, it's a very good example of how organizations can change the culture around a common problem. In this case, Schering-Plough helped healthcare providers and customers prevent unnecessary suffering—and even death—through health awareness and a change in mindset.

■ ■ ■

About Communications Strategies, Inc. (CSI)

Communications Strategies, Inc. (CSI), headquartered in Morristown, NJ, has been an innovator in marketing since 1993, with an emphasis on healthcare and women. The firm ranked among the top 100 public relations agencies in the U.S. and among the top 20 independent health care public relations agencies in the country. Specializing in bringing value to clients in consumer marketing, CSI addresses challenges in catapulting products into household names. Among its clients are companies such as Schering-Plough, Pfizer, Barr Pharmaceuticals, Teva, King, Daiichi, Organon, Ferring, Reliant, Sanofi Aventis, and many more. Since its inception, CSI has won numerous prestigious awards including Medical Marketing and Media Gold Award for Plan B One-Step, a half dozen MARCOM awards, PRSA Big Apple Award for Best Marketing Consumer Products Healthcare, the Clarion Award for Special Design, a Gold-level Bulldog Award for Healthcare Agency of the Year, the Bronze-level Bulldog Award for Small Agency of the Year, and many more over the years. To learn more about Communications Strategies, Inc., see www.cstratinc.com.

About Schering-Plough Corporation/Merck & Company

Schering-Plough Corporation was a United States-based pharmaceutical company, founded in 1851 by Ernst Christian Friedrich Schering, as Schering AG in Germany. In 1971, the Schering Corporation merged with Plough to form Schering-Plough. On November 4, 2009 Merck & Co. merged with Schering-Plough with the new company taking the name of Merck & Co. Prior to the merger, Schering-Plough had manufactured several pharmaceutical drugs, the most well known of which were the allergy drugs Claritin and Clarinex, an anti-cholesterol drug Vytorin, and a brain tumor drug called Temodar. These drugs are now available from Merck & Co.

■ ■ ■

If you found this innovation story interesting, see our enabling chapters entitled *A Business Case for Creativity and Creative Problem Solving*, *A Business Case for Strategic Partners and Alliances*, *A Path to Innovation Excellence*, and *Business Model Innovation*.

Inclusive Collaboration: Creating a New Dimension for Performance

An interview with Frances Hesselbein, President/CEO of the Frances Hesselbein Leadership Institute (founded as the Peter F. Drucker Foundation for Nonprofit Management) and former CEO of the Girls Scouts of the USA

When Frances Hesselbein was awarded the Presidential Medal of Freedom, the highest civilian honor in the United States, it was U.S. President Bill Clinton's way of recognizing her as one of the most highly respected experts in the field of contemporary leadership development. President George W. Bush Sr. also recognized her efforts by appointing her to two Presidential Commissions on National and Community Service. In 2009, Frances was recognized by the University of Pittsburgh when it introduced The Hesselbein Global Academy for Student Leadership and Civic Engagement. And in that same year, she received a two-year appointment as Chair for the Study of Leadership at the United States Military Academy at West Point. During her career, Frances has served on many not-for-profit and private sector corporate boards, including Mutual of America Life Insurance Company and the Bright China Social Fund. She also served as Chair of the National Board of Directors for Volunteers of America from 2002-2006. Frances is also the recipient of 23 honorary doctoral degrees, the editor-in-chief of the award-winning quarterly journal Leader to Leader, and co-editor of 27 books in 29 languages. She has traveled to 68 countries representing the United States and is the author of *Hesselbein on Leadership, My Life in Leadership, and More Hesselbein on Leadership.*

■　■　■

How might organizations grow and increase their value by changing their business models to reflect society's changing needs? And why is it important for today's organizations to specifically mirror the demographics of the customers and societies that they serve? This chapter illustrates how one leader in the Girls Scouts USA was able to produce a new dimension of performance by effectively leading change. It also describes how she continually reinvented the organization through inclusive collaboration and values-based innovation. Beginning with a story about a much-needed turnaround effort, this chapter also illustrates winning strategies that can be replicated by organizations in all sectors.

When Frances Hesselbein first began her career with a local chapter of the Girl Scouts USA (GSUSA), there was probably no way to predict how perilously close this U.S. institution would come to near collapse. Yet Frances might have been even less likely to predict how she herself would someday lead the effort that would save this long-standing and well-regarded organization. In her first leadership role with the GSUSA, Frances remained faithful to the original goal of making girls strong and developing them into competent women yet also felt that the way girls were being developed by the Girl Scouts USA was outdated. Believing that its leadership required more contemporary approaches, Frances knew that the focus should be on assisting girls to prepare for careers and to help them become independent.

With her promotion to the CEO role of the national organization 13 years later, Frances had the position power to bring about the kind of dramatic change that she had believed was needed from the start. And at that time, there was every reason to bring about that change—and quickly! She knew the decline in membership that had occurred over the previous eight consecutive years had put the organization's long-term survival at great risk and would continue to do so. With a goal to help the Girl Scouts USA become more viable and relevant, Frances worked diligently and collaboratively with her team, slowly breathing life back into the organization through a number of innovative, tangible, and measurable changes. Using Drucker's five critical questions, Frances and her team had asked: What is our mission? Who is our customer? What does the customer value? What are our results? What is our plan? Then she and her team members produced a concise but powerful and compelling mission: "To help each girl reach her own highest potential."

A History of Change

Frances was convinced that fulfilling this mission would require a significant culture transformation, yet when recalling how she had brought about meaningful change in her first role with the GSUSA, she knew this wouldn't be a first for her. Back in her early days with the Girl Scouts of America, she believed that, "No young person says, 'I can't wait to be a subordinate,'" and she quickly changed her local Girl Scout Council's traditional structure and language to eliminate terms such as "superior" and "subordinate." Frances had also changed the old hierarchical structure with an innovative new concept that she created called "circular management." Instead of remaining at the "top" of the organizational chart, with others "below" her, she placed herself in the middle of two concentric circles, with the idea of "supporting" those "around" her. In this way, all would function as members of a team, with no one designated as a "superior" or a "subordinate." Now it was time for Frances to bring about another transformation by once again incorporating circular management, this time at the national level.

Although she was committed to maintaining the organization's core values and principles, Frances was well aware that its practices needed to be relevant to prevailing needs. With only five percent of the organization's membership representing a racial or ethnic minority, she wanted to ensure that the Girl Scout's total membership, including the board and staff, would mirror the diversity of society. Viewing the changing demographics as a way to "serve in new and more significant ways than ever before," Frances wanted the Girl Scouts to include "every part of society." To accomplish that, however, she would need to construct a compelling business case and create an inclusive culture that would address societal needs as well as individual needs. She would lay the groundwork for the highly relevant and contemporary organization that she could now envision and she would ensure it with sound research and a formal study.

Sea Change

Frances retained Dr. Robert Hill, who she viewed as one of the best researchers in the country. To meet the needs of current Girl Scouts as well as potential future members, she would build a case predicated on Dr. Hill's research and a custom-designed study of the GSUSA. Then by using Dr. Hill's research and his study as catalysts for change, Frances would subsequently collaborate with consultant Dr. John W. Work III, who would provide diversity training and coaching to all Girl Scout USA leaders. She subsequently also partnered with a number of well-known and highly regarded educators. Dr. John W. Gardner, Jr., author and Stanford University professor, trained members of the GSUSA's board and Harvard Business School Professors Dr. Regina Herzlinger and Dr. James L. Heskett developed corporate management seminars for Girl Scout Executives.

However, to accomplish an effective turnaround at the scale that was required, Frances knew that it would be important to signal the change on all fronts, beginning with the GSUSA's long-standing icons. After collaborating with numerous consultants, educators, artists, designers, and trainers about how to innovatively and visually transform the organization, she and her team took the first step. By working with top designer, Halston, to, in Frances's words, "update the dowdy polyester uniforms that hadn't changed in 12 years." In addition, she and her team produced a new Girl Scout pin, but to ensure buy-in to further changes, they didn't force this change on anyone. Instead, they allowed scouts and leaders to choose whichever pin they would prefer to wear.

Frances and her team then collaborated with Saul Bass and other skilled artists and graphic designers to develop new handbooks, programs, and promotional materials that included videos and posters. All the new collateral featured girls from each cultural group along with captions that reflected their respective cultures and values. Moving beyond previous boundaries, GSUSA employees distributed this material and also began developing recruiting plans that included efforts to ensure diversity.

Results

As so often happens when people innovate, Frances and her team produced an unintended but highly favorable outcome. During the process of collaboratively designing and implementing the organization's transformation, she and her team had also effectively closed the previously existing chasm between local councils and the national organization. Now, in addition to a new dimension of performance, there was internal unification. Research conducted by the Chronicle of Philanthropy shortly after the turnaround showed that the Girl Scouts USA had become the most effective charity/non-profit of 100 other American organizations studied.

Tempting as it might have been to slow down and savor the fruits of their efforts, Frances and her team knew it was important to keep moving forward. Through ongoing internal and external collaboration, they continued to build the foundation that would support the more viable, relevant, and contemporary organization that GSUSA would become and continues to be today. Frances cites as evidence of that the many women leaders today who were once affiliated with the Girl Scouts USA and the 20+ NASA astronauts who were former Girl Scouts. Under Frances's leadership, membership had grown to 2.25 million girls and the organization's workforce—primarily volunteers—had grown to 780,000. To date, more than 50 million American women have participated in Girl Scouting, over a million of them as volunteers.

A New Chapter and Role

When Frances retired from her GSUSA CEO role, life clearly had other plans for her. Only six weeks later, she became the Founding President of the Peter F. Drucker Foundation for Nonprofit Management and the Editor-in-Chief of the award-winning quarterly *Leader to Leader Journal.* In these new roles, Frances was able to continue helping others create a new dimension of performance through diversity, inclusion, and cross-sector collaboration, and on a broader scale. One way she accomplished this was by collaborating with John Whitehead and James Austin at Harvard Business School with a specific focus on how organizations in the private and not-for-profit sectors could partner for mutual benefit. Another way was through the many publications that she authored and co-authored. And still another, was when she enabled good ideas, best practices, and examples of innovation to move across all sectors, around the world.

The Innovation Challenge

Few people would disagree that today's grand challenges call for change enabled by inclusive collaboration. In her book, *Leading for Innovation,* Frances and co-authors Marshall Goldsmith and Iain

Somerville reference Peter Drucker's definition of innovation as "change that creates a new dimension of performance." To that they add, "In today's turbulent times, bringing about such a change is one of the greatest challenges leaders face." Citing an article in the *Economist* that quoted Peter Drucker, these authors believed as he did, that the most effective way to manage change is to create it. Yet, Drucker had added, "… experience has shown that grafting innovation onto a traditional enterprise does not work. The enterprise has to become a change agent."

Frances said, "Today, leaders in all sectors must achieve systemic innovation and focus on performance and results during the most rapidly-changing and volatile times that I can remember." In *Leading for Innovation*, she and her co-authors describe the task as, "… being astute enough to catch a straw in the wind even before it becomes a trend, and then having everything in place when it emerges.…" Frances said, "To continually achieve that, we must partner with others—and, at the same time, deal with relentless change."

How is that best accomplished? Like values-based leadership, values-based innovation is based on the premise that people will perform at optimum levels if they're guided by well-communicated and inclusive missions, values, and guiding principles. Additionally, it's based on observations that employees are most apt to adopt the organization's values if leaders model behaviors that are congruent with the values set forth by their organizations.

Obstacles

Compounding today's ongoing change are the enormous pressures that leaders are under to perform—often on a quarterly basis. Yet Frances believes that the most significant challenge by far is dealing with today's crisis in leadership. As proof of this, she cited headlines and nightly newscasts about company presidents and CEOs, chairs of boards, and other leaders who have failed because of questionable ethics or poor leadership.

Frances described these leaders as "oblivious to fiduciary responsibility, disdainful of stockholders' and the public interest, disrespectful of the workforce, and unfaithful to their organization's missions," yet she also quickly pointed out that the leadership crisis isn't limited to corporate scandals, but crosses all three sectors. Frances also acknowledged that even leaders of high integrity face significant social, economic, and environmental challenges at present. That's because they're often tainted by the acts of other leaders with less integrity, and so most leaders today need to work at restoring trust. Acknowledging this, Frances said, "With today's highest level of cynicism and the lowest level of trust, leaders must ensure the inclusion that unifies and the language that heals." How is that best done?

Winning Strategies

In her 23 years leading the Institute, Frances has continually encouraged others to lead by example and to "manage for the mission, for innovation, and for diversity." Additionally, she believes that it's critically important to view opportunities, "not in terms of numbers and money, but of service...." Continually reminding others that "to serve is to live," she says, "... from the day we start a new job, we should start thinking about how and when we're going to leave the organization, institution, or enterprise far better than we found it." She suggests, however, that even the most effective leaders aren't usually able to bring about that kind of change single-handedly. They typically do it through inclusive collaboration—with team members, peers, and strategic alliances outside of their organizations.

Many people define global collaboration on a macro level, and they envision it occurring when country leaders and officials successfully work together. However, many leaders believe that global collaboration begins at the micro level, with individuals who pave the way for generations of future leaders by modeling the kinds of behaviors that enable successful collaboration. When former U.S. President Bill Clinton presented Frances with the Presidential Medal of Freedom, he recognized her leadership as CEO of the Girl Scouts of the USA and also as the Founding President of the Drucker Foundation and for her service as "a pioneer for women, volunteerism, diversity and opportunity."

Specifically referencing Frances's successful turnaround of the Girl Scouts USA, President Clinton said, "Frances... led them back, both in numbers and in spirit... and in so doing, made a model for us all. She invigorated the organization with her commitment to inclusiveness and to upholding the Girl Scout mission of empowering each Scout to reach her highest potential. She has worked to imbue other nonprofit groups with the hallmarks of true leadership: openness to innovation, willingness to share responsibility, and respect for diversity. In her current role ... she has shared her remarkable recipe for inclusion and excellence with countless organizations whose bottom line is measured not in dollars, but in changed lives. With skill and sensitivity, Francis has shown us how to summon the best from ourselves and our fellow citizens."

How exactly did Frances accomplish that during her turnaround effort at the GSUSA? By creating a strong business case for a more inclusive membership base and then implementing three powerful strategies: circular management, shared goals and objectives, and culture change.

Final Thoughts

Frances has often said that the kind of collaboration required for solving today's global challenges must occur collectively. Drawing upon her life lessons and guiding principles, she believes that winning strategies and solutions reside in the power of language, inclusive collaboration, and courage as well as in the organization's mission, values, and efforts to innovate. She added, "Courage is needed during periods of great divisiveness, but leaders can effectively build trust, inspire innovation, and bring the future to life when they formulate and communicate shared goals and objectives while acting in embracing and inclusive ways. Then those they serve, the future customers their organizations will find, and the people within their own walls, will eagerly partner with them."

Many leaders, tasked with bringing about change through others, need to relinquish some control. Frances said when they're able to accomplish that, "Then they often learn that leadership is a matter of how to *be*, not how to *do*—that it's the quality and character of a leader that determines performance—and positive results." She adds that when leaders learn how to "be," leadership becomes a *journey*, not a *destination*. And when that happens, leaders often transform *themselves* while they work at transforming *their organizations*. Frances reminds us that innovation is also a journey—and one of continual discovery that often leads to new and ever-changing interim destinations. What's more, since innovation is often described as a team sport, inclusive collaboration also plays a critical role in the innovation journey—and in creating new dimensions for performance.

A Look Ahead

Expressing great hope in the Millennial Generation—or what Warren Bennis called the "Crucible Generation"—Frances said she admires the value that these young people place on diversity, inclusion, and collaboration. She said, "Research suggests that they possess the qualities needed to heal and repair today's world, yet equally admirable are their global perspectives and their willingness to take responsibility for society's current challenges."

Frances is also optimistic about the leaders who will play a role in healing and unifying, yet she adds, "No single leader, organization, or sector alone will be able to address these challenges. To effectively innovate and, at the same time generate social value, leaders in the private sector, public institutions, and not-for-profit organizations will need to continue working closely together—but more globally. If we're to build a healthy society, organizations in all sectors must function as a large ecosystem made up of many smaller ecosystems—and that will only happen if leaders in all sectors are willing and able to go beyond the walls of their own organizations."

She added, "To meet today's grand challenges, leaders of businesses must become more socially responsible. And, to survive and thrive, leaders of not-for-profit organizations must become more businesslike." Frances is nonetheless encouraged by the number of partnerships developing between organizations in the not-for-profit and private sectors that already represent a major departure from traditional check-writing approaches to philanthropy. Additionally, she believes that cross-sector collaboration is already enabling the kind of partnerships that can build brand identity and goodwill for all parties. Looking ahead, she believes organizations in all sectors will increasingly uncover new business opportunities and revenue sources at the same time that they're facilitating social good. This will likely translate to an even broader dimension for performance when it's fueled by inclusive collaboration and values-based innovation.

■ ■ ■

About the Frances Hesselbein Institute

In 1990, Frances Hesselbein became the Founding President of the Peter F. Drucker Foundation for Nonprofit Management, named after the Austrian-born author, consultant, and educator often referred to as "the father of American management." In 2002, the organization became Leader to Leader Institute, giving the Drucker name back to the surviving family. With a unanimous Board of Governors decision, the Institute was renamed in 2012 to honor Frances Hesselbein's legacy and ongoing contributions. The goal of the Hesselbein Institute and its award-winning *Leader to Leader* quarterly journal is to showcase the best practices of highly effective global leaders and organizations and to connect the public, private, and social sectors with curated resources and relationships to serve, evolve, and lead together. By fostering leadership grounded in the passion to serve, the discipline to listen, the courage to question, and the spirit to include, the Hesselbein Institute works to create an open, responsive, global social sector through award-winning publications including a daily *Leadership Tip of the Day* newsletter, free global webinars, Skype sessions and keynote addresses, and a self-assessment tool based on Drucker's Five Questions.

■ ■ ■

To learn more about how the Frances Hesselbein Leadership Institute develops leaders, go to www.hesselbeininstitute.org. If you found this chapter helpful, see the enabling chapters entitled *A Business Case for Strategic Partnerships and Alliances, Change Leadership, Competition and Collaboration, Differences,* and *Shared Vision and Values.*

Natural Disaster Response: Dealing with Stronger and More Frequent Threats

An interview with Commander Hugh Griffiths, U.S. Coast Guard (retired), former USCG Innovation Program Manager, Office of Strategic Analysis, Washington, DC

A career US Coast Guard (USCG) officer with a diverse managerial and technical background, Hugh specialized in organizational innovation for government. Functioning as an Aircraft Integration Officer and an Aviation Engineering Officer, Hugh has implemented innovation and efficiency initiatives at numerous Coast Guard commands. He also served on the team that evaluated comprehensive recapitalization plans for all of the service's large mission resource systems, with a focus on fresh technical approaches. In 2009, Hugh was selected to revitalize Coast Guard innovation for the diverse 45,000+ member organization during an enterprise-wide push for modernization. A champion of strategically aligned innovation, complete idea management, and configuration management, his tenure as the Innovation Program Manager oversaw significant expansion of interagency collaboration and increased influence of private sector approaches to implementing change and efficiency. Hugh holds a bachelor's degree in Professional Aeronautics from Embry-Riddle Aeronautical University, a master of science in Quality Systems Management from National Graduate School, and a Certificate in Aviation Safety from the University of Southern California.

■ ■ ■

How can organizations adopt the U.S. Coast Guard's "always ready" posture when dealing with unanticipated challenges of unprecedented magnitude? This chapter illustrates how ad hoc teams, a culture of empowerment, and well-communicated guiding principles can help organizations respond efficiently and with flexibility. This chapter also illustrates how ad hoc teams can quickly pull together as high performing teams.

In 2012, when Hurricane Sandy reached the Eastern seaboard of the United States, it had already hit Jamaica with a vengeance and torn up six countries in its path. When Sandy intersected with an Arctic storm on its way north to become "Superstorm Sandy" it placed New York City firmly in its sights. Even then, it appeared to have the potential to be another Hurricane Katrina. When U.S. Coast Guard (USCG) crews from Sandy Hook, New Jersey stood watch along the Hudson River, they witnessed winds gusting over 90 miles per hour. Suddenly it was as if some malevolent god looking down from the heavens flipped a switch to prevent mortals from seeing the malicious onset of destruction until it was a *fait accompli*.

In what seemed like an instant, the brightly lit Manhattan skyline was extinguished and the horizon disappeared from sight. U.S. Coast Guard (USCG) personnel had only minutes to react before they were dodging entire trees to arrive on scene. Their advantage though was that most USCG crew members weren't encountering this kind of thing for the first time. Throughout its rich history, the US Coast Guard has adapted quickly and improvised operations based on experience in the same way as they had seven years earlier with Hurricane Katrina.

As Superstorm Sandy swept through the northern suburbs of New York, damaging winds blew steadily for hours. Residents who were afraid to open their doors and peer into the darkness could only hear trees that had steadfastly survived many hurricanes in the past falling on top of cars and houses from all directions. After approximately 12 hours, the storm finally left the metropolitan New York City area to do more damage in New England. And when the Sandy Hook, New Jersey crews on duty in New York finally returned home days later, they were totally unprepared emotionally for what they found. With Sandy Hook having been one of the hardest hit coastal areas on the entire U.S. northeastern seaboard, cars were pancaked on top of one another and houses were tilted at 45-degree angles, appearing to be hand-drawn images from some grim fairy tale. Yet the devastation didn't end there.

Bigger than Texas

In the days that followed, New York City subway tunnels were flooded, U.S. stock trading was suspended for two days, and most forms of transportation in "the city that never sleeps" came to a screeching halt. After that, there was only deafening silence for residents accustomed to honking horns, jack hammers, and other sounds of the city. In its fury, the storm left in its wake thousands of families in the metropolitan New York City area without power—or heat—as the late-fall temperatures dipped. When months passed and residents were still without heat and electricity, it appeared as if the nightmare might have no end.

To say that Superstorm Sandy produced unprecedented damage to the densely populated Northeast coast of the U.S. is an understatement. According to statistics compiled by CNN from local power providers, the storm left in its wake almost 7.5 million businesses and households without electric power in 15 states and the District of Columbia. Power provider Con Edison said it was the largest storm-related outage in recorded U.S. history, with a circumference estimated at roughly twice the size of the state of Texas. The result in the U.S. alone was 74 deaths and approximately 65 billion US dollars in damage.

After Sandy, many people who might have questioned whether there was such a thing as climate change (man-made or otherwise), put that question aside and instead braced themselves for what they feared might be the "new norm." Given the extensive power outages and damage that Superstorm Sandy caused, it still fell considerably short of the magnitude and scale of Hurricane Katrina, whose ferocity had been incubated and intensified by the warm water temperatures of the Gulf of Mexico.

Beginning of the New Norm

Going back in time to August of 2005, when Hurricane Katrina first hit land, gas stations quickly became overwhelmed and roads turned into parking lots. Katrina's wind-driven storm surge quickly pushed Gulf waters inland along the Louisiana, Mississippi and Alabama coastlines, invading 6 to 12 miles inland to depths of 25 feet above the highest high tide. Within a remarkably short period, the window of possibility for resident evacuations closed and only hours later, the levies protecting New Orleans failed.

As water continued to rush in, swift currents carried some victims away and left others stunned at having lost everything of value. Some people began moving to their attics and others clung to the roofs of their homes, looking down at the polluted waters swirling beneath them. Still others were trapped in hospitals or nursing homes. Within a matter of hours, it appeared as if the calendar pages had swiftly flipped from August to late October. The surreal scene in New Orleans looked more like some movie set for a haunted Halloween story. Corpses of early victims clogged streets and coffins, after being lifted from the city's above-ground cemeteries, were now hanging from trees.

The significant and unprecedented challenges that Katrina brought to New Orleans' various infrastructures could not be overstated. As a way to fully describe the unprecedented scope and magnitude of Hurricane Katrina, resulting property damage was estimated to be over $100 billion U.S. dollars and Federal disaster declarations showed that this natural disaster impacted a geographic area of 90,000 square miles or 233,000 kilometers—roughly the size of the United Kingdom. In addition to carrying uncontained sewage, bacteria, heavy metals, pesticides, and toxic chemicals, Katrina caused oil spills of over seven million U.S. gallons (26 million liters) from 44 facilities in southeastern Louisiana.

Seven Years Later

Fast forwarding to a sunny day in June of 2013 on the shore of the State of New Jersey, a crowd gathered around several people, recently injured and rescued from the turbulent waters after suddenly being swept off a jetty by a large rogue wave. Thankfully there had been no deaths, but after their rescue, injured victims learned that they had been hit by a meteotsunami (pronounced muh tay'-oh soo-nom-ee). This type of tsunami isn't caused by an earthquake but rather by weather conditions—often from storms occurring miles away. Was this meteotsunami nothing more than an anomaly? No!

This was not the first meteotsunami to hit the United States. The first occurred in 1954, when 10-foot waves struck a pier in downtown Chicago and killed seven people. Then in 1992, an 18-foot wave took out cars near Daytona Beach, Florida. And in 2008, a 12-foot surge poured into Boothbay Harbor, Maine. Yet the U.S. is not the only country to experience meteotsunamis. The largest ever reported produced waves of approximately 13 feet when it hit Nagasaki Bay in Japan in 1979. And in 2011, the United Kingdom was hit by a meteotsunami caused by a storm hundreds of miles away. Most unnerving, these meteotsunamis all had something in common: They all emerged seemingly out of nowhere and without warning materialized on calm sunny days—taking their victims by total surprise.

The Innovation Challenge

After centuries of research, scientists and meteorologists remain divided about the exact causes of the more intense and frequent weather-related disasters that occur in all parts of the world today. Many believe they're a result of rising CO_2 levels and an overall warming effect. Others take issue with this theory. Regardless of the cause, these events prompt serious questions. "Will we see more meteotsunamis and storms like Sandy and Katrina in the future?" "Will this phenomena take on the form of increasingly more formidable threats?" "Could storms of this nature, combined with rising sea levels, actually take out cities in coastal areas around the world, as has been predicted?"

The truth is, there are no definitive answers to these questions since each of these phenomena is different. We can learn, however, from how the U.S. Coast Guard has responded to each storm, with the intent of replicating its strategies in situations that call for quick and coordinated action. That said, of the many threats that the USCG has responded to over the years, Hurricane Katrina created unique and unprecedented challenges. What made this storm different? One reason is that it hit a major city, as opposed to the open waters to which the agency's members were accustomed.

The second reason was the challenge it posed regarding a multi-agency search and rescue missions on land that's been flooded. The third challenge for Coast Guard personnel was finding places to take evacuees. The fourth was providing evacuees with sufficient water, food, and shelter while heat indexes exceeded 100 degrees. The fifth challenge was getting fuel to USCG planes and helicopters when roads were inaccessible. And the sixth—critical to a 24/7 operation—was how to ensure that aircraft was properly serviced and maintained, despite supply system challenges, logistics breakdowns, and the inaccessibility of electronic maintenance records for review or updating.

What can other organizations in the public sector—and those in the private and not-for-profit sectors as well—learn about the methods and strategies used by the U.S. Coast Guard when responding to Katrina? In our interview with Hugh Griffiths, he described the ways in which the agency consistently ensures flexibility, efficiency, and decentralization, despite the many obstacles that surface during search and rescue missions.

Obstacles

Hugh said, "The biggest obstacle in dealing with Hurricane Katrina was the sad truth that evacuations should have occurred 24-48 hours earlier. Whether it was disbelief, complacency, lack of planning or an inability to act—or all of these things—the results were devastating. In short order, powerboats and helicopters replaced the wheeled emergency vehicles on land for the most part. However, they too faced challenges, given the atypical hazards of flooding, downed trees, power lines, and even fishing boats that were effortlessly pushed well inland. Adding to these compounded hazards were damaged military support infrastructures that hindered operations. And as Coast Guard and other rescue personnel worked diligently to help others, they struggled with damage to, or loss of, their own homes."

What does this tell us about preparedness? Can individuals, organizations, and communities adequately prepare for unprecedented disasters? And how might they respond better than some of the people and agencies did during Katrina? As a way of quantitatively describing one of the many challenges that Katrina presented, Hugh said, "The Coast Guard's total authorized strength on the fateful day the hurricane made landfall (approximately 39,000 personnel nationwide) can be roughly compared to the 36,149-member New York City Police Force at that time. To illustrate results compared to its numbers, it took an estimated 5,000 Coast Guard aviators, cuttermen, small boat crews, disaster response teams, maritime security response teams, and environmental strike forces to rescue 33,500 of the estimated 60,000 people who were in extremis during Katrina." How did the USCG accomplish such an incredible feat? And specifically, how was this small agency, more than any other, capable of assembling and deploying highly functioning teams on such short notice?

Winning Strategies

As a model of efficiency and effectiveness during Hurricane Katrina, the Coast Guard received unilateral accolades at the same time that local, city, state and federal entities were being harshly criticized for their failure to respond adequately. What made the USCG's response different? Hugh said, "The U.S. Coast Guard not only has an innovation *program;* it has an innovative *culture* as well. Members of the USCG possess innovation DNA that's been honed by a legacy of experience and lessons learned from a progression of previous disasters. Additionally, their organizational skill sets and team competencies are sharpened on an ongoing basis through continuous training, learning, and routine operations." Hugh also asserts that much of the agency's success is its adherence to seven time-tested core principals of operation, described in *U.S. Coast Guard Publication 1* and in the subsections that follow.

The Principle of Clear Objective

Hugh asserts that the essence of the first objective is that every operation should be directed toward a clearly defined and attainable objective. He also said the most significant action that leaders can take, while planning and executing any operation, is to communicate this overarching objective clearly to crewmembers. Hugh added, "Among its many missions and response operations, USCG is responsible for search and rescue assistance, marine environmental protection response and facilitation of commerce. That means in any disaster response such as Katrina, the agency's objectives are to rescue people, save property, respond to environmental hazards, and reopen waterways as soon as possible to facilitate recovery. In the case of Katrina, inaccessibility to the Mississippi River created major national commercial ramifications, but saving of lives and property was the priority and focus of the first response."

The Principle of Effective Presence

Hugh said that "effective presence," at its most basic level, means having the right assets and capabilities at the right place at the right time. He said, "During Katrina, standardized equipment and crews trained in standard well understood operating procedures were brought from every corner of the country, assembled, and scaled as needed, to conduct sustained 24/7 operations. With downed computers and other systems, USCG crews still needed to maintain aircraft maintenance records crucial to 24/7 recovery efforts. To accomplish this, maintenance and service crews used hand-written and hand-carried records in binders and created scheduling and maintenance status matrixes on dry erase boards while cohesive maintenance teams continuously rotated like NASCAR pit crews."

Hugh added, "In assembly-line fashion, mechanics worked with ant-like precision, washing, inspecting and fueling aircraft for their next missions." Pilots continuously coordinated records to maintain 100%

crew accountability, noting when rescue swimmers exited one plane and entered another. And pilots also continuously rotated in a process known as "hot seating," during which they left planes running as one crew left to rest and another continued operations.

Katrina also brought new challenges for helicopter pilots flying the missions. First, pilots needed to conduct search and rescue missions and avoid other aircraft in a free-fly zone. That meant operating without any defined communication plans or the usual assistance provided from ground-based traffic control. Second, even with vertically hoisted baskets and slings, rescue attempts were restricted because there was no easy way to get to the people trapped in their attics who were unable to break through roof-tops. Scott Price, in his report entitled "Darkest of Days" describes how on-scene crews met the challenge of "this new urban rescue environment." Following the innovation of a rescue swimmer who liberated a fire ax to get through roofs, USCG crews quickly located hardware stores and large chain stores to buy every saw and ax that they could find. Then they outfitted every helicopter with these tools so that when rescue swimmers were deployed from the air they could cut through rooftops.

The Principle of Unity of Effort

Hugh said most Coast Guard operations involve multiple Coast Guard units working in conjunction with a variety of governmental and non-governmental entities. Collectively, they focus their cooperative efforts on a common goal. Successful outcomes in these situations are incumbent upon a clear understanding of the objective and the role that each individual, unit, or organization is expected to take on. During surge operations, leaders must ensure both internal and external unity remain intact, as the Coast Guard simultaneously continues routine day-to-day operations in unaffected areas (i.e., other homeports) while conducting and coordinating high-volume "surge operations" (high-intensity efforts typically launched on short notice).

During these operations, USCG leaders and crews ensure internal unity through strict adherence to established chains of command. They do this by working with partners in state, local, and tribal organizations as well as other federal agencies, with local partnerships developed *before* a crisis. A key success factor of the USCG is the transparency that's implicit in the success of their unified operations. As stated in the U.S. Coast Guard "Pub 1" report, "Units must work with and around one another in an entirely open manner. Actions must be easily interpreted and understood. Lack of transparency can lead to doubt, confusion, or mistrust, and any of these can cause a mission to fail." Hugh said, "During Katrina, the USCG activated and adapted established emergency plans, quickly formed ad hoc partnerships with the limited local resources that were available. The USCG also adopted a variety of team generated innovative approaches to unique situations."

The Principle of On-Scene Initiative

"A major distinguishing factor of the USCG from other agencies—and other organizations in general," Hugh said, "is the latitude that leaders and crews have, to act quickly and decisively. Because people in the Coast Guard are well aware of the scope of their authority, they can take needed action without waiting for direction from higher levels. Personal initiative has always been crucial to the success of the Coast Guard."

Rapid action requires decentralization, and unity of effort is about getting many moving parts working together. "If there's one aspect of the Coast Guard's culture that distinguishes it from so many other organizational cultures," Hugh said, "it's the latitude afforded to responders. They're expected to assess on-scene conditions quickly and make rapid judgments about the assets and types of approaches needed. A good example of this during Katrina was when pilots on area-wide environmental survey flights restructured their mission profiles, which also allowed them to coordinate and act as communications relays critical to ongoing search and rescue efforts."

The Principle of Flexibility

To succeed in pursuing multiple missions with common assets—including people—Hugh told us that members of the Coast Guard must be able to adjust to a wide variety of tasks and circumstances. They must also function effectively despite limited resources, diverse responsibilities, and broad authority. Hugh cites as an example of The Principle of Flexibility how USCG personnel dealt with communications breakdowns in a city as dense as New Orleans. He said, "Despite damage to operating stations and a condemned hangar, pilots began flying primarily out of the Naval Air Station Joint Reserve Base in Belle Chasse, LA, just south of New Orleans. To enable these pilots to operate in and around New Orleans with restricted communications, members of the USCG produced yet another innovative solution: They divided the City of New Orleans into sectors, delineating certain geographic areas for designated crews as a way of avoiding confusion or overlap. Then each sector was given a unique operating frequency to limit inter-aircraft traffic to the communications of greatest concern."

The Principle of Managed Risk

This principle is similar to The Principle of Unity of Effort in that it too has internal and external aspects. The internal aspect is demonstrated by commanders' obligations that ensure their units are properly equipped and trained for their missions. Commanders must also assess whether to execute a given mission and how it should be executed. In this way, they carefully compare crew and equipment capabilities against particular operational scenarios. Hugh said, "The USCG manages risk proactively through standardized procedures, continuous training, ongoing drills and preventative maintenance that assure the highest state of readiness." During response operations, the agency also manages risk through time-tested and time-honored principles of safe operation that ensure people and equipment are "used within the limits of their capabilities." Continuing, he said, "USCG personnel during Katrina were able to quickly adapt core capabilities and competencies to deal with the unique challenges that were presented."

The Principle of Restraint

Members of the Coast Guard have a special obligation to exercise their authority prudently and with restraint. Hugh told how the USCG worked diligently during Katrina, to keep evacuated families together and to handle frustrated evacuees with sensitivity. In some situations, security teams were deployed to maintain order. However, not all situations lent themselves to these special units, such as when three armed men demanded that a USCG rescue swimmer hoist them to safety before other more critical victims. Hugh said, "Even amid the panic, crime, and chaos that was rampant in New Orleans, the USCG, which maintains federal law enforcement responsibilities, exercised responsibilities effectively and efficiently. They accomplished this while adhering to the principle of restraint, by diffusing all tense situations confronted during Katrina operations exclusively through the use of non-lethal force."

Final Thoughts

Although the devastating images of Katrina's victims will be indelibly imprinted in the minds of millions, many will also remember those who responded heroically by risking their own lives to save others. What lessons can be learned from the USCG's response to Katrina? Some organizations today have been able to deal with uncertain and sometimes volatile environments, yet others still struggle with rigid structures or practices that hinder performance as well as innovation. There is a huge difference between routinely "putting out fires" and being able to respond to rapidly changing circumstances through clear objectives and standardized, time-tested, replicable procedures.

The USCG's response to natural disasters illustrates how standardized procedures can be proactively and reactively deployed to manage risk, facilitate decentralization, and enable distributed decision making. Organizations in all sectors can learn from this, particularly from the way that advance planning and role clarity in advance of extreme situations can help people respond appropriately. Although most organizational challenges wouldn't meet the definition of a "disaster," we can see how organizational change might be less threatening to people who already know how to work in a decentralized manner and who are knowledgeable about their span of control as well as their individual responsibilities and authority.

Standardization, too, can play a key role in how well prepared people are, when responding to extreme situations—as can skills that have already been developed through the distributed decision making that occurs on a daily basis in many organizations today. In a natural disaster response, these aspects of a situation can make the difference between life and death. In rapidly changing markets and industries, they can also determine a life-and-death scenario with regard to organizational sustainability.

A Look Ahead

In looking to the future, we might ask if our changing weather is the result of natural cycles that recur every billion years or if it's the result of human beings who have polluted our planet. Despite an ongoing debate over a "clear cause," scientists have no answers to these questions. They can continue to analyze seismic activity and weather conditions to predict severe events. We can take some comfort in the fact that today's improved technology better equips us to predict, prepare, and respond to extreme weather, particularly hurricanes. However, our current science is somewhat limited in predicting meteotsunamis. What we can infer then, from the stories of meteotsunamis and storms such as Hurricane Katrina and Sandy? And what can individuals and communities do, to best prepare and respond to these types of events?

The weather phenomena that we're experiencing today should at least serve as a catalyst for ongoing research that allows us to predict natural disasters. However, it's critically important to have comprehensive response plans as well—constructed by individuals and city officials around the world. We see from the Katrina example how important it is to swiftly evacuate as soon as a major storm has been sighted. Leaving one's home and possessions is a difficult decision for most people, but the people who were indecisive—and those who minimized the threat of this storm—didn't live to tell how they might have done things differently. Officials from cities like New Orleans also learned painful lessons about how storms are unique and how each requires innovative and resourceful responses.

What role will the Coast Guard play in response to new and stronger phenomena? We know that the USCG, above all others, can be trusted to live up to its motto of "Semper Paratus" ("Always Ready"). We also know how it can be an example and an inspiration to leaders in all sectors.

■ ■ ■

About the U.S. Coast Guard (USCG)

Born as the Revenue Cutter Service in 1790, and created by the first U.S. Treasury Secretary, Alexander Hamilton, the USCG remains the smallest of the five armed forces of the United States. Now an arm of the U.S. Department of Homeland Security (DHS) it is the only military organization outside of the Department of Defense (DoD). It consists of a force of maritime professionals whose broad legal authorities, capable assets, geographic diversity, and expansive partnerships provide a persistent presence along rivers, in ports, in littoral regions, and on the high seas. Safeguarding the U.S.'s maritime interests and environment around the world, the USCG presence and impact is local, regional, national, and international, making it a unique instrument for ensuring maritime safety, security, and environmental stewardship.

■   ■   ■

If you found this chapter useful, also see the chapters in this book entitled *Courage, High Performing Teams, Personal Accountability,* and *Shared Vision and Values.*

Technology Hubs and Community Building: Activating, Growing, and Connecting

An interview with Iain Klugman, President and CEO of Communitech

As the architect of a five-year, $100-million-plus digital strategy, Iain Klugman and his team at Communitech delivered more than $900 million Canadian in economic impact in 2012. Before joining Communitech in 2004, Iain's career spanned leadership roles in both the private and public sectors, including Director of Global Branding and Advertising for Nortel, Executive Director of Communications with the Canadian Broadcasting Corporation, CEO of a provincial Crown corporation, and roles with the Privy Council Office and Industry Canada. Iain is currently the Chair of the Advisory Committee on Small Business and Entrepreneurship for the Minister of Industry. He sits on several boards and advisory committees, including the National Research Council's Industrial Research Assistance Program and Innovation Guelph. Iain holds an MBA from Wilfrid Laurier University, a Master's in Public Administration from Dalhousie University, and an HBA from Laurentian University. He subsequently completed the Advanced Program in Human Resources at the University of Toronto's Rotman School of Management.

■ ■ ■

What are technology hubs? What role do they play in helping start-up companies incubate new ventures? Can they also assist mature companies to grow and add value to their markets? And how do they facilitate collaboration among member companies? This chapter answers these questions with examples followed by ten winning strategies. Its particular focus is on a hub called Communitech, in Southwestern Ontario, Canada.

A story about Dr. Henry Luo, one of the first inventors in the world to develop the digital hearing aid, provides a good example of the kind of collaboration and cross-pollination that occurs in an innovation hub. Author Trish Crompton, in an article on Communitech's website, describes how Dr. Luo began his career in engineering, but coming from five generations of medical doctors, always wanted to help people hear. After completing an electrical engineering degree in China and a degree in biomedical engineering in England, Luo continued to focus on intelligent hearing aids. Limited by the technology of the day, however, he was, in Crompton's words, "like an artist without a canvas, waiting to paint his masterpiece."

Then after working briefly in Japan and the United States, Luo moved to the Waterloo Region of Canada to work for Unitron, a member company of Communitech. There he finally had the digital platform that he needed, but actually, it was two unusual catalysts that produced Luo's "aha" moment. Luo had previously learned from Don Hayes, Unitron's Director of Audiology, that people's reluctance to wear hearing aids was primarily due to the "shock sounds" that made other sounds indistinguishable and caused confusion and discomfort. Luo also learned from Hayes that the problem of acoustic shock had been plaguing hearing-aid wearers—and researchers as well—for over 20 years. That was, in part, because acoustic shock couldn't be eliminated completely. After all, hearing-aid wearers needed to hear shock sounds emitted by car horns, various types of alarms, and so on.

So what were those two unusual catalysts mentioned in Crompton's article? They were wine glasses dropping to the floor at different times and under different circumstances. Luo noticed that one made a sound during a noisy moment that was in sharp contrast to that made by another glass when it hit the floor during a quieter time. Realizing that he could modify the way a sudden impulse signal is detected and then control it in real time, Luo's discovery was a significant advance. After that, he developed the sophisticated algorithm that governs every Unitron hearing device today.

By detecting and isolating the acoustic shock from surrounding sounds, and dampening them as they occur, Luo enabled hearing aid wearers to distinguish conversation from other sounds brought about by acoustic shock. His subsequent work on digital hearing aids earned him the David E. Mitchell Award of Distinction, Canada's equivalent of the Nobel Prize. Since Luo's breakthrough innovation— and resulting patent for "AntiShock" technology—he has produced innovations almost every year. He says, "I love that what I do means people benefit and have better lives," adding that for him, that's "the biggest reward." Today, more than five million people wear intelligent hearing devices enabled by Luo's innovation.

Macro and Micro-Collaboration

Luo attributes his success in part to the caliber of the colleagues that surrounded him at Unitron. However, others like Luo say they benefit on both a micro level (through collaboration with colleagues) as well as a macro level (through collaboration that extends from other companies within the professional communities of their innovation hubs). In addition to providing tangible networking opportunities, hubs can create a collective mindset that encourages openness, risk-taking, and idea exchanges. These are what often produce breakthrough innovations such as Dr. Luo's.

A good example of how companies can work together synergistically—and collaborate on a macro level—is Canadian Tire, an almost $9 billion Canadian retail company that set up its Communitech innovation skunkworks in 2013. Canadian Tire leaders knew that retail in North America was changing with likely disruptions to their business if they didn't respond to changing market trends and customer demands. Consequently, their mandate was to extend the company's digital infrastructure via the web and mobile apps. Iain said, "By renting space at the Communitech Hub, Canadian Tires' skunkworks team was surrounded by 120 companies that were doing some of the coolest technological things on the planet. At the same time, web and mobile app developers had the ability to accelerate their ideas by talking with a major Canadian retailer, asking questions such as, 'Does this make sense?' 'Will retail customers ever buy this?' 'How do I sell to retail?' and 'Will you be a beta customer?'" As a sign of the experiment's early success, Canadian Tire expanded its innovation footprint in 2013 to a new "Digital Garage" across the street from the Communitech Hub, while retaining its original skunkworks space.

Over the last 30 years, technology hubs that support innovation have been springing up in increasing numbers, primarily in the technology sector. The most famous hubs in the United States are in Silicon Valley, Los Angeles, Seattle, New York and Boston. Outside of the U.S., they're found in Tel Aviv, London, Paris, Sydney, Moscow, Bangalore, and Sao Paolo, to name a few. In 1997, Communitech was created in the Waterloo Region in southern Ontario, Canada, whose winning strategies mirror those of most other successful hubs. Evidence of this is its 2012 ranking of 16 on Startup Genome's list of 20 of the world's' top startup ecosystems.

The Innovation Challenge

With the broad use of crowdsourcing strategies and open innovation, organizational success today increasingly comes from outside an organization's four walls—especially for start-up ventures or companies with limited infrastructures. Iain Klugman reminded us of how few entrepreneurs have the ability or capacity to grow a business from an idea such as the one that spontaneously sparked Henry Luo's imagination. Even fewer have the ability to translate their ideas into thriving multinational companies.

Conversely, mature companies, that have the resources, expertise, and opportunities, encounter different obstacles when they attempt to innovate. Even with well-defined growth targets, these companies find internal game-changing innovations challenging. That's because of the risk aversion that typically corresponds to an organization's long-term success. Stable workforces can inadvertently produce groupthink. However, when companies bring new thinking inside, this can be minimized and even prevented. For example, Iain paraphrased a recent conversation with the CTO of a large camera company who came to Communitech for support. The CTO said, "The challenge is that every time

I ask my 20,000 employees to innovate for me, everything they create looks like a camera. How do I change that?" Large companies are very interested in partnering with technology hubs to have their assumptions challenged and to think about radically different ideas. Iain reiterated, "They cannot do that in a closed environment." So how can innovation hubs help mature companies do this? And how do they create environments that support companies with challenges at both ends of the growth spectrum?

Winning Strategies

In past years, innovation hubs have evolved into ecosystems that add the greatest value for member organizations by providing expanded resources and support services. In the following ten winning strategies, the ways in which they've accomplished this are detailed, with a particular focus on Communitech.

Going Beyond Physical Space

Consistent with the way that most innovation hubs play a role in "hot housing," Communitech's 50,000 square-foot complex provides space for small, medium-sized, and large companies. However, in the same way that community centers provide services to constituents in specific neighborhoods, hubs like Communitech offer programs and services that go far beyond providing space. By offering services in the areas of legal, accounting, financial, insurance, and corporate real estate, hubs meet the needs of multiple members. In their local communities, regions, and countries, hubs can function as accelerators, to generate growth and create jobs. In their extended communities, hubs also bring together companies, services, government agencies, and academic institutions that can serve as invaluable classrooms for member companies and entrepreneurs.

Programs and services usually vary, based on the needs of member organizations, but most hubs provide R&D support, access to grants, and services that provide and develop talent. Hubs accomplish this by hosting events, facilitating networking opportunities, and sharing information about relevant laws, tax breaks, and venture capital financing. Some hubs also function as "brokers," that introduce member firms to one another and organizations outside of the hub, for purposes of potential partnering.

Connecting Entrepreneurs with Investors

We've said before that one of the most difficult tasks for almost any entrepreneur is finding money—specifically seed capital. We've also described the challenges of well-established companies when attempting to generate internally the next big idea. With that in mind, how does Communitech help entrepreneurs, established companies, and investors find each other—and at minimal cost? Iain said, "If you're a venture capitalist, and you want to do business in Toronto, you're going to have to invest $500,000 Canadian. Also, you're going to have to hire a business development person to put people on the ground, and that's like trying to find a needle in a haystack. So at Communitech, we create an advantage by assisting companies in finding the right kind of deals while significantly reducing transaction costs."

Iain also said, "By having the ability to connect with entrepreneurs, people at mature companies can infuse innovation into their organizations, often acquiring technologies or half-produced products that are almost market ready. Today, innovation hubs play an active role in enabling organizations to partner, acquire, align, collaborate, and more—based on the convening and the introductions that they can facilitate." Iain further explained, "A good example of this is an event run by Communitech called 'Founders and Funders' that pairs up entrepreneurial founders who are trying to raise capital with funders who are looking to invest. We run Capital Days, Collision Days, and Industry days—with lots of convening to build effective networks for people and businesses."

Iain continued. "At the same time that small companies can find avenues for their ideas and inventions, mature organizations can 'hoover up' the ones that they think have potential." Through various services, Communitech brings together potential partners to explore connections between business market needs, models, and technology capabilities. However, Iain added, "It's not enough for start-ups to create a company and hope that they'll be bought out by a company like Google. At Communitech, we also help people build businesses that are self-sustaining." That means the organization not only facilitates introductions but also plays a role in the venture capital system. By assisting start-up companies in accessing resources, Communitech can help them gain strategic advantage, particularly in competitive international marketplaces.

Facilitating Peer Connections

Reminding us that future leaders develop skills primarily on the job and through peer coaching and feedback, Iain proudly stated, "We run what is now the largest peer group in the world. In fact, we were founded with that in mind. Peer networks typically lead to unforeseen connections that often help member companies reduce transaction costs, and improve efficiencies, so Iain added, "We weren't only interested in being the best innovation hub in Canada—we wanted to be the best in the *world*."

Since peer networks typically lead to unforeseen relationships that often help companies reduce transaction costs and improve efficiencies, Iain said, "Communitech's 20-plus peer groups consist of over hundreds of participants with common job titles and responsibilities who are all helping each other build capability. Examples of these groups include groups for HR managers, sales leaders, developers, finance professionals, PR and communications people, executive assistants, and more."

Connecting Companies with Academic Institutions and Government Programs

Although the initial purpose of innovation hubs was to create a breathable bubble that would surround people in tech start-ups or academic settings, they now also enable organizations to pair up with large partners with capital and government agencies. In Canada, these include the country's National Research Council and its Industrial Research Assistance Program. In conjunction with these organizations, Communitech facilitates potential business partnerships that can support and accelerate business growth. Another good example is the organization's strategic partnership with Mitacs, a national, not-for-profit organization that helps companies innovate by connecting them with top talent and expertise at Canadian Universities.

Through Mitacs-Accelerate, companies are partnered with graduate students or postdoctoral fellows with research experience relevant to companies' research and development (R&D) challenges. Projects are then scaled according to type and duration while research grants from Mitacs ensure next-level innovation with a focus on commercialization opportunities. As a way of helping start-ups get the critical "leg up," Communitech promotes Mitacs programs to its members and ensures that they're aware of funding opportunities.

Creating New Markets

Another service that hubs can provide is helping interested parties explore uncharted territory. A good example of this was Communitech's "DATA.BASE" program, a service that aligned participants in academia and the private sector who wanted to capture and commercialize big data. Those at Communitech knew that when remote sensing technology and earth orbiting satellites for data capture were combined with other data sources and advanced analytics, they could provide new and improved commercial opportunities in numerous areas, such as port traffic efficiency. By working with a consortium of investors, Communitech helped to create a data-capturing network in 2014 that involved the use of several micro-satellites. Communitech periodically works with investors to launch new products or technologies such as this initiative.

Supporting Geographic Expansion

Iain pointed out that, as Communitech has grown, so has the organization's continuous need "to be nimble and quick at capturing opportunities and identifying issues." He said, "Today, companies face increased pressure to be more global and to generate international sales because there's a strong correlation between high growth and a global presence." As a result, some hubs like Communitech establish partnerships in desired markets with companies on the ground that are willing to provide space and support to companies that are trying to gain a foothold. A good example of this is the recent launch of the International Soft Landing Program by the Canadian Digital Media Network. This program is a national initiative, facilitated by Communitech, to connect tech hubs across the country. The first 30 companies that participated in it have found the program to be relatively inexpensive yet highly successful. This success is evidenced by a net $20 million Canadian in new sales in only a three-month period. Iain said, "We also bring in other resources, mostly through the Canadian Consulate and Foreign Affairs."

Developing and Retaining Talent

Other important fundamental services that hubs provide to member organizations are resources that enable them to attract, develop, and retain talent. Iain said, "We manage a job portal and recruiting events across North America in addition to talent development, which includes skills development and community outreach." However, as crucial as attracting and developing talent is, so is retaining that talent. Hubs can enable greater long-term retention within the community by tapping into world-class coaching and mentoring opportunities. Iain said, "Access to the right advice at the right time is critical to success, so we developed the "Startup Services Group," in which we work with more than 400 active startups. We have eight entrepreneurs in residence ("EIRs") who are here to coach the portfolio startups, and one of the unintended benefits is that start-ups also have access to the EIRs' networks of over a thousand tech firms."

Building Current and Future Talent Life Cycles

Communitech is known for supporting the entire talent lifecycle. Iain said, "You can have the best research and technology in the world, but unless there are people who want to grow up to be entrepreneurs, you're not going to have great companies. Becoming an entrepreneur must be a viable career choice. Unlike other organizations with a finite mandate focused on being an incubator or an advocate for larger organizations, we at Communitech look at all aspects of the ecosystem, which also includes youth outreach."

Communitech has been a supporter of the Business & Education Partnership of the Waterloo Region, which works with over 17,000 high school students to celebrate science, technology, engineering, math, and entrepreneurialism. Iain said, "We spend a lot of time helping people understand what it means to be a start-up because it's a different perspective on the world. Instead of saying, 'This is a terrible issue that the government should fix,' we teach future entrepreneurs to say, 'Wow! I've got an idea about how I can fix that and make a billion dollars at it.' It's a shift to viewing the world's problems as market opportunities rather than issues that somebody else should address."

Leading and Mentoring Entrepreneurs

"Concerning talent," Iain said, "in my mind, the scarcest resource we have in this country isn't natural resources or technology, it's the people who know how to make money—people who know how to build businesses." The lifetime contribution of entrepreneurs who can build billion-dollar businesses is invaluable. By strengthening ties between top executive talent and future leaders, communities and regions benefit from a much better connected and stronger talent base. Connecting mentors and protégés has been a long-standing recipe for sustained growth and is available to promising start-up companies through "Rev," an accelerator program that helps established early-stage companies find customers and increase sales. Launched in 2015, it addresses the needs of companies that have already proven there is a market for their innovations but need help to scale their revenue.

Achieving Long-term Growth of Communities, Regions, and Nations

Retention has become a concern of organizations in all industries and all geographies. As the "war for talent" continues, companies and regions must explore how to retain people in their particular geographic locations. We learned from Iain that regions are likely to have greater talent retention if they can create a feeling of belonging. He said, "If hubs invest in building a strong brand based on that, the long-term value is fairly significant." When describing why regional retention is important, Iain said, "We're trying to start and grow more companies because we think that, with the sun-setting of some industries and the fact that resources are often located elsewhere, we need to start and grow more companies. In this way, we also leverage the incredibly talented people and great entrepreneurs that we currently have in this region."

Evolving from Hubs to Ecosystems—or Hubs 2.0

Iain told us that, although technology innovation hubs have been evolving for decades, they have changed considerably in the last several years. What essentially began as incubators for entrepreneurs and emerging enterprises soon evolved into trade associations. Then hubs created opportunities for tech start-up operations, for established companies, and for academic partners to come together in a much larger ecosystem. Now people in member companies function less as independent entities and more as elements of systems that determine the fate of their entire communities.

Iain said that, within ecosystems, members align about the vision for the ecosystem. They support and cooperate while simultaneously competing. Iain said, "While that might seem contradictory when organizations view competition as both healthy and beneficial, they play a higher end game for all. The end results are high impact outcomes not only for companies but also for the communities that are supported by local interacting companies and individuals."

Iain elaborated on this by saying, "Today, we help businesses build company-specific ecosystems that sit on top of the tech ecosystem that we built here originally. When non-tech companies have opportunities to see what technologies are out there, it's quite valuable to them. Essentially, member organizations begin to support one another in some of the same ways in which we helped them network with each other initially. When organizations evolve to the point where they cooperate naturally and automatically, innovation hubs can provide new and additional services to more member organizations, making the situation a win-win for all."

Final Thoughts

When asked about some of the behaviors that Communitech encourages members in its ecosystem, Iain said, "The first is to color outside the lines. We want each person here to be a cheerleader. By cooperatively working together, we elevate the industry, region, and nation. That's because an ecosystem's success is usually the result of every person being focused on the same objectives. We all support companies in different ways, but we all have to work well together."

Another behavior that Communitech encourages is to "go for the gusto by injecting energy and enthusiasm into every relationship and interaction," Iain said. "A third important behavior is for people to do the right thing and act with honor and integrity, always working with the best interests of customers and potential partners in mind." He then described how a successful ecosystem requires commitment: "If you have the right commitment, things will work well, but it's important to keep in mind that ecosystems are not neat and tidy. They're not based on linear models. Instead, they're messy and organic, with no center of authority and no hierarchy. As the name 'ecosystem' suggests, they tend to be dynamic and fluid environments that don't—and can't—remain static. They effectively evolve over time but only if everyone is pulling together towards the same goal. And even then, it takes lots of hard work and a clear understanding that chaos and acceptance of failure are critical to the way an ecosystem functions."

Iain concluded with these thoughts: "With few exceptions, none of the value brought about by an ecosystem is possible for someone working alone in his or her garage. In fact, we continually see that people who network with others consistently do a better job of problem solving, experimenting, testing assumptions and innovating—and all in real time. So at Communitech, we continue to aim at building successful businesses by educating, developing, and enabling collaboration among a wide variety of people. By doing that, we help facilitate prosperity for everyone."

▓   ▓   ▓

About Communitech

Communitech is a member-driven innovation center in Waterloo Region of Ontario, Canada, supporting a tech cluster of nearly 1,000 companies that employ approximately 30,000 people. Communitech supports tech companies at all stages of their growth and development from startups to rapidly growing mid-size companies and large global players. A member of the Ontario Network of Excellence, which is funded by the Ontario Government, Communitech supports companies in commercializing innovation and technology, with the goal of creating a greater number of successful global businesses.

To learn more about the organization, see www.communitech.ca.

▓   ▓   ▓

If you found this chapter useful, also see our enabling chapters entitled *A Business Case for Strategic Partnerships and Alliances, Business Model Innovation,* and *Open Innovation.*

Urbanization and Social Change: Challenging the Status Quo

An interview with Katerina Cizek, Documentary Maker; Research Affiliate at Massachusetts Institute of Technology (MIT) Open Documentary Lab; and Director of HIGHRISE, National Film Board of Canada (NFB)

As a two-time Emmy-winning director and documentary maker working across many media platforms, Katerina Cizek is an internationally recognized leader in digital creation, with documentaries made for the web. In 2006, she received a Webby Award, the Internet version of an Oscar, for her documentary *Filmmaker-in-Residence* and an Emmy award in 2011 for *Out My Window*, the first in a series of National Film Board (NFB) documentaries entitled *HIGHRISE*. The series described the challenges of urbanization and vertical lifestyles in 13 major cities. Another documentary in the series, *One Millionth Tower*, reimagined vertical living and became the world's first documentary to use WebGL (Web Graphics Library) technology. In March of 2013, NFB HIGHRISE partnered with the New York Times to create a four-part documentary that traced the 2,000-year-history of human vertical life on the planet. The documentary won a Peabody, an Emmy, and a World Press Photo Prize for outstanding achievement in electronic media. In May of 2013, Katerina was named visiting artist at MIT's Open Documentary Lab, which is dedicated to exploring new technologies and storytelling practices of the future. Katerina holds a Bachelor of Arts with First Class Honors in Anthropology from McGill University.

■ ■ ■

The United Nations predicts that by the year 2050, approximately 64% of the world population and 86% of the developed world will be urbanized. In addition to producing rich and diverse cultures, urbanization can bring many economic and social benefits. However, unless there is careful planning by architects, urban planners, and city councils, the loss of community that's sometimes associated with urbanization can also lead to isolation, secularization, and weak social attachments. This is compounded when cities grow too fast and infrastructures are unable to support growing populations. Then urbanization can also result in conflict, poverty, social unrest, crime, and corruption.

The Innovation Challenge

Documentaries have traditionally been a powerful force for social awareness and social change, particularly when they include dialogue that gives disadvantaged people a voice and highlights ways to improve their situations. In the 1960s and 1970s, the National Film Board of Canada created a program called *Challenge for Change* with the goal of encouraging civic involvement. Recognizing that Canadian residents living in both rural and urban communities could be the true agents of social change, NFB placed media creation in the hands of the people featured in this series of documentaries. In 2004—exactly 26 years after producing the original series—NFB wanted to revisit the ideas of the program, using the same participatory methods but in the context of the digital age.

From International Human Rights to Digital Documentaries

When the NFB offered independent filmmaker, Katerina Cizek, the opportunity to reiterate *Challenge for Change* in a new digital age, she was intrigued. "I had always been inspired by the role that community media can play in challenging the status quo," she said, "and specifically in discussions about how to change the way things are. I know it can be a powerful tool by which community voices can make their way to a large audience." Then describing her work identity as a social justice documentarian, Katerina cited an early work with which she was involved entitled *Seeing is Believing: Handicams, Human Rights and the News.* The film featured case studies from around the world, as well as the 1960s Rodney King incident in Los Angeles, California. Katerina said, "This documentary enabled amateur filmmaking to find its way to the media and eventually to courtrooms. For me, it also reinforced the power of media and how the tools of media can influence key decision makers."

Working with NFB Senior Producer, Gerry Flahive, Katerina began a project called *Filmmaker-in-Residence*. Focused on downtown Toronto's St. Michael's Hospital, Cizek worked with physicians, nurses, researchers and patients to re-imagine inner-city healthcare. Producing a Webby award for Katerina and national and international acclaim for her new approaches in documentary production, *Filmmaker-in-Residence* was one of the world's first documentaries to be created and delivered completely online as a native platform for documentary.

Katerina said, "Prior to that, at the NFB, websites functioned only as a marketing tool. From *Filmmaker-in-Residence*, we learned how the web could give documentary new life, while at the same time enabling directors to continue using text, still photography, audio, and video as standalone media. Now they have the added ability to weave these things together to tell highly interactive stories. In addition, *Filmmaker-in-Residence* became a multi-directional learning process for Gerry and me—and also for the physicians and staff with whom we worked at St. Michael's. The result had huge impact in the way that it positively influenced provincial government in terms of health and education, childcare, and other issues—which was very satisfying for all of us."

The Nature of our Urban Planet

At the completion of *Filmmaker-in-Residence*, the NFB encouraged Katerina to continue her efforts with multi-media technologies, but with something of a broader nature. Attempting to successfully scale up what she had done at St. Michael's, Katerina contemplated the defining trends of the 21st century and focused on how urban areas were accommodating growing populations by building up and out. Wanting to depict urban life in a variety of cities throughout the world, she was particularly interested in Toronto's diversity and in the city's 1,189 post-war highrise buildings. Katerina knew that the diverse residents in these buildings could easily enable her to explore vertical living as a key component of the human and urban experience and as she says, "shape the future of our urban planet."

In 2010, Katerina and Gerry Flahive launched *Out My Window,* the first major global documentary of a multi-year NFB project entitled *HIGHRISE: The Towers in the World and the World in the Towers. Out My Window* captured the unique highrise living experiences of residents in 13 cities around the world, which included Toronto. Katerina said, "This documentary's focus on the differences in origin, age, race, and languages enabled it to become a metaphor for global urbanization and a storytelling prism that could shine new light on the challenges of urban life."

A Kaleidoscope of Ideas

In addition to raising awareness about some of the challenges of urban living, *Out My Window* won Katerina the International Digital Emmy for Non-Fiction. It also built the foundation for the next *HIGHRISE* project entitled, *The Thousandth Tower.* Equipped with digital cameras and rich points-of-view about vertical living, Katerina invited six residents in one Toronto highrise to capture their lives through words and images. Describing this as a "hyper-local documentary," Katerina said, "I knew that I needed to better understand the phenomenal diversity and human spirit that exists behind these gray concrete walls. Why? Because we're now living on an urban planet, yet we really have no clue about how these places work—culturally, politically, or economically."

As part of Toronto's Tower Renewal Project, the images and voices of these six highrise residents found expression in a public exhibit and event at City Hall. The over 300 people who attended included heads of schools, public administrators, politicians, architects, urban planners, students, and the mayor of Toronto. Katerina said, "These immigrant residents shared their dreams and concerns through poetry, photos, and a flag show that visibly represented their home countries. Yet what was really incredible was that the residents—who had barely spoken to each other in the past and had never spoken in public—shared their lives and dreams with hundreds of strangers at this event."

Learning from the six resident immigrants who had come from India, the Caribbean, and Ghana, Katerina says, "My eyes were really opened as to how highrise communities in the suburbs functioned—and how different they were from what I had initially perceived them to be." This insight inspired the next project in the series—*One Millionth Tower*. Katerina worked with documentarians and animators, urban planners and urban theorists, architects, academics, housing advocates, and ultimately residents—to reimagine vertical living and its possibilities. She aimed to shift the focus on urbanization from a macro to a micro perspective.

Katerina wanted to fully capture what she described as "the universal thread of our global urban fabric—the highrises that more than a billion people live in, and in particular, those falling into disrepair around the globe." She said, "People are facing challenges beyond deteriorating buildings. They're also dealing with inadequate access to social services and commerce, poor public transit or long-distance commutes, little or no community space between residential buildings, and no community play space for their children." Compounding the downside of urbanization, Toronto's highrises—unlike those in North America and other parts of the world—had spread into the suburbs, providing even greater challenges for residents who were isolated from the rest of the city and without access to mass transit or jobs.

Winning Strategies

In *One Millionth Tower*, Katerina and her crew exposed the deplorable living conditions of highrises though artistic expression, but with a new twist. After learning about some of the large-scale, nationalized tower renewal projects in Toronto and in Europe, Katerina saw that with careful planning, highrises could actually be "quite wonderful places to live." Inspired by stories about community and resilience among highrise dwellers, she collaborated with world-class architect, Graeme Stewart, who specialized in tower renovations that create or reclaim public space. Katerina then invited Stewart to work with residents to share in this leading edge, online, and fully interactive open-source documentary by showing them how to visually portray their current environment.

Shortly after that, the documentary team got together with the residents to imagine a more ideal setting—and to draw a future landscape on top of their depictions of their current environment. Stewart and his team of architects helped residents do this by showing them pictures of dramatic highrise transitions for inspiration. Residents were awed, in particular, by a re-clad, energy-efficient building in Moscow with cafes that spilled out onto courtyards and shops that helped to generate revenue. But Katerina didn't stop there. While Toronto residents dreamed of a new reality, she also worked with Mike Robbins, a computer developer at Helios Design Labs, to bring the residents' sketches to life through animation. Mike introduced a new technology, WebGL (Web Graphics Library), which turned the project into the first documentary built in open-source, in a 3D space directly within the browser.

Remix at its Best

Katerina says, "Around that time, two really talented animators approached producer Gerry Flahive, asking if they could also participate in the project. Through open-source technology, *One Millionth Tower* became a 3-D online 'space about a space,' in which people came in and out, as with typical re-mix projects where someone takes a concept and works with it for a while before passing it on to some-one else who builds upon it." Utilizing innovative technologies such as Google satellites and Google Street Maps, Katerina illustrated life in highrises while also showing how participatory urban design could transform places and spaces—as well as minds. "What was really fascinating," she said, "was watching how the initial communication and segregation barriers produced by different class, race, language, and world views eventually began to break down when residents worked on a joint effort."

A Serendipitous Outcome

We know that innovation is often serendipitous, but how could these efforts at re-imagining space really make a difference in the lives of residents? Katerina told us how serendipity prevailed when a representative from Kaboom—an American not-for-profit organization that builds playgrounds for dis-advantaged communities—called a Toronto Towers Renewal Office city official. The person at Kaboom said, "We had a sponsored playground ready to go in Toronto but then lost the community, so we're wondering if you might know of anyone who might be interested in getting a playground for free."

Remarkably, in only two weeks' time, there were hundreds of volunteers building a playground on the grounds of the Toronto high-rise that Katerina and her team had featured in *One Millionth Tower*. She said, "Even more incredible were the 100 or so residents who had volunteered to work on the project. None of them had previously known one another yet they were suddenly working side by side, bring-ing a collective dream into reality. Imagine that it only took a leap of faith and a simple act of envision-ing for residents to accept this gift when it came!"

A Manifesto for Interventionist Media

Katerina says, "*One Millionth Tower* suggests that social problems can be addressed and that it often only takes some imagination on the part of experts and non-experts alike." In reference to "non-experts," she draws upon Participatory Action Research (PAR), which requires that members of the community being researched are also engaged in solutions. In this way, non-experts and experts, together, develop knowledge about issues and opportunities, which leads to greater opportunities for effective social change. By utilizing this approach to her documentaries, PAR seeks to achieve successful and sustainable development by directly engaging members of local populations in projects that they'll benefit from. This, opposed to mainstream, top-down development approaches that exclude collaboration with the communities being researched. The PAR approach underscores the difference between participation as an end in itself and a process that can empower members of marginalized populations.

Citing a point from her ten-point "Manifesto for Interventionist Media," Katerina says, "Documentary makers involved in social change must go beyond simply telling a good story. While doing that, it's really important to respect peoples' social and political goals as well as the process by which those goals are to be achieved. That's why I think documentarians should ask themselves every day, 'Why am I doing this?' 'Who will benefit from this?' 'What positive change might it bring about?'" Katerina adds, "Those who are truly committed to making a difference should spend 10% of their time making a documentary and 90% getting it out to the world. They should also track the process and the results of their work by widely disseminating what they've learned—to the media, filmmakers, advocates, politicians, and policy makers or decision makers who are capable of taking action in addressing social issues.

Katerina told us, "Documentary makers rarely know how far reaching their work might be." Proof of that is the partnership between NFB HIGHRISE and The New York Times. In 2013, the two jointly launched *A Short History of the Highrise*, a series consisting of four short documentaries about life in highrise buildings. The first three films contain New York Times photo archives and the fourth and final film contains user-submitted images—all with the goal of educating people to the challenges of urban life and enlisting public support in dealing with those challenges. The whole series is augmented with an interactive layer for audiences to explore more.

Final Thoughts

Katerina told us, "Some of the most important discoveries of our times—in medicine, chemistry, and physics—have been serendipitous. People sometimes just happen to be in the right place at the right time and suddenly see things they didn't see before. If they're open to understanding that unintended insights can often become meaningful discoveries, the experience can have amazing ramifications. When people take time to listen, unexpected outcomes can challenge obstructionist or status quo elements, but it's equally important to apply insights—and know that they usually don't take hold overnight, so patience is often required. Equally important is the willingness to trust the viewpoints of others. People can often help us see innovations that we could easily miss, yet innovation doesn't always happen in group settings. Some of my most interesting insights have been the results of long conversations with people, where I've taken one person's ideas and shared them in other conversations, allowing others to build on the initial ideas."

Katerina concluded, "For me now, innovation is very intuitive. It's about breaking stereotypes and challenging traditional ways of doing things—pushing beyond boundaries—yet also building failure into the process. Unless you allow for both insights *and* failures, you'll never get anything new. People should be encouraged to take risks and launch their innovations even though they might be imperfect. Why? Innovation is typically an iterative process that gets better over time—and with the benefit of multiple perspectives. The lesson for many of us is to get our innovations out there so we can be part of the bigger conversation that's all around us—and then build on that." When asked about her greatest learning from her documentaries, Katerina said, "Serendipitous opportunity is key to innovation—looking in the right place, at the right time. There's no formula—only being present in the process and open to all the possibilities."

■ ■ ■

About the National Film Board of Canada (NFB)

Since 1939, the NFB has supported the work of extraordinary Canadian filmmakers, achieving international acclaim for all things cinematic, with a focus on social change. NFB films have influenced major social issues as well as filmmakers, leading with innovative digital content and distribution platforms for stories of global significance. An agency of the Government of Canada, the NFB reports to the Parliament of Canada through the Minister of Canadian Heritage. From its collection of 13,000 English and French productions, the organization has earned over 5,000 awards, including 90 Genies and 12 Oscars©. Under the banner of the *Challenge for Change*—which was recognized as one of the most respected and emulated media projects in the world—the NFB produced over 145 films. Many of them involved participants in a way that would eventually be replicated worldwide as a community-mobilizing vehicle by which marginalized people could express needs and concerns.

■ ■ ■

To learn more about *HIGHRISE,* see highrise.nfb.ca/. To learn about the joint NFB/New York Times project, go to www.nytimes.com/projects/2013/high-rise/. If you found this innovation story valuable, see our enabling chapters entitled *A Business Case for Creativity and Creative Problem Solving, A Design Mindset, Differences, Shared Visions and Values,* and *Storytelling.*

Closing Thoughts: Doing Well by Doing Good

An interview with Stephanos George Eapen, Principal Consultant at Innomantra Consulting Pvt Ltd.; Co-Founder of Strategy Regeneration; former Academic Programme Manager at CEDEP; and former Affiliate Professor at INSEAD

While functioning as the Academic Programme Manager for the General Management Program at CEDEP, Stephanos George Eapen managed academic relationships with multinational corporations and created management education programs for corporations such as L'Oréal, Tata, Danone, and Axa. At CEDEP, he learned about the work of Professors W. Chan Kim and Renée Mauborgne, creators of "Blue Ocean Strategy" and about the Value Innovation (VI) framework that is basic to the strategy. Inspired by VI, George co-founded Strategy Regeneration and spent a decade conducting research and providing consulting services around sustainability. He then moved to the INSEAD Centre for Social Innovation to further explore the application of the VI. Focusing specifically on innovation in strategy and management, George developed and delivered executive development programs and seminars at INSEAD and was later appointed Professor of Management Practice in Strategy at INSEAD's Middle East Campus in Abu Dhabi. George holds an MBA from INSEAD and continues to do extensive work in the area of social innovation within the U.S., Europe, and Asia.

■　■　■

When many of us think of game-changing innovation, we might envision new products and services, broad-reaching new applications, and sophisticated technologies. Because of this, we often believe that the most useful innovations come only out of private industry and through product innovation. In reality, process innovation and service innovation can occur in the public and not-for-profit sectors to the same degree that they do in the private sector.

Today, many leaders in public and not-for-profit organizations operate like businesses, innovating to ensure sustainability, maximize resources, and operate as efficiently as possible. At the same time, some

58

leaders in the private sector are improving profits while also taking pride in making the world a better place. Because of this, organizational missions in all sectors are converging to generate innovative new processes and paradigm shifts. These efforts are in sharp contrast to the typical thinking of years past. For example, over 40 years ago, the Nobel Prize-winning economist Milton Friedman decried the notion of corporate social responsibility in his book *Capitalism and Freedom*. Regarding it as a "fundamentally subversive doctrine," Friedman also expanded on his views in a New York Times article entitled, "The Social Responsibility of Business is to Increase Profits." In it, he described how, when business leaders talked about the value of social responsibility, it only helped "to strengthen the already too prevalent view that the pursuit of profits is wicked and immoral and must be curbed and controlled by external forces."

In 1999, Harvard Business School Professor Rosabeth Moss Kanter emerged as one of many thought leaders who began shifting some of the old thinking about social responsibility. In a Harvard Business Review article published at that time, she made reference to the concept of "Corporate Social Innovation." Moss Kanter wrote, "A great deal of business participation in social sector problems derives from the classic model of arm's length charity—writing a check and leaving everything else to government and nonprofit agencies." She also asserted, "Companies receive their benefits up-front through tax write-offs and the public relations boost that accompanies the announcement of their largesse." Moss Kanter added, "There is little or no incentive to stay involved or to take responsibility for seeing that the contribution is used to reach a goal. However well meaning, many businesses treat the social sector as a charity case—a dumping ground for spare cash, obsolete equipment, and tired executives on their way out."

Moss Kanter ended this article by writing, "It is important that businesses understand why the old models of corporate support don't create sustainable change. In partnership with government and nonprofits, businesses need to go beyond the traditional models to tackle the much tougher task of innovation." Since the time that Moss Kanter expressed these views, business schools such as those at Stanford and INSEAD created social innovation centers, and well-known global consultancies launched social innovation practices.

While the focus today continues to be on innovation, therein also lies the challenge: If organizations find it difficult to innovate in their own domains, then innovating in the social dimension is no small matter. And often, when business leaders do engage in social innovation, it's not always driven by altruism. It's because they've been prompted to introduce new technologies or to revise management approaches with the primary goal of greater profitability. Despite the many factors that might drive organizational leaders to innovate, however, it's evident that innovation can enable win-win scenarios that produce both social and business gains.

I'm pleased that one of the previous sections of this book features innovation success stories from all sectors, illustrating how leaders can universally apply a full range of innovation enablers. But how exactly might companies make money while also improving health and welfare? Several U.S. companies have found ways to do this, yet an excellent example is also the demonstrated success of a leading fertilizer manufacturer in India: the Coromandel Company. While maintaining the company's lead position, executives at Coromandel also developed a supply chain capable of handling over 1,000,000 tons of recycled garbage. By recycling with minimal development costs, the company produced unprecedented profits with this new line of business, yet there was an additional benefit. The low cost that Coromandel charged for recycling also meant that various companies and communities in India no longer needed to employ children as rag pickers—a practice that had previously exposed them to a variety of diseases when sorting through filthy garbage for recyclable bits.

With this, we can see how Coromandel's recycling business enabled it to make a profit while also meeting many of its sustainability initiatives, one of which was an effort to oppose and eventually eliminate child labor. Clearly, the company produced a win-win solution when it realized profits at the same time that it improved social conditions. With that, we might ask, "In what ways might other organizations replicate Coromandel's win-win scenario? And what might be some typical results?"

Some private sector organizations today are collaborating with those in the not-for-profit and public sectors, to build communities, enhance local environments, and counter crime. Companies today also catalyze awareness of health problems by working in partnership with not-for-profit and public healthcare organizations. In this book, you have learned how some organizations are also responding to global challenges that encompass extreme weather and natural disasters and to other challenges such as urbanization and social change. You have also seen other examples of how leaders are reducing the rich-poor gap in developing *and* developed countries through social innovation.

Today, social challenges that are emerging from a growing global population can also become business challenges—and opportunities. However, these challenges often exceed the problem-solving capability of any one individual. Some leaders are responding with expanded dimensions of performance that include more team problem solving and decision making enabled by inclusive and diverse collaboration. Other leaders are meeting today's challenges through sophisticated technologies that continually make the world a smaller place. And still others are forming collaborative partnerships across the globe that are enabling them to do well by doing good—thereby bringing new meaning to the old expression, "It takes a community."

■　■　■

To learn more about Innomantra Consulting Pvt Ltd., go to innomantra.com.

II. Innovation Enablers

The Starting Point is an Innovation Strategy

An interview with Deborah Arcoleo, Director, Product Transparency and former Director, Innovation Center of Excellence at The Hershey Company

Deborah Arcoleo has significant experience in the consumer packaged goods industry as an innovation practitioner, leader, and change agent. She has demonstrated expertise in driving business growth through innovation and in building innovation strategy, infrastructure, and organizational capabilities that have seeded creative and innovative thinking at leading companies. Prior to Hershey, Deborah was Director, U.S. Soup Innovation at the Campbell Soup Company and Director, Global Innovation with both the J&J Consumer Group of Companies and Pfizer Consumer Healthcare. She also spent 14 years in management consulting, including four at McKinsey & Company.

Deborah also also has significant expertise with the "fuzzy front end" of innovation as well as project management and stage gate disciplines. Her experience encompasses the strategic market assessment necessary to identify and qualify future growth opportunities by combining trends, consumer needs, and brand strategies for existing businesses and in white spaces. Deborah has led numerous innovation projects that generated new learning, created divergent ideas, and converged to produce business propositions that ensured balanced portfolios of longer-term innovation and closer-in renovation. She has a bachelor's degree in economics from Indiana University in Bloomington and a Master's in Organization Design and Effectiveness from Fielding Graduate University in Santa Barbara, California.

■　■　■

Every organization—whether it's in private, public, or not-for-profit sectors—needs an innovation strategy and an ongoing process to keep it current. These strategies are almost always embedded within organizations' strategic plans, and most of the time, outline the new or enhanced products or services required to meet financial objectives and customer or client needs. Formal planning provides opportunities for leaders collectively to map out their growth ambitions and strategic challenges and make choices about where they will or will not focus their resources. While planning is an important component of an innovation strategy, especially if resources are scarce, it doesn't address the whole picture. An innovation strategy is a foundational enabler.

There are two ways that leaders can optimize their innovation strategies. The first is to operationally define "innovation," and the second is to consider the changes that may be needed to ensure that the innovation strategy can deliver the desired results. One way of viewing the innovation definition is to see it as the "hardware" of innovation—where companies will focus their innovation efforts and the content of those efforts. The "software" can be seen as the process of envisioning the organizational implications of how narrowly or broadly innovation is defined. To clarify, the software dictates how businesses might need to change behaviors, practices and processes. The best innovation strategies, regardless of their breadth or focus, ensure congruence between the "hardware" and the "software."

Innovation Definitions

The starting point for effective innovation strategies begins when senior leaders discuss and align on a clear definition of what the word "innovation" means for the organization. For example, will it be limited to developing new or enhanced products and services? Or will it encompass business model innovation, internal business process redesign, or reinventing the customer experience? Will it be incremental, disruptive, or a balance of both? How broad or narrow will the innovation be in scope and scale, and how deeply will it impact the business? There are no right or wrong answers to these questions. Instead, the answers represent important strategic options for how far-reaching the organizational implications will be.

If leaders define innovation as only developing and launching new or enhanced product or service offerings, that could mean the business is able to meet growth ambitions with small-scale, incremental innovation. In that case, it's very possible that the organization structure, capabilities, and talent to perform this type of strategy already exist, and the level of change needed will be rather low. However, if the innovation definition extends beyond new products and services, leaders will also need to determine how and where it will be performed, who will be accountable for results, and how change will be managed. If growth ambitions or strategic challenges dictate a broader definition of innovation, it's highly likely that the organizational software—its capabilities, culture, talent, behaviors, processes, etc.—will need to be examined and gaps identified.

Organizational Implications

While most leaders are fairly adept at the hardware of innovation—defining where they want to play and how they'll win—they often fall short in understanding and addressing the organizational software implications of their decisions. However, there are ways to ensure this doesn't happen, and it's typically achieved through a series of questions and assessments. Starting with the organizational structure that will be most appropriate, leaders should determine which innovation activities will best be performed centrally and which will be more effective if embedded within business units or functions. Activities such as monitoring of trends, developing foresight, and scenario planning are often more efficient when done centrally. Developing product platforms based on consumer/customer insights is often more effective when done within individual business units.

Once leaders have defined innovation, determined its scope and scale, and made decisions about which innovation activities will be centralized or distributed, they must then ask key questions such as these: "What organizational capabilities and individual talents will be required to perform these projects with excellence?" "Do we have the best talent?" "If not, where will we need to go to recruit it? How will we attract talent, and do we have attractive career paths to retain it?"

Often, the most difficult assessment pertains to culture and behavior. Most organizations are hard-wired for predictability and ongoing operations, but when the innovation definition, scope, and scale are broad and far-reaching, leaders must take a deep dive into the needed software changes. Then, a solid change management plan must be established, and decision-making and human resources processes and practices may need to be altered. All this contributes to creating an "ecosystem" that's conducive to embedding and sustaining innovation behaviors.

Developing a robust innovation strategy—like formulating the right business strategy—requires thoughtful dialogue on aspirations and ambitions as well as a rigorous fact-based assessment of the current situation and what it will take to make needed changes. It also requires leaders with patience and persistence who can execute over the long run. Successful innovators view innovation as a complex end-to-end process with many different components, such as those captured in the following chapters. The chapter topics in this next section reinforce that a strategy is a necessary starting point, and they also address *enablers* of successful implementation—the other half of the equation.

Subsection I.
Inspiring and Encouraging Innovation

Inspiring and Encouraging Innovation: Creativity, Culture, and Collaboration

Introduction by Megan Mitchell

Do you know where the next game-changing idea might come from? I don't. Truth is, ideas can happen anywhere, and sometimes they come from the most unexpected sources. I begin this chapter with two examples of how creativity and innovation can manifest in unpredictable ways. The first is when a Sierra Leone, Africa neighborhood with power lines but no power, suddenly lit up. A self-educated engineer named Kelvin Doe had generated electricity for his family and neighbors by creating a battery from metal parts that he'd salvaged from trash bins. Equally remarkable is that Doe also invented a radio transmitter and a generator to power a community radio station that he managed.

Would you be impressed if I told you that Doe used only scraps to build all these devices? You might say, "Interesting but not earthshattering" until I tell you that, as the youngest person to participate in the Visiting Practitioner's Program at the Massachusetts Institute of Technology (MIT), this self-educated engineer delivered lectures to undergraduate engineering students when he was in his early teens. And at 16 years of age, he signed a $100,000 solar project pact with Canadian high-speed Internet service provider Sierra WiFi! If you think that Kelvin Doe is an anomaly, he is. However, if you search for child prodigies, you might be amazed at what you'll find. With Internet access, various technologies, and fresh unconstrained mindsets, child prodigies are becoming increasingly more common.

The second example of how innovation can manifest in unpredictable ways is Jack Andraka, a child prodigy from the State of Maryland in the United States. At 13 years of age, he won the Intel ISEF Gordon E. Moore $75,000 top prize for an important medical diagnostic test. What drove him to achieve this accomplishment, and at such a young age? After a close family friend died of late-stage pancreatic cancer, Andraka embarked on an ambitious mission. Knowing that this disease typically only gets diagnosed when it's in the late stages, he wanted to figure out how to detect this type of cancer earlier. Andraka's idea produced a new method of testing that was highly accurate and would cost mere pennies.

Wanting to further his research in a formal laboratory setting, Andraka identified approximately 200 labs and sent e-mails to them asking for space to help him advance his discovery. There was only one response, and it counted: Johns Hopkins pathologist and pancreatic cancer researcher, Dr. Anirban Maitra. Dr. Maitra encouraged Andraka and eventually became this child prodigy's mentor and sponsor. Maitra even provided the lab that enabled Andraka to do further studies.

Unlikely Sources?

As useful as it might be to ask where ideas come from and how they get supported, it's also important to ask what happens when ideas don't receive adequate support. Thinking about Andraka's story, what would have happened if Dr. Maitra hadn't been open to the potential merits of Andraka's discovery? Probably nothing—at least for a few years—and not until after pancreatic cancer had claimed more lives. Andraka, like Kelvin Doe, had a compelling passion, but few resources and little or no formal education in the sciences. What is truly amazing is that, despite this, he produced an inexpensive and fast detection test for a cancer that had eluded far more experienced and educated researchers. In fact, clinical trials are now underway to build on Andraka's discovery and further assess his simple test for accuracy and efficacy.

We all know, however, that great ideas like Andraka's and Doe's don't always translate into successful outcomes. In fact, we often see examples of this in business environments. So what's my point in sharing the ideas of Kelvin Doe and Jack Andraka? I'd like to put forth a provocative question: Would you have been open to their ideas and curiosity? Or, in Andraka's case, might you have been one of the 199 labs who dismissed his request? Consider your responses to these questions: Who, of the people you know, might be capable of advancing an idea that could improve performance or profitability—or perhaps even disrupting an entire industry? How often do you actively solicit or generate ideas instead of waiting for them to come to you? And do you know how to transform great ideas into valuable innovations?

Successful leaders know a simple truth: Although great ideas must often be supported by formal processes or structures, they come from human beings. Sometimes they're employees, sometimes they're leaders, and in other situations, they're people outside of an organization like suppliers or customers. And of course, sometimes they're intelligent young people like Andraka and Doe. Leaders can be innovative in their own right or their skill may lie in how they're able to inspire others to innovate. From these two examples, it's clear how some individuals with great ideas might be viewed as unlikely sources for game-changing solutions. They might even be the people you see every day, who are driven internally by intense passions, yet go unnoticed.

Leaders of Innovation versus Innovative Leaders

Here's something to contemplate—a quote from Kelvin Doe: "Creativity is universal and can be found in places where one does not expect to find it...perseverance and passion are essential to nurturing that creative ability." I couldn't agree more, but creativity is only a part of innovation. And although almost anyone can be creative, it takes an entirely different set of skills to *lead* innovation. The late UCLA professor Warren Bennis recognized this when he said, "There are two ways of being creative. One can sing and dance, or one can create an environment in which singers and dancers flourish."

What Bennis meant by this statement was that some leaders are innovators in their own right, yet others may excel at being "leaders of innovation," meaning they inspire and motivate others to innovate. In their 2011 book, *Innovative Intelligence: The Art and Practice of Leading Sustainable Innovation in Your Organization,* Weiss and Legrand assert that it's more advantageous for people to reframe the way they think about themselves as "leaders of innovation" versus innovative leaders. In either case, leaders must create the right climate for creativity to flourish, as opposed to simply being the most creative people in the room. They must also visibly model behaviors that bring out the best creativity in their people.

Innovation and Efficiency

You might guess why innovation is so important today, but I saw the need for strong innovation leadership over 15 years ago, when I was leading innovation at Pfizer Consumer Healthcare (PCH) Canada. As far back as the early 2000s, I witnessed how leaders were starting to see that the marginal improvement of the status quo was not going to be enough to maintain top-line growth targets. In fact, continuing the status quo was barely enough to sustain moderate sales growth. On top of that, leaders and employees almost everywhere were being asked to deliver more with less. In truth, not much has changed today. So what is the best approach when the plans that are in place are failing to deliver? Leaders need to get more out of all their resources (e.g., people, time, systems, and money) in new ways if their organizations are to succeed. To achieve and maintain a competitive advantage, they need to tap the creative potential of their human resources.

By continually encouraging employees to work at reducing the number of labor-intensive or duplicative activities, today's leading organizations have been continuing to streamline their operations. In doing this, they've also been freeing up employees' time to think more creatively. And they've been helping them become agile and resilient enough to differentiate and compete. At the same time, most successful leaders have known for years that there's a point of diminishing returns when they attempt to succeed merely by instituting cost reductions or becoming more efficient. In many ways, the contributors to this book address the question of how leaders can initiate and sustain innovation while still maintaining excellence in their daily operations. They know that, since efficiency has yet to trump innovation, nothing short of new thinking and innovative approaches will enable them to survive in today's highly competitive environments.

The Case for Creativity and Innovation

The 2016 World Economic Forum *Future of Jobs Report* illustrates the important role that creativity plays in today's environment. When experts identified the job skills required by 2020, they ranked creativity as number three of the top ten skills, compared to a number ten ranking in 2015. These experts also ranked two other vital aspects of innovation—complex problem solving and critical thinking—as number one and number two respectively. Why the change in ranking? Many business situations today already require breakthrough thinking. Leaders are already anticipating future implications, as indicated in the 2016 Jobs Report which states that, "By one popular estimate, 65% of children entering primary school today will ultimately end up working in completely new jobs that don't yet exist."

With projections like these, leaders and employees alike are moving beyond traditional analytical problem-solving approaches to employ creative thinking and creative problem solving. Knowing how important these skills are, how might leaders best teach, model and reinforce them? And what kinds of investments do organizations need to make, to teach and model innovation?

The Cost of Innovation

Depending on the scope of their existing strategies, leaders might need to go beyond incremental innovation and invest in potentially disruptive innovation initiatives, but does the investment always have to be monetary in nature? We can see from Kelvin Doe's success with mere pieces of scrap, and Jack Andraka's low-cost test for pancreatic cancer, how sheer creativity and passion can sometimes produce more significant innovations than even those with substantial monetary investments. Other efforts may require both tangible and intangible support, yet many public and not-for-profit organizations have made huge strides in innovation with very little financial support.

Make no mistake, however. Innovation isn't without a cost. What might not require deep pockets most often demands investments of time as well as a different mindset. For example, innovation can't be a part-time or volunteer activity that people engage in whenever they have a few moments to spare. For this reason, innovation shouldn't be addressed exclusively by task forces or CEO initiatives either. To be fully impactful, executives must insert an innovative mindset into the very fabric of their organizations and ensure that it's occurring in all the key functions. To accomplish this, they must have a fundamental belief in the creative power of their people. In line with this thinking, few should regard existing structures, current assumptions, and long-standing practices as so sacred that they can't be challenged and potentially enhanced.

The Innovation Challenge

A common theme in this book is about the need for leaders to inspire and encourage new and different thinking—through their employees and others associated with their companies. Leaders who aren't skilled at doing this can cause organizations to lose power and relevance. That's because today, the absence of new thinking and new approaches often *breaks* people and organizations. What's more, a demise of this kind can happen during both good *and* bad economic times.

A continuous stream of innovation certainly helps to maintain sustainable competitive advantage. And sometimes improved functionality of existing products and services or the creation of products and services in adjacent market categories can sustain an organization, but much more is usually needed to compete in today's world. Since we know that not all ideas are winners, it should be evident that we need to have lots of creative ideas to have any hope of translating some of them into innovations that drive value. Without robust creativity as a starting point, there is typically little or no innovation.

For musicians and other artists, creativity and innovation are givens, yet part of the innovation challenge for most business leaders today lies in the fact that very few of them outside of arts organizations appreciate the value of creativity as a raw ingredient for innovation. Why is creativity so important? Creative problem solving helps meet today's complex challenges as an adjunct to linear, analytical approaches. And today's challenges usually require diverse teams of people who can think creatively and draw upon a blend of different thinking, strategies, and methods for solving problems and making decisions. To foster creative thinking, leaders must create the right environment—one that welcomes ideas from everyone, regardless of rank or function. This chapter briefly describes how leaders build the right organizational culture and how they leverage various enablers that are essential components of that process.

In the chapter of this book entitled *Leading Innovation,* you'll see how leaders stimulate, support, and sustain innovation. In *Managing and Leveraging Innovation,* you'll learn how leaders achieve sustainable innovation through people, partnerships, and processes. And in this chapter, I tell a story about a highly innovative classical composer and conductor and illustrate how a combination of creativity, culture, and collaboration is needed to sustain innovation after the initial novelty has worn off, but first, let's examine the creativity challenge that exists today.

The Creativity Challenge

In some organizations, even the word "creativity" is taboo. You might wonder why that's the case. As an innovation consultant who works with many organizations, I see that, in some situations, it's because clients struggle to understand the difference between creativity and innovation—and the significant relationship between the two. Sometimes they even use these words interchangeably when they actually have very different meanings. Having a shared understanding of how creativity and innovation drive organizational performance is imperative today.

So what exactly is "creativity" and how is it different from "innovation?" While there are thousands of definitions of creativity, I define it as the act of bringing something new into existence—or something that may only be new to us as individuals. It doesn't have to be useful or meaningful; it's simply about our personal act of creating. For creativity to evolve into innovation, however, something of value must be produced. Therefore, innovation is often described as the output of the creative act of bringing something new *and of value* into existence. By contrast to how creativity comes about for individuals, innovation typically requires many people to bring ideas to life. Ideas can be the result of extensive planning or they can come about spontaneously. Drawing from my professional experience, I've identified three ways by which ideas evolve into innovations.

Three Ways of Achieving Innovation

In the same way that skilled physicians ensure better health outcomes by treating illnesses with multiple modalities, successful leaders initiate and sustain innovation by employing different and complementary approaches, based on their organizations' unique needs. What follows are my thoughts about accidental, deliberate, and systemic innovation, as well as the best approaches for supporting each.

Accidental Innovation

Some might call the outcomes of accidental innovations "lucky breaks" because they're often unpredictable, unrepeatable, and unsustainable. You can witness accidental or unexpected innovation when products or services designed for one application turn out to also be effective for others. A good example of this is when newly developed drugs for specifically intended conditions are discovered to be effective in eradicating others as well. Advocates of this type of innovation typically cite the accidental, yet monumental, discoveries of Madame Curie, Alexander Fleming, and Benjamin Franklin.

Somewhat less monumental, but just as exciting, was the invention of the famous Slinky toy. Richard James "accidentally" created it when he was developing springs for another application and one accidentally fell off the table. In the current atmosphere of intense competition, it would be imprudent to rely solely on accidental discoveries as a source of sustainable growth. Instead, leaders must actively build innovation competency and capacity and sustain it through organizational cultures and formal processes that support all three types of innovation.

Disciplined and Deliberate Innovation

Presenting a sharp contrast to accidental innovation is the second way in which innovation occurs. That's when people use a disciplined and deliberate approach by applying particular innovation tools, techniques, and skills in response to specific challenges or opportunities. The disciplined approach to innovation is both repeatable and sustainable, yet it's still only part of the total picture because it only addresses one challenge at a time.

While working in marketing and sales early in my career, and again in my role as Director of Innovation and Leadership Development, there were times when I needed to employ complex problem-solving skills on demand. Most of what I initiated fell within the category of what I refer to as "deliberate innovation." Often I had to take a disciplined and deliberate approach to seize an immediate opportunity or react to a pressing competitive activity.

Today, I continue to use a deliberate process to stimulate ideas in response to specific organizational challenges. By employing different tools, techniques, and frameworks, and then leveraging relevant insights, I help people solve challenges and seize opportunities in deliberate and focused ways. While this planned approach can be valuable for organizations that need to drive intended results and attack immediate problems, it's not always enough. For ideas to continuously flow, and have a chance at being implemented, organizations need an ongoing commitment to innovation—on multiple fronts and sometimes from both internal and external stakeholders.

Systemic Innovation

The third way to innovate is what I call "systemic innovation," where organizations focus on a day-to-day basis on the cultural conditions that foster innovation and allow ideas to come forward at any time from anyone. The culture must also ensure that individuals know their ideas will be heard and considered. In a way, ideas are spontaneous because we never know from whom or from where they will come. What we do know, is that when the conditions are right, creative ideas will inevitably surface. We can compare this to the way in which a farmer prepares a field for the growing season. When all conditions are right, things grow as they should.

Although systemic innovation might seem to be similar to accidental innovation, it's not. When innovation is accidental, it's because someone's discovery is unintentional. Systemic innovation is about people being intrinsically motivated to continually bring forward new ideas—not because they have to, but because there's an innate need or desire to do so. Systemic innovation is also about unconditional receptivity. When leaders can help people find a reason to innovate (for example, a meaningful purpose or goal that's aligned with the organization's goals), it guides their behaviors around *what* they do and *how* they do it. When systemic innovation is at play, people's minds often make connections both on and off the job. Most important is that spontaneous ideas occur more frequently when people feel empowered, comfortable, and safe. Then the personal and business impacts of their innovations are most likely to be sustainable.

I most appreciate the systemic approach to driving innovation because of its unlimited potential, abundant opportunities for creativity, and the energizing effect it can have on the human spirit to create. The one caveat is that it takes time and skill to build an environment for systemic innovation, so it's important for organizations to have the right kind of leaders and infrastructure in place to support it. What we're talking about is creating the right culture, which is necessary for the long game.

A Composer, Conductor, and Innovative Leader

In many chapters, the contributors to this book address the question of how to lead and sustain a climate that supports innovation. When thinking about the best ways to enable organizations to survive in today's highly competitive environments, I ask leaders questions such as these: "How might they reimagine the traditional ways in which they approach their work?" "How might they do more with less by leveraging the creativity of their existing talent?" "What might they learn from people who are masters at inspiring and encouraging creativity?"

I instinctively knew the answer to the last question when I heard the internationally renowned composer and conductor Eric Whitacre speak at a Coaching in Medicine and Leadership conference. His session was entitled "Building Community: Thousands of Voices." I immediately knew that his story about how he built a community could tangibly demonstrate the message I wanted to share with leaders. However, I was inspired before even hearing Whitacre's story. From the instant he walked on stage, I could see that he was a master at inspiring and encouraging others, but what made me come to that conclusion so quickly?

A local choir was on hand to support Whitacre's presentation, and what I found fascinating was how energized and ecstatic these young singers were by the opportunity to perform with him. Even more impressive was how infectious Whitacre's energy was for me as well. I soon found myself relating to the same magical quality of his style as these singers obviously were. However, the electric quality of Whitacre's persona was only one of the several reasons why I decided to interview him for this chapter.

First, I must point out that Eric Whitacre wasn't speaking at this conference to highlight creativity or innovation as a driver of organizational success. He was talking about how music can inspire, unify, and bring people together. But what I immediately took away was a perfect example of a leader who allows creativity, passion, and the pursuit of the unknown to challenge the status quo and create magic. I knew instinctively that I could share his story with business leaders to show the relevance that creative behaviors play in bringing about innovation.

Seeing Whitacre perform also reinforced a concept that appears throughout this book—that creativity and the process of "orchestrating" innovation are essential for achieving and maintaining sustainable innovation and competitive advantage. If Whitacre could so easily reimagine a traditional choir, in what ways might leaders employ his techniques to encourage people to innovate? Meanwhile, a persistent question kicked in: Why do so many leaders undervalue creativity—and the ability to dream—as important innovation drivers?

Beyond Charisma

We have featured several orchestra leaders in this book. I selected Eric Whitacre for this chapter, in part for how he has inspired millions, but not only as a composer and conductor. He's also a charismatic speaker, and most relevant to aspiring innovators—a leader who innovates through the use of technology. As a public speaker, Whitacre has addressed audiences at leading universities and prominent organizations worldwide, presenting at the United Nations Leaders Programme, UNICEF, *The Economist,* the Seoul Digital Forum, Google, TED Conferences, and others. He also led a debate at the World Economic Forum in Davos on the role of arts in society and the impact of technology on the arts. Additionally, Whitacre addressed the Ciudad de las Ideas Brilliant Minds conference, a celebration of the most provocative and innovative ideas in science, business, and culture.

Before interviewing Eric Whitacre for this chapter, I knew that many of his projects were the subject of scholarly works. I also knew that his compositions ranked among the most popular and frequently performed works in the early 21st century. And as the composer and conductor for the Eric Whitacre Singers, Whitacre had won a Grammy in 2012 for Best Choral Recording with his first album *Light & Gold.* So how did he achieve such incredible success—especially as such a young man?

A graduate of the Julliard School of Music in New York City with a Master of Music degree, Eric Whitacre recently completed five years as Composer-in-Residence at Sidney Sussex College, a part of Cambridge University. Viewed as a leading creative force in the choral world, he then began a two-year post in 2016 as the first-ever Artist in Residence with the Los Angeles Master Chorale. Today, Whitacre's success as a public speaker and musician continues to grow. As an example of his versatility, he collaborated with the legendary film composer, Hans Zimmer, to produce the "Mermaid Theme" for the movie, *Pirates of the Caribbean.* Other projects include a composition that he wrote for the Winter Dreams Holiday show at the Disney California Adventure Park and his creation of the Virtual Youth Choir in association with UNICEF, which premiered at the Glasgow 2014 Commonwealth Games.

The "Virtual Choir"

When considering all of Eric Whitacre's accomplishments, it's his creation and evolution of the world famous "Virtual Choir" that, to me, best characterizes him as a talented innovator and a living example of technology-enabled innovation. So what might leaders in business environments learn from the way in which he used technology to reimagine a traditional choir? And what, of Whitacre's leadership techniques might leaders replicate when encouraging people to innovate? To adequately respond to these questions, I need to first tell you how his Virtual Choir began.

Whitacre was profoundly influenced after receiving a YouTube video from a young fan who had produced a recording of herself singing the soprano part of one of his choral pieces entitled *Sleep*. He instantly told himself, "It would be amazing if I could get 100 people to do this, put it all together, and make a virtual choir." With that, Whitacre went to a studio, video-recorded himself conducting in total silence, and then uploaded the video to YouTube. After that, he put a call out to singers worldwide, inviting them to be a part of a "virtual choir" by uploading their own videos to YouTube. As the audition videos poured in, Whitacre was encouraged to keep going with his idea.

Like any successful innovator, Eric Whitacre didn't know exactly how this project would come together, but he did know that he couldn't do it alone. So when a potential partner stepped forward to offer technical assistance, Whitacre accepted the offer. Together, they collaborated to cut and splice the audition videos and, in so doing, challenged all the conventions of a traditional choir. They integrated all 185 recorded submissions, from people in 12 countries, into one brilliant production—one choir—and one transcending experience.

After only two months, the Virtual Choir video had attracted over a million views on YouTube. Commenting on this, Whitacre said, "It was all about connecting and creating—alone and together." Since then, the ideas for his virtual choirs have evolved in size, scope and artistry. Virtual Choir 4, "Fly to Paradise," featured over 8,400 singers from 101 countries. If you haven't seen one of these productions yet, you might want to put this book down and watch one online. As of the writing of this book, all four Virtual Choirs collectively have over 15 million views on YouTube.

Continuous Innovation

Innovators can seldom rest on their laurels. They need to find ways to remain relevant and fresh which usually requires them to push boundaries and take some risks. As a conductor who employs many elements at his disposal, Eric Whitacre continues to engage audiences creatively. And as a composer, he constantly thinks through not only a particular piece but also the dynamics of the environment in which it will be played.

In 2015, Whitacre was creating a piece called *Deep Field*, co-commissioned by the Minnesota Orchestra and the BBC Proms. *Deep Field* is his most recent piece for orchestra, chorus, and electronics. It was the Hubble Telescope Deep Field images that inspired Whitacre to write it. When thinking through the elements of the performance, Whitacre challenged a strictly followed "rule" employed in nearly every classical music performance.

After years of instructing audience members to turn mobile devices off before performances, Whitacre wondered what would happen if he asked people to do the opposite: keep their phones on. And just like that, another idea was put into motion—the development of the *Deep Field* app, which would enable audience members to see images and hear complementary music that they would play in response to the conductor's command during the performance. Imagine yourself as an audience member, listening to a beautiful composition while simultaneously gazing at images of far-away galaxies from the Hubble Telescope. How easy might it be to allow yourself to be magically transported into deep space through this highly innovative, technology-enabled multidimensional experience?

The Virtual Choir and Whitacre's *Deep Field* app are only two of many examples of how innovation often can start with a simple idea that seems to come out of nowhere, and when given a chance, grows to become something bigger than anyone might have thought possible. Whether companies are innovating within their categories or disrupting entire industries with innovations like the first smartphones, Uber, or Airbnb, they must continually fan the creative spark to take their inventions to the next level. Of course, a significant part of most leaders' jobs must also be dedicated to constantly innovating and reinventing over time.

Inspiration Near and Afar

What can we learn from Eric Whitacre's ongoing creations and from the way he inspires and leads others to create? Most of us have seen how new and novel ideas can be contagious. We also know that, if people are open to change, ideas can be customized and replicated in different environments. After meeting Eric Whitacre, I've incorporated his invention and subsequent ideas into the Strategic Leadership and Innovation class that I teach at the Schulich Executive Education Centre in Toronto, Canada.

I first ask participants questions such as these: "What do you think about a choir? What are the 'givens'—the things that you know for certain about a choir?" Their responses vary, and inevitably I hear comments such as, "They sing," "There is harmony," and "People sing at the same time." I smile when they say, "They're all in the same room." I ask these questions to help aspiring innovators become aware of how they must continually recognize their assumptions. Then I show them a video of Whitacre's Virtual Choir. These executives aren't only impressed; they also understand how assumptions can limit their imaginations and creative potential. You might reach the same conclusion by looking at how Whitacre reversed assumptions about smartphones: that they can enhance versus diminish the experience of classical musical performances. In this chapter, you'll also see what can happen when we challenge or reverse assumptions, and how we can open doors to something new and novel. So what, from Whitacre's Virtual Choir or *Deep Field* app, might you apply in your organization or classroom?

Innovation Strategy

To become innovations, ideas must have value and be brought to life by leaders who know how to inspire and encourage others. But that's not all. In her introduction to the enabling chapters in this book, Deborah Arcoleo, Director of Product Transparency at The Hershey Company and the former director of the Innovation Center of Excellence, tells us that an innovation strategy is most often the starting point for differentiation and competitive advantage. Arcoleo reinforces what many of us know about strategy: that it can set the course and guide the effort, but no plan by itself can make innovation happen—people do that. Then she describes why it's of vital importance for leaders to define the type of innovation that's right for their particular organizations. That's because it's a prerequisite for the kind of activities that need to follow.

Innovation strategy is not "one-size-fits-all." In other words, what's right for one organization may not be appropriate, or even possible, for another. Leaders must establish a shared understanding of what they're trying to achieve and how they'll accomplish it. For this reason, organizations can benefit from having a consistent definition of innovation as well as agreement on the behaviors needed to support it. Then leaders need to know, in a broad sense, what's involved in carrying out their organizations' innovation strategies and initiatives and what their individual roles will be. Eric Whitacre said, "If the music is well crafted, it's almost like you just add water to it, and it happens. The players know what to do with it. They know what their place is in it. If by the second time, you are not close to perfect, something has gone wrong."

The initial construction of innovation strategies largely determines successful execution. In general, it's good to ask relevant questions in advance, such as these: What goals are we trying to achieve? What kind of innovation are we looking for? Will we attempt product innovation or new business models? Will our innovation consist of new distribution channels or strategic innovation partners? Will we attempt growth organically or through acquisition? Only after leaders can discuss and evaluate their options can they establish meaningful innovation goals and objectives. Then, by taking the next step, they anticipate and identify the inevitable barriers and impediments to execution and decide how they'll deal with them. In this way, leaders can leverage some of the enablers that successful innovators use to inspire and mobilize their people.

Creativity, Culture, and Collaboration

With regard to "people" considerations, innovation must above all be aspirational. Blaine Lee, one of the original founders of the Covey Leadership Center, captured this concept well in his 1997 book, *The Power Principle: Influence with Honor.* He said, "The great leaders are like the best conductors—they reach beyond the notes to reach the magic in the players." But what about other leaders who don't appreciate the role that creativity plays in innovation? Or those who support the concept of innovation but view creativity as mere "fluff" or "feel-good activities" that don't produce meaningful results? This apparent lack of correlation between creativity and innovation sometimes means that these leaders don't know how to fully leverage their most precious resource—the creative potential of their people. However, it might also mean that they don't see the value of creativity because they haven't ensured that the right conditions are in place for creativity to thrive.

All stages of the innovation process, from idea generation to execution, require creativity. And asking questions at each stage is usually a good tactic for inspiring and encouraging people. Questions such as, "What if...?" or "How could you make that happen?" or "Have you looked at this opportunity from another perspective?" are usually effective ways to continually stimulate creativity and reinforce ideas by showing people that their opinions are valued. Some leaders seem to be instinctively skilled at nurturing the creative spirit whenever opportunities arise. They know that creativity and innovation aren't only about good ideas. Well aware of the need to provoke further thinking through questions, they also know that innovation is ignited and sustained by an occasional pat on the back and frequent words of encouragement.

In the chapters that follow, leaders and innovation experts show how three vital components set the stage for the crucial role that creativity plays in facilitating innovation and the top performance of individuals, teams, and organizations. The first element, and the one that feeds innovation, is creativity. The second is culture, which plays a foundational role in inspiring and supporting innovation. And the third component, collaboration, helps to both drive and *sustain* innovation. So let's now take a closer look at what enables creativity as well as what can inhibit it.

■ ■ ■

1. Creativity and Innovation

As previously mentioned, few business leaders recognize the raw value of creativity and its role in jumpstarting innovation. In part, it's because many organizations lack a shared understanding of the very words "creativity" and "innovation." That's understandable since these overused words have lost meaning for many people. However, once leaders can accurately define them and agree on how they relate to achieving their organizations' goals, the words become more meaningful.

Leaders must also define what kind of innovation they're seeking. For example, they ought to decide whether it will be incremental or disruptive in nature. Will it be new product innovation or new business models? Will it be new distribution channels or strategic innovation partners? Should the organization attempt organic growth or growth by acquisition? Only after these discussions occur can leaders establish relevant strategic plans to achieve their goals. And this is where the innovation challenge continues. Strategic planning must be a dynamic process. Leaders are required to continually decide on the best approaches for the execution of their plans, especially when long-standing goals and objectives that have been in place for years are failing to deliver.

The Creativity-Innovation Connection

As a first step to learning about the relationship between creativity and innovation, leaders must understand that creativity can occur without leading to innovation, but innovation—the lifeblood of many organizations today—is entirely reliant on creativity. If we accept that the expression of creativity is critical to organizational success, we must then ask what leaders need to learn about the creative process itself. For some, it's intuitive, and for others, it's hard work. So is there anything that leaders can do to make the creative process easier for themselves and others?

Although it requires a certain amount of discipline, the creative process can also be fun when it invites a sense of playfulness that unleashes people's imaginations. But how do leaders introduce playfulness into business settings where most people operate from only the analytical part of their brains? To fully ignite creativity in traditional work environments, some leaders use advanced problem-solving techniques that drive original thinking. Others immerse themselves and their employees in fresh experiences and stimulus, like field trips and presentations by guest speakers. And still others ensure that people engage with those who have different styles, backgrounds, and thinking processes. Of course, leaders who excel at innovation use all three of these methods, and even more.

A particularly compelling way in which leaders inspire creative potential is by helping people identify different types of creativity and assisting them in employing their own particular brand. When people see that their kind of creativity can make a difference, and honestly believe it, they reach a critical starting point. That's because beliefs drive the behaviors and actions that ultimately produce results. Visionary Henry Ford summed this up very simply when he said, "Whether you think you can, or you think you can't, you are probably right."

A Creativity Crisis?

Some experts believe that the devaluation of creativity begins early in life. And these experts describe how educational systems in many countries were designed to support the industrial age and are no longer able to equip students with the skills needed to become knowledge workers in a postindustrial age. We can see how Eric Whitacre values creativity as does one other highly regarded classical conductor featured in this book.

JoAnn Falletta, Music Director of the Buffalo Philharmonic Orchestra and the Virginia Symphony Orchestra, describes in an essay on her website how diminishing creativity may even constitute what she terms a "creativity crisis." She writes, "Creativity is key to our future—and that beautiful, personal gift of all human beings is often stifled." Falletta describes how she believes that happens. "Children...whose artistic and literary creations are so filled with imagination and dimension—grow increasingly more concerned with approval and become less poetic, more analytic, more predictable."

Falletta adds, "The non-nurturing of creativity is a true crisis, one of the most serious concerns facing us. If problems facing our world are to be solved, they will be solved by creative people with creative ideas. If we are going to make advances in medicine, psychology, physical science, and technology, these discoveries will be made, as well, by creative people." (See the essay "Music and the Mind" at joannfalletta.com.)

Indeed current education systems can hamper or even completely inhibit children's innate creative abilities. What's more, experts tell us that confidence in one's creativity often decreases through the school years and further diminishes by the time someone has been in the work world for even a few years. Is JoAnn Falletta's "creativity crisis" manifest within most organizations today? Unfortunately, in some it is, and you can find these organizations in all the key sectors—private, public, and not-for-profit—and in many industries.

Stimulating Responses

So how can leaders reverse the creativity crisis? If they were to accept that creativity is a natural part of being human, and a valuable innovation driver, might they then overcome the effects of it being unintentionally devalued and even squelched? The good news is that people are slowly waking up to the fact that we're all creative—and that we need to honor our own brand of creativity as well as that of others. This revelation is happening in the way we raise children and the way we treat other adults.

Many of us know that life is grander when we allow ourselves every opportunity to be creative, as it begins in childhood and continues throughout adulthood. We can also see that there have been some varied and positive responses to the creativity crisis. Take, for example, Peter Diamandis M.D., who founded the XPRIZE. This not-for-profit organization is a highly incentivized prize competition designed to change the world for the better by pushing the limits of what's currently possible. XPRIZE challenges range from a $30 million Google Lunar challenge to a $15 million competition to empower children to take control of their learning. XPRIZE leaders believe that good ideas can come not only from engineers, scientists, and mathematicians, but anyone and anywhere. Consequently, each challenge is set up to inspire broad-based creative solutions to some of the world's leading problems.

Another positive response to the creativity crisis is World Creativity and Innovation Week (WCIW), which is celebrated annually from April 15 to April 21. The event was created after a 2001 newspaper article stated that Canada was in a creativity crisis. The founder of WCIW, Marci Segal, has been instrumental in helping people learn how to use their natural abilities to generate new ideas, make new decisions, and take appropriate actions to achieve new outcomes. Today, schools, communities, and businesses in over 50 countries celebrate WCIW. In fact, beginning in 2017, the United Nations recognized April 21 as World Creativity and Innovation Day. From this example and that of the XPRIZE, we can see how creativity can be stimulated on an international basis, but let's also zero in on how it can begin at a very personal level.

Our Creative Nature

I often hear people say, "I'm not creative." What this often means to me is that they're simply not giving themselves enough credit. They might have a narrow definition of creativity or a limited understanding of what constitutes a creative act. Or they might believe that to be creative, one must work in the arts or have big radical ideas. This stereotypical thinking can also cause people to believe that smaller, less crazy, ideas—or different ways of thinking—aren't valuable. That's because these kinds of ideas often don't get noticed as much.

Since the beginning of time, humans have sought to continually improve the status quo. If you think about it historically, we have always looked for better tools and techniques by which to hunt and gather. As our world continues to evolve, so do the areas in which we continue to strive for improvement. This can be seen in our architectural design, improved methods of transportation, sophisticated communication devices, and so on. The desire to create is in our DNA, and we're all creative in very personalized and unique ways.

Recognizing the differences in creative styles, a researcher, Dr. Michael Kirton, theorizes that some have a preference to enhance what already exists, while others prefer to create something entirely new. With that, he developed the concept of Creativity Style and a corresponding instrument to assess it. His model, called the Kirton Adapter-Innovator or KAI, assumes that adaptive or incremental thinkers want to make things *better,* while innovators or disruptive thinkers want to make things *different.* If you place these two ways of thinking on each end of an imaginary spectrum, you can see that they both have merit and both drive value—just in different ways.

I mention the Kirton model because when people can expand their appreciation for the various types of creativity, they're able to see greater possibilities for themselves and others. And when they understand that it's human nature to be creative, and that each person is creative in his or her unique way, they often get energized. This natural ability is what empowers individuals to play to their strengths and enables them to contribute optimally to high performing teams.

Creative Beliefs and Behaviors

As a way to understand some of the creative behaviors and beliefs that support innovation, let's look at how they manifested in the launch of Whitacre's first Virtual Choir. The whole phenomenon may never have occurred if that young fan hadn't performed a creative and courageous act. When she expressed her creativity in a way that was uniquely hers, by uploading her voice to YouTube, she inspired Eric Whitacre to leverage her video in a new way—and a new idea was born. Each time that people build on the original ideas of others, thoughts evolve and take on new forms.

When Whitacre came forward with his idea about a virtual choir, and accepted help from someone with complementary skill sets, he was able to transform his vision into a reality, both technically and visually. Believing in the concept, he put his stamp of creativity on the process, but he also gave the idea time to incubate and take shape with continued input from others. Throughout the project, Whitacre lived with multiple uncertainties, but in the end, his combination of resilience, patience, and perseverance paid off with a groundbreaking innovation.

What's unique about the Virtual Choir is that although Whitacre had a revolutionary idea, no one—not even he—had a complete picture of the outcome in its early stages. Consequently, each person's contribution to the Virtual Choir demonstrated passion, openness to novelty, and ultimately, courage. Perhaps most important, people's leaps of faith reflected the right mindset for innovation. Essential to this project were their beliefs that they could contribute to something bigger even if they didn't know exactly how everything might play out. With this example, you can see how the attitudes of individuals and leaders are critical to inspiring people to act on their creativity.

There is something incredibly liberating about being around people who are both creative and passionate, perhaps even a bit fanatical, about what they strongly believe in. When passionate people act collectively and comprise a community in which each person contributes his or her unique talents, innovation comes to life in a big way. That's because passion—including a passion for innovation—can be highly infectious.

■ ■ ■

2. Culture and Innovation

Today, it's imperative that leaders keep pace with current trends, future trends, and converging trends if they're to continue meeting and anticipating consumers' needs. To do this effectively, they most often need to innovate. And to fully leverage innovation, they need to elicit the best from each employee. Successful leaders know that in the same ways that muscles increase with exercise, skills around innovation improve with use. As a result, they support innovation end-to-end by helping employees build or enhance their individual and unique competencies. They also visibly reinforce and embrace the behaviors that promote innovation. When employees and leaders dedicate their efforts to developing skills, they build innovation competency for themselves and their organizations. And when people also maintain positive attitudes about innovation, including the change that inevitably accompanies it, greater productivity and focus are logical outcomes.

The most successful innovation leaders know this. They also know that people's greatest strengths tend to stem from what they do well and what they love to do. Researchers at Gallup conducted what might be the largest study to date about employee productivity when they surveyed people in more than 140 countries from 2011 through 2012 for their ongoing *State of the Global Workplace* report. Authors Chris Groscurth and Stephen Shields, raise an important question about the results in their June 7, 2016 article (at gallup.com), "Managing in Tough Financial Times: Does Engagement Help?" Citing Gallup's extensive research about employee productivity, Groscurth and Shields indicate how, when people work in teams that focus on individual members' strengths, the result is 6 times higher engagement and 12.5 percent increased productivity.

These research findings validate why it's important for leaders to dedicate time and other resources to building and continuing to cultivate the right climate for strong productivity and the ability to execute high-impact strategies. Leaders must also consistently encourage and value new thinking and new ways of operating by ensuring that employees feel comfortable about suggesting new approaches and also experimenting with them.

Organizational Climate

When I asked Eric Whitacre how he encourages and inspires people, he said, "Most of the time it is fun, and it is light, and there is the sense of playfulness. That seems to inspire people because it awakens creativity...they've already got it, but [playfulness] allows them to feel *more* creative." This goes back to what I wrote earlier: Many people either don't realize they're creative or they've somehow forgotten *how* to be creative. While playfulness is one variable, many other behaviors are needed to stimulate the kind of creativity that leads to innovation. Today, a culture that encourages a positive environment and inspires the passion necessary for a steady output of ideas is essential, and leaders must set the tone for that kind of climate.

With regard to the ideal psychological environment for creativity and innovation, Barbara Fredrickson, a professor at the University of North Carolina at Chapel Hill, asserts in a September 2004 article entitled, "The Broaden-and-Build Theory of Positive Emotions," that the ability to make creative connections is enhanced when people experience positive feelings such as love and joy. In this article, she states, "When positive emotions are in ample supply, people take off. They become generative, creative, resilient, ripe with possibility and beautifully complex." (To read the entire article, published by *The Royal Society of Publishing*, go to rstb.royalsocietypublishing.org.) While some of you may have reacted hesitantly to the words "love" and "joy," I would invite you to consider other positive emotions such as respect, camaraderie, and inclusion. A broad range of positive emotions has a favorable effect on creativity.

Additional support for a positive work environment comes from Harvard professor Teresa Amabile, who has concluded that people are happiest when they generate creative ideas. Additionally, she believes they're more likely to have breakthroughs if they were happy the day before. In an article that she co-authored entitled, "Emotion and Creativity at Work," Amabile says, "One day's happiness often predicts the next day's creativity." (See this September 2005 article in *Administrative Science Quarterly* at the Cornell University S.C. Johnson College of Business website, www.joynson.cornell.edu.)

The implications of Fredrickson's and Amabile's findings are probably obvious. Leaders must create the right climate by dedicating time and resources, and they must also do it by consistently encouraging and valuing positive behaviors and new thinking. By allowing employees to feel comfortable about suggesting new approaches and experimenting with them, leaders create the right conditions for people to thrive. But is this easy? No.

Stress as an Innovation Inhibitor

Today, leaders must demonstrate emotional intelligence and resilience when dealing with the inevitable ups and downs of business and also with the innovation process. One significant challenge they face when innovating is the need to invent new ways of delivering value while also taking into account people's normal stress responses to change. Having opportunities to think clearly and creatively is what gives people room to breathe and the ability to solve complex problems. However, in today's constantly changing and unpredictable environments, it's easy for employees and leaders alike to succumb to the stress of the many tactical day-to-day tasks that compete with innovation agendas. And even when employees enjoy innovating, there are additional challenges when the change brought about by innovation isn't effectively dealt with and causes undue stress. I've witnessed how, when stress isn't managed carefully, it can kill even the strongest passion for creating.

I believe that stress is often caused by a perceived lack of options, whether it's of a personal or professional nature. Although too many options can also trigger stress, I see that less commonly. The point is that both can negatively impact creativity. Stress can be mitigated, however, when leaders understand its adverse effect on creativity and when they know how to help people manage it. Leaders also alleviate stress when they encourage multiple ways of approaching challenges and when they provide access to different problem-solving and decision-making tools. But that's still not enough to enable innovation.

Successful leaders know that stress can be overcome or reduced when people have opportunities to unleash their passions. So leaders need to know how to direct and channel people's emotions in constructive ways. They accomplish this when they enlist people's support and involve them in the creation of organizational visions and missions. These leaders also sustain innovation when they help people understand the unique roles that they can play in fulfilling shared missions, especially when those purposes represent departures from existing norms.

Employee Engagement

The experts cited in the *Leading Innovation* subsection communicate how critical it is to create a bias for action. This is what helps people leverage opportunities and maximize both personal and organizational success. When employees have the right skill sets, or they receive the right training to build them, a bias for action is often a natural result. But that only happens if leaders provide opportunities to apply what's learned. When they do, employees can then gain the confidence to play to their strengths. However, this still only represents part of the employee engagement picture.

The common expression, "Our people are our greatest assets" is true only in part. If people aren't sufficiently engaged, they can represent *untapped* assets. Conversely, the more engaged that employees are, the more likely they will be to leverage their strengths and passions and enable their organizations to succeed. There is a real power in engagement since it's the energy that pulls people forward, drawing out their skills and capabilities. It can also lift people to increasingly higher levels of performance without exhausting them. So how can leaders determine whether people are engaged? It's surprisingly easy to get a read on employee engagement. Asking questions such as these can help assess the degree to which people are engaged:

- Do people find their work to be energizing?
- Are their goals and values aligned with those of their organizations?
- Do employees think about their organizations' challenges during their time away from work?
- Are individuals in roles that play to their skills and passions?
- Are people able to leverage their talents and strengths on a regular basis and do work that they perceive as meaningful?
- Are their organizations developing them through on-the-job opportunities, stretch assignments, formal training, and coaching?
- Is there safe, healthy debate and open communication among employees and leaders?

If the answers to these questions are "yes," then many of the enablers of a climate for innovation are in place. If these questions are difficult to answer, or they produce "no" responses, it might be time to formally assess the culture. Without the ability to provide fertile ground for creativity, leaders might find themselves harvesting more weeds than great ideas.

Innovation Frameworks and Styles

Not all creative people are musicians, artists, or orchestra conductors, yet there are many types of creative intelligence, and many support innovation. In fact, I believe that almost everyone can contribute to an organizational initiative or creative endeavor. People do this in different ways and at different stages of the innovation process. Leaders who succeed at innovation have a fundamental understanding of basic innovation models or frameworks that, in turn, enable them to fully understand what's called for at different stages. Then they can match people's skills and abilities to the particular tasks within each stage. Effective leaders also match people's preferences to particular tasks. For example, they usually know which people prefer to work alone and which of their employees get energized by working with others. They also know that people will contribute to the innovation process when they're most excited about what they're achieving.

To help clients identify and leverage the different types of creative intelligence, I most often use the FourSight Innovation Framework, based on a theory by Dr. Gerard Puccio, Department Chair and Professor at the International Center for Studies in Creativity at Buffalo State University. The first stage in Puccio's innovation model describes the need to properly clarify and frame the innovation challenge or problem to be solved. Although this is one of the most important stages in many innovation models, people often rush through it. The famous (and late) University of Michigan professor C.K. Prahalad once said about the challenge inherent at this stage of the innovation process, "How we ask the question is extremely important to how we find the answer."

The second stage of the FourSight Innovation Framework is where people generate and select ideas, through brainstorming and other methods of idea generation and idea selection. This is the stage that people often associate with high creativity, and so it's sometimes difficult for people to move beyond it. The third stage is where ideas are further prototyped and developed, and evaluated by viability, cost, fit with the organization's mission and vision, and so on. The fourth stage of the FourSight Innovation Framework is about implementing the ideas that will best solve the organization's presenting challenges. Needless to say, all four stages are critical in taking an idea from inception to execution and for matching people's strengths to each stage—and leveraging them accordingly.

Individual Competencies and Alignment

In the *Leading Innovation* subsection of this book, contributors share how innovation competencies are developed in the same way as other organizational skills. When artfully leveraged, individuals' innovation competencies can collectively build organizational skills. For this to happen, however, leaders must continually attract, recruit, and retain the right talent. Eric Whitacre says, "I've discovered that the very best thing you can do with an orchestra is fill it with the best forces you can find. The better your baseline players, the better the *everything*."

In the section of this book, *Managing and Leveraging Innovation*, contributors discuss how important it is to translate strategy into action through people, partnerships, and processes. Some leaders have innate skills and abilities that enable them to do this, while others must develop them through formal training and coaching. However, I know from teaching executive education courses, that learning can be highly effective and even transformational. Successful organizations also know this, which is why their leaders dedicate resources to building both technical and "people" skills.

Innovation leaders appreciate that formal learning opportunities via courses or external programs can be critical enablers for both employees and leaders. At the same time, they ensure that their leadership development programs provide opportunities for retooling and resetting participants' thinking through immersion in new environments. By stepping away from the day-to-day responsibilities that can compete with innovation agendas, leaders can network and learn from others. This can help greatly in gaining fresh perspectives and new insights into how their organizations might operate more effectively and efficiently.

Form and Freedom

Another well-documented driver of creativity is the notion of freedom: freedom of expression, freedom to create, and freedom to take the approach that we feel is right to achieve a particular outcome. Sometimes it comes when we work alone, and other times it's a result of collaboration with others. For this reason, leaders need to be mindful of the environments they create and the behaviors that they model. In the chapter of this book entitled *Why This Book?* we learn that some orchestra conductors of times past led with an autocratic style that could be downright aggressive at times. These conductors might not have realized that musicians, singers, and other artists model their behaviors. For example, if musicians replicate an aggressive or authoritarian style, their performances will take on a different tone than if they're free to be creative and expressive. The same is true in environments outside of the concert hall.

If leaders want to get valuable input from most of their employees, they need to deliberately involve everyone. They must also keep in mind that some are extroverts and some are introverts. Extroverts are relatively easy to involve in the process because they get their energy through discussion and engagement with other people. By contrast, introverts prefer to process information internally, rather than thinking aloud. As the quieter members of their teams, introverts can appear to be uninvolved, but nothing could be further from the truth. Introverts usually only need to be away from the noise of the crowd and have opportunities to holistically reflect on and assimilate information and ideas. Successful leaders know how to draw introverted types into the fold, where they can shine and where their unique abilities can be fully leveraged.

When thinking about form and freedom, I'm reminded of how Whitacre's call for the first Virtual Choir gave direction and inspired people, yet also allowed individual singers to respond at their discretion and in their own way. Whitacre modeled innovative behaviors when he put his first-of-its-kind request on the Internet and invited people to co-create something new and untested. In this way, he demonstrated openness to novelty and encouraged passion. The result: 185 singers eagerly followed this open, passionate, and courageous leader into the unknown.

So in what ways do successful organizations inspire and nurture creativity, and how do leaders leverage it as a sustainable advantage? Some companies, like Google, offer free time to employees to explore the passions that ignite their imaginations because they may lead to growth opportunities. Other organizations allow freedom regarding where and when their employees work, including working from the comfort of their own homes. What challenges must leaders at many organizations overcome to shift their organizational culture to one that honors creativity and innovation?

Trust and Safety

In orchestras and business environments alike, a safe and supportive culture is essential. But what happens when people aren't allowed opportunities or resources to solve problems or unleash their creativity—or passions? And what happens if employees perceive the environment as unsafe or unwelcoming of their ideas? When people don't feel safe or valued, they may physically or psychologically disengage. This was evident when some musicians from a famous orchestra signed a petition to remove a legendary conductor. An orchestra leader who allowed musicians more latitude and creative expression replaced him.

How can leaders communicate that it's safe for people to contribute their unique ideas, talents and gifts? The answers to this question are imperative for leaders in almost any environment because, to feel motivated to perform at high levels, people must believe that they're being heard and their ideas are welcomed. If they don't feel safe, they may experience a sense of vulnerability that can cause them to be unproductive or to erect barriers that prevent spontaneity, creativity, and self-expression.

When this happens, leaders run the risk of losing not only the unique voices of a few key individuals but also those of the many people with whom these individuals interact. Then the overall result is that people's potential isn't actualized—a liability that very few organizations in today's competitive times can afford. Conversely, when leaders are thoughtful and deliberate about how they communicate that they value *all* individuals, welcome *all* ideas, and appreciate *all* contributions, they create the psychological safety that brings out the best in people.

Authenticity

Early on in many people's careers, my own included, there is often an urge to conform to the qualities of other successful leaders. After gaining some professional maturity, and having the right kind of reinforcement throughout their careers, some people finally feel safe enough for their authenticity to shine through. Eric Whitacre commented that he used to be concerned with what people thought about him as a composer versus an innovator and visionary. He said, "...at this age, all of that is slipping away... It's just here's what I like to do and I hope someone enjoys it." When I asked him how he inspires people's authenticity, he said, "I try to give people the space and the security to fail. When I'm leading [or] if I'm conducting a choir, virtual or real, I try to keep this big open heart and this sense of possibility, and there is no shaming—ever—in the process."

When the previously mentioned young fan uploaded her YouTube video to Eric Whitacre's website, she said it was Whitacre's genuineness that had inspired her as an artist. She told him that she hoped she could be as different and unique as he was when capturing passion and emotion in a piece. As previously mentioned, people's creative behaviors seldom manifest in the same ways, so the best approach for leaders is to encourage people to be their authentic selves. Then they can connect to an energy source within that allows them to come alive in highly personal ways.

Innovation is born out of bringing together diverse viewpoints and ideas. If leaders try to make everyone the same, creativity is less than what it can be. Successful leaders foster innovation through the celebration and embrace of diversity. They also remove the fear of being punished for being oneself—or for being different—because they know that when people become aware of what fires them up, they're better positioned to act on their internal drivers. To go one step further, when leaders help employees find their own meaning and connection to their organizations' missions and visions, they also begin to build a foundation for the confidence and courage that's needed for sustainable innovation.

Courage

I've often heard that the only fear greater than speaking in public is the fear of *singing* in public. In light of this, you might ask what could have driven one young woman to upload her Whitacre fan video to YouTube. Before the Virtual Choir became a reality, singers like her performed their choral parts alone in front of their cameras, and had no idea to whom or with whom they would be singing—or what the final choir would sound like. They simply watched Eric Whitacre conduct on a video and then they recorded their individual parts. What had compelled people around the world to participate in this project when it involved uploading their own solo voices and singing only a part of a creative work? And what force propelled Whitacre to create the first Virtual Choir?

When I asked why he pursued this idea without knowing how it would all come together, he said, "It was one of those electric ideas. I was just too dumb to know what I was getting into." Can you identify with this? Sometimes it's a gift when we don't know at the very beginning how we might execute an idea. Whitacre said, "I was able to stay dumb and naïve, and ultimately the momentum carried the idea." Should we conclude from this statement that his invention of the Virtual Choir was simply a result of good luck? Luck may have offered a helping hand, but much of the Virtual Choir's success was also a result of Whitacre staying the course and having the courage to see his idea through. Of course, the choir's success was also due to the singers who were brave enough to post their videos.

Whitacre's role in creating this most unusual innovation, and in modeling the behaviors that support innovation, aptly illustrate how a culture that supports courage and risk taking can bring forth the ideas and creative thinking that are so critical for innovation. So here are three important questions that the Virtual Choir story might raise: How often do people talk themselves out of taking risks? How often do traditional organizations stifle risk-taking when positive outcomes aren't readily apparent? And how do most successful leaders enable employees—and their organizations—take the required risks for innovation?

Risk Taking

Risk is a very important consideration when driving innovation, especially personal risk. How do we get people to overcome their fears of making mistakes or looking foolish? Leaders foster personal risk taking when they create a safe environment for people to share their thoughts, make decisions, and take action. All of these steps require courage because they trigger people's fears about speaking up and potentially failing.

A perfect example of this is visible during brainstorming. Some people set up rules that state, "There are no bad ideas." But people know there are terrible ideas, and they hesitate to share ideas when they don't know how they will be received. And let's face it—there are bad ideas. So to set the right climate for a brainstorm, what I prefer to say is, "There are bad ideas; however, all ideas are welcome when we're diverging and generating options. So let's have some fun and not worry about what anyone thinks just yet." After all, most ideas, simple or outrageous, help to move a process along and enable other possibilities. Bad ideas are weeded out when people converge and select the best ideas to move forward, and when leaders play a critical role in helping overcome fears around bringing forward all ideas without the fear of negative repercussions.

Of course, innovation requires more than the generation of good ideas, so leaders must also help employees manage personal risk throughout the innovation process, and in a variety of ways. One is by creating guard rails that prevent catastrophic failures and make risk taking safer. This can be done by setting up systems to test ideas at earlier stages of the innovation process when the cost of not succeeding is lower. Another way in which leaders help to manage personal risk is by rewarding desired behaviors and reinforcing everyday courage. When doing this on an ongoing basis, they continue to help employees move beyond fear and other internal barriers.

The Power of Failure

Most senior leaders didn't get to where they are because they failed many times in their careers, so they face a significant challenge when communicating a message that failure is a natural and inevitable part of innovating and learning. Why is this shift in conventional thinking so difficult for both leaders and non-leaders? Because most of us hate to fail, and we carefully avoid opportunities where there is even a remote possibility of failure. The irony of all this is that children stumble hundreds of times when they're learning to walk, and no parents expect any less. So why do we, as adults, expect perfection in even our most preliminary attempts at creating something that has never existed before? The answer to these questions is a simple one: We have been conditioned to avoid failure.

The most successful leaders adopt a "growth mindset" toward themselves and others by the ways in which they continue to encourage risk taking and also by how they redefine failure. In her book *Mindset: The New Psychology of Success*, Carol Dweck writes about the power of the growth mindset. That's when people see failure as a stepping-stone for personal and professional growth rather than a fixed event. They witness this when they see leaders take risks and sometimes fail. Employees are encouraged by leaders who admit occasional failure. Why? Because it makes leaders seem more human. In organizations that fully support disciplined experimentation and innovation, people are rewarded for generating ideas and taking risks—even if they don't mesh well with other organizational goals and objectives or if the timing isn't exactly right.

So what are the important takeaways about courage and risk taking? To counteract fear and judgment, leaders need to actively support people while they're learning—especially when they're stumbling. Their skill lies in recognizing whatever stage of the innovation process people are in and responding to their needs through continued support. When leaders do this skillfully, they encourage people to walk—and then ultimately run—with greater ease. This not only builds and increases innovation capacity in individuals; it also builds capacity for people who work in teams.

■ ■ ■

3. Collaboration and Innovation

In his book *Social: Why our Brains are Wired to Connect*, Matt Lieberman, Ph.D., asserts that human beings have a "neural seesaw" between two separate sections of the brain—one for analytic thinking and one for "social thinking." Lieberman says about this, "Getting us more social is the key to making us smarter, happier and more productive." If we accept that social thinking is essential for connecting with others, and for successful collaborations, we agree that people need to engage consciously with others to best facilitate the creative process.

By stepping beyond traditional analytical problem-solving to use more advanced techniques, people usually reach greater heights and produce better outcomes. And when they collaborate with others, no matter the degree, it changes how well innovation works. Whitacre described this by relating it to how he conducts. He said collaborations are a "dance between the players and the leader," and then further described the metaphor when he added, "While handing the reins back and forth to one another, sometimes people need you, and sometimes you need them. Sometimes you let them drive, and sometimes you drive." About supporting collaboration, Whitacre said, "When I'm at my best as a leader, I'm most flexible and responsive, and I am present to exactly what is happening in front of me, not trying to force my vision on my group."

Workspace and Workplace

How do successful leaders unleash the power of collaboration in their organizations? To answer that question, let's revisit our orchestra metaphor. It's relatively easy for symphony orchestra leaders to connect with their musicians because their work environments haven't changed much in hundreds of years. By contrast, business environments are just the opposite. Today, many online idea portals allow people to meet, collaborate, and develop ideas from inception to launch in ways that overcome traditional resource barriers. Today's physical work environments have changed dramatically as well, but workspace still plays a significant role in innovation.

Some leaders leverage physical space by dedicating places where people can meet both formally and informally and by designing that space to support how they interact and collaborate. Targeting where people have frequent informal contact with one another is a hot trend now. So in addition to carefully designing workspaces, leaders ensure that informal seating, coffee lounges, and kitchen areas also provide opportunities for real-time connections, often even eliminating the need for e-mails and meetings.

Another way in which leaders foster communication is to walk around and connect with people one-on-one and in group settings. Even in our virtual world, where leaders manage remotely and sometimes across entire continents, it's necessary to directly connect with people to know what they're thinking and feeling. Successful leaders know that if there is to be collaboration, almost every touch point between them and employees is an opportunity to build relationships and to inspire and encourage thinking outside the norm. Consequently, if leaders want fresh thinking or buy-in to organizational initiatives, they need to use every relevant means of communication. Dialogue is the best framework because it involves both talking and listening, with the aim to fully understand and be understood.

Leaders use conversation not only to foster collaboration but also to get work done more effectively. That means helping people to connect the dots and to also break down barriers between various work groups and functions. When encouraging people to innovate, it's especially important for leaders to also "walk the talk." That means ensuring that their behaviors are consistent with what they preach. It also helps when leaders continually reinforce their organizations' goals and objectives. And since innovation is typically a process of discovery, almost everyone can benefit from provocative questions that leaders put forth to push boundaries. By encouraging these types of questions, they can create "opportunity mindsets."

In reference to "workspace" and "workplace," Whitacre says, "[The Virtual Choir] seems to have captured the poetry of the human condition—that we will simply go to any lengths necessary to find and connect with each other. The technology does not matter." At the end of my interview with him, I asked if he knew what had inspired his fan to upload her video to him without any invitation. He believed she might have been looking to meaningfully connect with like-minded people to create an extended community. He also said, "I think she somehow infused into that video a sense of longing [for that kind of community], and I somehow channeled it. Now I think her original intention is embedded in all virtual choirs, which I just find extraordinary."

Teamwork

Most of us aspire to be a part of something bigger. Would the Virtual Choir have been such a success if it hadn't provided an opportunity for individual singers to feel as if they were part of something larger? It's difficult to say. Whitacre said about being part of a bigger picture, "There is something that happens when you get people together with a shared intention. Something transcendent happens at that moment, something fundamental to who we are as people."

I agree with Whitacre on this point, and I believe the real magic in innovation occurs through team-work, where individuals play to their respective strengths, and at the same time, receive support from other individuals with complementary skills and competencies. Some of the experts featured in this section of the book underscore that no one person can outperform a team, particularly on a long-term basis. That's because, when mobilized, teams can generate a multiplier effect, particularly when people align in support of a compelling goal. As a way to increase the multiplier effect, leaders often assemble project teams or task forces that are comprised of people with skill sets that uniquely qualify them to solve particular problems. When their tasks are completed, these teams might disband.

No matter how teams are put together—or for what purpose or duration—successful leaders leverage the engagement of group members. This strengthens the power of teams and enhances collaboration. But what, exactly, makes high performing teams so powerful? Is it their common purpose? Shared goals? Diversity? We can witness the majesty of an orchestra's performance when we see how teams of musicians play together and strive for the same goals by using a variety of different instruments. The diverse sounds are aligned and in harmony. Orchestra conductors ensure that different instruments come in and out of a musical piece at the appropriate times so that they're complementary versus contradictory.

The way that successful innovation happens in organizational settings is similar. Different viewpoints from various functions are often combined to create robust solutions. This is what happens when people with complementary strengths participate at various stages of the innovation process that call for their unique skills, competencies, and functional expertise. Then leaders, like skilled orchestra conductors, can orchestrate in ways that achieve alignment, balance, and harmony. This is truly the way to drive outstanding performance.

Technology-Enabled Collaboration

We can see how technology has the potential to be a great enabler of collaboration, limited only by the imagination. Today, smart enterprises are co-creating with consumers and business partners to strengthen relationships. As repertoires for conversing and connecting expand, technology will likely continue to be a critical tool for attaining new levels of interaction and for mobilizing people to address business goals collectively. When we apply these concepts to the hyper-competitive business environments of today, we see that there's a continual need to challenge the notion of how and where people need to be, to achieve the collaboration that facilitates sustainable innovation.

Whitacre has shown how the technology in smartphones can be used to enhance experiences in concert halls. One famous musical organization, the Metropolitan Opera ("The Met"), has also proven that audiences don't even need to be in a concert hall to enjoy its live performances. In 2006, this organization launched "The Met: Live in HD" where it broadcasts, in high definition, a series of live performances in movie theaters across the world. How's that for an example of the many ways in which organizations can expand their consumer bases by reversing assumptions and leveraging technology?

How might this paradigm-shifting behavior inspire you to think differently about how you create? Eric Whitacre has demonstrated that people don't need to be co-located to create together. Today, many organizations are growing regionally and globally, with geographically dispersed colleagues bound together by shared objectives and challenges. Conversations can happen almost effortlessly—not only through e-mail and virtual meetings but also web-based technologies such as idea management software and organization-wide idea platforms. Not surprisingly, enterprise-wide technologies can do even more than this. They can also give voice to those who we might think of as "hidden innovators"—introverts who might not feel comfortable about speaking in group settings but who shine in the virtual arena.

In other situations, these tools allow for collaboration that might not be possible for some people in real time. For example, asynchronous chats enable individuals who work night shifts, rotating shifts or irregular hours to do their job from home—and even collaborate with others from home. The technology of Whitacre's Virtual Choirs facilitated the participation of thousands of people—all from remote locations. Now imagine similar possibilities in business settings, where current or commercially available technologies can provide a voice for all employees.

Crowdfunding

When looking at innovation-enabling technology from another perspective, however, we might ask what happens when innovators don't have the luxury of working in companies where it's easy to connect with others. Many of them can still use the Internet to create awareness for their projects and to facilitate the collaboration needed to raise money, enlist support, and get projects funded and off the ground. A good example of this was Eric Whitacre's online campaign to partially fund the production of the Virtual Choir 4. It enabled him to raise over $122,000 from over 2,000 backers.

Other good examples are the many crowdfunding sites that help innovators gain traction, such as Kickstarter. De La Soul, an American hip-hop group, says about this organization, "Kickstarter is one of these platforms that gives you space to work with people who know you, love you, and support you." It's amazing that, by early 2017, 13 million people have backed a Kickstarter project, almost $3 billion has been pledged, and over 120,000 projects have been successfully funded.

■　■　■

Exemplary Leadership

Looking back on my various leadership roles and the types of innovation initiatives in which I've led or been involved, one visibly stands out as an excellent example of both deliberate and systemic innovation. After acquiring Warner-Lambert in 2003, Pfizer Consumer Healthcare (PCH) set about achieving growth targets for over the next five years, with innovation as the primary driver.

In my role as Director of Innovation and Leadership Development for PCH Canada, I participated in the effort to help the company become the fastest-growing consumer healthcare business in the world. Our goal was to empower the many, rather than the few, by employing a two-pronged strategy. We accomplished this by applying deliberate innovation practices that drove early wins and built capability for large transformational projects. Our second goal, and the more important lever for the long term, was to use a systemic approach that would create the right conditions and climate for sustained innovation.

In Canada, we aligned strategies and goals with global targets, while also helping employees gain a thorough understanding of innovation. One of the many ways in which we accomplished this was by providing skills training to the individuals who were facilitating transformational projects that supported deliberate innovation. We also made e-learning available to all employees as a way to create a common language that included definitions of words like "innovation." We also viewed the physical work environment as a strategic innovation enabler, and whenever possible, leveraged it for improved workflow and informal communication. We then examined performance metrics, incentives, rewards, and various methods of recognition to ensure that they'd support the right behaviors for producing the best outcomes. We also engaged in the process of continuous improvement.

Centralized and Local Approaches

To encourage risk taking and also recognize the accomplishments of colleagues around the globe, Pfizer's most senior global leaders established a prestigious and much coveted team-based global award for innovation. Ever present was also messaging from senior leaders, who consistently reinforced progress, both on and off stage. Specific tools, frameworks, and policies like these were used to systematically tackle our largest challenges and opportunities while we continued to improve and reinforce other aspects of the organization's culture.

Although the company's global headquarters guided most of the culture-building efforts, each country had the freedom to leverage and tailor strategies locally, for maximum impact. A good example of this was one of PCH Canada's first targeted initiatives, a project that used a deliberate innovation approach to tackle the cumbersome product promotions process. By the end of the first month, issues were clarified and the project team had already identified almost one million dollars in savings.

Another targeted initiative tackled work-life balance. One key outcome was a program called "Freedom 6-to-6" that prohibited employees from sending (or consequently receiving) emails from 6:00 pm to 6:00 am. This enabled employees to take a deliberate break from normal work hours to rejuvenate. As one of many culture initiatives, Freedom 6-to-6 was a strong starting point because people needed to feel fresh and creative to be able to perform optimally. The result? With better work-life balance, both internal and external customers were better served by this program.

In 2006, Pfizer Consumer Healthcare celebrated World Creativity and Innovation Week in 25 countries. Each country was invited to celebrate in a way that was relevant to their local organization while honoring the overall company values and behaviors for an innovative culture. Thousands of employees participated in this week-long event, furthering their ambition to build an innovative culture.

Tangible and Intangible Outcomes

While I was involved primarily in the Canadian efforts, I felt honored to be a part of the entire initiative. It was exciting to see our results as well as the innovations that occurred around the globe. A good example of the impact of PCH's innovation initiatives was manifested in metrics that showed significant increases in efficiencies, sales, and profits. With both tangible and intangible outcomes, you can easily see how the business benefited by employing deliberate efforts to develop creativity and by encouraging and developing the behaviors and skills that produce sustainable innovation.

The outcomes of this initiative could also be seen in employee opinion surveys, specifically the positive response to a question about whether the company was doing the right things to be innovative. The rise in the company's creative energy was reflected in high engagement and many new ideas. In fact, more than ten years later, some employees still reminisce about how empowered and inspired they felt at that time in the company's history—an excellent example of how to sustain innovation long after the initial novelty has worn off.

It's important to note that the Pfizer consumer business of today has an entirely different portfolio and leadership after the acquisition in 2009, of pharmaceutical giant, Wyeth, which already had its own consumer business. So why is the Pfizer consumer business completely different now? In 2006, after years of successfully executing its innovative strategy and driving change, Pfizer Inc., the parent company, was able to sell the Pfizer Consumer Healthcare division to Johnson & Johnson (J&J) for over $16 billion USD. The lucrative deal allowed Pfizer Inc. to focus on its pharmaceutical business and future acquisitions, while also making J&J the world's largest consumer healthcare company at that time. Also important to note is that when J&J integrated the PCH division, it adopted many of PCH's successful innovative approaches, which still exist and help the business to thrive today.

Concluding Thoughts

What can be learned from PCH's innovation success story? It illustrates how innovation can start and sustain itself when people are inspired, encouraged, and intrinsically motivated to improve the status quo. Hank McKinnell, the CEO and Chairman of Pfizer Inc. during that time, epitomized successful leaders of innovation by the manner in which he gave permission to take the necessary risks to succeed. In one town hall meeting, he said, "Doing things differently doesn't mean doing things better, but doing things better always means doing things differently." In effect, McKinnell told PCH employees that the only way toward growth was to try new things, even if it involved failure. This holds true for almost every person and organization today.

Leaders enable and reinforce sustainable innovation when they continue to support new ideas and innovative behaviors—both tangibly and intangibly. This is what truly inspires, motivates, and drives potential innovators to seek improvements to the status quo. People then innovate not because they *have* to, but because they *want* to. Inspiration and motivation, such as that witnessed in Eric Whitacre, are powerful forces. An excellent example of this is the young singer and fan who had been inspired by Whitacre's creativity and authenticity. She, in turn, and quite unintentionally, inspired him to create his first Virtual Choir, and has since become a songwriter and composer herself. The potential ripple effect of one person's courage to create something new is virtually unlimited. The eventual creation of 4 virtual choirs with 8,400 singers from over 100 countries is a great illustration of this.

In closing, I'm intensely proud of the experts who contributed to the chapters in this subsection and others in this book. I feel privileged that they allowed us to generously share their best practices, innovation tips, and winning strategies. You'll no doubt learn something from each and every one of them. I look forward to hearing your thoughts or reactions to this section of the book, but until then, I encourage you to orchestrate innovation by finding your authentic voice and inspiring others to find theirs. Then have fun innovating and producing the kind of music that can take people and their organizations to new heights, transforming them in sustainable and life-changing ways.

Megan Mitchell
Principal, Mitchell Consulting
Program Director, Centre of Excellence in Innovation Management
Schulich Executive Education Centre, Schulich School of Business, York University, Canada
www.meganmitchell.ca
megan.mitchell@me.com
Twitter @mitchellmegan

Chapter 1

A Business Case for Creativity and Creative Problem Solving

An interview with Jay Aquilanti, Group Creative Catalyst Director, Yellow Shoes Creative Group, Disney Parks Marketing and former Director, Franchise Management at Walt Disney Imagineering

■ ■ ■

"Creativity is the generation and initial development of new, useful ideas. Innovation is the successful implementation of those ideas in an organization. Thus, no innovation is possible without the creative processes that mark the front end of the process: identifying important problems and opportunities, gathering relevant information, generating new ideas, and exploring the validity of those ideas."

— *Teresa Amabile*

Orchestra leaders and jazz musicians alike know that creativity drives innovation, but many leaders in business environments fail to attach enough importance to it. Although most say they would like to be more creative, their focus tends to be on putting out fires, which is understandable but limiting. Only a few understand the role that creative problem solving plays in effective and efficient decision making. Consequently, few organizations have formal processes for creative problem solving; for integrating those processes into day-to-day business operations; and for encouraging, recognizing, and rewarding creativity.

Well-known innovative organizations such as Google and 3M—as well as many smaller, lesser-known ones in the private, public, and not-for-profit sectors—know the importance of carving out "creative time." Additionally, they understand the need to support good ideas with resources and infrastructures that facilitate implementation—and innovation. Creativity and creative problem solving are necessary parts of the innovation process, which begin with what many call "the front end of Innovation," or the "fuzzy front end," for short. "Fuzzy" informally describes the "creative (or right) side" of our brains, as opposed to the "linear and logical (left) sides," which have historically been valued in most traditional business environments. Successful innovation leaders know that both are needed for "the back end of innovation" as well, which is where actionable ideas are executed.

We selected Jay Aquilanti for this chapter because of his experience as a trained practitioner and facilitator of creative problem solving at The Walt Disney Company. Jay has worked in a variety of functions and locations for Disney Parks, beginning his career with the company in 1993 after earning a Bachelor's Degree in Political Science and Romantic Languages from Bishop's University, in Quebec, Canada. Jay has developed expertise in the various marketing and sales disciplines and has spent the last 19+ years actively engaged in facilitation of creative problem solving. In this interview of Jay, we learn how leaders and facilitators can build and leverage creative ideas for enhanced organizational performance and competitive advantage. Please join us as Jay makes a business case for creativity and creative problem solving.

QUESTIONS AND ANSWERS

How do you define "creativity" and "creative problem solving"?

For the most part, I support the notion of a standard dictionary definition—"the use of imagination or original ideas, especially in the creation of artistic work." I say, "most," however, because what I struggle with is the limiting term "artistic" within that definition. Creativity might manifest in a more obvious manner through "artistic" work, but it is much more than that. Rather, I prefer to define creativity as the habit of continuously doing things in new ways to make a positive difference. To me, it is an approach in thinking differently AND making that a habit. It's being open to possibilities, taking risk and having the willingness to examine and express those possibilities. In defining creative problem solving, I view it as a disciplined process whereby one really works hard to determine the right challenge, explores the data at hand, brainstorms ideas to solve the challenge, and eventually moves those ideas to action.

Why should leaders be concerned about creativity and creative problem solving?

Organizations need innovation to grow, thrive, and sustain themselves, but also to remain relevant to their customers. Creative ideas fuel the innovation pipeline. In fact, it's difficult to envision innovation without creativity.

Is there such a thing as being too focused on creativity?

Only if a leader focuses on creativity for creativity's sake, without a plan of action or accountability for next steps, when attempts are made to translate ideas into actions. To apply creativity effectively, one must continually ask, "What is the business need?" and "Where do we need to apply innovation?" If there's no link that allows creativity to drive innovation, time and valuable resources can be wasted.

How do leaders create the right environment for creative problem solving?

Leaders create the right culture, not only modeling, but also by supporting key creative behaviors. That is the foundation for new ideas to thrive and for people to garner success. If we think of a farmer's field, we know that fertile ground is needed for crops to grow. Paying attention to culture is akin to farmers paying attention to the soil in which they plant things. The culture that recognizes, supports, and allows ideas to grow lays the groundwork for success. If leaders are open to ideas, if they encourage and reward collaboration, and if they encourage risk taking, the odds are good that a lot of ideas will come forward.

How do idea generation and creative problem solving play roles in driving innovation?

Idea generation, or brainstorming, is a deliberate step in solving problems. It plays an important role in that it's the forum to deliver many potential solutions to a problem. I'm positive that there's a direct correlation between the number of ideas generated and the ways of getting to "the innovative idea." Edison had failed 1000 times before his light bulb was a success. The act of deliberate idea generation and creative problem solving allows the mind to consider the question of "What else?" It also allows for openness to new opportunities, new ways of doing things, and in the end, a way to foster innovation.

How can organizations ensure that creative ideas will translate into added value?

In my experience, four critical elements are necessary for the kind of creative problem solving that translates ideas into action. First, with regard to "belief," leaders need to support an idea strongly enough to stand behind it. Second is what I would call "a path," which is a plan of action to align resources and support. Third is accountability, ensuring people are responsible for those next steps. And fourth is risk-taking. It's critical to celebrate risk-taking and accept some degree of failure to encourage experimentation. The last factor is the most important because it creates an environment of experimentation, and real innovation happens when leaders and employees feel that it's safe to go outside their comfort zones.

How important is it for people to properly identify a business problem that needs to be resolved?

It's absolutely critical to identify the issue and find out what's really going on. It can be tempting to jump right to "the idea," and spend too little time determining the actual need or clarifying the issue. But without this discovery, you can find yourself off track, unable to address the root cause of the problem or trying to solve the wrong problem. Asking the right business questions to begin with is time well spent.

When is brainstorming most successful?

If done properly, brainstorming can provide the playground for people to dwell in the possibilities and a place where people's thoughts and ideas can intersect with others for exponential results. It really works out the creativity muscle—the brain. In my experience, there are three key elements to a successful brainstorm: the environment, facilitation, and expert guidance.

Environment is about setting the right tone. It's important to get out of the boardroom and to brainstorm in a place that engages the different senses and inspires different outcomes. It's also important to create an environment that is welcoming for people with different styles. I use these guidelines to set the stage: (a) communicate that every idea is accepted, (b) separate divergent from convergent thinking, (c) encourage collaborative behavior and building on ideas, (d) provide a safe environment where there's no judgment about expressing an idea, and (e) have FUN.

Strong facilitation is critical to reaching the best outcomes. If discovery is done well, idea generation sessions begin with the right question to ideate against. Successful facilitators make the question inspiring—one that others will WANT to answer and that will get them excited. A clear flow of ideas and a plan of exercises allow for divergent and convergent thinking, diversity, and variety. Successful facilitators also embed energizers into the session and vary activities to keep energy levels up. Lastly, brainstorming tends to be most successful when a trained facilitator is utilized. He or she can keep a session on target by acting as an unbiased leader and by allowing the owner of the problem to fully participate.

What are some barriers that leaders or facilitators encounter when trying to generate creative ideas?

Some of the biggest barriers are trust and lack of time or clear goals. There tends to be a ticking clock associated with any creative idea session—from the amount of time dedicated to the session itself to the expected outcomes of the session. When we take time to establish a clear goal from the start, idea generation and results are so much better. But the biggest barrier to idea generation is attitude, and ensuring trust in the process and the people doing it. Brainstorming takes courage, open-mindedness, and collaboration to allow participants to dwell in the possibility of "what if." When they do, it's easier to achieve success.

How can facilitators and leaders encourage effective creative problem solving?

While there are many tools and techniques for deliberate creativity, I believe the level of success and strength of creative problem solving has to start with creating an environment that supports the right mindset. It's fostering a setting that builds trust and risk-taking and allows for a degree of failure. It's celebrating risk-taking—particularly if it helps to advance a solution. It's empowering teams' curiosity. For leaders, that's about modeling the desired behavior and asking questions that inspire creative problem solving. For facilitators, it's about creating a session with activities that honor style differences and bring out the strengths needed for formulating and refining the right questions, generating and enhancing ideas, and effectively executing ideas.

Why is it important to accommodate different creativity styles?

The rubber hits the road when we all have the awareness of different styles as well as the expertise to bring those diverse styles together—effectively and safely for each person. In closing, it's in that diversity—that collaboration of thought and the collective strengths—that the magic happens. Creative style can be as personal and individual as one's fingerprint, and everyone has the ability to bring something unique and brilliant to the table. Involving and rewarding everyone on a broad scale is what adds value to an organization—and makes innovation not only attainable but sustainable.

TAKEAWAYS

- Start with setting the right environment for creativity by making it comfortable for all participants to contribute every day.
- Encourage collaboration and leverage differences.
- Develop the habit of learning to live with ambiguity. Live in the question.
- Defer judgment and help others learn to live without immediate answers.
- When answering critical questions, say, "I wonder if ...." for different possibilities.

TAKING STOCK

- Is my organization doing enough to set the right environment for creativity to thrive?
- Do we have people with the right skills to lead deliberate creative problem solving?
- Are my organization's leaders aware of different creativity styles and how to leverage them?

■ ■ ■

To learn more about creativity, consider reading one of the many books about Imagineering. If you found this chapter useful and want to learn more, also see our chapters entitled *A Culture of Innovation, A Design Mindset,* and *Leadership Development.*

Chapter 2

A Culture of Innovation

An interview with Julie Anixter, Executive Director, AIGA; Co-Founder and Editor of Innovation Excellence; and former Managing Director, Tom Peters Company

■ ■ ■

"One of the biggest responsibilities of management is to look after the corporate DNA."

— Andrew Rolfe

Contemporary conductors sometimes enable musicians to express their creativity by passing their batons to them. This distribution of power translates to the type of music that's selected as well as how it's to be played. Jazz ensembles exhibit an even higher degree of power distribution, as well as many of the other characteristics of a culture that supports communication, collaboration, and teamwork. If a culture of innovation is at the heart of any successful orchestra or jazz ensemble, can we safely assume that it's also basic to unleashing the creative potential of individuals, leaders, and teams in most other venues? If so, how do leaders build and sustain cultures of innovation?

An organization's culture is heavily influenced by the amount of information that's shared, how problems are solved, the ways in which conflict is resolved, and how decisions are made and implemented. Another powerful influence on culture is the way that its members view the risk, experimentation, and failure that are the hallmarks of successful innovators. For this chapter, we interview Julie Anixter, a practicing innovator with 20 years of global experience. Today she is the Executive Director of AIGA, the professional association for design.

Prior to Julie's current position, she held roles as the Chief Innovation Officer, Maga Design, CMO for Brand-image and Desgrippes Laga, Managing Director of R&D for The Tom Peters Group, and Chief Learning Officer for Anixter International. She has consulted with diverse clients in both public and private sectors that include Aetna, Avery Dennison, Blue Cross Blue Shield, Chanel, Ian Schrager Hotels, P&G, the US Air Force and Navy, Sun Chemical, Xerox, and many others.

In 2011, Julie also worked in conjunction with other leading innovators to launch innovationexcellence. com, one of the largest crowd-sourced communities for innovation practitioners. At present, she functions as its chief editor. The mission of Innovation Excellence is to curate Innovation 3.0, creating a knowledge exchange and marketplace that connects practitioners, communities and organizations to make innovation more broadly accessible. Julie earned a bachelor's degree in art from Oberlin College, a Masters of Science in Learning Sciences from Northwestern University, a Master of Fine Arts from the University of San Francisco, and also studied design at the University of California, Berkeley. Please join us as Julie describes the elements that characterize a culture of innovation.

QUESTIONS AND ANSWERS

Please share your definition of "a culture of innovation."

Cultures of innovation are most often characterized by high engagement, high involvement, and highly collaborative teams of people who generate, build on, and support each other's ideas. A culture of innovation draws from both internal and external sources, optimizing all its relationships to create value and improve the status quo for the majority of its stakeholders. These cultures typically operate from two basic premises: First, that innovation needs to be part of everyone's job, and second, that disciplined experimentation is not merely tolerated, but intentionally sought out, as a way of learning.

How do leaders typically build and sustain cultures of innovation?

Even though the CEO is usually the pivot point or lever that's ultimately accountable for leading growth and innovation, boards too, have responsibility for this because of their involvement in governance, planning and strategy. Strong boards realize that great cultures are assets like no other, so they fully appreciate the importance of installing "initiators" or "builders"— not "maintainers"—into CEO roles. Cultures of innovation also require enlightened leadership that understands how transformational growth occurs—through the intentional development of new products and services and new business models for both the short and long term. These leaders also understand that today's world is highly connected and transparent, so they value networks. Although it's important for leaders to foster innovation, it's also critically important that they model the behaviors needed for innovation, which includes valuing diversity.

Would you address why diversity and inclusion are so important for innovation?

Diversity is the backbone of innovation, and here's why: Many times people debate over which is more effective—radical or incremental—yet there is little to debate, as they must co-exist side by side in the real work of any organization. Different types of people are needed to support each of these methods of innovation. There's the noble warrior class—the ninjas who will roll up their sleeves and acquire, transform, merge, dismantle, or destroy that which is not working or which needs to be reinvented. These folks will do whatever needs to be done to usher in the new—and gladly—since they have no nostalgia for "the way things were—or are." They are much more motivated by the future, and they're absolutely essential for radical innovation. Then there are the gardeners, who cultivate, nurture and pay attention to growth on a daily basis. You need both.

Because organizations also need incremental improvement and sustained innovation, people are valued who are willing to work within the system to bring about gradual change. In truth, most people can't handle radical change very well—at least not of the "burn-the-ships" variety—so both types of people are required, even though their co-existence generates conflict. Skilled leaders know how to deal with the conflict that comes with differences—and they're good at helping others deal with it as well. They know that, when companies leverage differences, they benefit greatly from the richness that different styles, approaches, and perspectives bring to complex problem solving and decision making.

What can leaders do to redefine fear and communicate the message that innovation is a trial-and-error process that involves detours or "mistakes"?

Fear of failure is a debilitating energy. Fear-based management is the antithesis of an innovative culture. For these reasons, I love that you've included this question and also that it's about "redefining fear" instead of "getting rid of it." We all know that fear rarely goes away on its own. While no one wants to fail, growth requires learning, and learning through experimentation inevitably results in some failures—at least initially. Effective leaders can build tolerance for failure by supporting disciplined approaches for gathering insight, for analysis, and for experimentation—all of which can mitigate fear of failure. Now one last point: Many people question whether play is needed for innovation—and whether organizations should encourage it. I believe that play is a necessary exercise because, within the context of innovation, play isn't really play—it's more like fitness for the brain and emotions. When people feel safe in their environments, play is a natural outcome—and another way to mitigate fear that can inhibit.

How can leaders create environments where employees are involved and feel challenged?

Let's start by acknowledging a painful reality: Many leaders and employees are not challenged in ways that engage and involve them—and so they often feel underutilized and underappreciated. I've spent 25 years with employees and leaders in different industries all around the world, and I wish I could say that work cultures are on a powerful evolutionary trajectory of engagement and involvement.

Experience tells me that only a fraction of organizations know how to engage and challenge talent productively and most don't even see the value of it. I believe there isn't a human being alive who doesn't want to make a difference—that's the gift of the human spirit—and in today's innovation economy, there are a multitude of tools and approaches for creating high engagement, high involvement cultures. What's ironic is that organizations are rife today with challenges, and they can certainly provide the tools that would fully engage people in addressing those challenges. What happens when challenge and involvement are missing? Atrophy and de-volution. However, effective leaders know how to prevent this by involving employees in some of their organizations' most serious and pressing challenges.

What other key elements need to be in place for an innovative culture?

Organizations that foster cultures of innovation invest in them, specifically allocating resources for systems, programs, and processes that support innovation. These resources support innovation teams, new strategic projects, innovation forums, myriad pilots, and so on—with "myriad" being the operative term. That means not only one innovation project, or one leader who champions innovation, or one approach or methodology—but many. While I could point to many factors and requirements that create robust innovation cultures, the greatest of all is the investment that leaders make in sourcing the right people who can introduce new ideas. Then organizations need to provide the resources to make those ideas real. As Tom Peters once said, "You can't shrink your way to greatness."

Not every organization can provide "thinking" time—as 3M, Autodesk, Google, and others do—but innovation doesn't always require heavy financial or time investments. Often organizations only need to provide basic tools and give people opportunities to innovate. Of course, it's important to reward people when they do, but rewards don't have to be monetary. What's important is to create a process that allows people to work on the ideas that they're passionate about. When people have a shot at taking their ideas across the finish line, that's often a reward in itself. Public and private acknowledgement and recognition for contributions are also rewards that don't cost anything, yet have amazing impact. In fact, most serious innovators would pay to be able to do the work they love.

How can leaders use shared vision and values as good starting points for innovation?

Leaders need to communicate support for innovation as well as why it's needed. They must also provide people with a sense of direction through authentic, clear, communication. Strong visions can often compensate for the natural fear that people experience when doing things that haven't been done before. However, there's a world of difference between the "shelf-ware" or platitudes that often fail to inspire—and more often evoke cynicism—and the visions and values that provide foundations so real that people could stand on them. Visions need to go beyond rhetoric and must be explicitly articulated and tacitly modeled in the behavior of leaders.

Values are the new currency of social intelligence, and they're critically important for conveying to people that their work has value and meaning to the organization. Values can keep people aligned to their highest and best selves while also easing the legitimate friction that every successful innovation culture faces. Equally important, leaders need to visibly demonstrate that they're living their values. This might mean taking tough stands to ensure that projects with different time horizons and risk profiles will receive the right resources at the times they're needed. It might also be by providing support to employees who have experimented and had setbacks or failures with early efforts.

Could you describe the role that trust plays in risk taking and innovation?

Trust isn't only the bedrock for a culture of innovation—it's a basic foundation for business survival. Innovation—or any process that requires something new—requires courage and trust. If innovation also requires a suspension of "having all the right answers right away," then trust in leaders, or in the organization's systems or its capacity to learn, is essential. It's impossible to over-value the trust that's required for innovation. I don't mean only trust in leaders, the organization, or one's team, however. People must also trust themselves and their own personal compasses—commonly known as the courage of their convictions. One of the hallmarks of great innovators is their ability to take calculated risks, fortified by trust in their own intuition.

Leaders in start-up cultures are increasingly admired and looked at as having the goods required to innovate—passion, purpose, and a personal sense of mission. Yet leaders in all organizations are capable of building cultures that entrust people to look for what's needed or missing—and then empowering them to act on their most important ideas and dreams. This sounds simple—and in theory, it is—because it's about helping people fulfill a profound need that they have at work: to be trusted to use their imaginations in creating something new or better. If I had to choose one element that's most important in creating and sustaining a culture of innovation, trust would be it!

TAKEAWAYS

- Boards must require investments in innovation and leaders must provide the necessary strategic roadmaps and tools.
- Failure must be redefined within the context of experimentation and learning.
- Managers and team leaders need to work harder at matching people with work they're passionate about and then challenge them to create new value.
- Vision and values can be important as guiding forces—but only if they're authentic.
- When it comes to innovation, the power of trust cannot be underestimated.

TAKING STOCK

- Is my organization providing the necessary tools for innovation?
- Do our leaders know how to cultivate and sustain a culture of innovation and all that it entails?
- Have we built a foundation of trust that enables experimentation and the calculated risk taking that's needed for innovation?

▩   ▩   ▩

To learn more about Innovation Excellence, go to www.innovationexcellence.com. If you found this chapter helpful, also see *Alignment, Differences, Employee Engagement, Meaning and Purpose,* and *Shared Vision and Values.*

Chapter 3

Alignment

An interview with Scott Williams, CEO of Maga Design and former Chief Information Officer for the United States Naval Aviation Command (NAVAIR)

■ ■ ■

"Just as your car runs more smoothly and requires less energy to go faster and farther
when the wheels are in perfect alignment,
you perform better when your thoughts, feelings,
emotions, goals, and values are in balance."

— Brian Tracy

We hear it time and again: Innovation is a team sport. While this claim assumes effective teamwork, what role does alignment play in high performing teams? Orchestra leaders must align the efforts of 100 or more musicians. Jazz musicians perform with fewer players, but the nature of their constant interactions could be thought of as even more challenging. How do successful leaders in all disciplines achieve alignment on strategies for optimal performance?

When people are aligned as teams—rather than simply working as groups of individuals, their diverse skill sets and competencies can produce an effective complement. Blind spots can be identified and offset, and strengths can be built on and leveraged. When looking closely at what makes for strong teams, we see that individuals at all levels are focused on organizational goals as well as individual and team priorities. In today's multigenerational and otherwise diverse populations, alignment is especially challenging, yet vitally important. Sometimes even the most well-aligned, well-intentioned, and capable teams get off track and lose momentum. That's why effective leadership is so critical for alignment.

Leaders with good people skills can assess where problems are occurring, at both individual and team levels, and realign teams by ensuring that people possess the necessary skills. Leaders must also ensure that team members are exhibiting behaviors that support success. It's valuable for leaders to view the ongoing fine-tuning of teams as a highly essential task and a personally rewarding activity. Ensuring alignment can be time-consuming hard work, but the rewards are significant and the alternative is untenable. For this chapter, we interviewed Scott Williams, the CEO and founder of Maga Design, who tells us how organizations build alignment, sustain it, and restore it once it's been lost.

Working with clients in the public sector such as the U.S. Navy, the U.S. Air Force, and U.S. Postal service—and with private sector clients such as Aetna, Dell, IBM, Pepsico, and QuinetiQ—Scott and his team help organizations ensure alignment. A pioneer in the use of visual information mapping, he and others at Maga Design utilize a proprietary process that creates physical and virtual maps as representations of collective strategic thinking. Combining 15 years of Navy technical and business innovation experience with commercial marketing and brand strategy acumen, Scott assists organizations in meeting a wide range of challenges. Before founding Maga Design, he served at the U.S. Naval Aviation Command (NAVAIR) for 15 years, most recently as the Deputy Chief Information Officer.

QUESTIONS AND ANSWERS

How do you define "alignment," and why do you believe it's important?

Alignment is a primary responsibility of leadership and the optimal state for organizational performance. It's about the effective and shared coordination of vision, mission, goals and strategies to achieve goals. By default, alignment needs to occur on an enterprise-wide basis and start with the executive team. Even though it doesn't directly get people to their intended destination, it's like the North Star that continually guides our journey.

I was privileged to work for and with great leaders in the U.S. Navy, like Admiral Joseph Dyer, who led NAVAIR during Admiral Vern Clark's tenure as the Chief Naval Officer. Dyer and other leaders were extraordinarily committed to alignment, and they worked very hard to achieve it. We, at the U.S. Naval Aviation Command (NAVAIR), were part of larger joint U.S. military's operations but we too had a large number of people—22,000 who worked across 10 different bases. We took alignment very seriously because when someone is on a carrier or an airplane, or operating a weapon system, alignment isn't only mission critical—it can mean the difference between life and death.

What role does alignment play in enabling optimal performance?

Alignment is not simple to achieve, yet it starts with a simple premise. The simple premise is that, if people know what their jobs are and—more importantly—exactly how and why they contribute to the organization's core purpose, leaders have a shot at leveraging the best that people have to give: their discretionary energy. This is what George Labovitz, the author of *The Power of Alignment*, calls the "main thing" —when individuals and the team know their purpose and how to perform in their respective roles to achieve it. Think of how critical alignment might be to the world's greatest sports teams or orchestras. Although they're made up of individual players, these folks know how to play at their best with others—to produce results together. Alignment is all about optimal human performance when teams of people perform with coordinated precision.

How can organizations build cultures that facilitate alignment?

There's an expression lately that goes something like this: "Culture eats strategy for lunch." Shawn Power at Fast Company coined it in his book by that name, and I agree with it completely. Culture is really about norms—the way that people understand "how we do things around here." It's shaped by leadership, values and purpose. When leaders make values and purpose clear, and teams understand them well enough to bring them to life, organizations have the right conditions for alignment. Without effective leadership, there is no hope for alignment.

How do leaders build alignment within their own teams?

It sounds so simple but it's anything but: Clear, consistent communications about values, mission, and the expectations are mandatory. Here's what we've learned in our work: Organizations today are living and working at such speed and pressure—and with such high digital-to-noise ratios—that no matter how well or how often intentions are verbalized, they often aren't enough. It's not that talk is cheap. It's just that it doesn't last. That's why we at Maga believe in creating images and artifacts that are persistent—that last. And we're not alone in the belief that the visual is as important as the verbal. We help people visualize strategies, future states, and key messages. With teams, we help team members see themselves represented collectively in those future states.

How do leadership and personal styles differences play a role in achieving alignment?

Let's say, for the sake of argument, that there's a spectrum of styles, and that those styles represent fierce opposites. On one end of the spectrum is someone who likes to "tell" and on the other, one who likes to "ask." This is one of many opposites on the styles spectrum. Often the traditional view of leadership and communications styles focuses on telling, rather than asking—and on finding "the right way" of doing things, and as the "only way." Alignment is only possible when leaders bring diverse styles together and create a place for them all. Effective leaders know how to harness or coalesce different styles. With them, alignment is code for "To serve the larger mission, all styles are welcome here."

How do emotions play a role in teams or companies that fall out of alignment?

Emotions are like the weather—they just are. Good leaders bring empathy and emotional intelligence to this most human dimension of the organization. As author George Labovitz teaches, "Aligning teams and organizations is a balancing act that involves sensing, setting direction, connecting the dots, and making adjustments." This balancing act is a primary leadership challenge—one that requires tremendous ongoing emotional intelligence, patience, and commitment.

What happens when there are conflicting feelings, priorities, or values?

Well, since there are always going to be conflicting feelings, we're probably not talking about divine intervention. Conflict is a necessary part of human nature and it's not something that we can, or would want to, eliminate. Successful organizations aren't aligned because of a lack of conflict. They're aligned because their leaders care enough to include everyone in the vision. Fundamentally, people either care about the mission or they don't. So when we think of alignment as a verb, rather than a noun, it's what leaders do to get people to care. In other words, it's about securing buy-in and commitment through personal engagement.

What tools are available for ensuring alignment or restoring it once things have gone off track?

Anything that coalesces the team can be a tool for realigning. At Maga, we use maps to help leaders and teams align around a worldview. The purpose of our information visualization processes is to co-create a picture of the future that represents key stakeholders' vision and intent. But there are many other tools that work if they fall within the category of co-creation or collaboration on shared themes.

What typically happens when leaders—and their teams—aren't well aligned?

A simple answer: The mission fails, the business falters, and people lose confidence in the leaders' ability to lead.

How is alignment sustained, once it's been built?

Success is a great enabler. When a team or organization succeeds at achieving the mission or the goal, and the work produces tangible results, it begins to sustain itself. I'm not an expert about the Fed Ex, Apple, or Disney cultures, but I know that a cadence of authentic communications about the work, and ongoing clear acknowledgement of the work and effort required is what contributes to sustainable missions. When communications are top down and bottom up, we call it a drumbeat. It enables most everyone to see, hear, and participate.

How can alignment be restored once it's been lost?

That will depend on the severity of the misalignment. However, people usually realign in the same way that they restore trust that's been lost: one conversation and one committed action at time.

TAKEAWAYS

- To achieve alignment, leaders must create a culture from a collective vision of the organization's "main thing" or reason for being, and then continuously refine and adapt that vision.
- As a way of sustaining alignment, leaders continually ensure that everyone has line of sight and knows how and where he or she individually contributes to that vision.
- Effective leaders, create a two-way cadence—a drumbeat—of top-down and bottom-up communications.
- Executives must understand that enterprises are made up of human beings who have discretionary energy. They will contribute and align only if their hearts and minds are engaged.
- When conflicts arise, candid discussions should be initiated among all parties to reassess whether the vision is shared and what steps should be taken to realign.

TAKING STOCK

- Do we have an aligned organization in which all employees can see themselves in the vision?
- What current initiatives should be addressed to ensure that team members are aligned—and that they stay aligned?
- Are there any obvious examples of poor alignment that need to be quickly addressed? If so, when and in what ways should it be addressed?

■　■　■

To learn more about Maga Design, go to magadesign.com. If you found this chapter useful, see other enabling chapters in this book entitled *A Business Case for Strategic Partnerships and Alliances, A Path to Innovation Excellence, Buy-in, Sponsorship, and Commitment, Employee Engagement,* and *Shared Visions and Values.*

Chapter 4

Competition and Collaboration

An interview with Sally Van Duyn, Principal of Van Duyn and Associates and former Director of Organizational Development at the University of Texas System

■ ■ ■

"New ideas come from differences. They come from having different perspectives and juxtaposing different theories."

— Nicholas Negroponte

When musicians compete among themselves to continually achieve higher levels of mastery, it can be a motivating force for them as individuals and for their fellow musicians. In scenarios like these, there can be a direct parallel between healthy competition and innovation. However, many people question the value of competition in a work context like today's, that's sometimes more focused on collaboration. Does the current trend to eliminate silos and foster teamwork render competition obsolete? How might competition and collaboration coexist in organizations today—and *should* they? Can too much collaboration lead to groupthink? Can too much competition be unhealthy? Can competition and collaboration be utilized in synergistic ways? If so, how might leaders ensure the right balance? And what happens when they're out of balance? Can they each sometimes hinder, as well as enable, innovation?

For this chapter, we interview Sally Van Duyn, a consultant and facilitator who has witnessed the advantages and disadvantages of both competition and collaboration in her various engagements. She has over 20 years' experience working with leaders and teams in both private and public sectors, at national, state, and regional levels. With expertise in the areas of organizational change management, strategic planning facilitation, leadership and team development, and executive coaching, Sally's services include the facilitation of shared visions, development of team agreements, design of customer assessments, the creation of transitional implementation teams, and assistance in outsourcing.

When facilitating team building and partnering workshops in conjunction with the Restoration of Texas State Capitol Project, Sally worked on over 50 major design and construction projects with numerous project teams. Other clients have included NASA, the University of Texas System, University of Texas Medical Branch, George Washington University, the Baylor School of Medicine, and the State University System of New York (SUNY). Sally holds a Master of Education from the University of South Alabama and a Bachelor of Science from Auburn University and is certified in a number of assessment instruments. Please join us as Sally describes how, if balanced properly, competition and collaboration can enable innovation.

QUESTIONS AND ANSWERS

How do you define "competition" and "collaboration," and how can each help to advance organizational strategies and initiatives?

Competition can occur when people strive, as individuals, to perform at their highest levels—often to gain advantage. When competition is healthy, it can provide incentive for people to improve their organizations' performance while they enhance their own. By contrast, collaboration is a process where people share ideas, solutions, and knowledge. When engaging in idea generation, collaborators bring different views and build on them, with the goal of "adding to," not "taking from" each other.

How might various technologies support collaboration, competition—and innovation?

Groupware, SharePoint, Skype, WebEx, employee portals—and even e-mail—can greatly expand the number of people who are able to participate in idea generation. Today, web-based idea generation and idea management systems make idea submission easy; however they shouldn't be thought of as simply electronic "suggestion boxes." Custom-designed software can enable crowdsourcing, and it can also foster competition through idea contests. In addition, it enables people in multiple locations to collaborate by transferring knowledge or discussing similar projects, technologies, and solutions.

In what ways might collaboration enable innovation?

Today's problems are highly complex. Often exceeding the efforts of dedicated individuals, they require multiple perspectives and approaches in addition to strong abilities and work ethics. In addition to complex problem solving, collaboration can enable innovation when teams are highly motivated to perform and when they bring unique experiences, specialized expertise, and a wide range of skills. When people from different divisions, functions, or teams share information and work toward shared visions and common goals, collaboration can facilitate robust exchanges of ideas and perspectives in the same way that it can prevent redundancies and is useful in anticipating and dealing with implementation barriers. However, to fully innovate, organizations need to collaborate with stakeholders and others, both internally and externally. That means boards, customers, lawmakers, vendors, industry experts, members of special interest groups, and so on.

Can competition also enable innovation?

Executives who put a high priority on individual performance view competition as a strategy that works as well with employees as it does in the marketplace. To keep the bar high, these leaders provide opportunities for individuals to compete in much the same way that athletes do: internally, against themselves—and externally, against others. Those who favor competition also tend to compete among themselves—by securing the best available talent and the resources to differentiate and by ensuring that the people who perform the best, and contribute the most, receive the greatest recognition and rewards.

Some of these leaders produce amazing results because they create environments that are highly challenging. They, themselves, tend to have a zeal for competition because it's what makes them feel most comfortable or most energized. When they also encourage their people to compete, it can stimulate and get the juices flowing for innovation. Organizations known for innovation often fuel competition in much the same way that these types of leaders do—through innovation contests, individual spot awards, and team awards. These organizations have learned how to tap the desire of certain individuals to compete at the same time that they leverage the collective intelligence of teams.

Are there situations where competition and collaboration can each inhibit innovation?

When collaboration is carried too far, it can sometimes take too much of people's time, diverting energy from potentially more important or timely projects or tasks. Additionally, collaboration can inhibit innovation when it's used to solve problems or make decisions when issues require immediate action. It can also inhibit when valuable time is invested on inconsequential matters, particularly those that don't warrant significant discussion. Most apparent is when too much collaboration inhibits innovation because of too many collaborators. They can sometimes produce solutions that are either overly complex or not targeted appropriately, because of attempts to incorporate too many different perspectives into a single result.

Competition is sometimes viewed as a force that can compromise teamwork. It can also be an innovation inhibitor when leaders work from the assumption that, if a little bit of competition is healthy, more is undoubtedly better. Unaware that not everyone is energized by competition, these leaders can unwittingly pit people against each other through misguided attempts to raise the bar. People can feel burned out in environments that require them to be constantly "winning" or "always on." Symptoms of this are obvious inhibitors of innovation, such as general fatigue or malaise, or other innovation inhibitors such as information hoarding, cliques, and oppositional forces that stall projects or initiatives. Excessive competition can erode a strong esprit de corps that leaders have inspired early on and have been working diligently at maintaining.

When people compete to the extent that they don't listen to each other, they're unable to build on the ideas of others. This can eventually create a culture in which some people no longer talk about what they're thinking. They also stop sharing ideas and no longer challenge the status quo. Divisions can then occur, often resulting in hostilities or subcultures that focus on individual or political priorities, rather than shared goals that support the organization.

How do cultural differences play out, with regard to competition and collaboration?

Some people have grown up in families or cultures that favor competition and the ways in which it can invigorate and motivate. Others grew up in environments that discourage individualism and favor collectivism. It's critically important for leaders to balance competition and collaboration as a way of respecting and leveraging cultural differences, yet communication is equally important. I've seen people benefit from informal "team contracts" or agreements that can serve as catalysts for communication. These "contracts" often provide the structure to safely talk about cultural differences and help people leverage them.

In what ways can diverse styles and different work methods impact collaboration—and innovation?

Many people believe that heterogeneous groups outperform homogeneous groups. While that's often true, the challenge lies in managing the conflict that's inevitable when people have to deal with diverse team members. Differences can be evident when some people like to plan and others like to keep their options open—or when some people are highly organized and others prefer spontaneity. Differences are also apparent when some people approach their work with passion and visible emotion—and others pride themselves on their objectivity and controlled emotional responses. We can see how these differences can result in conflict, yet they aren't the only areas where there is potential for conflict.

People with extroverted preferences like to (and might even *need to*) think aloud, while those with introverted preferences like—and often *need*—time to reflect and process information before expressing opinions. In cultures where individualism is highly valued, leaders often favor those who quickly come forward with ideas and comments. Additionally, these leaders often overlook and fail to reward introverted types for their contributions. In truth, introverted people can sometimes be much more creative than their more expressive counterparts because they tend to approach issues from a more holistic perspective—taking time to consider all angles, rather than "shooting from the hip." From these examples, we can see that differences have the potential to significantly create conflict or add value.

It seems that competition might come naturally to some people. Is this also true of collaboration?

Successful collaborators come in all shapes and varieties but they exhibit some common behaviors and personality traits. Good collaborators are most often open and respectful of others. They're people with strong group problem-solving skills who are often naturally cooperative. They're also willing to take calculated risks and to look for better ways of doing things. Those who are able to respectfully disagree and find common ground are especially successful. Are people born with these skills and attributes? Some are—and others have to work diligently to develop these traits. Organizations can help these employees become better collaborators through skills training and coaching.

Do leaders need to balance collaboration and competition—and if so, how do they do that?

Competition is inevitable among leaders, but if it becomes a predominant theme, it can negatively impact teamwork, organizational alignment, and innovation. However, competition doesn't have to occur at the demise of teamwork and synergistic performance. It can be effective when it's well-defined, when expectations are clearly communicated, and when it's monitored to ensure that it stays healthy. When leaders effectively balance competition and collaboration, they create dynamic environments that get the best from both competitors and collaborators.

Leaders who favor competition need to provide opportunities for collaboration—to tap the benefits of those who work best together, rather than against others or themselves. And conversely, leaders who favor collaboration need to occasionally add stimulation and challenge through healthy competition. By facilitating both, leaders can help employees bring ideas to fruition in ways that allow everyone to "win."

TAKEAWAYS

- Today's complex problems often require large and diverse communities of problem-solvers and collaborators to achieve advantages from both collaboration and competition.
- To leverage these diverse communities, it's important that leaders value differences.
- In order to innovate, leaders must ensure that competition and collaboration are well balanced.

- Technology provides opportunities for employees to compete, collaborate, and innovate virtually.

TAKING STOCK

- Is my organization currently maintaining a good balance between competition and collaboration?
- Do we leverage competition and collaboration as a way of fostering innovation?
- Does our technology adequately support competition and collaboration in our virtual environments?

■　■　■

To learn more about Sally Van Duyn's work, go to vanduynconsulting.com. If you found this chapter helpful, please also see *Differences, Employee Engagement, High Performing Teams, Open Innovation, Idea Management and Virtual Collaboration*, and *The Physical Environment.*

Chapter 5

Differences

An interview with Corinne Miller, Founder & Principal Consultant at INNOVATING RESULTS! and former Director of Motorola University at Motorola Corporation

■　■　■

"It is ironic that companies so often pretend to celebrate 'diversity' while systematically stamping it out. The kind of diversity that really counts is ... diversity of thinking."

— Gary Hamel

In the same way that skilled jazz musicians and successful orchestra leaders leverage differences in their musicians and their instruments, business leaders also leverage differences—and for the same reasons. They must ensure that they differentiate in their own unique ways. Companies in the private sector often believe they've achieved diversity through increased globalization. Although a global presence has produced greater diversity in today's organizations, it doesn't mean that differences are being fully leveraged for tangible results.

How do successful leaders move their organizations beyond the hype that's so often associated with diverse and inclusive work environments, to achieve favorable outcomes? They ensure that their workforces mirror the demographics of their customers or clients. In addition, they often place diverse talent on project and work teams to solve today's complex problems. Yet, highly functioning teams don't simply happen when diverse people are brought together. And although diverse teams tend to produce better results, the challenges inherent in their team dynamics are usually significant. This might lead readers to ask whether efforts to leverage differences are really worthwhile and whether the costs outweigh potential benefits.

To address these concerns and others, Corinne Miller draws from her consulting expertise and experience in both line and staff roles, and in technical and leadership positions, at Motorola, Rockwell International, Northrop Defense Systems, and TRW. In this interview, she shares how successful organizations achieve strategic advantage by leveraging differences. Propelled by her passion for employee learning and development, Corinne joined Motorola University and served as its director, utilizing her previous experience to create its first innovation training portfolio and to achieve tangible business results. Today she functions as an innovation consultant, trainer, and coach, helping companies apply innovation practices to everyday problem solving. Combining the science and artistry inherent in successful innovation, Corinne is also an experiential artist who creates fine art paintings that include real pieces of their subjects as well as embedded microchips that tell their story.

Corinne has taught in the Lake Forest Graduate School of Management MBA program, where students benefit from her broad experience in engineering, learning & development, program management, communication, business operations, quality management, and innovation. In 2014, she received the Faculty of the Year award at Lake Forest Corporate Learning Solutions. Corinne holds a BS in Mathematics & Computer Science from the University of Illinois in Chicago and a Master of Science in Communication from Northwestern University.

QUESTIONS AND ANSWERS

How do you define "differences" within the context of most organizational settings?

Although differences such as gender, race, and ethnicity are sometimes obvious, others aren't, and they can have a profound impact on leveraging innovation. Differences in the workplace include educational levels, cognitive and creativity styles, life experiences and perspectives, professional expertise and skill sets, and more. These differences are most evident in the ways in which people take in and process information, solve problems, make decisions, and respond to conflict. Although gender and culture are two important determinants of differences, there are many others that drive how people view and respond to authority, give and receive feedback, as well as how they work independently or in teams. Although the factors that drive diversity are complex, diversity is often made more complex than needed. One way to keep things simple is to view differences as forces that shape a person's thinking and to think of the aggregate results as simply "diversity of thinking."

When is diversity of thinking most evident in work settings and how is it best leveraged?

Differences are most evident when individuals work in teams to solve problems and make decisions. Diversity of thinking is critical to all four stages of a typical innovation process: problem identification, idea generation, exploration of potential solutions, and implementation. Organizations best leverage differences when they identify and match the strengths of particular styles with each of the four stages of innovation. By that I mean, when leaders identify and assign people to teams who are highly skilled at generating ideas, building on initial ideas, screening them, and executing.

Does any particular thinking style trump other styles?

No—all are needed! However, I've noticed that many people put significant focus on the "front end of innovation," having great admiration for those who put forth unorthodox ideas or approaches. Often, this results in overlooking or minimizing the efforts of unsung innovation heroes—those who move ideas along and translate them into action. I personally saw this play out when I introduced an innovation program at Motorola that focused on educating and implementing diversity of thinking. We taught leaders and practitioners how to identify and leverage differences by encouraging healthy exchanges at all stages of the innovation process. It was both amazing and satisfying to watch the "aha moments" and to witness first-hand how diverse thinking at each of the four stages resulted in better problem solving and more elegant solutions. From that experience, I concluded that it's important for leaders—and for employees—to know that the innovation process not only *benefits* from diversity of thought—it *demands* it!

What are some of the inherent challenges with differences and heterogeneous teams?

Although different styles and approaches can add value, they can also cause miscommunications, misunderstandings, and personality clashes. We know from assessment instruments such as the Myers-Briggs Type Indicator (MBTI) that frustrations can arise when some people approach problem solving and decision making with their heads first, followed by their hearts—and when others do just the opposite. We also know that out-of-the-box thinkers can be frustrated by those whose approaches tend to be more grounded and practical—or who adhere to traditional approaches, claiming, "That's the way we've always done it."

The MBTI distinguishes, among other things, how people process information differently—how extroverts think aloud and in real time—while introverts prefer to reflect and process before communicating. Other differences that the MBTI identifies are those which exist between types who like to plan and those who like to "play things by ear" or "go with the flow." There are many opportunities for impatience or frustration unless people are convinced that differences can truly improve outcomes. But that usually happens only when people can personally participate in the process and directly observe the results, as the leaders at Motorola did.

How can the challenges resulting from differences be resolved so that they don't generate conflict?

First, it's important to know that it's not conflict that inhibits innovation, but an inability to deal effectively with the conflict. Leaders typically view conflict as something that they need to squelch as soon as possible—or totally avoid or ignore—in hopes that it will go away. Conflict rarely goes away. When inhibited, it tends to go underground and then resurface in passive-aggressive behaviors. What's ironic is that leaders who work diligently to extinguish conflict don't realize it's a key force for people to share and build on ideas. Skilled leaders know how to re-channel conflict into collaboration—an important ingredient for enabling both incremental and breakthrough innovation.

So what happens when differences aren't understood or valued?

When differences aren't understood, people may personalize them instead of seeing their value. This can cause relationships to suffer, which in turn, can negatively impact team performance and produce organizational siloes and turf wars. Another negative consequence is when employees (and leaders) are placed in jobs that don't fit well with their preferences, skill sets, or personalities. In these situations, they're not able to play to their strengths because they're continually required to function outside their comfort zones.

To avoid or minimize this, leaders must be selected on the basis of their ability to identify a variety of different styles, and who can recruit for those differences—as well as unleashing them in current employees. Leaders who stereotype on the basis of "left-brainers" or "right-brainers"—who view "right-brain types" as "weird," or who prefer to be around people who think as they do—will likely miss the opportunity to play to strengths. Or they might struggle in their efforts to recruit and retain the kinds of employees whose core strengths are needed to meet organizational challenges.

How can leaders foster innovation by leveraging differences?

When innovation leaders make deliberate attempts to seek out people with different styles, they send a message that differences are valued, rather than merely tolerated. This builds the foundation for a culture that makes people feel welcomed, respected, and able to openly display who they are, instead of superficially conforming to others' ideals. This results in people feeling more energized, creative, and engaged. But to facilitate innovation, leaders need to do more than simply leverage differences.

At the idea generation stage, leaders need to provide a variety of tools and techniques to elicit ideas from all team members. Successful leaders accept the fact that some people feel shy about expressing differing views in group settings—particularly in highly political environments. These leaders know that introverted types (who like time to process), or those whose cultural predispositions determine their comfort level with verbal expression, might like to communicate in other ways. That's why it's so important for leaders to help people use tools and methods that best suit them and to employ relevant tools and methods throughout the *entire* innovation process.

One way to do this is to define specific steps in an innovation challenge or project and then identify the skill sets and thinking styles required for each step. By establishing formal processes with defined steps, and communicating what the expectations are for each step, they can match people's styles and skills accordingly. Successful leaders also build an innovation structure that provides accountability mechanisms along with ways to reward and recognize contributions. Successful innovation leaders also provide coaching or mentoring and they take corrective action when it's necessary.

Have some sectors or industries excelled at leveraging differences?

In my work with clients in a number of industries, I've noticed that technology companies seem to be the most comfortable with differences, and also with employees who challenge the status quo. First, because the tech industry is constantly changing, tech leaders encourage people to challenge traditional ways of doing things. Second, since its inception, expert talent had to be imported from all corners of the globe. In short, the tech industry's initial challenges with diversity—and what its leaders learned about the "secret sauce"—occurred decades earlier than most other industries. That said, there's every reason for organizations in all sectors and industries to learn from tech companies and replicate the practices that have continued to make them successful at leveraging differences.

TAKEAWAYS

- Today, organizational effectiveness and competitive advantage are reliant on diversity of thought.
- Leaders must understand the role that diverse perspectives play in all stages of the innovation process and be able to attract and retain people with the right mix of different styles and strengths to ensure diversity of thought.
- The innovation process must include specific steps and varied tools and methods for all personality styles to share, and it must employ diverse perspectives at each stage of the innovation process.

TAKING STOCK

- How well do my organization's leaders and employees understand and demonstrate that they value differences—and view them as a business necessity?
- What parts of our innovation process define specific steps for exchanging diverse perspectives?
- How could focused training and coaching for leaders and employees help them leverage differences better at each stage of the innovation process?

■　■　■

To learn more about Corinne Miller's practice, go to innovatingresults.com. If you found this chapter useful, please also see our chapters entitled *A Culture of Innovation, Competition and Collaboration, Employee Engagement, High Performing Teams,* and *Leadership Development.*

Chapter 6

Employee Engagement

An interview with Susan Perry, Vice President, Change Acceleration at Comcast Spotlight, a division of Comcast Cable

■　■　■

"Those who have changed the universe have never done it by changing officials, but always by inspiring the people."

— Napoleon Bonaparte

Many studies have verified that high employee engagement scores translate to high productivity and strong financial returns. However, Marin Alsop, Music Director for the Baltimore Symphony Orchestra tells us that symphony musicians historically rank among the lowest in job satisfaction. How do leaders like Marin Alsop change that scenario? And what might other leaders learn from her? When musicians and employees alike have a voice in problem solving and decision making, they feel that they're a part of something meaningful. This greatly helps with engagement and commitment, yet there are also other factors that drive these two important innovation enablers.

Organizations whose employees are engaged and excited about the work they're doing have a far better chance of achieving goals and objectives than those whose employees are simply putting in "face time." Yet when people think about high engagement, they might assume that the most engaged employees work for organizations that are top-paying and employers of choice. Clearly there is evidence to the contrary. Some of the best examples of high employee engagement are not-for-profit organizations, which typically aren't the highest payers, but where the driving force for motivation is often a compelling mission, a dream, or a shared goal. We also see this in start-up or turnaround situations, where employees are highly energized by complex problem solving, "creating from scratch," or by "creating something better."

In this chapter, Susan Perry illustrates how high employee engagement is basic to a culture of innovation. Passionate about her role at Comcast Spotlight, Susan supports the business through strategic human resources consultation and talent management. She is a graduate of Comcast's prestigious Executive Leadership Forum, a PDI (Professional Development Institute) Executive Coach, and a senior HR leader with more than 25 years of HR experience that includes the successful start-up of an internal fee-for-service HR consulting practice.

Susan has held a variety of senior human resource leadership positions in industries that include newspaper and magazine publishing, high technology, and professional services consulting. She received her MBA from Simmons Graduate School of Management in Boston, MA. She is also a graduate of the Women in Cable Telecommunications' Betsy Magness Program, which partners with (CCL) The Center for Creative Leadership to provide focused instruction and discussion on key management challenges and opportunities for today's senior women leaders. Susan is a member of the Society for Human Resources Management, Women in Cable Telecommunication and the Cable and Telecommunications Human Resources Association. Please join us as she describes the key role that employee engagement plays in facilitating innovation, regardless of industry.

QUESTIONS AND ANSWERS

How do you define "employee engagement"?

I witness employee engagement when I see a group of employees going the extra mile—taking ownership and performing at high levels within their areas of responsibility. I believe that engagement is also about employees being fully aware and connected to the organization's goals. When they're clear about what's needed to accomplish those goals—and willing to run through walls to make that happen—that, to me, is the essence of employee engagement.

How do you think employee engagement fosters innovation?

When employees are engaged and invested, they tend to view the business as their own. They ask what they can do to solve problems and resolve challenges—and innovation becomes a by-product. Engaged employees help to create innovative environments by trying new things and innovating in their own unique ways. This kind of innovation is even further enhanced when organizations utilize collaborative teams. In collaborative environments, people's frames of thinking and their approaches expand exponentially—especially in cross-group and virtual team collaborations.

What are some of the challenges in ensuring engagement and innovation in today's virtual world?

One of today's biggest challenges is the need to meet current demands without the in-person connections in which relationships can best develop and provide leverage to advance the work. I believe that conversation and connections are vital for innovation—and that they're best facilitated with at least some face-to-face contact. Creating opportunities to enable those connections is important—even if it's as infrequent as once a year. I advocate for a blended approach, and with today's technology, that's easy to accomplish if in-person opportunities aren't easily available.

How might effective communication promote high engagement and innovation?

In my opinion, communication and alignment form the foundation for engagement, which in turn, facilitates innovation. However, I also believe that all communication must be congruent with the key drivers of organization strategy. We invest a lot of time and energy in our communication strategy to ensure that all messaging is aligned and easily understood. In that way, we have a working playbook from which to execute our plan. Since our efforts are proactive and intentional, they inform both communication and action.

Do you also have specific initiatives for facilitating collaboration?

We bring employees together in as many ways as we can—to leverage diversity and to create an inclusive environment. That can mean brown-bag learning sessions or something as simple as staff meetings or special meetings dedicated to discussions about how best to meet customer needs. In addition to involving employees in meetings, we provide mentoring opportunities with senior leaders. These efforts help employees increase confidence and enable them to develop a number of important skills. Mentoring is also a great leadership development initiative in that it allows mentors to see the organization from different perspectives. So to summarize, good communication, opportunities to connect, and diversity of thought are all basic elements in collaboration, and leaders need to actively work at encouraging all of these things.

How do you achieve the alignment that's so critical for innovation?

Without an understanding and true embodiment of the organization's goals, it's difficult for employees to view their roles in the big picture and ultimately perform to their fullest potential. I believe that three important factors are necessary for understanding and embodiment, since they are what help to drive connectedness and engagement. The first factor is the need to bring people together at all levels and across all functions to actively explore ideas and discuss how they can personally impact collective goals and objectives.

The second factor relates to opportunities for people to weigh in on how best to accomplish goals and objectives. The third regards alignment between individual goals and organizational goals. This is why we invest time and energy each year to bring employees and leaders together to participate in processes by which organizational goals cascade to meaningful individual goals. We see evidence of alignment in our business results and also in our positive employee engagement survey scores. And this is why we believe that engagement and alignment are key drivers for strong performance and innovation.

What role do you believe employee surveys play in employee engagement and innovation?

Assuming that employee surveys are well designed, they're basically an organization's report card for measuring leadership's role in ensuring employee engagement. Organizational leaders receive valuable information, and surveys can provide roadmaps for what leaders need to continue doing as well as what they might need to change. One of the most powerful ways to stimulate engagement and innovation is to involve employees in focus groups and enlist their feedback and ideas in response to what surveys reveal. However, there's one caveat: There has to be follow-through and action on any promises made by leaders because that builds the trust necessary for innovation.

How do you typically address potential problem areas that surface in surveys?

We know that it's important to address problem areas quickly. Since early problem identification and action are keys to success, we share survey results right away and conduct a deep-dive discovery process in areas of concern. We try to determine what was happening at the time of the survey that might have driven a particular response, and then engage folks in a dialogue about these areas, promptly discussing actions to be taken, and then following through. We see how this translates to high engagement and high performance.

Equally important, while surveys are a great resource, we wouldn't want them to be the primary way that we learn about problems, so in HR, we maintain a constant pulse by being well integrated with our leaders and various teams. This enables early problem detection and quick action. Each year, I look forward to opportunities to meet with employees to develop action plans in response to areas of concern. I believe that one of the reasons why our employee engagement levels are so high is that we do what we say we're going to do—and I take great pride in that. One of my greatest rewards as a leader is shared ownership and accountability, and an appreciation for the importance that the organization places on that.

Now that we've talked about how employee engagement can foster innovation, how do you think leaders might inhibit or stifle it?

When I think about innovation, I think about discovery and learning and sharing, so when leaders aren't facilitative and they don't create a supportive environment, employees don't feel that they're playing an important role in the company. Then innovation invariably suffers. Employing a "my way or the highway" attitude definitely inhibits innovation. As a leader, I know that I may not always like what I hear, but if I'm not open to asking questions or gaining input, I lose valuable opportunities for new thinking and I risk stifling *both* innovation and engagement.

If you had to choose a single driver of employee engagement that has the greatest impact on innovation, what would that be?

You can probably tell that I believe it's vitally important to create a culture in which leaders and employees have good interaction opportunities. This is needed not only to gain and maintain a pulse on what's important, but also for creating the relationships that are foundational to a shared purpose. When meetings are well facilitated and good questions are raised—such as how can we create an extraordinary customer experience—organizations are often rewarded with great ideas and innovations.

In fact, I've experienced something almost "magical" when leaders leverage well-facilitated experiences by bringing all employees together and creating ways to integrate the various functional areas. When this happens, people can more easily align, and they're also better able to manage change because they've played an active role in it. This also helps to foster an appreciation for different perspectives that often creates energy and synergy among people. In my experience, meaningful interactions are what truly build an inclusive environment that can open the doors to new and innovative ideas and the successful execution of those ideas!

TAKEAWAYS

- To foster employee engagement and innovation, all communications efforts, meetings, training, and other development initiatives must be congruent with the organization's overall strategy and critical drivers.
- Alignment at all levels is vital to ensuring an understanding of what's mission critical so that employees can feel a part of the effort and know how they can support the organization.
- Conversation, connection, and collaboration are also critical factors that result in diversity of thought and a shared purpose that, in turn, facilitates employee engagement and innovation.

TAKING STOCK

- Do my organization's leaders communicate through their words and actions, that collaboration, engagement, and innovation are important—and necessary?
- How do we currently define employee engagement, and do we formally measure it?
- Do we provide opportunities for employees to participate in strategy development and collaborate in implementation?

■   ■   ■

If you found this chapter helpful, be sure to also see the chapters entitled *A Business Case for Creativity and Creative Problem Solving, Buy-in, Sponsorship, and Commitment,* and *Shared Vision and Values.*

Chapter 7

Executive Development

An interview with Alan Middleton, Ph.D., Executive Director, Schulich Executive Education Centre and Assistant Professor of Marketing, Schulich School of Business, York University

■ ■ ■

"As we look ahead into the next century, leaders will be those who empower others."

— Bill Gates

Leaders typically drive innovation by setting the tone for it, dedicating resources, and providing highly visible and impactful support. Nowhere is the challenge of leadership more evident, however, than when formal schooling ends and real life education begins—especially for newly appointed leaders. Maestra JoAnn Falletta, Music Director for the Buffalo Philharmonic Orchestra and the Virginia Symphony Orchestra, tells us that much of an orchestra leader's job involves continuous learning. However, she also comments on how ill-prepared most college graduates are with regard to their knowledge (or lack of knowledge) about various aspects of leadership.

Business leaders often start with the same deficiencies, learning about the ways of the world through ignorant risk taking balanced by healthy doses of hand slapping. With luck and persistence, leaders experience success. Unfortunately, as some leaders advance to more significant levels, they often don't take as many risks as they used to. Many have found a formula for success that works for them and so they have little reason to change. These leaders hope that the success in the first half of their careers will carry them through the second half. Fortunately, successful leaders resist this thinking, and instead, achieve results through innovative strategies and approaches. However, many more leaders fall within the first scenario, relying on past successes, becoming risk averse, and failing to develop skills for the future. With regard to innovation, it's easy to see that there are obvious implications with the latter scenario.

We interviewed Alan Middleton for this chapter because of his strong background and expertise in management, consulting, and executive development. After a 25-year career as a marketing practitioner with Esso Petroleum in Oslo, Norway and UOP Inc. in Chicago, USA, Alan rose to the position of Executive Vice President and Board Director of J. Walter Thompson (JWT) worldwide. He then served as President/CEO of JWT Japan before leaving to complete his Ph.D. at the Schulich School of Business in Toronto, Canada. There he currently teaches and functions as Executive Director of the Schulich Executive Education Centre (SEEC), which trains over 10,000 managers and executives domestically and internationally. Alan also taught at Rutgers Graduate School of Business in the U.S. and at business schools in Argentina, China, Russia and Thailand.

Alan co-authored the books *Advertising Works II* and *Ikonica: A Field Guide to Canada's Brandscape, and* wrote chapters in several other books. In 2005, he was inducted into the Canadian Marketing Hall of Legends in the mentor category. In 2012, Alan was awarded the Association of Canadian Advertisers (ACA) Gold Medal for contribution to the marketing communications community and the Queen Elizabeth II Diamond Jubilee Medal for services to the literacy community. Please join us as Alan talks about how executive development is needed to compete effectively in global markets.

QUESTIONS AND ANSWERS

How do you define "executive development," and how does it enable innovation?

Both questions are answered best with an analogy to the advertising world. Most great advertising ideas don't get killed; they die the death of a thousand cuts. Innovation can also be like that. Good ideas often get modified to meet the competing needs of different stakeholders. Innovators—like good advertising people—need to be creative and innovative, yet at the same time, disciplined, rigorous and factual. The challenge is in knowing what to be—and when. Executive education teaches leaders how, by providing tools and building the skills needed to overcome pre-existing training and traditional mindsets.

What are the most critical skills that executive development can help to build?

Adaptability and collaboration are by far the most critical skills that need to be built or enhanced. Adaptability means having the creativity to come up with new ways of operating and getting things done, regardless of the barriers. Successful entrepreneurs continually look for ways around barriers and adapt their approaches to explore new paths. Real experience and learning, and applying that as they go, creates avenues for them to achieve. They can explore the roadblocks and find ways to go around them. Collaboration means being able to appreciate different viewpoints, and being able to get the best out of everybody, as opposed to focusing on the lowest common denominator. This means being open to different perspectives and learning how to use them. People can be trained to do that, but please note that collaboration is not compromise. Collaboration means working together to find better and new solutions, not simply creating smaller solutions to meet the needs of only a few stakeholders.

Why don't more organizations provide executive development in innovation?

There are three main reasons. The first is discomfort. When people are asked to step outside their comfort zones, it requires admitting that they need development in certain areas, and that's often met with resistance. People want to feel they're already capable. The second reason is fear. Organizational structures tend to resist innovation rather than encourage it. Learning new ways of operating, such as establishing new systems, is perceived to be hard work.

Executive development is resisted because it means potentially changing behaviors as well—particularly those which have made executives successful in the past. Informal systems can often be the best way to work around structures that require change and innovation, but even then, people need to move past fear. The third reason why organizations don't provide more executive development is ignorance. Often disruptive innovation requires changing a business model, which executives view as too much work and too much risk. More importantly, a new business model might not be profitable in the short term.

Is executive education currently focused on developing the skills needed for innovation? If so, has this produced any changes in teaching methodology?

An increasing number of innovation programs, program components, and centers of excellence are popping up for good reason. We long ago stopped running project management sessions strictly for project managers. The programs are still popular because we now arm any manager or executive with the ability to manage projects—especially across silos. The same is true for skills in creativity, innovation, agility, and resilience. These skills need to be built in all leaders, not only those with "innovation" in their titles.

Creativity is also central to the collaboration that's so necessary for innovation, since part of innovation is having different perspectives and learning how to employ them through collaboration. We use an exercise to enhance a collaborative mindset. We call it "Doing the Pig." When we ask, "What is a pig?" people might say, "It's an animal that is pink and often covered in mud." Then we explore,

"What is a pig to a farmer? To a religious person or vegetarian? To a butcher? To a child?" The point about defining a pig from different perspectives is at the heart of innovation.

Creativity, as a means of dealing with change, is consistently showing up in many executive education programs today. Teaching methodology has become more creative as well, and is evolving in two ways. One is with increased interaction and learning between students and faculty—with a greater emphasis on participant interaction and less lecture. Executives learn best from each other, from methodologies such as peer coaching. The second way is with increased action learning—working on real life issues—and focus on just-in-time learning that coincides with business challenges.

We ask leaders or executive teams to bring real business issues into training now—particularly those issues with internal sponsorship and that have measurable goals so that learning can be linked to actual projects. We also provide coaching to participants, to reinforce learning. For us, there is no better demonstration of competency building than solving complex problems, seizing opportunities, and ultimately delivering results—and so our teaching methodologies work toward those outcomes.

How can some of the barriers to executive development be overcome?

The best way for organizations to overcome barriers about executive education is to require leaders to actively and consistently encourage innovation—by walking the talk. Only then can they encourage employees to learn as they go, even if that means taking paths that can produce initial failures—if there is also learning. That said, organizations have become increasingly impatient with development and training. We've noted an increase in informal learning, through various seminars, "lunch and learns," and so on. However, in these venues, few participants are held accountable for recording, reflecting, and sharing learning. If learning is oral, rather than written, retention of new information can be as low as 10% after three days.

To overcome barriers to successful executive development, organizations need to view it as a process that happens over time—not over a few days or by a single course. Typically, 10% of development happens through executive programs, which are often the best places to learn new skills and make valuable contacts. However, 90% of leaders' development happens early in executives' careers—on the job, through stretch assignments, and with coaching and feedback. For leaders to effectively innovate, they need to be provided with suitable learning opportunities—inside and outside the organization.

What are the implications of not developing executives and other key decision makers?

In 2011, the Organization for Economic and Co-Operative Development (OECD) identified upgrading the skills of management and executives as critical in two key areas: productivity and innovation.

According to the OECD, North America is falling short of its investments in executive education, with the U.S. ranking 31 of 59 countries and Canada ranking 25. Who is ranking the highest today? Despite a population of over 1.3 billion people, China invests more in leadership development on a per capita basis than do countries in North America and Europe. The implications of this are self-evident.

There are also implications for organizations that don't develop leaders early in their careers. When people enter the working world, they tend to be full of great ideas and aren't jaded by life. We find that people returning to do an MBA, other graduate work, or executive education programs as little as five years after graduation have become much more cynical. Most often their creativity has been stifled because they've learned to work in systems that typically don't encourage out-of-the-box thinking. Advanced educational institutions must work diligently to re-frame this "off-kilter" orientation. And countries other than China, who want to compete successfully on a global scale, must make significant investments of time and money in leadership—or risk falling behind their global competitors.

What capabilities do executives need to develop in order to foster innovation?

To put my answer in context, the capabilities that most leaders need to develop are skills to deal with disruptive change. What we've seen in the past few years is nothing compared to what we'll see in the next ten. The old phrase in ecology, "A butterfly that flaps its wings in one part of the world causes a hurricane in another," will continue to be evident. A good example is how flooding in Thailand can affect the supply chain in the automotive parts industry in North America. In fact, we already find this kind of change happening in every aspect of business today, and it demands agility and resilience.

The specific capabilities or qualities needed to drive innovation are also patience, consistency, and an ability to self-manage. Executives today need to re-think the way they do things—sometimes on a dime—in order to go in new directions. Strategy has new meaning today as well. It's not a fixed end point or direction anymore; it's becoming more about the way that organizations get to where they need to go—with many modifications along the way. To be successful, executives need to continually be on the lookout for new ways to do things—which is where innovation and business success come from.

TAKEAWAYS

- Leaders need to develop competencies to deal with an environment of constant disruptive change.
- Critical leadership assets include agility, resiliency, and creativity.
- Formal learning associated with action learning—where participants apply learning to real-time business issues—is an excellent way to develop capability.
- To better compete on a global basis, countries and organizations need to invest in leadership and executive development.

TAKING STOCK

- Is my organization developing leaders for the challenges that they'll face tomorrow as well as today?
- Are the executive development methods that we're currently providing relevant to today's organizational challenges?
- Does my organization make it "safe" for executives to apply what they learn?

■ ■ ■

If you found this chapter useful, also see *A Business Case for Creativity and Creative Problem Solving, A Path to Innovation Excellence,* and *Change Leadership.*

Chapter 8

High Performing Teams

An interview with Wes Pringle, President, Fluke Corporation (a subsidiary of Fortive Corporation); Senior Vice President of Field Solutions for Fortive Corporation; and former Senior Vice President at Whirlpool Corporation

■ ■ ■

"If you want to go fast, go alone. If you want to go far, go as a team."

— African Proverb

Regardless of how talented creative geniuses might be, they seldom achieve the level of innovation that teams can. Executives are well aware of this when they assemble teams to complete projects, to explore, and then seize specific business opportunities. In the same way that businesses today rely on high performing teams to distinguish themselves from their competition, symphony orchestra conductors rely on teams of 100 or more musicians to generate income through recordings and performances. Yet despite the power of teams, many organizations still fail in their attempts to drive beyond the status quo. The true value of high performing teams lies in their skill sets and in their ability to leverage diverse thinking and strong functional competencies. Nowhere are these factors of effective teamwork more evident than in a jazz ensemble, where musicians need to actively listen, collaborate, and support each other.

Most of us know that to achieve this level of performance, it takes more than assembling the most talented people in a room and expecting that brilliant outcomes will automatically result. Teams need to be built over time. As with most relationships, members of teams usually encounter obstacles at some point. What are the factors that determine whether teams derail or perform at high levels? What happens when creative genius is multiplied and accessed in real time? To answer these questions, we interviewed Wes Pringle, who has had extensive experience with teams at different organizations. Prior to Fluke, Wes worked at Whirlpool Corporation, a company that's consistently cited as a leading innovator. While at Whirlpool, he held the positions of Vice President of Kitchen Aid & Jenn-Air, Senior Vice President of Brand Business Teams, and Senior Vice President, Integrated Business Units, in which he led a number of global businesses.

Before joining Whirlpool, Wes progressed through a series of sales, marketing and general management roles at Pfizer Consumer Healthcare, Warner Lambert, and Johnson & Johnson, in both Canada and the United States. Originally from Winnipeg, Canada, Wes earned his MBA from The Richard Ivey School of Business at the University of Western Ontario and a Bachelor of Science from the University of Manitoba. Please join us as he shares his thoughts about the qualities that make for great teams, about the conditions that need to be present for innovation to thrive in teams, and what leaders can do to leverage the power of teams in their efforts to drive innovation.

QUESTIONS AND ANSWERS

Would you please share your definition of a "high performing team"?

I think corporations get confused about what high performing teams are. When I think of teams, I think of small groups—sometimes no more than three people—who understand an opportunity space well, are committed to a shared outcome, and demonstrate a high degree of respect and trust for each other.

In what ways can high performing teams enable innovation?

First, problems in organizations are often too complex for one individual to solve. Second, although individuals can produce great ideas and elegant solutions to problems, it's typically high performing teams that help organizations achieve predictable, sustainable, and reliable outcomes. Third, it's rare to have someone with a fully baked marketplace-ready idea. Experience proves that the best innovations come from an iterative process within teams that allows team members to bounce ideas around, find flaws with the golden nuggets, and make ideas better. Great innovation is organic and is based on the kind of mutual respect that enables team members to share freely and improve on ideas without fear of repercussions. High performing teams function with the intent of making ideas as strong as possible.

If high performance teams are valuable in building a culture of innovation, why are there so few?

It takes time to create high performing teams because trust is key, and it's most often developed through shared experiences, which require time. There would probably be many more high performing teams in companies if people didn't move around as much as they do now. Every time people leave intact teams and new players need to be assimilated, it can destroy what's taken time to create because it requires that teams continually rebuild.

We've noticed that some people seem to be obsessed with the "hero mentality," as opposed to valuing what successful teams can do for organizations. Why is that problematic?

Most often, a hero is someone who is motivated by self-interest and is good at internal marketing. A hero culture implies there are internal winners and losers, and that can lead to unhealthy competition—a significant barrier to high performing teams. Although some individuals can be exceptional in terms of their ability to drive innovation and performance, each team member of a high performing team usually plays a different role and provides a missing perspective or necessary piece. I strongly believe in the power of individuals on teams, which is not the same as believing in a hero culture. To achieve consistent innovation in organizations, the hero mentality in many corporate cultures must change because no individual—no matter how talented—can continually innovate or consistently outperform a high performing team.

How are high performing teams best formed and what are good ways to jumpstart them?

Leaders need to put something out there that is compelling—some challenge that surpasses individual needs and goals. That typically involves a lot of listening to find out what's right for the strategic vision of the business and what people feel passionate about. Leaders also have to be consistent about listening and exploring to identify a challenge that has staying power. When a team is in start-up mode, leaders need to ensure that the team vision is repeatedly and consistently brought forward and reinforced so that each team member can personally relate to it and buy in. Leaders must get this buy-in to achieve shared meaning and purpose, and they also need to celebrate early wins because team members need to see and feel progress. Even the smallest wins can be evidence that the team is moving in the right direction, and this is what builds both confidence and trust.

What's the best way to harness the power of teams to innovate and create value?

A highly successful leader and early mentor of mine once said, "The role of a senior leader is pretty simple: First, you need to have the right people on the team with the right training and skills. Second, they need to know what's expected of them. Then third, you need to make it as easy as possible for them to get the work done. If you don't have the right people with the right skills or people who know what's expected of them, leaders are forced to micro-manage." The highest performing teams tend to produce fantastic ideas because they're empowered. When people are empowered, they're committed at deeper levels to shared outcomes. Leaders must focus on enabling teams and then super-charging their efforts. Then they can harness the power of teams, rather than limiting the power in the traditional pyramid structure—where everything has to go through a very small funnel. When leaders know how to ignite the entrepreneurial zeal of employees on high performing teams, organizations can become unstoppable.

How can leaders maintain the momentum needed for high performing teams?

Ideally, high performing teams have goals that go beyond financial outcomes. They also include goals that speak to how they're fundamentally going to make things better for their customers. If they can get there, that is what truly drives commitment to a different level. These kinds of goals are extremely powerful because most people like opportunities to make an impact, leave a mark, or be part of something greater than themselves. Team goals pave the ways to continually accomplish this. It's where the potential is greatest for exceptional team performance.

Leaders should also know what undermines team performance. Sometimes they must facilitate agreements between team members about how they want to behave with each other. This creates the right climate for trust to build. Effective team leaders frequently look for opportunities to recognize individuals and for team members to recognize each other, showcasing behaviors that are connected to team success.

What is the best way to assess and evaluate team effectiveness and performance, when people are typically measured and rewarded individually?

Of course all teams and team members should have specific measurable goals that clearly showcase their collective accomplishments and performance. Within teams, the higher the organizational level, the more "team" goals should be the centerpiece of someone's performance appraisal. In other words, few employees at more senior levels should have their performance based on individual projects or achievements. Their success is more dependent on their ability to motivate, develop and lead others. This can best be measured by whether the teams they are deeply connected to are achieving what they need to.

How can leaders help teams recover from setbacks?

If a setback is due to the financial performance of a project or innovation, leaders might simply need to help team members look at what could have been done differently. Most importantly, this needs to be done with shared accountability and an eye toward learning. If the setback was due to a team breakdown, leaders must evaluate whether team members had the right skill sets and if they knew what was expected of them. Then leaders need to help team members take responsibility and recover—especially if the team is still intact. If trust was broken, that will be more difficult, and it will take time to repair. When teams derail because of a break in trust, it's most important for team leaders to uncover the reasons and then help the team move forward in constructive ways. Sometimes the leader may need to change one or more members in such circumstances. Then, before attempting to move the team back to a common goal and shared purpose, leaders usually need to help team members contract with one another for better outcomes in the future.

What are critical competencies for people who lead innovation teams?

Leaders must first have the ability to work with team members to construct a meaningful vision for the project or intended innovation. Leaders of innovation teams must also be able to identify each person's role and unique contributions. Knowing that everyone brings very different skills and perspectives, effective teams leaders typically ask, "What makes each person special on this team?" Defining this helps to tap into each person's strengths. Team leaders must also be focused, clear and consistent. Their intentions, principles, and behaviors must be understood. They must be authentic and have empathy as well as an ability to connect with team members so each person feels it. Lastly, an effective leader must have the courage to try new things, take risks on behalf of the team, and even risk failing— particularly if something can be learned from it. Most importantly, effective team leaders must instill confidence that they will advocate for the team and that they will put the team's interests first.

What was the best innovation team in which you were a member, and what made it special?

One of the most outstanding innovation teams I was part of was an innovation team with a higher order goal—to find ways for people to use more products to help them quit smoking. Although the project team had financial goals for which it was accountable, knowing how many lives we had the potential to save was the real power behind the team. We saw that its potential impact could go way beyond financial performance because we had a mission and vision that were literally tied to life or death—and that was a very powerful driver of innovation. Since then, I've repeatedly seen that finding the "greater good" in any activity is a powerful way to amplify the team's motivation and drive.

TAKEAWAYS

- Strong teams typically outperform even the most creative individuals in delivering innovative results.
- Leaders must ensure that teams have the right people, a compelling shared vision, the capabilities to perform, and knowledge of what is expected of them.

- Whenever possible, leaders should conspire to innovate for great outcomes and create significant goals for teams that allow them to go above and beyond financial goals.
- When teams derail, leaders need to help team members recover by analyzing what went wrong and then facilitating a rebuilding process.

TAKING STOCK

- Does my company allow teams to stay together long enough to become high performing teams?
- Do our leaders have the right skills to help team members play to their strengths?
- How is my organization currently inspiring innovation through teamwork?

■　■　■

If you found this chapter useful, also see *A Culture of Innovation, Buy-in, Sponsorship, and Commitment, Competition and Collaboration, Employee Engagement,* and *Shared Visions and Values.*

Chapter 9

Idea Management and Virtual Collaboration

An interview with Luis Solis, Chief Operating Officer, Digital Roam Inc.; Managing Director at Innovation Alchemists; former President (North America) and Innovation Evangelist (SaaS) at Imaginatik plc

> "... when we add information technology to the mix of creativity and knowledge, we
> get a particularly potent combination: capabilities to represent, deploy, and
> track knowledge coupled with technologies to promote collaboration
> across divergent disciplines and perspectives."
>
> — John Kao

A jazz ensemble is certainly among the best examples of how people co-create and collaborate to produce something new or different. And few people would dispute the fact that technology has further enabled people to build on ideas by providing opportunities for virtual collaboration. In the introduction to the first section of this book, we learned about how the widely acclaimed composer and conductor, Eric Whitacre, worked with a tech-savvy partner to build a "virtual choir" of vocalists throughout the world. This is one of many inventions enabled by virtual collaboration—both inside and outside the world of music.

When comparing the accomplishments that virtual collaboration often creates when enabled by advanced idea management systems, we see how it can enhance new products and services as well as enhancements to products, services, and business models. In fact, organizations in all sectors can benefit from ideas about how to streamline their processes and improve the experience of various stakeholders. For example, the collaboration that occurs in connection with idea management often brings combined value through employee empowerment and increased employee engagement. And when leaders embrace social media in purposeful ways, they're able to leverage different perspectives that often transform the cost, scale, and speed at which their organizations can make things happen.

Additionally, when leaders solicit ideas from people at all organizational levels, collaboration and idea sharing become a natural part of doing business and an integrated element of the organization's culture. How do leaders best evaluate, screen, and act on ideas? We interviewed Luis Solis, who responded to that question and others, drawing on his many years of experience helping organizations create sustainable innovation capabilities and fuel growth. Through enterprise software and consulting services, Luis likes to make big things happen, particularly at technology firms in transition. A graduate of Stanford University in Business (MBA) and Law (JD), his experience spans roles as business executive, entrepreneur, C-suite advisor and private equity investor. Luis is regarded as a global expert in enterprise collaboration and SaaS business software.

Beginning his career at the private equity firm, McCown de Leeuw, in Palo Alto, California, Luis subsequently served as VP-Business Development at GE Capital with a focus on supply chain outsourcing and technology investments. He also founded and managed Symbius, a technology supply chain consultancy. And before joining Imaginatik, Luis was the CEO and Board member of GroupSystems, an enterprise decision-support software company that grew 410% under Luis's leadership. In 2014, Luis published the book *Innovation Alchemists: What Every CEO Needs To Know To Hire The Right Chief Innovation Officer*. He addresses the CINO leadership opportunity in large organizations, from corporations to cities and nation states. Please join us as he discusses the value that idea management and virtual collaboration can bring to organizations.

QUESTIONS AND ANSWERS

How do you define "idea management"?

Idea management is a business process by which ideas are deliberately collected and leveraged for business value. Importantly, ideas can be sourced from inside or outside the organization, and from employees as well as third-party experts. Usually, the best ideas represent an amalgamation of idea fragments.

How do idea management and virtual collaboration support innovation?

Ideas have mostly existed in the shadows—trapped in people's heads, or at best, given the light of day during discussions in meetings, or brainstorming or collaboration around a project. Such ad-hoc use of ideas vastly undercuts their potential. What if a great idea from a meeting could instantly be available to everyone in the company? When leaders begin to capture and share ideas methodically, they practice idea management—and achieve business value. Ideas are synonymous with the fuzzy front end of innovation, the large end of the innovation funnel, where "creative collision" can occur. Creative collision is often a by-product of quantity, not just quality, so it's mission critical to source ideas from highly diverse stakeholders. Today's technology enables organizations to accomplish this from anywhere in the world, and when this process is managed well, the results can be dramatic. Even single ideas can save or create many millions of dollars—or they can lead to innovative new strategies with incalculable benefits.

What are some of the reasons why organizations purchase advanced idea management software?

During the past 20 years, enterprise software has transformed business. Many organizations today use sophisticated software systems to manage every aspect of their operations, from talent management and customer relations to global supply chains. However, relatively few organizations use software to stimulate or manage ideas for growth, even though most business leaders know that ideas fuel innovation and innovation drives business success. Today, powerful software platforms exist to help organizations collect, develop, and leverage ideas systematically—as value-creating business assets. These same systems then facilitate the development of robust business cases and, ultimately, the launch and scale-up of growth ventures. Some leaders have found that software-enabled idea management provides useful information in the form of dashboards that manage the idea funnel, highlight unsuspected innovators, and discover powerful ideas in remote places.

How does technology-enabled idea management differ from the simple suggestion systems of the past?

Collecting ideas is the easy part. Collaboration and creative collision are where the heavy lifting and great business value resides. Today's advanced idea management platforms feel like consumer applications, in that they incorporate social media elements, but at the same time, they utilize robust decision-making tools and even light portfolio management. Deployed via an SaaS format in the Cloud, today's systems empower enterprise change on a global scale. Access is easy; transparency and participation reinforce accountability; collaboration supports idea development, and embedded workflow ensures constant communication among end-users and participants. Enterprises can tap the passion, hearts, and minds of stakeholders in ways that suggestion boxes were never intended to do.

What happens when leaders get inundated with large numbers of ideas?

The quantity of ideas is highly correlated with innovation success because a large front-end funnel expands possible outcomes. The key is to avoid inundation by employing a proper system that captures ideas, affinitizes them, and reveals uncommon patterns and insights. With some systems, powerful algorithms and analytics "spotlight" the best ideas to be leveraged, and also "spotlight" the uncommon innovators in the organization.

Many organizations use an "idea challenge" model to get results. How is this organized?

It's important to know that asking for ideas means being very clear about what you want to do with them later. So idea challenges typically begin with a definition of goals and objectives, at the management level, and end with a charter statement. We can think of this part of the idea management process as "discovery." Once the stage has been set for discovery, other stages follow, such as ideation, decision making, and result. But let's begin by talking about the first stage.

In discovery, it's critical to align idea management with business objectives and initiatives. It's also important to remember that, although ideas can be enabled by software technology, people create them. Talented innovation leaders know how to recruit internal sponsors and how to help sponsors craft initiatives to generate widespread participation and results. In my book, *Innovation Alchemists*, I show how the Chief Innovation Officer's role as "Discoverer" manifests itself in collaboration and connections. They actively engage with a diverse circle of collaborators, from fellow innovators and scientists to ethnographers, designers, marketers and engineers who will share valuable insights as nuggets for larger opportunities...[because] discoverers tap outside catalysts.

Equally important to collaboration are efforts to create purpose around ideation, since they help to ensure that ideas are being directed toward clear goals. Celebration is equally critical, and so it becomes quite important to think in advance about rewards and recognitions that will steer desired behaviors.

And then the process continues to the ideation stage?

Not yet. The last stage of the discovery process requires the team leading the initiative to set a timeline for submitting ideas; for formulating key expectations for results; for selecting the range of participants; and for identifying subject matter experts and review team members. Then the process can move to the ideation stage, which is the main phase of idea submissions and collaboration.

In the ideation stage, participants submit ideas for a specified period, using a carefully designed idea form. This tool asks for key information related to the idea in conjunction with goals and follow-up objectives for the challenge. Ideas are open for various forms of collaboration, (e.g., commenting, remixing, and sharing/forwarding). Voting and group prioritization from the "crowd" are also important activities during the challenge, as they help sort and screen for the most promising ideas. This is where virtual collaboration can provide additional input that can be leveraged.

Moving to the decision-making stage, how does idea generation software enable decision makers to take in an appropriate amount of information and make sound decisions from it?

Idea management systems usually include a variety of mechanisms for filtering, screening, prioritizing, and scoring ideas. But there are two categories of screening: by the "crowd," and by reviewers and managers. Ultimately, experts and managers must get involved before ideas are chosen for funding, development, or implementation. Often, a reviewing panel will take the most promising ideas—informed by crowd-based voting and screening—and then perform in-depth reviews. But before then, multiple reviewing tools might be used, depending on the nature of the challenge. When ideas are relatively straightforward and non-technical, simple voting schemes work best, but when ideas are more complex, they often require "head-to-head reviews." In these cases, reviewers are presented with side-by-side comparisons of two randomly selected ideas, and after comparing a statistically significant set of idea pairs, comparative data can illustrate which ideas have the most merit.

Moving to the results phase, can idea management software track progress on projects in pipelines? Can it also identify where projects might be stalling and in need of intervention?

Advanced idea management systems track projects that come from ideas. Stage-gate workflows can be freely customized, as well as some steps in exploring, developing, and launching ideas. An integrated dashboard, combined with analysis and measurement tools, helps to track overall results; to diagnose problems with particular projects; and to chart progress against metrics. During the Results phase, worthwhile ideas might be funded, developed, directly implemented, or documented for potential future use.

What types of companies use idea management platforms and what are the advantages?

They're used by companies that believe wisdom resides in uncommon places or with uncommon people, even outside of the corporation. That's why P&G is committed to open innovation and why The World Bank challenges employees to help solve hunger, health, and habitat issues for more than 180 member nations. Many organizations still believe that experts or siloed teams have all the answers, but our experience with thriving global brands shows otherwise. The search for disruptive innovation and breakthroughs—and the commitment to deep engagement with employees and stakeholders—inevitably leads to new ways of working. Additionally, the central role that idea management plays in innovation is immense—and most organizations have only begun to explore the bounds of its potential.

TAKEAWAYS

- Idea management is a powerful enabler for employee engagement and support from stakeholders with change initiatives.
- Technology-enabled idea management vastly increases the quantity and quality of ideas available for innovation.
- Enterprise-wide idea generation can produce substantial savings or increased revenues from improved products, services, and processes.
- Mass collaboration can assist organizations in innovating faster and better, to achieve or maintain competitive advantage.
- Cloud solutions for idea management allow organizations with scale or complexity to efficiently move selected ideas into business case formats, in which they can be invested and managed to completion.

TAKING STOCK

- Could my organization benefit from a formal idea management process that utilizes collaboration, large crowds, and social media elements?
- Could a technology-enabled idea management strategy make the idea-to-new-results process a repeatable, differentiating capability?
- Does our senior management team have the vision, courage and passion for doing things in better ways so that we can set ourselves apart from the competition?

■ ■ ■

To learn more about Luis's book, go to www.innovation-alchemists.com. If you found this chapter helpful, also see chapters entitled *A Business Case for Creativity and Creative Problem Solving*, *A Path to Innovation Excellence*, *Business Model Innovation*, *Employee Engagement*, and *Open Innovation*.

Chapter 10

Resilience

An interview with Christie Knittel Mabry, Ed.D., HR Leader for Biogen in North Carolina and former Director and Vice President at GE, Blue Cross-Blue Shield of North Carolina, CGI/CARQUEST, and SciQuest

■ ■ ■

"Highly resilient people can dance and flow with disruptive change because they have many attitudes and perspectives that let them be both involved and detached from the action."

— *Al Siebert*

Successful orchestras and jazz ensembles have many of the same qualities as successful organizations in all sectors and industries. One important quality is staying power. In part, that's determined by an organization's resilience. Researchers have studied resilience to learn about the kinds of strategies that are employed to build it. Their work reveals that resilience is compromised when individuals, teams, and organizational leaders resort to "safe behaviors" that can inhibit or stifle innovation. Conversely, when people feel that they're in control, they're able to view challenges as opportunities. This enables them to be more creative, more open to new possibilities, and more resilient in the face of obstacles or disappointments. In turn, it allows them to freely commit to a new course and to innovate. But resilience isn't only important for individuals; it's also a success determinant in teams, as team members freely collaborate to build on each other's ideas and when they routinely challenge the status quo.

For this chapter, we interviewed Dr. Christie Knittel Mabry, who cites the work of various researchers and shows how organizational leaders can help build and maintain the confidence, trust, and collaboration that foster resilience. As a Board Certified Coach, Christie draws on 24 years of experience from leading organizations in 6 different industries. Prior to Biogen Idec, she spent the first 11 years of her career in a variety of positions at GE Capital. A graduate of GE Capital's Advanced Leadership & Facilitation Network, Christie was a master trainer and facilitator of GE's legendary Work-Out and Change Acceleration Process (CAP) models, a fully trained GE Six Sigma Master Black Belt, and a co-facilitator for the Work-Out of GE's legendary Session C succession planning process.

Post-GE, and prior to Biogen Idec, Christie was also a professor and administrator at Peace College and had held leadership roles in human resources and human resources development at SciQuest, CARQUEST, and Blue Cross and Blue Shield of North Carolina. She has presented her research at major national and international research conferences and has served as president of several professional associations. Christie earned her Ed.D. in Adult Education and HRD from North Carolina State University and her executive coaching certification from Duke University. Please join us as she describes how organizations can achieve sustainable innovation by becoming more resilient.

QUESTIONS AND ANSWERS

How do you define "resilience"?

I resonate with Reich, Zutra, and Hall's definition of resilience in their *Handbook of Adult Resilience*. They conclude that resilience has two key components. The first is recovery, defined as the ability to rebound from stress and; the capacity to regain equilibrium quickly; and then the ability to return to an initial state of healthy homeostasis. The second and typically overlooked component is sustainability. Sustainable resilience means that the recovery continues along a positive trajectory and can potentially grow in a way that one's life and work might be transformed for the better.

How can resilience be an enabler for innovation and what happens when it's compromised?

I believe that the capacity to innovate is rooted in a mindset of learning from constant change and growth. Although change is a constant, it is still a very difficult concept for many people – both intellectually, as well as viscerally, and is challenging to organizations. The capacity to be resilient lies at the heart of innovation. Resilient people are more comfortable with change because they understand that change is an inherent and healthy part of life. They view themselves as capable of managing, and working through change, and so they have high self-efficacy. Resilient people expect that something positive will come of the change, and they extract learning and meaning from it, often finding the proverbial "silver linings." As a result, they're often transformed for the better, and from this, I believe that resiliency is a core competency for innovation. Conversely, when resilience is compromised, people in organizations can waste valuable time, energy and resources resisting innovation. In the end, they may not only fail to thrive, but also be doomed to fail.

What factors impact resilience in individuals? How can fear and negative events trigger behaviors that compromise resilience?

I like the concept of "hardiness," that Maddi and Khoshaba identified in their book, *Resilience at Work: How to Succeed No Matter What Life Throws at You.* I believe "hardiness" is central to the capacity to be resilient. If the constellation of attitudes and skills that comprise hardiness is not present, it will likely have a negative impact on resilience. The three factors of hardiness are commitment, control, and challenge. Commitment means continual belief in the goal that contributes to personal enthusiasm to stay the course. Control is about agency, or self-efficacy—the inherent belief that a person can affect the change. People with high control typically have an internal locus of control that allows them to trust their own judgment, instincts, etc. Challenge is about a belief system that some good or meaning can be made from the situation. People high in "challenge" typically have a view that all will work out in the end and that they may, quite possibly, be better or even transformed.

What happens when individuals and teams lack resilience and what factors in organizations tend to compromise resilience?

Teams that lack resilience resist the inevitable changes that are part of organizational life. They often disengage or withdraw from problems, fight the change based on their lack of comfort with it or continually seek direction. All of these behaviors can translate to energy wasted and missing vital opportunities to innovate. Several factors compromise resilience, and a primary one is a low-trust organizational culture. These are cultures where reflection, sense-making, and ongoing learning are not encouraged. They're also organizations that don't have practices for supporting people by giving them opportunities to stretch into new and different roles, and they're cultures that penalize people for taking risks. Additionally, rigid command-and-control cultures can compromise resilience because they inhibit experimentation and independent decision making. Negative emotions such as fear can also compromise resilience, risk-taking and innovation. These emotions cannot be avoided as they are part of the individual human experience.

Command-and-control leadership reinforces the concept that the locus of control resides outside of anyone who isn't at the top. As such, it can negatively impact people's desire to engage with change or to feel as if they can extract meaning from change. This has obvious implications for innovation as well as for resiliency, since innovation is dependent on the ability to deal effectively with change. Restrictive policies and procedures can limit trust, dialogue, experimentation, risk-taking and sense-making in organizations.

What are some effective strategies for building resilience at all levels of the organization (e.g., in individuals, teams, leaders)?

Executives must legitimize the concept of resilience as a core competency that enables employees to manage change and contribute to innovation. Leaders must attend to the culture issues previously mentioned. Additionally, leaders must understand, model, discuss, and teach resilience. Culture change begins at the top. Modeling, discussing and teaching not only makes them more authentic and accessible, but also legitimizes resilience as a central quality for meaning making, innovations and progress. Another strategy is legitimizing emotional intelligence as a core competency, which enables hardiness and resiliency. Emotional intelligence has as much to do with knowing when and how to express emotion as it does with managing it.

How can stories contribute to helplessness in organizations? And how might a compelling vision be empowering?

Stories are powerful in an organization's culture. Stories that reinforce a belief system that change and leadership only happen at the top or by a single hero create, and sometimes elevate helplessness. If a vision is compelling and the stories support the vision, employees can begin to place themselves as powerful and purposeful actors within that narrative. Stories that reinforce mutual support and collaboration help build conditions for resiliency and innovation. As we know from the research and from our own experiences in life and in work, this sense of purpose and agency is central to resilience and managing change.

How might communication help to build resilience by eliminating the element of surprise?

It is unrealistic to believe that leaders will ever eliminate surprises that occur during change, although, through ongoing, honest and transparent communication, they can minimize a lot of it. Leaders can begin to think about, talk about, and train employees to be more "hardy"—something that will help people to better manage their reactions and make sense of surprises.

How can leaders encourage people to take time to build trust, given today's demanding workplaces?

I believe that the ability to collaborate—to do it freely and well—implies distributed power and the opportunity to experiment, play, and learn. Certainly it's a challenge for leaders to encourage collaboration and trust, yet both are essential for high performance and for innovation.

TAKEAWAYS

- Leaders must legitimize the concept of resilience as a core competency that enables managing change and innovation.
- Organizations must teach and coach leaders and employees about the core concepts of resilience. They must also help them understand root causes and what happens when resilience is not present.
- Training in emotional intelligence skills should be done to enable self-awareness, self-management, awareness of others' needs and relationship management. These are key factors in generating the best conditions for resilience, risk-taking and innovation.
- Leaders must reinforce policies and practices that increase collaboration, mutual support and resiliency.
- Executives must create cultures where resilience and innovation can flourish.

TAKING STOCK

- Does the culture of my organization support the trust, sense-making, collaboration, mutual support, and ongoing learning that is critical to innovation?
- Do leaders in my organization allow people to experiment, take risks, or stretch to take on opportunities that might help them grow or become more innovative?
- Do the stories that we tell in my organization empower? Or do they create or elevate helplessness?

■　■　■

If you found this chapter helpful, please also see *A Culture of Innovation, Courage, Employee Engagement,* and *High Performing Teams.*

Chapter 11

The Physical Environment

An interview with Paulo Carmini, Vice President, Northeast Region, Steelcase

■ ■ ■

"Innovation comes from people meeting up in the hallways ..."

— *Steve Jobs*

Without a doubt, symphony orchestra musicians and jazz musicians need the right acoustics to perform optimally. They also need the right settings in which to perform, as do people in business environments. Realizing how important strong performance is to organizational success, leaders at Skype knew they needed to attract, inspire, and retain top talent. With that, they conducted a survey in the U.S., to identify the needs of highly sought-after technology professionals and found that "quality of the work environment" ranked among the top three factors in job satisfaction.

Successful organizations like Skype ensure high-quality work environments through design elements such as open offices, healthy cafeteria choices, and fitness centers, as well as work areas with natural light, outdoor views, and comfortable seating. Their settings also acknowledge different work modes, allowing employees to stand and walk around, as well as sit throughout the day. What challenges do leaders have, in providing physical settings that facilitate creativity and innovation and enhance job satisfaction?

At the same time that leaders must ensure the well-being of their employees, they must also manage high real estate costs. That means finding ways to make the most efficient and effective use of space. Although technology has in part offset the high cost of space today through alternative work styles, it has also created an interconnected work environment that is challenging to manage. To learn about how organizations meet these types of challenges, we interviewed Paulo Carmini, a leader who has personally observed the ways that work gets done in various and different parts of the world.

With responsibility for P&L management, sales and distribution, Paulo currently oversees Steelcase's Eastern Canada region as well as the New England states in the U.S. Prior to his current role, he served as the Managing Director for Steelcase Middle East, and before that, as the Area Sales Manager for Eastern Canada. Please join us as Paulo describes how the right physical environment can maximize job satisfaction while also fostering the creativity and collaboration that are so vital to innovation and success in today's competitive environments.

QUESTIONS AND ANSWERS

How do you define "the physical work environment" today and its ability to foster innovation?

The work environment today is not simply about cubicles, tables, and chairs. In the past, traditional offices were created as a sort of "cubicle land," where people were secluded and had very little contact with one another. Today, mobile technology allows for more things to be done in more places, so physical space should be designed to provide a better opportunity for people to focus, collaborate, learn and socialize. Innovation has often been described as a "team sport," and if that's the case, then team members need easy access to one another. In the physical work environment, that means creating a variety of meeting spaces and dedicated project spaces that allow team members to meet informally and spontaneously, unhampered by the need to search for available conference rooms.

We know that Steelcase conducts ongoing research to identify specific needs and trends. What findings can you share with us, in regard to designing space that promotes innovation?

Steelcase employees study and learn about job satisfaction and office solutions through two internal groups. The Workspace Futures team conducts ongoing research and the ARC team provides consulting to clients and their design professionals. By showing clients how to link their strategic goals with their workplace strategies, Steelcase employees help them leverage their real estate as a competitive asset. Much of the research conducted by Steelcase confirms the importance of what we refer to as an "interconnected workplace."

There are five key workplace issues to keep in mind, and I'll talk a little about each of them. First, current economics dictate that organizations optimize every square foot of real estate. If employees are out of the building or away from their offices or dedicated workstations, sometimes as much as 70% of the time, do they all really need dedicated offices or workstations? Organizations that analyze current needs and construct their workspaces around them are better able to align their workplace strategy with their business strategy. This also requires an understanding of how work really gets done.

What are the other key workplace issues?

The second key workplace issue is design that enhances collaboration and enables it to be a natural way of working. At Steelcase, we look at three types of collaboration: informative, evaluative and generative. Generative is the most important for innovation because it's where co-creation happens. To facilitate generative collaboration and tacit knowledge exchange, organizations need to create project spaces that allow integration of digital and analog sharing of knowledge. Project spaces also need to facilitate sharing of ideas and different perspectives and support small groups of people who can join in, connect, and disconnect with minimum disruption to the flow of ideas—whether they're participating physically or virtually.

It seems that organizations need to first attract, develop, and engage talent. How does the right physical work environment help with those efforts?

This relates to the third key workplace issue. When people come to work, they want to be engaged and feel energetic. With the need to solve today's complex problems through greater collaboration and high engagement, the physical environment needs to allow people to be active, to connect, and to collaborate in ways that really get things done. Yet that's not enough, so I'll next describe the fourth key workplace factor: Leaders need to communicate the purpose of their organization. The physical environment can be a way to integrate the organization's strategy with its brand and its culture. The workplace is a tangible reflection of these factors, and so its overall design and spaces for interaction should build and reinforce organization's purpose, brand, and culture.

Today, the concept of well-being seems to be getting a lot of attention. Would you please describe how the physical environment can enhance well-being?

The fifth key workplace issue regards the cognitive, physical, and emotional well-being of an organization's leaders and employees. In fact, well-being is one of the biggest trends we need to look at today, and it means going beyond simple ergonomics, acoustics, lighting, privacy, etc. It also means allowing users choice and control over where and how they work, and providing them with a range of spaces that allow them to choose the places to support the work they are doing at a particular time.

So how do leaders enable choice and control in their physical environments?

In Issue 63 of Steelcase's online magazine 360.steelcase.com is an article entitled "Creating an Interconnected Workplace," which summarizes elements to consider when designing work spaces.

It puts forth the challenge of dealing with the complexities of competing in today's interconnected world and says there is a need to understand that, first, people need technology. Second, people need people. And third, people need spaces that effectively bring technology and people together.

All this translates to what Steelcase calls a "palette of place" (meaning individual and group space) and a "palette of posture" which includes a range of solutions that encourage people to move about, rather than simply sit all day. Steelcase's research shows that people are most productive when they're able to switch between a variety of positions or postures throughout the day. Workplace design can provide mental stimulation and can be physically energizing if it supports varied postures and different work modes. Additionally, configurations like work cafés can allow people to meet, eat, relax, work, socialize, and network—all important activities for creative problem solving and decision making.

Do changing demographics have an impact on the physical work environment?

The physical environment can definitely hinder collective learning, collaboration, and performance if it fails to take demographics into consideration. Space must be tailored to the way work gets done today across the diverse range of demographics that exists in today's workplace—and that includes generational, professional and cultural diversity. As a leader in various office solutions, Steelcase began operations over 100 years ago when its business consisted solely of the manufacture of office furniture and equipment. Yet today the company offers clients an entire portfolio of products and services that include interior architecture, furniture, and technology solutions for corporate, education and healthcare environments. What caused Steelcase to expand its former business model? Changing demographics and changing needs.

Does this mean that brick-and-mortar offices, as we currently know them, could become extinct?

Definitely not. Although the traditional nine-to-five job is dead, and many people work virtually, the need for brick-and-mortar is more important than ever. A recent study conducted by Steelcase confirms this. In North America and Europe, 86% of organizations offer alternative work strategies, ranging from home offices to hoteling and other mobile options. However, these organizations have found that less than 10% of their employees choose to work remotely on a routine basis. In that same study, 72% of people said the office provided the best environment for enhancing their interactions with employees. That makes a case for brick-and-mortar offices, but it doesn't eliminate the challenge of having to pay for them. The focus should be on real estate optimization designed to support the different work modes employees are embracing today.

So how can organizations efficiently utilize space while still meeting the needs of today's workforce?

It's important to know that efficient work space isn't just about compression, and that it's possible to provide people with spaces that allow them to excel while allowing the company to better leverage their real estate. At Steelcase, we refer to this as "don't just shrink—re-think," and that means exploring how underutilized spaces—such as corporate cafeterias—can be activated to support the way people want to work today. Understanding how to create spaces with the vibe of a coffee shop and the functionality of a well-planned office, can provide real estate that is utilized effectively all day long, and that's the most important measure of all for space.

What are other important considerations, when trying to create space that meets current needs?

We need to also look at the role of technology. Today, mobile technologies have allowed more work to be done in multiple places. The notion of "distributed work" is a prevailing trend where people collaborate all over the world with extended partners via e-mail, web-based platforms, and high definition video cameras. Mobile technologies have also changed how work is done. By enabling people to work in coffee shops, hotels, and even on public transit, mobile technologies raise the question, "How is technology best utilized and leveraged, to create a sense of community that drives high engagement?" Think of the concept of "palette of presence," where work environments support virtual and physical connections with the same degree of attention. Trust is the foundation for strong collaboration, and today virtual connections are becoming as prevalent as physical ones for global teams, so spaces should enable physical and virtual connections to happen naturally.

Another consideration is a change in the traditional model of employment, as it encompasses the creative or contingent workforce. When organizations contract to bring in people for specific projects, they need to allocate space for those people, but they also need to provide appropriate space for regular employees to collaborate with the contingent workforce. Other considerations are the erratic schedules and longer workdays of today's work environments. Employees with clients, customers, or team members in different time zones often need to begin their work days earlier or later—going beyond traditional work hours. When organizations provide work cafés, people can work alongside colleagues with similar working hours, and work better when they have access to nutritious food, as opposed to snacks from vending machines.

To summarize, successful organizations today maximize investments in their real estate by designing work places that augment their employees' collective performance. That means workplaces must change as human behaviors change. If space shapes behavior, then the right physical environment can help people feel appreciated, energized, and inspired. Leaders who know how to leverage their organizations' physical environment can effectively compete in both local and global environments.

TAKEAWAYS

- Leaders must ensure that workspaces are designed to meet both current and future needs.
- To facilitate innovation, workplace design must support informal communication and collaboration.
- Leaders should leverage their work environments as strategic tools to support business goals.
- Insights from research regarding future trends can be used effectively to meet emerging needs and create physical work spaces that help people work best.

TAKING STOCK

- Is our work environment flexible enough to support the different ways in which people like to work?
- Does our workplace provide an environment that stimulates the creative process?
- Do we effectively facilitate learning and global team activity in our current work spaces?

■　■　■

To learn more about creating the right conditions for innovation, see our chapters entitled *A Culture of Innovation*, *A Design Mindset*, and *A Path to Innovation Excellence*.

Closing Thoughts:
Innovation Prowess

An interview with George S. Day, Ph.D., Co-Director of the Mack Institute for Innovation Management at the Wharton School of the University of Pennsylvania; Geoffrey T. Boisi Professor; Professor of Marketing; and former Executive Director of the Marketing Science Institute

Dr. George S. Day is the past chairman of the American Marketing Association. He has consulted at numerous corporations such as General Electric, IBM, Metropolitan Life, Unilever, E.I. DuPont de Nemours, W.L. Gore and Associates, Coca-Cola, Boeing, LG Corp., Best Buy, Merck, Johnson & Johnson, and Medtronic. His primary areas of activity are marketing, strategy making, organic growth and innovation, organizational change, and competitive strategies in global markets. George has authored 18 books in the areas of marketing and strategic management. His most recent books are *Peripheral Vision: Detecting the Weak Signals That Can Make or Break Your Company* (with Paul Schoemaker); *Strategy from the Outside-In: Profiting from Customer Value* (with Christine Moorman); *and Innovation Prowess: Leadership Strategies for Accelerating Growth*. George won 10 best article awards and one best book award, with 2 of his articles judged to be among the top 25 most influential articles in marketing science in the past 25 years. He was honored with the distinguished Sheth Foundation award in 2003 and the Mahajan Award for career contributions to strategy in 2001. In 2003 George received the AMA/Irwin/McGraw-Hill Distinguished Marketing Educator Award and in 2011, he was chosen by his peers as one of 11 "Legends in Marketing."

■ ■ ■

Growth leaders are often characterized by their innovation prowess—their skill in successfully bringing more and better initiatives to market and their ability to also improve innovation productivity. Today, as always, these skills and abilities provide critical advantages. According to Arthur D. Little, top performing organizations are five times as productive as average performers. This means that they realize five times as much output in terms of new product revenues or profits for the same investment in R&D and in new product development costs and time.

In my most recent book, *Innovation Prowess*, I describe three entwined elements of innovation that are exemplified by the majority of highly innovative organizations. I call them the "Three Cs of Growth Leadership": capabilities, culture, and configuration. In this chapter, I'll describe how leading organizations leverage these three elements.

The First of the Three Cs: Capabilities That Enable Innovation

Capabilities are bundles of closely integrated skills, knowledge, technologies, and cumulative learning that are manifested in organizational processes that can enable an organization to execute. Three widely recognized capabilities ensure superior innovation prowess and help to maintain competitive advantage: open network capability, market learning capability, and adaptive development capability.

Open network capability refers to the ways in which organizations tackle opportunities with one or more collaborators, to accelerate innovation, share risk, and produce a broader range of possible solutions. Collaborators usually bring two kinds of risk: "co-innovation risk" and "adoption chain risk." Co-innovation risk stems from dependence on others to innovate in parallel. Adoption chain risk is the extent to which partners need to adopt their innovations before consumers can actually access their full value propositions. Both of these risks need to be managed with different action plans, but if synergy can be achieved, it is a small price to pay for the potential benefits of open innovation.

Market learning capability is evidenced by leaders who actively seek, share, and act upon insights via market sensing, sense-making, application of insights, and learning from market feedback. Relevant and actionable information can also be sought internally, from what's stored in an organization's knowledge system and from the tacit knowledge of its leaders and employees. For findings to be relevant, however, they must be converted into usable insights and distilled so they produce coherent patterns. Organizations with strong market learning capability actively seek and integrate lessons from market responses, asking questions to determine whether their efforts have yielded the desired response, and if not, why not. They also ask how their processes and methodologies can be improved.

Adaptive development capability is descriptive of the phase-gate or stage-gate development processes that are used by successful innovators to evaluate whether to bring innovation concepts to market. When the development process is segregated into a natural sequence of steps needed to move a chosen concept to launch, each stage begins with "go–no go" decision points and a review by senior leaders who evaluate progress and decide whether to proceed to the next stage. This enables "pay-as-you-go" project funding, with resources available only when there is acceptable progress. The most capable organizations have replaced "one-size-fits-all" stage gate templates with heavy-weight versions for breakthrough innovations and light-weight versions for those that are incremental. They've also modified standard approaches to eliminate lengthy and time consuming preparation of deliverables. Teams present only brief documents with a few back-up slides so that gatekeepers are simply informed about the risks and decisions that need to be made.

The Second of the Three Cs: Cultures that Support Innovation

Business literature is replete with examples of how efforts to build new innovation capabilities or to improve an organization's configuration will succeed only when supported by certain cultural attributes. Culture can be defined as an organization's shared values and beliefs as well as how its leaders define and model behaviors that support its mission and value proposition. Although innovation leaders typically employ a variety of different business models and strategies, their cultures have at least three factors in common: First, leaders in highly innovative organizations accept that their customers or clients will migrate to better solutions regardless of who might provide them. They also know that the likelihood of failure for any innovation initiative is high when it goes beyond the organization's current capabilities. As a result, they continually enhance their products and services—and create new ones. Most importantly, they resist the temptation to keep investing only in core businesses.

Additionally, leaders in highly innovative organizations define failure as an opportunity to identify and eliminate mistakes through iterative processes. These leaders are willing to embrace the high risk of innovation failure over the even greater risk of competitive defeat that typically comes from standing still. These leaders inspire risk taking by encouraging employees to pursue new ideas and opportunities despite their risks. This sends a powerful message that leaders will stand behind their employees and support their efforts. However, a second key cultural factor in these organizations is the way that leaders focus on the future, downplaying both past and present successes, and only devoting energy to pursuing the next success. The third distinguishing factor is that leaders and employees don't seek out and attempt to replicate best practices—they *create* them.

The Third of the Three Cs: Configuration for Execution

Configuration is the structure of the organization that identifies specific responsibilities and account-abilities for achieving targets. It also determines how success should be measured, and allocates resources. It establishes incentives for individuals and teams and then assigns rewards for people who perform at full potential. Configuration only works, however, when all members of the C-suite concur with answers to questions about who, at the highest level, will be accountable for reaching the growth objective. Additional considerations regard how decision makers will keep score and what key innovation metrics will be used. In addition to effectively structuring the organization, C-suite members must also identify and agree upon the organization's persistent inhibitors to growth.

One major growth inhibitor occurs when leaders attempt to force–fit breakthrough initiatives into existing business models and onto infrastructures built for current products and services. Diffused accountability is a second major growth inhibitor and occurs when accountabilities aren't effectively established, or enforced, because of a lack of clarity. Successful innovators usually dedicate budgets or strategic reserves for non-core opportunities to ensure that innovation opportunities aren't smothered or starved of resources. They also work at preventing diffused accountability by communicating clear goals and expectations about intended outcomes. They ensure accountability through aggressive portfolio reviews and through small, cross-functional teams whose members ensure that projects aren't competing for resources and working at cross-purposes.

In closing, growth laggards must continually evaluate the three C's to learn what might be holding them back and to constantly seek improvements. Growth leaders, too, need to constantly seek improvements in order to stay ahead of the game. One thing remains certain for both: there's no room for complacency if leaders are to sustain innovation prowess and continue leveraging the 3 Cs that enable it.

■   ■   ■

To learn more about Wharton's Mack Institute for Innovation Management, go to mackinstitute.wharton.upenn.edu.

Subsection II.
Leading Innovation

Leading Innovation: Shaping, Stimulating, and Supporting

Introduction by Andrea Zintz, Ph.D.

On May 9, 2003, after the Florida Philharmonic Orchestra finished playing to an audience of 1,300, Trey Devey, the orchestra's executive director, came on stage to announce this might be its last concert. In his May 14, 2003, *New York Times* article, "As Funds Disappear, So Do Orchestras," Stephen Kinzer quoted Devey: "If you have the potential to help us and be a hero, then call us. We need a hero." Kinzer commented, "No one called, at least, no one with the necessary resources." Later Trey Devey issued a statement saying the orchestra was "temporarily suspending operations and terminating the employment of musicians." The Florida Philharmonic never reopened its doors. This type of closure isn't unusual for orchestras or businesses. For many, it's the norm.

Symphony orchestras struggle, as do many organizations in our ever-changing world. Recent studies conducted by the nonprofit research organization, the Brookings Institution, reflect these challenges. One study revealed a steady decline in business dynamism and aggregate productivity in the U.S. during a 30-year period from 1978 to 2011. The number of companies created and the number that close determine business dynamism, a key driver of innovation. It is vital to productivity and sustained economic growth. Bottom line, this study shows that businesses in the United States have, for 30 years, been collapsing at a faster rate than they're forming. Adding to concerns about this downward trend is the fact that business dynamism has been declining in all 50 states. (For more detail, see the March 22, 2014 report "Declining Business Dynamism: It's for Real" by Ian Hathaway, of Ennsyte Economics, and Robert E. Litan, of the Brookings Institution, at brookings.edu.)

New Rules, New Ways of Operating

Although many U.S. companies have recovered from the Great Recession in 2008-2009, the game has changed substantially since that time—not only for orchestras but businesses in almost every industry and sector. Old rules no longer apply, and today's executives must think in new and creative ways if they're to keep their organizations economically viable. So what is the meaning of this constant threat for organizations? Times of uncertainty, radical change, and opportunity elevate the importance of leadership.

JoAnn Falletta, Music Director of both the Buffalo Philharmonic Orchestra (BPO) and the Virginia Symphony Orchestra (VSO), is well aware of the implications of change and the opportunities it can create. As a guest conductor with leading orchestras around the world, she has seen the many orchestras in both the United States and Europe that have either failed in recent years or been struggling financially. Having taken both the BPO and VSO to higher levels, Falletta describes on her website (www.joannfalletta.com) what she perceives to be the necessary skills of leaders today in her essay "The Compleat Music Director." (Merriam-Webster defines "compleat" as having all necessary or desired elements or skills.) She says, "In extraordinary times it is extraordinary action that makes the difference. The 21st century is not a time for maintenance of the status quo." However, maintaining the status quo has no place in JoAnn Falletta's modus operandi. Innovation is evident in her selection of music as well as her leadership style. Under Falletta's direction, the Buffalo Philharmonic released 12 CDs in only 10 years' time, with 2 of them being Grammy winners.

Falletta's national and international reputation further reinforces her success. Following an appointment by George W. Bush, she served on the National Council of the Arts from 2008 to 2012. Musical World, an organization that connects artists, managers, and presenters worldwide (www.musicalworld. com), references *The Washington Post's* praise of Falletta as having "Toscanini's tight control over ensemble, Walter's affectionate balancing of inner voices, Stokowski's gutsy showmanship, and a controlled frenzy worthy of Bernstein." The National Endowment for the Arts' website cites *The New York Times'* description as "one of the finest conductors of her generation." (See arts.gov/about/national-council-arts/joann-falletta.)

New and Fresh Approaches

One of the hallmarks of Falletta's success at programming is her skill in delivering a blend of classical and contemporary music. Although classical music enthusiasts rarely seem to tire of the music of Western Europe from the 1800s and early 1900s, other audiences want something new. Why? Because we live in an age where people demand new and different experiences. When considering how jazz has seemed to fare better with younger audiences than classical music, it might be due to the love of change. Since the 1920s, when jazz first emerged, it's been always changing. That's because the focus of jazz is primarily on improvisation, where musicians continually experiment to produce something new and different.

As a creative leader who has mastered both orchestration and improvisation, Falletta has, for much of her career, blended old and new approaches to music as a way of responding to the preferences of today's younger and more diverse audiences. In addition to conducting the music of classical composers such as Beethoven, Mahler, and Mozart, she's introduced more than 500 works by American composers and artists. (See bpo.org/staff-members/joann-falletta/.) Falletta stands as a clear example of a leader who is committed to continuously staying attuned to the evolving needs of customers as well as attracting those who may become future customers. This leadership practice is also critical to generating and modeling new and fresh approaches to products and services that go beyond the world of music.

Part Conductor, Part Historian

Through extensive research, Falletta has discovered a significant amount of music by contemporary composers. In a YouTube video of the CBS Sunday Morning Show (circa 1992) at joannfalletta.com, Falletta says, "…[this] really changed my life in a very joyful way because I was looking at music that had never been played." While directing at the Women's Philharmonic early in her career, Falletta also located works possibly lost to the world—obscure scores that would probably not have seen the light of day had it not been for her efforts. Many of these scores were the works of previously unknown women composers and conductors. In her February 23, 2001 interview with Jeremy Siepman, Falletta tells why these scores were unknown.

Falletta found works produced long ago by women composers who were virtual unknowns. She said, "In many ways I'd had a very traditional conductor's upbringing…and women composers don't tend to be a part of that. But when I went to San Francisco to work with the Women's Philharmonic Orchestra, I discovered a wealth of music from the past…" By resurrecting the work of these women, Falletta not only brought life to music that might have remained buried; she also honored these women's contributions posthumously.

Years later, when Falletta was functioning as Music Director of the Buffalo Philharmonic Orchestra, an unexpected event led to what she refers to as one of the most interesting projects that her orchestra has ever embarked upon. (See the 2011 YouTube video "JoAnn Falletta: Naxos CD Tyberg's Symphony.")

A Fact Straight From Fiction?

In the chapter of this book *Inspiring and Encouraging Innovation*, Megan Mitchell shares what she describes as three ways by which innovation occurs. It can happen (a) accidentally, (b) through disciplined and deliberate actions, and (c) systemically, by building a culture in which innovation is a likely outcome of employees feeling safe and highly motivated. She asserts that the most successful leaders leverage all three. For example, when Falletta researched buried treasures from the past, she was employing disciplined and deliberate innovation. The organizational cultures that she built at both the BSO and the VSO are examples of systematic innovation. And what was about to present itself in the form of accidental innovation would closely parallel the discoveries and ultimate innovations of Benjamin Franklin, Madame Curie, and Alexander Fleming.

In an interview captured in the 2011 YouTube video "JoAnn Falletta: Naxos CD Tyberg's Symphony," Falletta tells the story. Calling it "almost an example of fact being straight from fiction," she describes how, on one of many rainy days in Buffalo, New York, she was returning to her dressing room from rehearsal when she saw an elderly man in a raincoat, dripping wet, holding a huge shopping bag. When he asked for a few minutes of her time, Falletta graciously agreed. She quickly learned that the man was Dr. Enrico (Henry) Mihich, a physician at the Roswell Park Cancer Institute in Buffalo. Although very curious about the contents of the shopping bag, Falletta listened patiently as Dr. Mihich told a story that she hoped would describe what was inside.

Mihich related how when he was a young boy, his father, Milan Mihich (also a physician), had provided music lessons for him by retaining the services of a composer and musician named Marcel Tyberg. Henry Mihich told how Tyberg had become not only a beloved teacher but also a welcomed guest and friend of the Mihich family. Mihich also described difficult times back then, when many people throughout Europe were fleeing their homes to avoid consignment to Nazi death camps. Still curious about what was in the large shopping bag, Falletta nonetheless continued to listen patiently.

She learned that, when Marcel Tyberg realized he was personally at risk of arrest and deportation for his Jewish heritage, he had entrusted all of his musical scores—symphonies, masses, and chamber music—to Dr. Milan Mihich (Henry Mihich's father) for safekeeping. The understanding was that the Mihich family would protect these scores until Tyberg could "return" to Italy and reclaim them. Of course, he never fulfilled that intention. The Mihich family felt deep sadness when news arrived that Marcel Tyberg had perished in the death camp at Auschwitz. Most amazing, however, was that they continued to maintain the charge of his musical scores, even as they too were forced to flee from their home.

With each move they made throughout Europe, trying to ensure their safety, the Mihich family members took almost nothing with them except these scores. In time, Henry Mihich inherited the responsibility for all of Marcel Tyberg's scores, yet despite his many attempts to rescue these works from oblivion, he'd had no success. After his move from Europe to Buffalo, New York, Mihich had learned about JoAnn Falletta. And now it appeared as if he might be ready to reveal the contents of the large shopping bag and ask for Falletta's help.

For the Love of Music

Although Falletta felt quite moved by the admiration that Dr. Mihich still had for his former teacher and how determined he had been to find a way to share Tyberg's compositions with the world, she saw a serious challenge. Much as Falletta wanted to help, when Tyberg's Symphony #3 finally emerged from the shopping bag, she noticed it was handwritten on what was now yellowed and crumbling paper with some parts missing and others barely legible. When Falletta also saw that the score was composed in a European style of music calligraphy, she knew it would take "a very long time to decipher."

Acknowledging how busy she was with conducting two orchestras, her better judgment might have been commanding her to say "no," but her heart overrode it. Falletta said, "There was something very compelling about Henry's love for this composer and about the mystery of this music too.... So I agreed to take this shopping bag filled with original manuscripts, and I spent a long time over the next few months trying to decipher [them]." So what was the outcome of the mysterious scores? Once deeply immersed in the project, Falletta discovered several reasons for feeling compelled to promote Tyberg's work. In addition to honoring Henry Mihich's request, she discovered that Tyberg, like herself, was exceptionally skilled at blending different types of music. In much the same way that she continues to combine classical and contemporary music, Tyberg had mixed music from two different worlds—by taking parts from the older music of the 19th century and integrating it with the 20th-century music of his time.

With the help of Naxos, the largest classical music label, and assistance from people at the Foundation for Jewish Philanthropies, Falletta ultimately succeeded in deciphering one of Tyberg's works and getting it out to the world. In 2008, she conducted the world premiere of Tyberg's Symphony #3—more than 60 years after he had composed this piece and entrusted this score and others to the Mihich family for safekeeping. His Symphony #3, an incredibly complex piece composed for a large orchestra, is now available in CD format, and people at Naxos, who have seen the value of Tyberg's work, are currently in the process of deciphering his other compositions.

What does the Marcel Tyberg story tell us about JoAnn Falletta—not only as a person but also as a leader who has established herself as a prominent innovator? (For more information about the recovery of Marcel Tyberg's work, also see the 2014 YouTube video "Giving Voice to a Lost Composer: JoAnn Falletta Explores Tyberg.")

Head and Heart Leadership

In a section of this chapter entitled "The Power of Inquiry," I describe how effective leaders operate inside their authentic curiosity. I also compare a mindset of curiosity to one that is judgmental. What would have happened if JoAnn Falletta had been put off by, or had given into conventional thinking about the senior man outside her dressing room, sopping wet and holding a large shopping bag? She, instead, chose a mindset of curiosity over a judgmental mindset. The speed at which she was able to do this, and her willingness to listen nonjudgmentally to Henry Mihich's story, is an indication that Falletta, like other very special leaders, had likely developed this skill after years of intention and practice. Then again, it may have come naturally to her.

An October 6, 2011 *Belfast Telegraph* article quotes JoAnn Falletta as saying, "[Music is] about what the heart of the composer is saying to the heart of the listener. It's about the human element behind the technical artistry. At its core, music is all about people and touching those people." (See the *Belfast Telegraph* article entitled "At its Core, Music is All about People and Touching Those People.") In this chapter, you'll learn more about JoAnn Falletta through detailed accounts of her leadership ability as told by VSO board members, musicians, and others who have worked closely with her or who know her well. You'll see how she has created an organizational culture within the VSO that inspires and encourages systemic innovation. This is where the cultural conditions that foster innovation are firmly entrenched, and the trust levels high enough that people feel free to come forward and express ideas, and suggest better ways of operating, without any active solicitation from leaders.

Power, Authority, and Gravitas

In a video aired in 2012 on the WHRO TV show "What Matters," host Kathy Lewis celebrated Falletta's 20th anniversary with the VSO. In this video by Kim Wadsworth, it is evident how she captured detailed descriptions of Falletta's personal and leadership attributes. Some of the people featured in it view Falletta as a leader "with heart," who is "humble," "very warm-hearted," and "incredibly compassionate," "gifted," and "inspirational." Others see her as someone who has "a good head on her shoulders"—a strong leader who is "full of dynamism and confidence," "poised" yet "energetic," and "enthusiastic yet balanced." (Video "What Matters – JoAnn Falletta: 20 Years With the Virginia Symphony," posted to YouTube by WHRO TV in 2012.)

Michael Tilson Thomas, currently Music Director of the San Francisco Symphony, was once quoted as saying, "A conductor's authority rests on two things: the orchestra's confidence in the conductor's insightful knowledge of the whole score and the orchestra's faith in the conductor's good heart." If we view Tilson Thomas' quote as a recipe from which music directors lead and promote innovation, we can see how it requires the two essential ingredients associated with JoAnn Falletta's style: "head" and "heart." Leaders must have the "head," which symbolizes their technical competence and expertise as well as the "heart," which enables them to relate to and engage others.

Leaders who are self-aware and in touch with their emotions usually have an ability to remain composed in the face of complexity and uncertainty. JoAnn Falletta seems to have the heart to lead and the demeanor that can contribute to a leader's gracious impact in a turbulent world, but the kind of leadership that stimulates creativity and innovation calls for something more. Orchestra leaders must also be able to command authority, and that was something Falletta had to learn. While working with conductor Jorge Mester, she realized the importance of discontinuing the self-effacing ways in which she was dealing with musicians. In fact, Falletta had to work diligently to project the commanding presence that might come naturally to others on the podium. That effort would become one of the many factors that propelled her to where she is today.

The Grammy awards for Falletta's orchestras and many additional awards for her personal achievements reflect not only her technical expertise but also her ability to inspire exceptional performance. The measure of these qualities is in the results. Falletta helped two orchestras achieve increasingly greater prominence, particularly when many others throughout the United States were failing. She most likely didn't accomplish this solely through leadership by the heart, however. Leaders like JoAnn Falletta, who employ a "head-and-heart" leadership style, must be able to balance leadership from the heart with an uncompromising commitment to excellent performance and strategic focus.

An Exemplary Leader

In the Kim Wadsworth video of Falletta's 20th Anniversary celebration is a brief statement about Falletta from John Paul Lindberg, retired VSO Principal Timpanist who played for the orchestra for 46 years and also served as President of Local 125 of the American Federation of Musicians. Lindberg best describes Falletta by saying, "You'd have more luck striking gold in the Yukon tomorrow than you would to find another conductor that's comparable to JoAnn Falletta."

When profiling innovative orchestra leaders based on their unique capabilities and professional contributions, I chose Falletta as an exemplary role model and an ideal example of a leader who sets high standards of performance, inspires innovation, and possesses the attributes to introduce the changes that typically accompany innovation. Her depth of professional knowledge and her competence in these areas contribute to her excellent performance as both a conductor and a leader of innovation— on stage and off.

Before taking on her first leadership roles, Falletta earned an undergraduate degree from the Mannes College of Music in New York and subsequently completed her masters and doctorate degrees at the Juilliard School of Music. Upon graduation, she started an orchestra, the Jamaica Symphony (later called the Queens Symphony), and afterward conducted the Milwaukee Symphony Orchestra, the Denver Chamber Orchestra, and the Women's Philharmonic in San Francisco. She then became the music director of the Long Beach Symphony Orchestra in California. In addition to her current roles as the music director of the BPO and VSO, Falletta functioned as the principal guest conductor at the Brevard Music Center at Brevard College, North Carolina, and as Principal Conductor of the Ulster Orchestra and the Ulster Youth Orchestra in Northern Ireland. In August

2012 she led these two groups in a strong debut at the BBC's prestigious Proms, held annually in London.

Under JoAnn Falletta's leadership, the BPO and VSO have also risen to higher levels of prominence. The BPO won a double Grammy Award in 2009, became one of the most recorded orchestras in America, and gained recognition as one of the leading orchestras for the Naxos label. The Virginia Symphony Orchestra recordings also earned a double Grammy as well as other Grammy-nominated discs. The VSO has also been ranked among the top ten percent of professional orchestras in the United States and has made critically acclaimed debuts at the Kennedy Center and Carnegie Hall. Falletta is often invited to guest conduct many of the world's finest symphony orchestras. She has received many prestigious awards for conducting, including the Seaver/National Endowment for the Arts Conductors Award, Stokowski Competition, Toscanini Award, Ditson Award, and Bruno Walter Award for conducting. She also received the American Symphony Orchestra League's John S. Edwards award as well as 11 awards for creative programming from the American Society for Composers and Publishers (ASCAP).

Gender Barriers

Adding to the many challenges that most leaders face is the very thick glass ceiling for women, people of color, and those from other cultures. Inclusiveness remains as a unique but persistent barrier for female orchestra leaders like JoAnn Falletta. In an August 1999 article in *Living Prime Time* magazine titled, "JoAnn Falletta: Brings New Perspective to the Philharmonic," author Edward Yadzinski, a long-standing member of the Buffalo Philharmonic Orchestra, wrote about her BPO appointment. He said, "…One would think that by now the issue of gender should have been long settled and closed. After all, women on the concert stage are today no less likely than men to appear as featured soloists, whether the role is that of an instrumental virtuoso or as a diva on the operatic stage."

Yadzinski continues, "Likewise, the ranks of major symphony orchestras have long reflected an appropriate balance—on all instruments, there are as many women as men with tenured positions in various roles as principal or section players. Even in the world of symphony orchestra management, one finds a fair distribution of executive responsibility between both men and women at all levels. It seems that only the position of principal conductor has remained a domain apart—as if some mystic credo forbids genuine access to women." Unfortunately, not much has changed since his 1999 article.

When leading innovation, seeking and cultivating different perspectives are essential ingredients in achieving successful outcomes. During an interview by Emily Deroo, featured in the April 19, 2012 edition of the *Buffalo News* ("Bringing Music to the Western New York Community"), Falletta addressed gender issues and other diversity challenges that she had faced early in her career. She said, "I was very fortunate to start my professional conducting career at a time when gender issues were becoming increasingly less significant and noticeable. I have tremendous respect and admiration for the true pioneer women conductors—women who really struggled at a time when it was not...possible for them to be appreciated as fully as they should have been." Evident in this last statement is Falletta's humility because her path to becoming a world-renowned conductor and music leader was not without difficulties and gender barriers.

Authenticity

Even though she led the student orchestra at the Mannes School (at 18 years of age), Falletta needed to persevere there, to pursue a career in conducting. The Mannes School was concerned about the number of years that it would take to prepare for a conducting career as well as the unlikelihood of Falletta landing a job afterward. Although at first severely discouraged by this, Falletta was ultimately successful in convincing administrators at Mannes to approve her transfer to the conducting program. And after earning her bachelor's degree from Mannes, she also received a master of arts in orchestral conducting at Queens College. At Julliard, Falletta needed to persist once again to gain entry to the school's conducting program. As a result of her struggles at both Mannes and Juilliard, she demonstrates great sensitivity toward the challenges that women continue to experience in the world of symphony orchestra conducting.

Self-advocacy often develops the inner strength necessary to advocate for others. Successful leaders of innovation often demonstrate the kind of advocacy that JoAnn Falletta has when behaving like role models for those who aspire to take risks and advance. In a February 23, 2011 Naxos.com article, author Jeremy Siepmann describes Falletta as "a formidable activist, doing more for the cause of women than many a more strident colleague." (See "Women at Work—JoAnn Falletta Talks with Jeremy Siepmann.")

When Siepmann asked Falletta when she had decided to "take up arms against tradition," she humbly replied, "Oh I never did...I wanted to be a conductor when I was nine years old. And for years, I was quite unaware that women weren't 'supposed' to conduct...I think in a way my naïve attitude was very good. I went into the profession simply because I had to for sheer love of music. I certainly didn't do it to prove anything, to change anything." When leaders like Falletta behave in alignment with their authenticity, they contribute an essential ingredient to the executive presence that attracts followership. Employees then become inspired to trust and to follow these kinds of leaders.

The Leadership Challenge

In "The Compleat Music Director" (www.joannfalletta), Falletta writes, "Often the very survival of the institution will hinge on the skill of the maestro." Expanding on this, she explains that it's not only skills in conducting and musical talent, but also management acumen in planning and scheduling as well as interacting with staff and musicians, dealing with conflict, and fostering feelings of community, common purpose, and solidarity. Added to this list is the task of motivating people and the need to retain talent, particularly a new generation of employees with different needs and values. There's also the challenge when launching innovation strategies—whether incremental or disruptive—of adeptly addressing fear and resistance. To achieve success, leaders must be as skilled in coaching, mentoring, and managing performance as they are at planning, organizing, and scheduling. That often means addressing challenges at three levels: individual, group, and organizational.

Going far beyond their expertise in conducting, music directors of symphony orchestras must link the objectives of their organizations to possibilities and options that introduce an element of newness. At the same time, they must preserve successes of the past. Competing priorities and ever-increasing demands for higher quality can be difficult for managers in any sector. In the private sector, this often translates to speed in getting products and services to markets ahead of the competition. Leaders in all sectors must be skilled at working with both individuals and teams to build a shared vision and common purpose that creates a sense of community among critical stakeholders.

Inspiration is the key to engaging people to align with their organization's mission, vision, and purpose. Inspirational leaders involve key stakeholders in problem solving and decision-making, but even then, participation is often a challenge—particularly when working with people who might not share the same standards of excellence. Highly successful leaders such as Falletta don't let differences in standards get in the way of raising the bar on performance. They deliberately push followers to reach higher levels. Robert Cross, VSO Principal Percussion and Artistic Director for the Virginia Arts Festival, says about this, "JoAnn has this great way of…finding works that are challenging and new for the orchestra so they can continue to grow."

Old and New Approaches

Piggy-backing on Falletta's style of head-and-heart leadership, a blend of different approaches can be ideal for managing both a future focus and day-to-day processes. An excellent example occurred during the 1980s and 1990s when a few thought leaders intentionally exaggerated the differences between leaders and managers. In an attempt to elevate the discipline of leadership development they polarized two roles: "leaders" and "managers." With that distinction, they associated "leadership" with people and "management" with processes. Also, in this differentiation, managers became associated with compliance through "positional power" (i.e., their rank) and leaders were viewed as having "personal power" that enabled them to influence by inspiring, teaching, and coaching.

Predictably, these old distinctions between management and leadership placed managers on the back seat of the innovation bus. In the innovation domain, leaders were the strategists and managers were those who executed the strategy. When globalization, technological advances, and increased competition dictated organizational change on a large scale, leaders as characterized in this model, launched a battle against the status quo while managers fought to maintain current ways of doing things.

As the millennium approached, thought leaders combined the functions of managers and leaders. The combined roles under the title "leader" replaced that of "manager," with the notion that leaders needed to be managers and managers needed to be leaders. These same thought leaders defined the act of managing as that of building the foundation for organizational performance and success, and reinforced that base of support through the act of management. This meant specifically achieving goals and working through people to produce measurable and sustainable outcomes. By gaining a complete understanding of the responsibilities of individuals tasked with leading innovation, we can see how these old stereotypes need no longer create conflicts. For example, some leaders like to challenge the status quo, and others prefer to build on past successes. The volatile economic conditions and increased competition in today's markets dictate a need for both of these essential activities.

The Innovation Challenge

The innovation challenge takes on a wider scope than the leadership challenge. Most business leaders outside of the tech industry know that attracting funding for research and development or innovation projects can be a critical leadership challenge. In trying times, these activities can mean the difference between life and death for an organization, particularly if financial difficulties preclude innovation—the lifeblood of most organizations today. What are some of the specific innovation challenges that symphony orchestra leaders face in the 21st century? And what, besides securing and retaining the right talent, do leaders in various sectors and industries need to do today to build environments that support creativity and innovation?

Falletta views the way in which not-for-profit organizations in the United States must sustain themselves through donations as the most difficult part of her job. When music leaders lack adequate preparation for this challenge, the problem runs even deeper. In "The Compleat Music Director," she says, ""I am convinced that no one leaves the conservatory with more than the sketchiest idea of the meaning of the title music director." She adds, "It is the rare conductor who has significant marketing or development experience" when accepting a position with an orchestra. "Even rarer is the music director who will not spend…countless hours with…experts…analyzing, fund-raising, and reaching out to his community constituency."

Leaders in the private sector come up against an equally daunting challenge. It manifests in the way by which most organizations typically measure financial health: short-term views often based on quarterly earnings. For many leaders, the fundamental innovation challenge lies in getting their colleagues to take a long-term perspective and see innovation as an investment in their futures. Funding for innovation remains a persistent challenge for most leaders outside—and sometimes even inside—the tech industry.

Forward Focus and Design Mindsets

To achieve sustainable innovation, successful leaders often look backward (as Falletta did when retrieving valuable work from the past) and forward (as when she responded to the tastes of new audiences and added contemporary music to her repertoire). With all the responsibilities that support sustaining business as usual, the act of leading is very much about growing the future. Consequently, many leaders learn from the past and apply lessons to the present. To achieve future growth, leaders anticipate trends in the market and set a clear direction so that followers know what to do and how to set priorities.

That means visualizing the future, articulating it to others, and ensuring that employees share their organization's vision and commit to it. At the same time that leaders anticipate the future, they develop plans to leverage it for a competitive advantage in target markets. Visions often trigger innovation by inspiring ideas about what might be possible. When leaders put forth their concept of the future, they open new possibilities for their organizations and maximize their execution. Leaders must be able to create and execute multiple strategies. The competencies required to accomplish this include:

- Ensuring the support of people and processes
- Leveraging long-standing organizational capabilities and assets while adopting new approaches
- Tracking performance and analyzing gaps between what should be happening and what isn't
- Managing processes that support efficiency, effectiveness, and customer satisfaction
- Ensuring compliance with regulations and organizational rules
- Demonstrating a commitment to sustaining successful results

These essential behaviors ensure that customers and shareholders get what they expect on a consistent basis. To achieve this, leaders must also empower, coach, and hold their employees accountable. And to accomplish all this, it's essential that leaders attract and retain the right talent; value both hard and soft skills; and create a culture that supports innovation. They should also cultivate and maintain a design mindset—a way of thinking that continuously evolves and adapts to ever-changing environments. In this respect, leaders today must function as accomplished jazz musicians who aren't anchored by a score in the way that symphony orchestra musicians are. A design mindset plays out for leaders in three ways: long- and short-term focus, space to create, and strategies for incremental as well as disruptive innovation.

Long-Term and Short-Term Focus

Leaders must do more than merely *react* to today's challenges. They must also be proactive. To survive and thrive, they need to take both short- and long-term views in the same ways that JoAnn Falletta has done, to help her orchestras survive. By engaging in comprehensive strategic planning and keeping a pulse on their respective markets and constituencies, leaders remain acutely aware of potential challenges in both the near and distant future. Out of necessity, however, these leaders usually make major decisions from a "quarterly economics" perspective. That means focusing monomaniacally on how quarterly profits might be impacted by changes in their markets and by the decisions they make in response to them.

Leaders at companies like Amazon have done things differently. Crediting this organization's success to the various technologies that it employs, Amazon's leaders have been using a very different strategy since the company's inception. They've even created a new paradigm by continually reinvesting rather than merely focusing on short-term gains. They've also leveraged technology as a way to enter new markets and disrupt existing ones. Amazon's business model raises a question, however: "Can this strategy possibly be viable in the long term?" Most organizations have found that the right balance between short- and long-term strategies is the best assurance of sustainability. Time will tell whether Amazon will be able to reframe its financial management strategies in the same way that it has successfully introduced virtual operations to the marketplace and significantly undercut its many competitors.

Space to Create

Years ago, in the industrial age, leaders expected people to produce with machine-like efficiency, relying extensively on data to measure the productivity of their human resources. From this came piecework and time-and-motion studies in manufacturing environments. Today, executives are taking a different tack—and they need to. Currently, workers bring a new perspective about work output—to find meaning in what they do. Instead of being focused on the quantity of work that people could produce, as their predecessors were, leaders are responding to employees' needs to express themselves through quality work that's driven by creativity and innovation. As an example from the symphony orchestra, Principal Flute of the VSO, Debra Wendells Cross, said about JoAnn Falletta: "She's very fluid, and she allows us the freedom to have our own voice."

Freedom and space to create are imperatives in motivating and retaining a new generation of talent. Progressive organizations in the private sector, such as Google, and those in the public sector, such as the US Army, realized this when they created "white space." What is white space? Leaders at Google and the US Army view it as open discussion forums in which employees can talk to one another informally and exchange ideas. They also see white space as unstructured time in which people can explore areas of professional interest.

Famous for their company's "20% Time" (later called "Google Time"), Google's leaders encourage employees to devote 20 percent of their time to projects of their choice. Google Time also allows people to explore options independently rather than waiting for approval from company leaders. Besides encouraging active involvement on the part of employees, leaders at this company enable them to gather information and conduct detailed market analysis, saving time typically spent in additional approval processes. Although Google's leaders established 20% Time years ago, they still credit many of the company's key innovations to this enduring strategy.

Disruptive and Incremental Strategies

Although there is much emphasis today on disruptive innovation, JoAnn Falletta says in The Compleat Music Director, "...Orchestras do not develop through the splashy applause of concert nights...[they] develop slowly—through every valuable minute of rehearsal, through every score we choose, through every audition we hold." Some companies in the private sector have also developed in this way. Toyota and Honda achieved significant growth by successfully implementing a business strategy they call *kaizen*, which calls for incremental changes and a particular focus on improvements in quality and efficiency. Through *kaizen*, these companies made small changes that ultimately allowed them to disrupt the well-established American auto industry.

Kaizen has also proven useful for driving internal innovation, specifically process improvement that can enhance day-to-day operations. In addition to ensuring functional effectiveness in operational productivity and efficiency, *kaizen* can improve the functionality of enabling functions such as human resources, finance and accounting, and legal. Because it isn't practical for organizations to reinvent everything on an ongoing basis, *kaizen* plays a significant role in most innovation portfolios. With today's business climate being what it is, however, most leaders can't succeed entirely with a *kaizen* mindset. In most organizations today, business strategy reflects this with its shift from small, *kaizen*-like improvements to approaches that have the potential for disrupting the way entire games are played. Good examples of this are companies such as Netflix and Zappos, which have significantly challenged established competitors, and indirectly invited others to replicate their strategies.

Are there some disadvantages to employing a disruptive innovation strategy? Disruption typically entails more risk and requires significantly more resources than those needed for incremental change. In addition to their high cost, disruptive innovation strategies can be a frightening proposition for both leaders and employees because people instinctively know that this form of innovation tends to produce significant change. The fear that accompanies disruption is why most executives prefer incremental innovation. Despite the cost and risk of disruptive innovation strategies, however, they must be included in most innovation portfolios if organizations are to grow and keep pace with competitors.

A Model for Innovative Leadership

An active leadership-followership partnership creates the right environment for innovation. In the chapter *Inspiring and Encouraging Innovation*, we learn that this kind of collaboration is essential at every stage of the innovation process—from idea generation to execution. Most of us sense that command-and-control methods don't work well with today's followers, particularly artistic staff and a new generation of employees. Most successful leaders use them only temporarily, with those who are new in their roles. So how might leaders achieve a leadership-followership partnership that fits well with today's workforce?

Michael Tilson Thomas, Creative Director of the San Francisco Orchestra, illustrates a method that he uses with this metaphor: "Old-school conductors liked to hold the lead in their hands at all times. I do not. Sometimes I lead. Other times I'll say, 'Listen to one another and find your way.'" How might leaders in all sectors and industries replicate Tilson Thomas' approach and use it as a foundation for creative and innovative thinking? What else might they do to create an environment that fosters sustainable innovation?

Shaping, Stimulating and Supporting Innovation

Based on over 35 years of experience as a leader and consultant, I believe there's an effective leadership model for daily operations and for sustainable innovation that works well for leaders, regardless of their experience level. This leadership framework is also very useful for managing the change that inevitably accompanies innovation. Consisting of three distinct and often overlooked intentions, the goal of this model is to shape, stimulate, and support innovation. These distinctions are each described in detail in the following three subsections of this introductory chapter.

▓ ▓ ▓

1. Shaping Innovation

To successfully shape innovation, leaders must first look strategically at the external landscape, as Joann Falletta did, when she saw the need to blend classical with contemporary music. Leaders like her must take into consideration market forces that determine the value that their organizations bring to the marketplace. Many problems require delving into root causes. An important habit of mind for shaping innovation is to see the whole system. This practice requires leaders to notice recurring patterns, attractors, and factors that can seem entangled until they detect the connections. Leaders who can see the whole system, and hold opposing ideas without the need to reconcile them, can shift from either/or thinking to choosing several possible solutions and experimenting with a few in a small way.

Leaders also shape innovation by creating structure, taking long-term views, and allowing time and space for creative thinking and idea generation. These three leadership actions significantly enable the collaboration and experimentation that's necessary to meet future challenges through innovative thinking. In a similar way to how orchestra leaders encourage ongoing excellence, so too must leaders in business settings. They must shape the right mindset for others by providing structural, developmental, and social support. And before leaders can accomplish this, they must secure the right resources—including talent with the right skill sets and behaviors.

The Right Talent

Business leaders and orchestra leaders alike are dependent on top performers. In fact, a very critical way in which leaders shape innovation is by bringing in people with the right kind of perspectives and skill sets. When doing this, they create balance and build the necessary capabilities. By recruiting the best talent, they can deploy the right people in the right roles at the right time. At the idea generation stage of the innovation process, it's imperative for leaders to gain the buy-in, sponsorship, and commitment necessary for investing in new ideas and approaches. Then they must continually develop talent at all stages, from idea generation to implementation.

To achieve innovation breakthroughs, leaders must have access to intellectual energy and be capable of divergent thinking. To evaluate their current direction and continually stay ahead of the competition, many leaders today are making changes to existing recruiting profiles. They're deliberately hiring a broad range of people with varying strengths and personal characteristics such as focus, perseverance, courage, and tenacity—important factors in shaping innovation. Of course, new hiring practices also require leaders to appreciate, recognize, and reward these new skills sets and behaviors.

Historically, a company's view of an ideal hire was someone who had broad practical experience as well as knowledge of the industry. While in the past that was usually an internal candidate, leaders eventually found themselves limited by hiring only from within, especially when this tended to recycle old ideas and perpetuate the status quo. A common strategy now is to partner with research organizations, universities, and other sources of intellectual energy that can be imported and developed. This practice prompted leaders at progressive companies such as Apple to take another tack. By recruiting individuals from outside the company's industry, these leaders could rely on new employees to infuse new ideas and also challenge current thinking and established business practices.

Hard and Soft Skills

Another limitation of past hiring practices was the tendency to recruit only people with strong technical skills. Today we see some new trends, the most prominent of which are changes in the admissions policies of medical schools. At one time these schools only accepted applicants with hard science backgrounds, yet when graduates began practicing as physicians, they were often unable to relate effectively to people, including patients.

Knowing this, administrators in medical schools began to accept liberal arts applicants in addition to those with backgrounds in the hard sciences. In fact, today, one school even mandates that once admitted, students must visit art museums to understand what various artists are attempting to communicate through their work. The goal is to produce physicians with both technical and soft skills who can relate to patients' human conditions as well as their medical issues. How might leaders also apply this practice in the public and private sectors?

Many organizations today are attempting to attract talent with both soft skills and hard skills, such as those taught in STEM education, with its focus on science, technology, engineering, and math. Attracting and recruiting talent must then be followed by intentional onboarding practices and attention to retaining employees with required skill sets and leveraging their abilities and efforts. Leaders, like employees, need both the technical and administrative (hard) skills and emotional and relationship intelligence (soft) skills. One way to ensure that employees learn them is by having them engage in dialogues that stimulate new ways of thinking and operating. When leaders teach employees how to communicate, such as by skillfully and strategically asking questions, listening, and sharing ideas, they promote employees' abilities to influence through participation in problem-solving and decision-making.

A Culture of Innovation

The way business gets done is heavily influenced by an organization's culture, which consists of the attitudes, values, and habits expressed through its norms or unwritten rules of behavior. In some cultures, the "crisis du jour" mentality sometimes naturally occurs and is a compelling factor for employees who persist in adhering to familiar ways of working. Skilled leaders counter this by listening, asking questions of themselves and others, and exploring creative ideas. These practices are critical elements in creating a culture of innovation and also in establishing leadership credibility. In fact, one might define a mindset of curiosity as one of the most challenging, yet valuable, aspects of sustainable innovation.

To co-generate win-win solutions with employees, leaders must, on a daily basis, help create and model constant dialogue. This is how they match actions and decisions to the standards professed in vision and value statements. Since the most skilled leaders "ask" more than "tell," they model and elevate the ability to ask questions skillfully, and in so doing, they strategically build leadership skills in others. To create a culture around innovation, leaders must identify the current practices and behaviors that yield rewards as well as practices that serve as obstacles to innovation. Since people tend to behave according to what's rewarded, leaders must then identify normative behaviors and ask, "What is the prevailing success model in the organization?"

To sustain an innovative culture, leaders must also focus on the practices that their organizations will need in the future, such as those which connect to the vision and strategy. This type of ongoing examination ensures the behaviors that are necessary to achieve innovation goals and objectives, such as growth plans. It also establishes a common language and clear expectations for practices needed across the organization. If the stated vision and policies are at odds with what gets rewarded through both formal and informal means, employees will do what yields success. Since innovation and change typically require risk taking, it's reinforcing to show appreciation to people when they experiment and learn from failure. Leaders should also recognize employees when they advocate for something that they believe is important and when they achieve something great in the face of obstacles such as skepticism and resistance.

On a final note, the value of new thinking and new behavior is immeasurable, and most innovations result from diverse (heterogeneous) teams. However, human beings are hard-wired to intuit whether another person is a friend or foe, so we tend to favor collaboration with others we trust. Leaders must keep in mind that diversity can also run counter to existing cultural norms, creating new tensions that require skills in change management. Human resources professionals must actively engage leaders in diversity efforts, and in addition to performing simple transactional work, must function as teams of internal consultants, supporting all members of their organizations in creating a culture of innovation that values and embraces diversity.

Trust and Safety

The level of trust is also a potent factor in creating an environment that fosters and sustains innovation. If employees don't feel safe enough to take risks and experiment with the new behaviors that support organizational goals, then the chances of introducing innovation will be slim to none. When attempting to build trust, leaders must be willing to listen deeply for what may underlie employees' requests or demands. For example, these might include issues arising from complaints, work commitments that have made work-life balance difficult, and processes experienced as unwieldy. Leaders must help create and model dialogue on a daily basis, and cogenerate win-win solutions with employees.

Risk tolerance is also an essential element that drives innovation. Successful leaders help employees summon courage for new tasks and develop new behaviors or skill sets by tapping into the principles to which they're most committed. Another way in which leaders help employees build risk tolerance is when they create effective risk management strategies and establish guidelines and guardrails for employees. Creating psychological safety in an organization's culture makes it easier for employees to raise potential risks and discover mitigation strategies before any possible disasters can occur. Leaders of innovation reinforce risk tolerance by recognizing and rewarding people who exhibit trust, take calculated risks, and demonstrate a willingness to continue innovating.

■ ■ ■

2. Stimulating Innovation

What might business leaders learn from the ways in which orchestra conductors encourage imagination and innovation with their artistic staff? In "The Compleat Music Director," JoAnn Falletta said, "The technical and personal communication skills required on the podium are enormous...any conductor who does not fully devote himself to the constant development of his musical understanding is failing to recognize the single most significant requirement of his profession...then secondary to the depth of one's musical aptitude is the *communication* of that knowledge."

Leading from the inside out, Falletta's opinions about professional growth illustrate the importance of one's mindset to being a learning leader while also attending to the development of others. It's important for leaders to keep learning, stay current, and share knowledge through means that include teaching and coaching. The *Belfast Telegraph* article previously cited quotes Falletta as saying, "...I love working in different places around the world. If I stayed in the one place, I wouldn't keep learning so much. There are such riches out there and discovering them helps me grow as a musician. When I learn new music, it changes me."

Equally important for leaders wishing to innovate is the act of initiating conversations that stimulate new thinking. When they do this, they manage the creative energy that helps shape an innovation culture and helps employees see that they're assets worthy of an investment of time and energy. Beverly Kane Baker, Principal Viola of the VSO said about Falletta's contributions, "To have wonderful music played, you must make sure that your musicians feel good about themselves—and feel good about what they are doing...she is a master at that." What follows are several other ways in which leaders can stimulate innovation.

Meaningful and Inspiring Visions

Just watch the faces of members of an audience when they're responding to a powerful musical performance to witness how leaders might stimulate their employees to innovate. What we don't see in a musical performance is how each person is drawing from his or her interpretations based on life experience, memories, preferences, and dreams. Despite that, we know that inspiration is powerful. A shared vision is equally compelling. Why? Because leaders help people offset their fear of change and uncertain futures by jointly creating a picture of a better tomorrow.

Communication of shared visions and values is critical for inspiring high performance at the individual, team, and organizational levels. Two-way communication ensures alignment between employees' goals and ambitions and strategic agendas. As human beings, we all "make meaning," and since all meaning is socially constructed, leaders can be a powerful force in creating it. On the whole, leaders want their people to experience a feeling or have a dream because these are what help to overcome fear and what will ultimately endure. We've probably all watched leaders stimulate people when speaking passionately about their missions and visions as well as what personally moves them.

Leaders can also encourage employees and other critical stakeholders by helping them see how their unique roles contribute to the organization's mission and vision. To be sufficiently stimulated to innovate, people benefit from frequent communication about how the work they're doing connects to a greater good. Then they can relate the importance of their roles in the ways in which their work makes a significant difference. Examples of meaningful activities or outputs might include clear and accurate information for enhanced decision making, help in cures for diseases, or products and services that improve people's quality of life in general.

Author and educator Jim Kouzes shares that leaders must also be able to show how an innovation itself has value and can be brought about in meaningful ways. In our interview for this book, he said, "People don't think of life in statistics or metrics." Kouzes believes that the ways in which leaders communicate with employees reflect the meaning of desired innovations. What employees tell themselves about their roles, responsibilities, and goals concerning certain innovations is of equal importance. When people commit to a shared vision collectively, they often feel a part of something larger than themselves—and that's what creates synergy.

Italics and Punctuation

Orchestra conductors are no doubt among the most visible leaders, regardless of their sectors or industries. After all, what other leaders stand on podiums so every individual within their sphere of influence can see them? Restricted in their ability to communicate orally, conductors can only convey their intentions through their batons, their hands, their facial expressions and their entire bodies. That means they can only affect others' behavior nonverbally through signals.

These gestures are among the few ways in which conductors must achieve alignment among musicians, and they're most visible to their audiences. In a November 9, 2016 article "Conducting Power," author Mus'ab Abdalla references a study conducted in 2012 that's cited in the November 26, 2012

NPR article, "Do Orchestras Really Need Conductors?" (at www.npr.org). Abdalla describes how Yiannis Aloimonos, of the University of Maryland, and several colleagues enlisted orchestral players from Ferrara, Italy to answer the question contained within this article. Infrared lights and cameras were used to determine whether a conductor's movements influenced musicians or musicians influenced the conductor. Using mathematical techniques originally designed by Nobel Prize-winning economist Clive Granger, computers were used to analyze the patterns of the infrared signals.

What was the outcome of this study? It revealed that the movement of the conductors is the real influencer of control. Also, when this study compared a veteran conductor with an amateur, the skill of the more experienced conductor produced superior music to the amateur's as determined by music experts who only heard the music, rather than seeing who was conducting it. This small study would seem to confirm the power of a conductor's nonverbal communication because while on stage, they aren't able to communicate in the same way that other leaders do, or in the ways in which they might when directing offstage. (To access Mus'ab Abdalla's article go to sites.psu.edu/leadership/2016/11/09/conducting-power.)

Through only body movements and other nonverbal communications, conductors signal when particular instruments must come into play. They do this while also establishing the mood and timing in the performance. Michael Daniels, Principal Cello of the VSO says about JoAnn Falletta's ability to set the mood, "One of the things that is magical, I think, is that she's able to draw all the musicians into what she is feeling at the time when she's conducting." Given the uncertainty associated with experimentation and charting new ground, employees look to leaders for signals and for manifestations of both behavior and mood that indicate whether they're well supported—or not.

Signals and Other Motivators

What can leaders learn from orchestra conductors about the power of nonverbal communication? James Levine, Music Director of the Metropolitan Opera with leadership positions at the Ravinia Festival, the Munich Philharmonic, and the Boston Symphony Orchestra, provided reassurance concerning signals. He did so with his famous statement: "Great cataclysmic things can go by, and neither the orchestra nor the conductor is under the delusion that whether they make this or that gesture is going to be the deciding factor in how it comes out." However, the late Cleveland Orchestra leader, George Szell would profoundly disagree with this. Known as a "literalist"—a conductor who follows the composer's score to the letter—Szell said, "Conductors must give unmistakable and suggestive signals to the orchestra."

David Wick, former Principal Horn of the VSO, said about JoAnn Falletta, "What I react to most is the expression we see on her face. She's able to communicate the emotional content of the music, and she's not doing it in a choreographed kind of way. Some conductors sort of plan ahead what they're going to do, and when they're going to look at the audience. This is all coming straight from her heart, and it's very infectious." Leaders are communicating almost all the time, whether on stage or not, and consciously aware or not. This communication occurs when followers interpret nonverbal communication, as well as action or non-action, as signals. Followers also attribute meaning to a leader's nonverbal messages when they share their perceptions with others. For this reason, effective leaders in almost all environments benefit by consciously giving clear and unambiguous signals. They also provide the necessary vision and structure while still allowing their partners latitude in expression.

Keep in mind that although signals enable leaders to exercise their authority, neither employees nor musicians are likely to tolerate dictatorships today. Neuroscience studies have confirmed that human brains are hardwired to see the lack of autonomy as a threat. People feel safer with the ability to make choices. Consequently, leaders must stimulate with signals that strike the right balance between structure and freedom. How else might they also communicate in actions as well as words?

I've seen managers use the "symbolic act" as a clear signal. A Johnson & Johnson executive who I greatly admired employed this strategy when he took on a new leadership role in Corporate Administration. This leader questioned a long-standing unpopular policy that allocated all award travel mileage to the company. By subsequently changing the system to assign award miles back to the traveler, he sent a strong signal. Without words, he showed that he could listen and act in the best interest of hardworking employees who had to travel for work. Leaders like this one engage in symbolic acts when they clearly and thoroughly communicate plans, visions, and goals while simultaneously encouraging people to challenge the status quo and question long-held assumptions. One way that leaders can do this effectively is the way in which they seek out and obtain the answers to questions.

The Power of Inquiry

Most successful innovators would tell us that the innovation journey is often complicated. When stimulating innovation, two habits can help leaders. The first is asking questions that open up new possibilities in thinking. The second is taking multiple perspectives. When leaders try out the point of view of someone whose ideas are usually dismissed, they can learn and bring about value from the diversity of thought. For example, when a question asked inside an old model can only be answered from outside it, a paradigm shift occurs. In the same sense, innovation—in processes, products, or services—can represent a response to a new question or to an old question asked in a new way. That's why innovative leaders thrive on inquiry.

Innovators often search for new questions and new answers because they know that if they keep asking the same questions, they'll keep getting the same old answers. To produce a new response, and potentially create a different future than expected, one must ask a new question. The juncture at which a new inquiry opens up a new path often occurs at the very moment that it's asked. The difference between leaders who are innovative and those who aren't depends in large part, on the way in which they ask questions of themselves and others. Because of that, no question exists apart from its delivery.

Just as important is the way that leaders deliver a query and their intention because this can speak louder than any words. Whether they ask questions of themselves or others, leaders' inquiries can come across as requests, invitations, or missiles. Those who are skilled in the art of questioning deliver questions in a constructive manner rather than as attempts to intimidate, criticize, or show how much they know. Effective leaders such as JoAnn Falletta operate inside their authentic curiosity. To further clarify, the salient differences between a mindset of curiosity and one that is judgmental include a person's flexibility, respect for another's point of view, and ability to operate in a resolution seeking mode. Since a mindset is a coherent set of attitudes, the power of leadership resides in the capacity to observe and choose a particular mindset from which to operate, strengthening a mindset of curiosity while taming a judgmental one.

Leaders demonstrate presence, vulnerability, and authenticity when they ask provocative questions and engage with others in a transparent manner predicated on integrity. This conscious choice is a discipline that becomes easier with intention, practice, and reinforcement. For JoAnn Falletta, it resulted in the recovery of Marcel Tyberg's Symphony #3, which was one of the most exciting projects for the Buffalo Philharmonic Orchestra—and no doubt one of the most soul-satisfying personal outcomes of her many years of hard work.

Strategic Communication

Because many orchestra leaders also lead employees in addition to musicians, they have a broader range of responsibilities than do conductors. Therefore, like leaders in business environments, they must be skilled at nonverbal, oral, and written communication. Most leaders find it difficult, if not impossible, to stimulate engagement and connection through speeches and one-way communication tools such as PowerPoint presentations. Instead, they rely on strategic narratives, or storytelling, as powerful tools for communicating their authenticity and energy as well as the content of their messages. Stories can also convey leaders' emotions, help people remember essential ideas, and in other situations, cause them to take action. When establishing the context for messages, leaders can also use stories to incorporate their unique experiences and learnings.

Strategic narratives are also a moving force in creating emotional connections with people, so when leaders speak in authentic ways, they can use a powerful motivating force. In this way, stories can also create meaning. When well communicated, messages can also raise the level of engagement necessary to take on risk and overcome a variety of obstacles. And since storytelling is highly personal, we can all—with some good material and a certain degree of practice—become compelling storytellers.

Two-Way Communication

As powerful as storytelling can be, we know that leaders need to do more than telling. They also need to listen. Just as important, leaders shouldn't feel they're held hostage to what they hear when they solicit input from others. Effective communicators are respectful of their audiences without feeling bound by them. In other words, they actively listen to what's being said without feeling the need to agree or take action about suggestions.

In much the same way that orchestra conductors interpret the work of composers from their musical scores, business leaders must be able to understand and translate their organizations' missions, visions, and values. They must also communicate them in ways that help their employees carry out goals and strategies, solve problems, and overcome obstacles in the process. For example, when helping employees overcome obstacles, leaders can facilitate conversations with people by using a central idea to open up thinking and solicit ideas for overcoming obstacles. Leaders who do this well find it especially valuable when participants in these conversations also commit to new behaviors that will enable them to translate ideas into actions.

To accomplish this, leaders must provide details about expected deliverables and be explicit and precise about specific roles, tasks, and responsibilities. They also need to ensure that others hear their messages. However, when leaders attempt to stimulate creativity and innovation, they need to do more than communicating compelling visions or engaging in two-way communication. Conscious communication that builds trust is vital for building strong partnerships and for leaders to function as sponsors and coaches. Then leaders can inspire and motivate by illustrating what might be possible while continually aligning employees' goals and ambitions with their organization's agenda.

■ ■ ■

3. Supporting Innovation

Leaders must provide support to their followers through skills and competency assessment and then through developmental efforts that often include coaching and mentoring. They also encourage innovation through their sponsorship of specific initiatives and by recognizing and rewarding their employees' efforts to achieve agreed-upon targets.

Sponsorship

Beverly Kane Baker, VSO Principal Viola, said about JoAnn Falletta, "She came on board and...built us up. She challenged us musically, which was wonderful, but she also nurtured our musical soul." Sponsorship support is vital to this type of nurturance, and so is validation and praise for work well done. This kind of assistance can mitigate the threat response that many employees experience in the face of change, such as that related to uncertainty, status changes, shifts in relationships, changes in levels of autonomy, and perceptions of what's fair or unfair.

Sponsorship is evident by how conductors respond when people in the audience applaud their efforts at the end of performances. Those who effectively sponsor others share in the applause by turning to their musicians and signaling them to bow. The most successful orchestra conductors and business leaders today use an egalitarian leadership style that's consistent with the current workforce. These leaders know that without employees, there would be no organizations, and without musicians, no one would hear the music.

Successful leaders of innovation like JoAnn Falletta understand how important it is to build and sustain partnerships with their employees and with all other key stakeholders. They also know that sponsoring their efforts and continuing to provide support is just as critical. Sponsorship shouldn't be viewed as a blank check, however. Leaders must hold people accountable for results by rewarding high performers and also by taking timely corrective action with those who aren't meeting goals and objectives.

Leadership Assessment and Development

Employee partnerships are essential for generating the proverbial spark that leads to innovation. The entire innovation process—from idea generation to execution—is based on leaders' commitments to followers, as well as their dedication to evolving themselves as leaders. This process ideally begins with formal and accurate skills assessments and continues with both structured and informal development efforts. As a way to move development beyond classrooms and coaching, leaders frequently assign people to meaningful projects that require the application of newly acquired skills and experience. Applying new skills generates confidence and competence with new practices and habits.

Leaders demonstrate commitment most effectively when they sponsor initiatives that develop employees. Through formal coursework, coaching, and on-the-job training, leaders can strengthen their benches with potential skilled replacements at the same time that they help people close skill and competency gaps. And because research has proven that learning is more powerful when it's experiential, leadership best practice is to also include special projects, international assignments, volunteer roles on boards, and other developmental initiatives in a potential leader's development plan.

When leaders create a deep "innovation bench," they also optimize employee retention. Building and—equally important—sustaining innovation requires an effort to expand capacity. While leaders create a lineup of both current and potential internal candidates, they also develop and support their organization's innovation potential and capabilities. Here's a warning about a common mistake that's easily made, however, when formulating training and development initiatives. Leaders sometimes predicate new projects on the competencies needed to address the existing business—and business as usual—rather than anticipating skills necessary for the future.

When leaders look at development as the foundation for both current and emerging competencies, they ensure sufficient preparation of high potentials. And when leaders link skills requirements to both present and future strategies, there's another benefit: This linkage often becomes aspirational and possesses the power to engage employees as they develop the required skills and experience, based on the direction of the organization.

Change Management

Successful leaders don't only look inward at their employees and the various functions that need to work together seamlessly for innovation to occur. They continuously look outward, at the always-evolving requirements of the market, converging trends, and new technologies. Changes in the market can lead to innovations and new processes, both internal and external. Because innovation invariably brings about change, leaders must be especially skilled at initiating and managing it. With this in mind, how do successful leaders overcome the fear and resistance that go hand-in-hand with many innovation initiatives?

Effective leaders build and reward flexibility and courage while helping employees manage organizational change. They accept the human impulse to retrench in the face of uncertainty. They're also intentional about engaging with others and sensitive to their perceptions and emotions. This way of engaging requires self-awareness as well as an understanding of others and their needs. During times of change, leaders with these qualities can be a stabilizing force and anchor for followers. Consider what VSO Principal Oboe Sherri Lake Aquirre once said about JoAnn Falletta: "She has become our lifeline. When [she's been away and] comes to the podium, there's a global sigh. Ahhhh, JoAnn's back."

One way in which leaders can manage change effectively is by making a clear distinction between the predictable and the unpredictable, and communicating that difference to employees. Then it's easier to determine the optimal response and elicit support for it. In predictable environments, cause and effect can be seen, analyzed, and handled through sound decision-making, expertise, and the application of best practices. However, when the causal relationship is unpredictable, leaders must continually scan, experiment, and learn through trial and error methods. When leaders help employees examine what may be at risk for them personally, and assist them in facing what might be lost by the new reality, they can assess people's concerns accurately and find options to help them adapt to change.

Another way in which leaders take some of the fear out of change is by involving employees in the change process. That means inviting their thoughts and suggestions and facilitating creative problem solving and decision-making. By encouraging people to suggest changes of their own, no matter how small, leaders can increase people's risk tolerance. And during times of change, when things are already in flux, it's a best practice to encourage employees to challenge long-held assumptions and question the status quo. When leaders see all this with an eye to what's possible for themselves and their stakeholders, they can also create shared visions that illustrate what success might look like for everyone—and then help mobilize people to achieve it.

Culture Transformation

When an existing culture doesn't support change, leaders must transform it. Change often forces a rethinking about how an organization must operate. In conscious transformational change, leaders intentionally choose to help people develop and function effectively and efficiently. Because every transformational change effort is a pioneering effort, no one can accurately predict the organization's path—or how long it will take to get where it needs to go—only that it has embarked on a journey that is vital to its survival and growth. The strategic planning process typically requires leaders to proactively seek and incorporate all relevant information from entities and forces that may have an impact on the organization's ability to succeed. So when planning, leaders should consider the needs and impact of principal subcontractors and suppliers as well as employees and other internal stakeholders.

To effect culture change, leaders must also define, model, and reward new norms and behaviors. Additionally, they must be prepared to address negative behaviors when they emerge, especially those with the potential to dismantle the infrastructure that's being created to change the organization's culture. Leaders can prevent some problems by highlighting new and positive behaviors and by showing how they will bring about success in conducting business. To do this, many craft a "leadership ideal"—a model to which others can also aspire. A primary goal might be the empowerment and mobilization of employees. Another might be a sense of urgency. However well intended, many culture transformation efforts can stall due to current agendas that hijack people's focus on the future, so leaders must engage in ongoing efforts to stay the course.

Regularly revisiting plans and goals is one way of staying on track. However, continual review and examination can be among the toughest disciplines for any organization. If leaders don't sustain a focus on the future, and what's needed in the present to get there, constituents can assume that proposed changes are simply part of a temporary initiative that will quickly come and go. Their hope might even be that everything will then return to normal. Often employees try to "wait out" new initiatives with the hope that they can eventually go back to what was comfortable and familiar, even if it was a way of doing business that they didn't enjoy very much.

Communication and Change

Culture transformation efforts also demand that leaders tell the truth at all times. That means being very careful not to overstate successes or over-exaggerate problems and obstacles. While negative messages can dampen enthusiasm, positioning everything with a favorable spin can undermine the credibility of leaders and jeopardize an entire culture change effort. In addition to communicating honestly, leaders must also do so frequently. Although it can be difficult to repeat the same messages about commitment to the vision and its connection to the evolving change, unless leaders regularly reiterate that message and give plans keen attention, commitment will wither. Then momentum can slow or come to a complete halt.

Communication in the midst of a culture transformation effort should frequently include simple messages that are consistent with new values and attitudes. It's also essential that leaders recognize and reward the people who function as champions of change and change agents. Being out in front as they so often are, these employees can feel lonely, and at risk, so they usually need support from leaders who can recognize and appreciate their vulnerable positions.

■　■　■

Exemplary Leadership

In their book, *Credibility: How Leaders Gain and Lose It, Why People Demand It*, Jim Kouzes and Barry Posner wrote about a then-new Johnson & Johnson start-up created in the early 1990s called Ortho Biotech Inc. The authors' particular focus was on the management board's attempts to shape Ortho Biotech's culture to support the contributions of its diverse constituencies. One of the many challenges for leaders at this J&J start-up was to convince skeptical physicians of the efficacy of its product and to ensure that insurance companies would add the new drug to their lists of approved medications. I had the privilege of serving on this company's management board.

In a February 21, 1994 cover article in *Fortune* magazine, reporters John Huey and Richard Sookdeo also referenced the work of this J&J start-up. Their article, "The New Post-Heroic Leadership," begins with a Chinese proverb that holds, "Of the best leader, when he is gone, they will say: 'We did it ourselves.'" This idea represented my thinking and that of my peers when we took on the challenge of building an intentional culture. Huey and Sookdeo also said, "Increasingly, the crucial challenge facing the would-be post-heroic leader is less about how to structure a company than about how to get people who are truly not like you, or even one another, to pull in the same direction..."

During our culture transformation process, we encountered two potential barriers that could have derailed our efforts had we not addressed them early on. One regarded the way in which the parent corporation previously rewarded most managers for facilitating quick action by telling people what to do. In Ortho Biotech's early days, some managers were still explaining, defending, or attempting to solve problems without listening to employees' input or ideas. The second potential barrier concerned leaders' reactions to employees who were demonstrating new behaviors that supported the organization's desired culture. Because culture changes demand focus and effort, these leaders were concerned that employees might be spending too much time on the culture change process instead of their "real" responsibilities.

For our start-up operation to succeed, we would need to ensure alignment, mutual respect, collaboration, and a balance of creativity and rigor. Since most of Ortho Biotech's leaders, and many of its employees, had previously worked for the parent company, it would also be necessary to develop a new culture by intention that would force a shift from an organizational culture that people knew and with which they were comfortable. To facilitate that change, we as senior leaders needed to build a distinctive internal culture with a foundation of common purpose and shared values.

Collaboration and Culture Transformation

To turn insights into new strategies for marketing and selling our product, we would have to reshape our mindsets and practices from the outside in. An external focus meant ensuring the exceptional customer attention that would shape the organization's strategies. In turn, that meant stimulating the employee population to adopt the right behaviors for excellent customer focus, communication, and collaboration. The development of Ortho Biotech's culture would require vigilant leadership to champion sustained attention and action in support of our shared vision, values, and desired behaviors. We were committed to providing that, knowing it wouldn't be easy.

Members of the management board started by recruiting new talent from a variety of sources with a commitment to diversity of race, gender, and experience. We then created a culture change committee by drawing from a cross-section of employees by level and department who would function along with board members. We followed this action with a series of meetings called Adventures in Cultural Enhancement (ACE). Aimed at bringing the employee population closer to our draft vision, these meetings encouraged employees to challenge the vision, experience a feeling of participation, and become aligned in identifying the new behaviors that would support this new culture. ACE helped us successfully keep the organization's vision front and center, focusing on the long term as the priority.

Organizational Alignment

To ensure alignment with a common set of goals, we posted six priorities for the calendar year inside the elevators in the building, where everyone would see them. Knowing that a creative recognition and rewards system would also be needed to reinforce new behaviors, we designed a peer recognition system that any employee could use to acknowledge desired behaviors in highly visible ways. From the ACE experience, employees volunteered to join affinity groups, whose roles were to research and recommend to the management board ideas and solutions that would positively contribute to the Ortho Biotech culture. Our culture change committee also assigned a management board sponsor to each affinity group, to openly communicate approval, help point out positive progress and benefits, and celebrate results. This support created psychological safety and encouraged employees who were leading the change process to demonstrate new behaviors.

So was Ortho Biotech Inc. successful? Within six years, this J&J start-up grew from 40 employees to 1,000 and achieved profits of over $500 million. What can you learn from this company's bold leadership and culture change initiatives? Almost any leader can replicate Ortho Biotech Inc.'s efforts since these are not only what's needed to achieve success in a start-up operation, but also in most organizations of any size and stage of their lifecycle. You can also see from the Ortho Biotech story how successful leaders develop and demonstrate competencies for shaping, stimulating, and supporting innovation. By taking a personal interest in helping others grow, and committing to what's possible, leaders like the ones at this J&J start-up are who make innovation happen.

Concluding Thoughts

Reflecting on the key takeaways from successful leaders, people in almost any sector and industry must assertively reinvent their games and accomplish this by setting the stage for creativity and innovation. Similar to the way in which orchestra conductors bring forth music, organizational leaders can lift and inspire their followers to elicit new thinking that's balanced with successful execution. To do that, leaders must identify current needs and anticipate future ones. Then they need to accurately position and continually reposition their organizations for successful outcomes. What might you learn from the examples of JoAnn Falletta's "head-and-heart" leadership style?

The late Anita Roddick, British environmentalist, human rights activist, CEO, and founder of The Body Shop, once said this: "You have to look at leadership through the eyes of the followers, and you have to live the message. What I have learned is that people become motivated when you guide them to the source of their own power and when you make heroes out of employees who personify what you want to see in the organization."

The thought leaders and practitioners who we interviewed for this section of the book expand on this and other leadership strategies expressed in this chapter. By addressing a broad range of topics, they share their experience, the results of their research, and their best practices. I thank them for that, and I also want to invite you to visit my website and express any thoughts, reactions, and ideas that were prompted by this chapter.

■　■　■

Andrea Zintz, Ph.D.
President, Strategic Leadership Resources
azintz@strategicleadershipresources.com
www.strategicleadershipresources.com

Chapter 12

A Business Case for Coaching

An interview with Marshall Goldsmith, Ph.D., Founder at Marshall Goldsmith Group; Executive Coach; Internationally Renowned Thought Leader; and Best-Selling Author

■　■　■

"Coaching isn't an addition to a leader's job, it's an integral part of it."

— George Odiorne

Even though leaders of symphony orchestras work with highly qualified creative talent, they continue to help musicians achieve mastery by playing to their strengths. Musicians in jazz ensembles work with each other as peers, diligently practicing as a way to continually improve their performance. Successful business leaders must also do this, while taking on additional responsibilities. The need to manage remotely, deal with the increasing rate of change, and leverage differences in today's diverse workforce are only a few of the challenges that they face daily. Today, they must manage gender and generational differences, different thinking and creativity styles, and a variety of different approaches to problem solving and decision making. For these reasons and others, coaching is needed more than ever—not only to assist leaders in managing day-to-day business, but also in facilitating innovation.

Coaching can also help leaders manage conflict and ensure the alignment and collaboration that's needed for innovation that's both incremental and breakthrough. Typically employed to address leadership challenges with current and potential future leaders, coaching is often combined with succession planning and leadership and executive development programs. Organizations most often provide development opportunities to senior leaders, yet many also extend coaching to designated replacements for key positions and employees identified as high potential. For this chapter, we interviewed Dr. Marshall Goldsmith, who has worked with over 70 major corporation CEOs and their teams and was named by *Forbes* as the number one executive coach in the world.

Marshall was named by the *Wall Street Journal* as one of the top 10 executive educators and by *The Economist* as one of the most credible consultants in the new era of business. The American Management Association ranked him as one of the 50 great speakers and business leaders who have influenced the field of management. Marshall has also consistently been top ranked among the top 10 most influential thinkers in the world by Thinkers50, regarded as the "Oscars of Management Thinking."

Marshall's work has also received national recognition from the London Business School, Academy of Management, the Institute of Management Studies, The American Society of Training and Development, The Center for Creative Leadership, The Conference Board, and the Human Resource Planning Society, as well as the *New Yorker*, and *Harvard Business Review*. Serving on the faculty of the University of Michigan and Dartmouth's Executive Education program, Marshall has authored or edited over 35 books, which have sold over 2 million copies, been translated into 30 languages, and have become bestsellers in 12 countries. Please join us as he describes how leaders can achieve positive, measurable change and behavior for themselves and their teams.

QUESTIONS AND ANSWERS

What is your operational definition of "coaching"?

Behavioral coaching helps successful leaders achieve positive long-term change for themselves and for the leaders who report to them.

What are ways in which organizations can leverage coaching in the service of innovation?

Examples of this are role modeling—leaders publicly standing up for what they believe. Other ways are through transparency, by effectively managing the business, and by letting go and forgetting. It's difficult for leaders to "let go" of running the day-to-day affairs of business to facilitate innovation—mainly because of the possibility of cannibalization. Most leaders fear cannibalizing their products and services, so creating an environment that fosters and leverages coaching is often critical in developing innovation competencies.

Since so much about innovation involves the ability to deal with risk, what do you do if feedback points to this as a development need? And what do you do if your client doesn't accept it?

If feedback indicates an issue with risk-taking, I deal with it. However as a general rule, in the coaching process itself, I don't argue with clients. I have a simple system. The competency is either required or optional. There is no use in arguing about it. With this approach, I minimize the amount of time it takes to get long-term change.

Would you please share your views on how well leaders typically deal with conflict?

Leaders often don't handle conflict well. They can get defensive and argue. Yet, knowing how to deal with conflict is critical for alignment and collaboration. To enable this, I use a process called "Feed-Forward" where leaders ask for suggestions on what they could do differently, take notes, don't promise anything, and fight their initial urge to talk. Leaders can learn better when they truly listen versus compose.

How do you help leaders build competencies to deal with conflict effectively?

Leaders learn not to be right, but to sell decision makers or make peace with the outcomes. People usually do things because there is a payoff for it. We get positive reinforcement and we think what we're doing is fine. This is true for most top executives. People flatter and cajole, and executives buy it. I help executives open up the blind spots. It's all about building new habits in areas that are new to them. Basically, I tell them, "What got you here won't get you there."

We can all fall into the superstition trap. As mentioned in an interview with Fast Company in 2004, "In many cases, the higher we climb the organizational totem pole, the more superstitious we become. Superstition is the confusion of correlation and causality. One of the greatest mistakes of successful leaders is the assumption, "I behave this way, and I am successful. Therefore, I must be successful because I behave this way." The higher up a leader advances, the more he or she is going to win. I teach leaders to listen and learn—and to help others be winners.

Would you say more about dealing with blind spots?

I give leaders feedback. Leadership is not only about what we say but about what others hear. Are others important? Are their perceptions important? What is right and wrong is not important—it's about perceptions, and changing others' perceptions isn't easy. Follow up is key. It's the only way to change perceptions. We don't see what's actually there, but what we think is there. We sometimes impose our thinking onto reality—and that creates blind spots.

Do you believe that peer coaching works? If so, what should organizations do to ensure that peer coaching programs encourage new and different approaches that support innovation?

Peer coaching works great! Ford's CEO Alan Mulhally conducts weekly follow up sessions with the people he works with and helps them to focus on how to help each other. His philosophy is to help more than judge—to "shine the light on what's happening versus trying to hide from it." Again, follow up is key. I use daily questions as part of the process. I challenge myself daily with questions such as:

"How happy were you today?" "How meaningful was today?" "How many times did you try to prove that you were right?" In peer groups, we discuss our responses to these kinds of questions with each other. This is a great way for people to express ideas and to build the foundation for collaboration, which is so important for innovation.

You use daily questions in your coaching practice. How does this work and how does it facilitate innovation?

I have achieved amazing results using questions, but the questions should be active versus passive. I ask, "What can be done to engage?" Passive questions are, "How engaged are you?" and "Do you have clear goals?" You get externally based answers to questions like these. People often use judgmental projections when responding. When active questions are used, such as, "Did you do your best to improve your own engagement?" they focus on their own behaviors. Then they're not victims. It's difficult for victims to be innovative, so coaching often needs to provide options that encourage people to give up victim-like behaviors. I also use 360 feedback, which is essential for clear and honest information. My clients agree on what's most important and then they must follow up with stakeholders on an ongoing basis to ensure alignment, which in turn, facilitates innovation.

How does the coaching process build leadership capability for innovation?

Innovation is focused on organization change, while coaching is focused on behavioral and individual change. I work with top management to achieve the optimal environment for innovation and change. My focus in coaching is taking a micro versus a macro approach. I help leaders confront issues about themselves and support them in helping others to confront themselves. I assist leaders in creating the environment for honest, upward feedback, creativity, and risk taking, which provides the culture that facilitates innovation. In this process, the key variable is not the coach, but the coaching client. I don't make coaching about how good the coach is, but instead, about how good the clients are.

TAKEAWAYS

- Keep coaching about the client, not the coach. Come at coaching from the perspective of what's inside the client versus what's inside the coach.
- Use measures to assess coaching for behavioral change.
- Make coaching voluntary, not mandatory.
- Start with the top level. If the CEO or person in charge doesn't want to engage in coaching, it won't be supported by others either.

- The most powerful coaching tools are questions. Make them active and about behavior.
- Choose executive coaches carefully! Don't tell coaches your problems. Let them prove they can add something of value.

TAKING STOCK

- Would feedback and follow-up from professional coaches assist us in uncovering blind spots and conflicts that might be blocking innovation?
- How can we make coaching a business practice for every leader—not only those at senior levels?
- What coach or coaches would be qualified to help us with organizational innovation? (i.e., Do they know about strategy? Will they understand the culture and issues?)

■　■　■

To learn more about Marshall Goldsmith's work, go to www.marshallgoldsmithgroup.com. If you found this chapter helpful, also see our chapters entitled *A Culture of Innovation, Change Leadership, Executive Development, Leadership Assessment,* and *Leadership Development.*

Chapter 13

A Design Mindset

An interview with Nicolas Maitret, Principal at SYPartners & Adam Schorr, Founder of Rule No. 1 and former Principal, SYPartners

■ ■ ■

"You know you've achieved perfection in design, not when you have nothing to add,
but when you have nothing more to take away."

— Antoine de Saint Exupery

As a symphony orchestra conductor, jazz musician, and educator/Honorary Associate of the Royal Academy of Music in London, Dominic Alldis epitomizes a design mindset—clearly evident in a jazz ensemble. Dominic says, "In jazz, each song is the starting point of a creative journey." To begin or continue on this journey, orchestral leaders and business leaders alike must resist business-as-usual behaviors when situations call for new thinking and approaches. By operating with a design mindset, successful leaders approach each task or challenge with an open mind and a desire for customized solutions.

Given the absence of a universal definition of "design thinking," however, people often struggle to understand it. Some view it as a blend of both art and technology—a more creative way of solving problems than traditional, left-brained analytical approaches. Others view it as getting to root causes, identifying needs, or facilitating the transformation of many requirements into one holistic solution. Still others view it as less of a process or discipline and more of a mindset. In this chapter, we interview Nicolas Maitret and Adam Schorr, who talk about the impact of design on innovation and describe the difference between "design thinking" and a "design mindset."

Nicolas leads projects at the intersection of branding, innovation, and transformation, with deep expertise in both design and business strategy. Over the past 15 years, he has designed a wide range of products, services, and environments. At SYPartners, he's helped AARP, Johnson & Johnson and IBM bring to life new visions for their businesses and brands; imagined customer experiences for Old Navy, Yahoo!, Blue Shield and Target; and designed exhibits for Nike and IBM. Nicholas served as creative director on IBM's award-winning THINK exhibit, an immersive multimedia experience at Lincoln Center that commemorated the company's centennial. The exhibit is not a permanent installation at Epcot. Nicolas holds an MFA in industrial design from ENSCI and an MBA from ESSEC Business School, both in Paris, France.

After 16+ years as a consultant, marketer, and innovation practitioner, Adam started Rule No. 1, a consultancy dedicated to helping companies be the best version possible of themselves—living their unique purpose and values in their culture and in the market. He recently spent six years at SYPartners focusing on the intersection of brand and culture—helping companies create distinctive brands and fully activate their people to bring those brands to life. He's partnered with senior executives at leading companies such as IBM, Hyatt, JetBlue, Celgene, and Metlife, to codify company purpose, values, behaviors, and vision; define brand identity and strategy; design leadership development and workforce engagement programs; and shift mindsets and behaviors to fuel brand, culture and performance. He began his career at McKinsey & Company, consulting on strategy and organizational change and also worked at Pfizer as a brand manager on Sudafed, Listerine, and Efferdent. At J&J, he built a new innovation capability to unlock non-traditional revenue streams. Adam earned a BA in Speech & Drama from Yeshiva University and a PhD in Psychology from the University of Chicago.

QUESTIONS AND ANSWERS

First, how do you distinguish between "design thinking" and a "design mindset"?

We don't use the term "design thinking" because we believe it creates a false dichotomy between thinking (coming up with ideas) and making (bringing those ideas to life). We prefer the terms "design approach" or "design mindset." Design thinking, as a concept, emerged when designers, once relegated to the making part of design, began to take part in strategic conversations. They were then able to influence the approach to problem solving rather than just the execution of the solutions. "A design mindset" takes that notion a step further and implies a fusion of creative thinking and making—of theory and practice—in all aspects of business.

How can organizations employ a design mindset to enable innovation?

We define innovation as any new idea, strategy, or product that challenges the status quo and creates new value. Organizations have to think expansively and constantly come up with new ideas in order to compete today. One of the ways we help clients build this innovation muscle is to get them in the habit of starting with simple yet potent questions, such as these: "What do people want that they aren't currently getting?" "What does the organization need to achieve?" "What is it uniquely good at?" Understanding what problem we're actually trying to solve is the critical first step of the design process. Often, this questioning process yields tremendous clarity, and from there, an organization can begin iterating possible solutions. Leaders need to recognize, however, that a design mindset never turns off, and that this cycle of identifying worthy challenges and coming up with new solutions is perpetual.

Can a design mindset also be a vehicle for organizational transformation?

Organizations themselves are a result of design—and that design can always be more deliberate. Organizations are made up of systems, which in turn are made up of individuals with different opinions, needs, and desires brought together to achieve some particular set of goals. Approaching organizational transformation with a design mindset means understanding the interconnectedness of these systems and, therefore, the obvious and subtle structures that make up an organization. The same questioning and iterating process used for external innovation can then be applied to redesigning the organization from the inside out.

We've used this approach with clients to design comprehensive brand systems that extend to every part of the organization. We've also helped create wholly new HR systems with skill-building programs and incentives that more clearly align with the organization's purpose in the world. Organizations are living entities, constantly influenced by events, behaviors, and forces both within and outside their walls. Nothing stays the same for very long, so transformation, like innovation, has to be constant. That's where a design mindset—and a perspective that things are never truly "done"—can make a difference.

What are typical barriers that organizations face when attempting to become more innovative?

The lack of a clearly articulated purpose is the biggest barrier to meaningful innovation that we see with clients. We believe that every organization needs to start with purpose, or their reason for being. It's the central idea that animates an organization and motivates people to show up every day to do the work.

From that clearly articulated purpose, an organization can then begin to identify the traits of what we call its "corporate character"—how it looks, sounds, thinks, and performs. An organization's corporate character dictates the way it innovates as well. Some organizations are risk-averse while others are more tolerant of mistakes. Some are suited to incremental innovation while others attempt more disruptive leaps. Some drive innovation through marketing—packaging existing solutions in new ways—while others focus on engineering—developing products based on new materials and technologies. Some innovate through strong internal R&D while others grow through acquisition and integration. And some develop new products and services while others build unique processes and business models.

In any case, innovation is not a monolithic concept. It has as many personalities as there are organizations. Recognizing what is true about themselves can allow organizations to innovate in a way that is uniquely suited to their particular ways of being in the world. Some of the most painful innovation mistakes we've seen have happened when organizations have ignored their unique innovation personalities and forced things through that just didn't resonate with the larger truth of the organization's corporate character.

What role does prototyping play in innovation?

The willingness to prototype is a defining characteristic of a design mindset. In the constant dialogue between thinking and making, prototyping is about making concepts real. It's what pushes thinking forward and strengthens ideas. It's what answers the question, "How will this show up in the world?" There's a misconception that prototyping sits strictly in the realm of designers, who might possess sophisticated drawing or other technical abilities to bring something to life. Not true. Prototyping can take many different shapes—a sketch, a mockup, a simulation, a flow chart, a back-of-the-envelope calculation.

The point is experimentation—to bring fidelity to a nascent idea and begin to see how it might actually work. Building prototyping into an organization's process will inevitably lead to greater comfort with failure, which is essential to any innovative culture. Prototyping is basically an ongoing cycle of try and fail, try and fail. The point is the trying. The failing just leads to better future attempts. Teams should prototype early and often. Don't wait for the idea to be perfect to put it on paper. Put it on paper to make it perfect.

How do you approach branding and how does it relate to innovation?

To us, branding is the expression of who you are and what you do. In that sense, brand and culture are one. We lead brand conversations that center on the question, "What do we really value and how can we behave in ways that communicate that?" These conversations go far beyond traditional notions of brand and extend into every corner of every system within an organization. Innovation is, therefore, first focused not on a website or a product launch, but instead starts at the very core of what the organization actually does in the world. A company working on a major turnaround, for example, would need to first come up with a central animating notion about who it wants to be in the world before getting into the specific tactics of "rebranding." Or an organization moving into a new market would need to articulate clearly how that shift fits in with its larger story and purpose before designing the campaign announcing it.

Today, employees and customers can identify and call attention to even the smallest gaps between what an organization says it stands for and how it actually acts. Truly authentic brands live in constant dialogue about how their actions align with their purpose, pushing new thinking and new expression forward through innovation, and staying true to corporate character at every turn.

What skills and competencies should designers have in order to thrive in today's complex environment?

We seek designers who can apply a combination of systems thinking and creativity to their work. This means they're able to understand the interconnectedness of factors, to see challenges from multiple angles, and then come up with new solutions. People who think this way tend to have boundless curiosity, deep motivation to come up with ideas, and courage to go far into complexity.

TAKEAWAYS

- As a fusion of thinking and making, a design mindset prompts organizations to ask the right questions, see the interconnectedness of challenges, and come up with creative solutions.
- Every organization has a unique corporate character that serves as a touchstone for every decision it makes. Clearly defining what that character is should be the first step for any organization seeking to become more innovative.
- Prototyping is an essential part of the innovation process that allows designers to quickly test new ideas.

TAKING STOCK

- How might we encourage all of our employees to realize that they are, in fact, capable of participating in the design process and to do their work consistently with the end user in mind?
- Can we use a design mindset for organizational transformation efforts where alignment is critical?
- Could we utilize prototyping to enhance products, services, and processes?

■ ■ ■

If you found this chapter useful, also see *A Culture of Innovation*, *A Path to Innovation Excellence*, *Change Leadership*, and *Shared Vision and Values*.

Chapter 14

Buy-in, Sponsorship, and Commitment

An interview with Ray Specht, Founder & CEO, Specht Leadership Consulting; former Industry and Legislative Affairs at Toyota Financial Services and Vice Chair at Toyota Financial Savings Bank, Toyota Financial Services

■   ■   ■

"Individual commitment to a group effort—that is what makes a team work, a company work, a society work, a civilization work."

— Vince Lombardi

Successful symphony performances and jazz performances alike require a collaborative effort among musicians, conductors, and even audiences. To ensure that musicians perform effectively, orchestra leaders must ensure buy-in, sponsorship, and commitment. These are critical for alignment and for effective day-to-day operations of almost any organization, and they're especially important when innovation initiatives are being introduced or implemented. Large-scale, enterprise-wide innovation and change initiatives require coordinated action to deal with a number of moving parts. With that, it's important to keep in mind that the people involved will typically react with different mindsets, experiences, points of view, and biases.

How can innovators secure buy-in and sponsorship in spite of the significant and inevitable obstacles that usually occur with even the smallest change? With concerns about job eliminations often associated with large-scale change, today's economic challenges tend to exacerbate normal fears. It takes skill and expertise to implement innovation strategies today. To ensure success, leaders must obtain buy-in and ensure alignment early on, and then it's critical to sustain buy-in, sponsorship, and commitment throughout the innovation process.

We interviewed Ray Specht for this chapter because of his personal expertise with this topic as well as his experience with Toyota, world renowned for consensus management. Ray was Vice Chair for Toyota Financial Savings Bank (TFSB), an entity that provides products and services to Toyota and Lexus dealers across the country and issuer of the Toyota Rewards and Lexus Pursuits Visa credit cards. He also provided strategic guidance on federal and state legislation for Toyota Financial Services (TFS) and worked in conjunction with TFS Corporate Communication, Legal and Compliance; and Toyota Motor North America, Washington DC.

Prior to joining Toyota in 2004, Ray served as Chair, President and CEO of Volkswagen Bank USA. He also held a number of other senior positions at several banks including Cendant's Wright Express Financial Services, Fidelity Investments' Fidelity Trust Company, and John Hancock's First Signature Bank and Trust. Ray earned a Bachelor of Science degree in Accounting, graduating magna cum laude from the University of Massachusetts. He also holds a Masters in Strategic Communication & Leadership, graduating with honors from Seton Hall University. Ray has served on many not-for-profit boards including the National Association of Industrial Banks, the Conference of State Bank Supervisors, Safe Nest, Las Vegas Global Economic Alliance, and Boys & Girls Club.

QUESTIONS AND ANSWERS

Please tell us how you define "buy-in," "sponsorship," and "commitment."

I believe there are varying degrees of buy-in, but primarily, it's about mutual agreement. Sponsorship is a higher level of buy-in that involves a commitment to both personally support the innovation and take responsibility for success and those involved with it. Commitment means agreement to do something that involves one's personal and functional support.

Why are buy-in, sponsorship, and commitment so critical to the success of innovation initiatives?

Without buy-in, sponsorship, and commitment, innovation can't be nurtured or leveraged for competitive advantage. In most companies, sponsorship must begin with the board and senior management. Because innovation requires a change from the status quo, it's paramount to communicate messages over an extended period—maybe even years—about why the innovation is needed and why individuals and the business will benefit from it. This rationale particularly needs to be communicated by key stakeholders who are in positions to make the innovation a success—or a failure.

Why are stakeholders especially important to large-scale, enterprise-wide initiatives?

Large companies have many levels of separation, both vertically and horizontally. A very significant aspect of effective communication is how it relates directly to the core meaning and purpose of the initiative for each stakeholder. This typically involves describing a "noble purpose" or "greater good" as to why the innovation is needed. Buy-in, sponsorship and commitment must be ongoing and nurtured over years—even after a change initiative or innovation has been implemented.

What are the critical competencies required for obtaining the buy-in, sponsorship, and commitment that are essential for innovation?

I believe there are ten critical competencies, all of which can be considered leadership competencies. This is because without strong leadership skills, it's difficult to achieve alignment with peers and employees, and then motivate them to rally around and support the desired change or innovation. Often the level of confidence in the change or innovation is in direct proportion to the level of confidence in the organization's leadership. Leaders are almost always being observed to see if their actions are congruent with their words, so it's critical that they effectively model the ten competencies.

The first competency is communication. Leaders must have presentation skills that enable clear, concise, and passionate messages. Communicating with high energy is important because change requires a lot of energy on a consistent basis. The second competency is persistence. Leaders shouldn't take "no" or "maybe" personally. They need to push on, despite obstacles. Perseverance and tenacity are numbers three and four. They include resilience in the face of obstacles or setbacks. This is important because leaders need to stay positive and clear about the end goal.

Competencies five and six are trust and honesty. These are also critical because they form the basis for credibility and advocacy—especially when leaders have to communicate messages about difficult issues. Competency seven is subject matter expertise. People must have faith in the leaders who are change-makers. Flexibility is number eight. When implementing something new, it's necessary to quickly adapt to organizational, market, customer, and economic changes. Competency nine is a sense of humor. This helps leaders mitigate the stress of change.

I've saved one of the most critical competencies for number 10, and that's compromise. In organizations, leaders rarely achieve 100% initial buy-in of their desired change or innovation; 80% is a good start, and with success, one might be able to achieve 100%. However, effective leaders accept that compromise is a necessary part of advancing agendas that takes into consideration the needs of others.

How important is a compelling vision in setting the stage for innovation?

Vision may be the most important aspect of innovation and change management. Without a vision, there is no direction. The vision also must be simple and clear so that all readily understand it. The fewer words the better. Most important, the vision needs to be embraced and owned by key stakeholders, and the vision must be supported by strong research. That means having, and communicating, a deep understanding of the current state and the desired outcomes.

How can leaders maximize the success for innovation or change initiatives in the launch stage?

Constant communications across the company are imperative, and the content is also important. Sponsors or project teams need plans that are well defined for key stakeholders. Plans should contain timelines and convey a sense of urgency that's consistent with organizational realities. Ownership and accountability for success should be imbedded in the plans, and projects or intended innovations broken down into many pieces or segments. Efforts without a solid plan will most often result in a project or innovation that dies a slow death.

How do differences in mindsets, experiences, and biases impact the challenge of gaining and sustaining buy-in, sponsorship, and commitment?

People have different past experiences that cause them to react to change in unique ways. Organization culture plays a huge role, as well. The culture has to enable and nurture change and innovation, and the persons responsible for the change must understand how the culture will impact the project. Each company that I've been a part of has had radically different cultures, and that has taught me the importance of communicating with different stakeholders in ways they understand and appreciate. This includes using a style that's consistent with that organization's cultural norms.

What do you believe are the most critical influencing strategies for gaining stakeholder support for an innovation?

In addition to sending messages that are consistent with the organization's culture, innovators must be passionate about the innovation or change that they're trying to introduce or implement. Many people will look to them to determine their emotional stake in the project. Innovators also need to present facts in ways that enable people to understand the reality of the situation. There has to be a shared understanding for others to take part in advancing change. And so it's important for leaders to communicate frequently and in a variety of ways that are aimed at group and individual levels. It's important to use all of the tools available, such as newsletters, email updates, periodic company meetings, and lunch and learns. Communication should also be two-way, so it generates dialogue and ensures shared meaning. Leaders should make it a goal to have a series of incremental wins because the credibility of the project or innovation will be determined by many small successes that gain the confidence of various internal and external stakeholders. At the same time, they must accept mistakes and "failures" along with successes. This helps to create a safe place for implementing innovations and change.

How do you believe new leaders in an organization best deal with fear and resistance?

New leaders, often eager to make their mark, sometimes err by initiating change for the sake of change—or are perceived as doing that. To maximize success, they must be willing to learn about, and accept the culture of their new organizations and adopt or enhance key behaviors that typically generate success in that business. Even when change might be viewed as advantageous, there is usually fear associated with it. Successful new leaders help to alleviate that fear by illustrating why the change initiative or innovation is necessary. Listening is crucial during times of change. If leaders don't listen to the fears at play, then those who are fearful won't be able to hear important messages or buy into the change. People need to be heard, and all leaders must proactively draw out fears and address them to achieve buy-in, sponsorship, and commitment from others.

TAKEAWAYS

- Buy-in is about mutual agreement, with sponsorship and commitment involving higher degrees of alignment. Sponsorship involves personal support and commitment most often means personal and functional support.
- The greatest success arises from sponsorship and commitment that cascade from the board and senior management.
- It's important for leaders to communicate the "noble purpose" or "greater good" that will be brought about by an innovation or change initiative.
- There must be a shared vision that is simple and clear enough that all understand it, and it must be supported by a well-defined project plan with clear assignments and timelines.
- Leaders who champion innovation or change initiatives should consider how an organization's culture might provide support or produce resistance, and how to adapt to achieve success.

TAKING STOCK

- Who are the critical stakeholders in my company that are needed for buy- in and sponsorship, and what are the meaningful differences that innovation will provide for them?
- Are our senior leaders committed to innovation and open to the change that will come with it?
- Is our vision clear, simple and compelling and shared by all?

■　■　■

If you found this chapter useful, also see our chapters on *Change Leadership, Competition and Collaboration, Employee Engagement, and Shared Vision and Values.*

Chapter 15

Change Leadership

An interview with Dan Cohen, Ph.D., Retired Principal, Deloitte Consulting LLP and Best-Selling Author

■ ■ ■

"And one should bear in mind that there is nothing more difficult to execute, nor more dubious of success, nor more dangerous to administer than to introduce a new order of things; for he who introduced it has all those who profit from the older order as his enemies, and he has only lukewarm allies in all those who might profit from the new."

— Niccolo Machiavelli

Skilled orchestra leaders and jazz musicians know that the success of their productions depends on the ability of musicians to adapt to change. This requires a willingness to try fresh, new approaches that can not only help to increase ticket sales but also facilitate mastery. When orchestra leaders are willing to go beyond traditional pieces and tailor their productions to changing tastes, they can successfully grow their organizations and ensure sustainability. To adapt and achieve sustainability, executives in all sectors often need to grow their organizations. At times, this requires taking dramatic measures, and with that often comes large-scale change—and risk.

If change isn't managed carefully, it has the potential to put an organization's entire infrastructure at risk. However, in his book, *The Heart of Change*, Dr. Dan Cohen tells how, when change is managed well, it can provide an opportunity to meet both current and future needs. In this chapter, Dr. Cohen describes the best ways to involve leaders and employees in change initiatives and new processes. In addition to the many tips he offers, Dan Cohen also shares best practices for transforming change-averse behaviors into those that embrace and support change and ultimately enhance organizational performance. As the Chief Executive Officer of Stuart Advisory Service Group, he focuses on large-scale organizational transformation and strategic change. Dan has over 35 years of experience consulting to and working in industry and also brings a strong background in the energy and public sectors.

During his 15 years at Deloitte Consulting LLP, Dan developed the firm's first global change leadership methodology and was the lead architect in the design of Deloitte's Strategic Change methodology. Prior to his career in consulting with both Deloitte Consulting LLP and Ernst & Young, he worked in the manufacturing, financial and real estate industries for more than 15 years, in various executive human resource capacities. In addition to his lectures at many major universities, Dan has appeared in television and radio interviews and has delivered presentations and provided counsel to executives at major corporations around the world. He obtained his Bachelor of Arts from Adelphi University in New York, Master of Arts from the University of Detroit in Michigan and Ph.D. from Ohio State University.

QUESTIONS AND ANSWERS

How do you define "change leadership"?

I see change leadership as a set of proactive actions and activities designed to prepare and engage stakeholders to achieve and sustain a desired outcome.

How do you see change leadership moving behavior toward enabling innovation?

Leaders must separate the people side of innovation from the process, technology, and policy side. This latter set of concerns is not change leadership. If you set a direction and are clear about what you want to achieve, then it's about helping the employee deal with the behavior and actions that must occur to make that a reality. What are the strategies and processes required? What must occur to make that happen? How different is the new technology from the old, and what behaviors are needed to carry it forward?

What are some of the greatest challenges with regard to change leadership?

The biggest issue I find with change leadership is generating a clear emotional understanding of the problem or opportunity and letting go of current behavioral habits. When I look at all the things that go wrong with a transformation, it typically comes back to the fact that people throughout the organization do not identify in their "gut" that there is a problem or that what is being undertaken will yield something better than what already exists. If people don't see a problem, why would there be any motivation to change what they're doing?

Of all the challenging emotions, complacency is the most formidable. It rests on the premise that we want to exist in a pleasurable state and altering our behavior causes discomfort. So, if the pain does not outweigh the gain, why change? It therefore falls on leadership to demonstrate that the innovation they are seeking will result in a better organization. In order to achieve transformative change, leaders have to do more than send e-mails written by their communications staff or show up at the occasional meeting to "rally the troops."

What, specifically, should leaders do to ensure that innovation is successful?

Leaders need to do three things: (1) demonstrate that they have a deep understanding of what it is they are doing; (2) model the behaviors needed for the change to take hold; and (3) hold others accountable for results by measuring results. So first, they must be able to answer the what, why, and how questions of the transformation: "What are we doing?" "Why are we doing it?" "How are we going to achieve results?" This requires clarity about the problem or opportunity and what the future looks like and how they're going to get there. Leaders must speak to a working vision which resonates with their people. Furthermore, frontline leaders must take these messages into their communication with their teams on a day-to-day basis. By crafting a shared vision, values and behaviors, leaders can converse about the meaning of the changes in a very personal way.

Next, leaders must model the behaviors involved with the change. If they introduce a new technology such as SAP, they should actually use it themselves. For example, if leaders are introducing a new way to conduct an audit, they need to lead an audit in order to model the new approach and demonstrate their commitment. Finally, leaders need to hold others accountable for the new behaviors and measure performance outcomes so that everyone can see there are consequences associated with performing in accordance with the transformation.

How can leaders raise the feeling of urgency?

Leaders can raise urgency by engaging the workforce and attacking the existing complacency. People have to move, not be moved, out of their comfort zones. This is done most effectively by getting people to see the problem so that they can identify with the need to innovate, rather than feeding them facts and figures about innovation. Since writing *The Heart of Change Field Guide*, I have found that 97% of the people I have spoken with about change have told me that it was the 'inner passion' to succeed rather than the logical presentation of facts that drove their behavior to make the change a success.

You speak of "Guiding Teams" in your book *The Heart of Change*. How can Guiding Teams be engaged in the innovation process?

The membership of Guiding Teams must include middle management. Top leadership can't implement a major transformation until the middle is on board because that level has daily contact with workers. Start looking at the change on a division-by-division and country-by-country basis. Create teams for each division that extend right down to the lowest level. This process should be based on the breadth of the change and to what extent it affects the organization. Wherever there is a logical group to be led, Guiding Teams can help. Having fewer members is generally better—less than 12 is best.

How can Guiding Teams generate the trust and emotional commitment among members to sustain the leadership that's needed through all stages of change?

When building Guiding Teams, it's critical to get middle management involved to create the leverage needed at the bottom of the organization. In order to do this, they must set up interlocking teams, where the members of one team are the leaders of the next team below. They need to think of this process as linking pins. If CEOs or CFOs talks to their EVPs about financial transformation, then they must also talk with their directors, who must then talk to their managers, and so on down the line.

Imagine the follow up and accountability involved with getting people to see where the organization is going and why. Buy-in must occur at each level of the organization to achieve the commitment necessary for making change happen. If this is not happening, people need one-on-one conversation with their leaders to resolve the problem. At the end of the day, the Guiding Team leader needs to generate alignment around the direction of change and take the appropriate action to move things forward.

How can the Guiding Team best create and communicate bold strategies?

The change process must touch the heart of people. This involves creating the strategy with this question in mind: "How far out of the box are people willing to go?" The strategy must make business sense, show margin, and be sustained for the long term. In the public sector, it must demonstrate public accountability and enhance the public's agenda. The Guiding Team members must be willing to explain the change when they're challenged so that people believe they are being dealt with in a fair way. They should focus communication on what to do and how to get there. People need to believe that leadership is committed to the strategy rather than just supporting it verbally. Minimal verbal support implies, "I'll root you on but I really do not want to get involved." Change leadership means getting people to see that leaders are serious about the change and willing to engage them to align with it.

With a major transformation, leaders should reflect upon how often they get the company together beyond conducting town hall meetings. It is critical for leaders to interact with people. Addressing the masses and sending out emails is demonstrating communication, but leaders need to use multiple channels. It's more about engaging the stakeholders in ways that cause them to see your commitment to making the change a working reality.

How can leaders make it politically safe and socially acceptable for people to embrace behavior change and help employees remove barriers?

First, leaders should identify the barriers that are either obstacles or objections. Obstacles are represented by physical structures such as processes, software, performance management, and organization design. These obstacles can be overcome. Objections, on the other hand, are people-related and take the form of resistance. Leaders must be able to identify causes. Are they dealing with skeptics or cynics? Skeptics need communication to see the outcomes and value from the change. Another way to remove barriers for people is to make it safe for them to take calculated risks by thinking of failures as investments in improvement.

How can organizations best deal with people who can't or won't make the desired behavioral shifts?

If you're talking about the cynics who scoff at new ways of behaving, leaders must deal with them as saboteurs who are committed to the status quo. There are also those who are trying to change, but are having difficulty. Leaders should work with those who are genuinely trying by demonstrating that they care about them and are willing to go the extra mile. It's also important for leaders to have a time frame in mind regarding when they should expect to see changes in action or behavior—and have a tough conversation about it. To lead change, leaders must demonstrate accountability and hold others responsible.

TAKEAWAYS

- Leaders must demonstrate a deep understanding of the change, the reasons for it, and how this translates to behavior changes that drive desired outcomes.
- The need for change must go beyond logical persuasion, quarterly town hall meetings, and emails. Leaders must create visceral motivations that compel people to feel committed to change.
- It's critically important for leaders to model behavior change by their own actions and behavior.
- To create leverage, the senior team must ensure that Guiding Teams consist of mid-level managers who are powerful in shifting away from old behaviors to drive new habits.
- Senior leaders should also ensure that training and other change initiatives are targeted at building the competence and confidence for new behaviors.
- Leaders must hold people accountable through straight talk, performance measures, and firm action.

TAKING STOCK

- Is my organization communicating a compelling reason for the change, with clear behaviors tied to measurable outcomes?
- Is our vision for the change robust and shared by all stakeholders?
- Are there communication strategies in place that will generate two-way communication about the change?

■   ■   ■

If you found this chapter useful, also see our chapters entitled *A Culture of Innovation*, *Buy-in, Sponsorship, and Commitment*, *Differences*, and *Employee Engagement*.

Chapter 16

Courage

An interview with Louise (Yochee) Klein, Psy.D. and Merom Klein, Ph.D., Co-Principals of Courage Growth Partners in the U.S. and Tuval, Israel

■ ■ ■

"The main thing we have to fear is fear itself—nameless, unreasoning, unjustified terror which paralyzes needed efforts to convert retreat into advance."

— Franklin D. Roosevelt

Courage is evident in most jazz ensembles, where musicians play without rehearsals and compose as they go. Today, a number of contemporary orchestra leaders are also making significant changes to their repertoires, with some even expanding classical music to include a variety of other musical styles. This kind of dramatic change often generates fear in musicians in the same way that change can produce fear among people in other environments. What do we know about the power of fear? It's an uncontested fact: Fear inhibits innovation. In the face of constant change, scrutiny, and tight timelines, many forces stimulate fear.

Unless people know how to overcome or transcend it, they can shrink back from it—often becoming paralyzed in the face of threats and even when being asked to commit to a bold new opportunity. Fear can be contagious when threats are magnified out of proportion to the solutions that will neutralize them. Fear can sometimes discourage possibility thinkers who dare to reach higher or to ask tough questions. The antidote to fear is courage, and it's courage that's needed to stimulate boldness and brilliance. Courage also illuminates new possibilities and ensures the successful performance of individuals, teams, and organizations in all settings.

It takes courage for any leader to anticipate and manage change rather than waiting or hoping for permission to act. Ideally it starts in the C-suite, yet C-suite members face additional challenges: nervous investors, board politics, and a complex array of special interests—inside and outside their enterprises. Courage is a critical choice for all who overstep formal authority to achieve the extraordinary and to change the game. Courage is also essential for the luminaries who raise red flags or propose solutions before game-changing ideas or strategies have gained acceptance or popularity.

For this chapter, we interview Dr. Louise (Yochee) Klein and Dr. Merom Klein, who work with innovation leaders in a variety of industries to build courage, spark imagination, and ignite brilliance. Yochee and Merom have lived and worked on four continents and in dozens of countries. Together, they bring 25+ years of business experience. Their research on courage draws from military psychology, innovation management and entrepreneurship, as well as sports and performing arts. Yochee earned her Psy.D. at Widener University in Professional Psychology and has over 20+ years of experience as a business psychologist and executive coach. Merom earned his Ph.D. at Temple University in Organizational Psychology and brings expertise as an entrepreneur and inventor as well as a business psychologist and leadership expert.

Merom and Yochee provide innovation coaching for teams, and team leaders, who are developing new cures, new devices, or new delivery or quality systems. Their book, *Courage to Lead*, describes how five Courage Activators power real innovation. Their most recent book, *Lead from the Middle: 5 Courage Activators for Business Leaders*, provides vivid examples and practical "how-to" advice on powering innovation in cross-functional teams, matrix structures, and business transformations. Merom and Yochee's clients include ARAMARK, Johnson & Johnson, Merck, IBM, Israel's Electric Corporation, Abbott, ING, the MRC and NASA. Please join us as they describe how leaders build courage.

QUESTIONS AND ANSWERS

How do you define "courage"?

Courage is a choice, not a character trait. Actually, according to our research, it's about choices that we make when demonstrating courage rather than withdrawing or getting paralyzed. These decisions help us engage, rather than run away or get belligerent—when we face adversity, discomfort, uncertainty or opposition. These choices constitute the 5 Courage Activators that make us adaptive, resilient, and agile in the face of danger. We call them Will, Purpose, Rigor, Candor, and Risk.

Will is demonstrated when we approach challenges with energy, spirit, and optimism—rather than resignation or defeatism. Purpose is evident when we choose lofty and audacious goals over those that are easily attainable. Rigor is present when we coordinate and orchestrate so that resources, time and energy are used efficiently. Candor is apparent when we solicit and learn from feedback, rather than justifying or defending our actions. It sharpens our thinking and facilitates learning. And finally, Risk is manifest when we make ourselves vulnerable in our efforts to build trust so that we and our teammates can empower and support each other in win/win partnerships.

Is courage something innate or can it be developed or enhanced?

We intentionally use the word "activators" because research shows that we are already hard-wired for courage, yet it can also be enhanced. Neuroscience researchers at the Weizman Institute in Israel discovered an area in the cerebral cortex that lights up when we fear something, yet draw closer to it to face it adaptively. Certainly we're all born with this "courage center," yet it takes practice to learn to use it as a way of overriding the more primitive fight-or-flight reflexes that shut down our ability to innovate and generate new possibilities.

We may need to override it when we feel stifled by politics, criticism, by a culture or personality that rubs us the wrong way, or a "big boss" who doesn't like the breakthrough ideas we put forward. We like to use Israel's first prime minister David ben Gurion's definition of courage—what he called "special knowledge." It's to know how to fear what we ought to fear, without getting stuck or disabled by that fear—and to be rational enough to not fear what we ought not to fear.

Specifically how do these 5 Courage Activators enable innovation?

Anything that's a real innovation—a game-changer—is going to stimulate discomfort. Working out the kinks or problems inherent in any big ideas creates tension in teams. The early adopters who "get it" want to run full-speed-ahead, jumping every hurdle in their way. Late adopters, who are threatened or turned off, often dig in their heels, find the flaws, and throw up obstacles that can block the critical path forward. It takes skill and courage to harness the discomfort, making it generative and creative, rather than combative.

Leaders who master the 5 Courage Activators equip their teams to thrive with this tension. They don't buy into one of the biggest myths about innovation: that people are most creative and generative during brainstorming—when there is no criticism, no debate, no naysaying, and when every idea gets appreciation and gold stars. Research does not support that myth; instead, it shows that creativity is greatest when team members can argue and debate—and use diverse perspectives to sharpen everyone's thinking.

We're not talking about those debaters who push others out of the way in their own pursuits—or who are so disrespectful that they leave a wake of fear, insecurity, and instability. Those behaviors stifle innovation, yet so do overly indulgent and generous leaders who encourage employees to maintain the status quo or who create benign conditions that don't require change. It's important that bold behaviors are employed when needed, and they must also be balanced by strength of heart.

In what way might dissatisfaction with the status quo build courage?

According to Israel's ninth President, Shimon Peres, dissatisfaction is the cultural DNA that makes Israel such a powerhouse for innovation. "We are always dissatisfied," Peres said. "Give us a desert and we ask, 'How can we make it bloom?' Give us two million immigrants and we ask, 'How can we build a high-tech economy and put them to work?' Give us disease and we ask, 'Where are the algorithms that show us what works, so we can spend our healthcare resources wisely?' We are never content when we see an unmet need or an imperfection," he says, and Peres was right. If people are satisfied, complacent, and willing to live with a certain level of inconvenience—or hunger, or illness, or ignorance—they don't need courage—and they're also not going to foster innovation.

Could you talk more about how courage sparks innovation?

It's important not to give in to fear, even if things get personal or if people whose interests are threatened come at us on the defensive. We also have to know how to embrace the hard work that comes with innovation, because anything that hasn't been done before is going to take a lot more effort and problem solving than tried-and-true pedestrian solutions. Focusing on the adversity, obstacles, or hardships of life can be overwhelming, but if we flip our perspective to the joy of discovery, and to building and creating, it's exhilarating. That requires knowing how to transform our fear so that it puts us on alert, prods us to act, and sharpens our thinking, rather than shutting it down. Another way to deal with fear is to know to deal with things such as criticism, naysaying, risk assessments, debates, or conflict without reacting out of fear. It's also knowing how to get past the fear of being alone—and without support—before our ideas catch on. This is a common trait of effective innovators.

What happens when courage is compromised?

Here's a good example: Let's say that someone has suddenly become incapacitated by a disease and family members react in a variety of ways. Some shut down in fear, throwing up their hands in resignation. Others move past that initial reaction, seeing how even a terrible disease can be a trigger for innovation. If we look back in time, we see that history is replete with examples of scientists who viewed these kinds of challenges as "calls to action" and subsequently made brilliant discoveries. Think what would have happened if they'd given in to their initial fear responses. Their brilliance would have been untapped, and millions of other people would not have benefited from their efforts.

How might leaders unwittingly compromise courage, and how can that be resolved?

Leaders can compromise courage in many ways, but two in particular stand out. One way is through hierarchy traps—when they get so focused on "what the boss wants" or what their roles are—or aren't—that they wait for permission or approval rather than taking action. The second way that they can err is by bringing people together in flat matrix structures, task forces and boundary-less teams, thinking that they will free people up to innovate. Without the security of knowing where they sit on organization charts and what their roles are, it can be daunting for people to step up and speak out.

The third way that leaders can compromise courage is with a bias against creativity. They might say that they want imagination, creativity, and initiative on their teams, yet research tells us that they often prefer to work with people who make them feel comfortable and secure. Sometimes leaders even marginalize or demonize people who bring creative, out-of-the-box thinking—or who take initiative. We can't blame leaders for creating hierarchy traps or for their biases against creativity. These actions and feelings are as natural as our fight-or-flight instincts, but leaders often need to be assisted to develop the courage to diagnose and overcome their biases against creativity.

You don't have to be a CEO or a department head to resolve those problems. That's why we talk about "leading from the middle." You just have to see what's happening and make the choice to transcend fear—and bring the team to a higher level of attention with a joke, a focusing question, or an affirmation of your company's core values. The 5 Courage Activators give leaders in the middle a roadmap to "flip the switch" and take teams from defending their positions or waiting for permission into a creative, generative, adaptive dialogue that produces real innovation. The research is clear: Courage is often compromised when people are reaching for high aspirations or doing things that are dangerous or politically sensitive. When leaders see courage is compromised—to lead from the middle flips that around.

What strategies can leaders employ, to build the degree of courage that's needed for innovation?

Leaders must communicate the message that courage is part of everyone's job, rather than something that's reserved for stretch assignments. Leaders must inspire—and *require*—courage, which means holding themselves and others accountable. Some leaders are too willing to be bystanders—or even worse, sometimes willing to join forces with those who resist change. Yet other leaders make things too easy—by handing out gold stars for work that isn't yet well baked or good enough. If they're courage-literate, leaders know how to resist these temptations, and they're skilled at pulling employees into the game and engaging them. They also effectively communicate their expectations and consistently recognize and reward courageous behaviors. They're the leaders who know how to build the courage needed for innovation, by lifting people up, moving them through their fears, and ennobling them.

TAKEAWAYS

- Leaders must reinforce the factors that build courage and ensure that they're not promoting comfort with the status quo or taking away reasons to innovate.

- Courage needs to be inspired—and required—by teaching people how to transcend fear rather than indulging it—and then recognizing and rewarding courageous behaviors.
- Leaders must also hold themselves and others accountable for courage by making it part of everyone's role and by reinforcing the link between courage and innovation.

TAKING STOCK

- Are my organization's leaders building courage or unintentionally stifling it?
- Could we be doing more to recognize and reward courageous and innovative behaviors?
- Are we effectively communicating our expectations about courage and innovation—and helping leaders support them by balancing boldness with strength of heart?

■ ■ ■

To learn more about Courage Growth Partners, go to couragegrowthpartners.com. If you found this chapter valuable, also see *A Culture of Innovation, Employee Engagement, High Performing Teams,* and *Meaning and Purpose.*

Chapter 17

Human Resources as a
Strategic Business Partner

An interview with Patricia Hamrick, Global Vice President, HR and Vitaliy Rusakov, President at Alcoa Fastening Systems & Rings (now Arconic)

■ ■ ■

"The magic formula that successful businesses have discovered is to treat customers like guests and employees like people."

— Tom Peters

Partnerships are as critical to orchestras and jazz ensembles as they are to organizations in all sectors and most industries. Orchestra leaders function as coaches and lead diverse groups of people in the same way that business leaders do today. And Human Resources leaders actively partner with leaders in the businesses that they support, functioning as skilled internal consultants who help people deal with the challenges inherent in multigenerational, multicultural, and highly distributed workforces. Human Resources leaders and various specialists within the profession also play a pivotal role in leading organizational change and strengthening relationships between employees and leaders to maximize collaboration and performance. As a result, it's not unusual to see HR functions today charged with the responsibility of building and sustaining cultures of innovation.

To facilitate innovation, effective HR leaders must know how to manage the change that accompanies it. They must also understand that prescriptive processes, practices, and policies need to be changed or discontinued—as do fragmented or outdated organizational structures. HR leaders also need to assist leaders in identifying the right talent and then developing and retaining it. In this chapter, we interviewed a powerful leadership team: Global Vice President of HR, Patricia Hamrick, and President, Vitaliy Rusakov.

Patricia has responsibility for developing and executing the division's global HR strategy, which encompasses talent acquisition and development, employee engagement, diversity, performance management, and innovation. Prior to joining Alcoa, Patricia worked for Johnson & Johnson's Consumer Sector, managing worldwide human resources for the Neutrogena franchise. She later assumed responsibility for the J&J Consumer Supply Chain organization in both Latin and North America. Before J&J, Patricia worked for the Network Centric Systems Division of Raytheon Vision Systems and at Pacer International. She holds a Bachelor of Arts degree in English from UCLA.

Prior to his current role, Vitaliy was the Vice President and General Manager of Operations at Alcoa Fastening Systems North America Aerospace, where he had responsibility for a number of California-based businesses as well as one in Suzhou, China. Beginning his career in the fastening business, Vitaliy worked at Fairchild Fasteners, which was acquired by Alcoa in 2002. Before Fairchild, he functioned in consulting roles with the global consulting firm Bain and Company. Vitaliy holds an MBA degree from Georgetown University in Washington, DC and two Bachelor's degrees from Kiev University: one in Linguistics and Education and another in International Economic Relations.

QUESTIONS AND ANSWERS

Would you both describe what a strategic partner does and why it's important for HR professionals to function as strategic partners?

Strategic partners work at aligning the goals and objectives of their functional areas, departments, or divisions with the broad goals and strategic direction of their organizations. As strategic partners, HR professionals can enable innovation by playing a key role in helping organizations lead change. They also help in recruiting, developing, and retaining top talent. Equally important, they support experimentation and learning. As business partners and change agents, HR professionals can also provide sounding boards and function as internal consulting resources.

What can HR professionals do to help organizations build and sustain cultures of innovation?

HR professionals can influence and help build a culture of innovation. They also help in leading the change that comes with that, but HR shouldn't be charged with owning innovation because that needs to be part of everyone's job. If HR is held solely accountable for innovation, no one else will have skin in the game. Equally important in building a culture of innovation is that it shouldn't be thought of as one size fits all. To make innovation happen, HR and other leaders need to consider the desired future state and what the organization wants to drive. That way, the right people are hired and subsequently put on the right teams.

HR also needs to ensure that highly creative and innovative people are identified during recruitment efforts and then developed, recognized, and rewarded. But that's not the extent of HR's role.

Organizations frequently hire external consultants for their honest opinions, and they have a right to expect the same from internal consultants. In the same way that consultants need to, at times, skillfully confront organizational leaders, HR professionals must do this too, backing up their positions with facts and data whenever possible.

What are the best ways for HR to recruit creative and innovative talent?

Word of mouth and the organization's reputation are most important for recruiting top talent, so the HR function must work at protecting and continually enhancing the organization's reputation in its recruiting markets. When interviewing candidates, HR needs to play an active role in evaluating potential innovators by looking for certain competencies and behaviors. To do this, it's important to know what drives people—at work and outside of work. For example, we know that people with interesting hobbies often add value professionally, so we ask candidates about their hobbies. We might also ask questions that determine whether they're curious about things. Since organizational fit is very important, we also ask questions to determine whether they're interested in the kind of work that we do. We know that innovators tend to be self-starters who set ambitious goals. They're also not afraid to take chances—and even fail—so we ask candidates what they're failed at. We also look for evidence of focus, courage, perseverance, and tenacity—all important enablers of innovation.

Have you changed any of your recruiting practices to incorporate other ways of identifying creative and innovative talent?

Yes. To drive better recruitment of future innovators, we recently enhanced our recruiting process by including plant tours that allow candidates to interact directly with engineers and numerous senior and cross-functional leaders. In this way, they know exactly what our division does, and through direct observation and interaction, we're able to carefully and intentionally select the best candidates. This often translates to identifying and selecting the candidates with the greatest potential to innovate.

How can HR help leaders motivate and retain highly creative and innovative employees?

Once we've identified creative people during the recruiting process, another challenge begins. Certain leaders can find it difficult to manage creative people because they typically want more than what they have and they typically try to improve things by challenging the status quo. The people who lead these kinds of employees sometimes need to reframe their expectations of them. Instead of viewing them as demanding or annoying, leaders need to see these employees as people who can bring value through their fresh set of eyes and unique perspectives.

At Alcoa, HR professionals work at incorporating employees' desires and aspirations for their current roles while simultaneously managing expectations regarding future roles. Rather than simply determining where the company itself would like to utilize employees' talents, we know that we need to play to people's passions and strengths—especially those of highly creative and innovative employees. This alignment—between what employees want and what we want of them—is critical for retention, for innovation, and for strong organizational as well as individual performance.

How can HR develop or revamp traditional recognition and reward systems to encourage innovation?

Sometimes technology can minimize—or even eliminate—the personal connection that employees and managers have, during face-to-face conversations about personal and organizational needs. In fact, it might already be time to throw out traditional performance management systems. They're often regarded as nothing more than check marks, as opposed to the performance contracts that they were intended to be. We know that it's very important to recognize and reward strong performance—and also creativity and innovation—and we believe that's best done through pay-for-performance systems that differentiate and reward top performers who give 100% and who drive big change.

However, HR professionals might need to, at times, help their organizations maintain flexibility around performance expectations. If the performance process or the performance goals are too rigid, they won't allow for the experimentation that's a necessary part of innovation. Rigid goals and expectations can have negative repercussions for any employee, but especially those who are highly creative and innovative, so we also need to ensure that everyone is getting recognized and rewarded in ways that make sense.

If you had to describe the most important element in a culture of innovation, what would that be, and how might HR support it?

The organization must create an environment that provides latitude for people to play, work, and take calculated risks. HR leaders, too, need to be comfortable about taking risks and about introducing change without fear that their positions will be jeopardized. Through training and individual coaching, leaders can be taught how to support risk taking and learning by providing guard rails and reinforcing innovative behaviors even if people aren't successful at their initial attempts to innovate. Change management is also critically important. To be innovative, one has to make changes to the status quo. Innovation won't happen if leaders can't get people to buy into and support necessary change.

What advice would you give to an HR leader who wants to help build a culture of innovation and function as an effective internal consultant and strategic partner?

At Alcoa, there's no question about needing the HR function at the table, but in organizations where this isn't the case, HR leaders shouldn't have an exclusive goal of obtaining a seat there. Their goals should instead be about wanting to contribute something valuable. In some organizations, the HR function might not even report to the same position as its peers do, but that doesn't have to be an insurmountable barrier.

HR leaders shouldn't wait to be "invited" to the table. They should assume that their function and that they, personally, belong at the table. This means leveraging their professional expertise, learning the language of business, and leaving "HR speak" behind. If they do this, HR leaders can demonstrate their value in problem solving and decision making at senior levels. To do that, however, HR leaders must have intimate knowledge about their organizations' business, culture, dynamics, and strategic direction. In demonstrating that knowledge, however, they can get their feet in the door and then continually grow their influence and credibility over time.

What advice can you give other senior leaders about how to leverage the HR function to positively impact innovation?

It's most important that HR functions as a strategic partner. For an organizational leader, that means picking the right HR people and allowing them to take risks as well as giving them latitude to develop innovative employee recruiting and retention methods and techniques. It's also good to involve HR partners in projects that aren't directly related to HR because that strengthens the function, creates greater alignment with peers, and provides different perspectives. This also makes output stronger.

It's also important to enable HR leaders as change agents by continually encouraging and rewarding them for asking why things are done in certain ways or how they might be done differently. The key role of the HR function in fostering innovation is to influence and transform—and that typically requires courage and tenacity. Knowing that, leaders with responsibility for HR functions need to visibly and actively support these functions and their leaders, so that credibility is built and maintained in both the short and long term.

TAKEAWAYS

- HR should facilitate innovation but not own it because innovation needs to be everyone's job.
- The HR function should play a pivotal role in building a culture of innovation through effective talent acquisition, talent management, and change management.
- HR professionals can provide value by coaching leaders about how to support the experimentation, risk taking, and learning that's critical for innovation.

- HR professionals need to have latitude to develop methods and techniques that attract, develop and retain innovative employees. They also need to discontinue policies and practices that inhibit innovation.
- Senior leaders need to hire HR leaders who can function as effective partners who actively contribute to implementing their organizations' visions and goals.

TAKING STOCK

- Does our HR function have the right leader, influence, and resources to enable innovation?
- Do we use HR policies and programs to build the future—or defend the past?
- Is our HR function empowered to reinvent itself and its services? If not, what could we do, to further empower it?

■ ■ ■

If you found this chapter useful, also see *A Culture of Innovation, Change Leadership, Courage,* and *Leadership Development.*

Chapter 18

Leadership Assessment

An interview with Harold Weinstein, Ph.D., Co-Founder TA-DA (DA (Talent Assessment and Development Advisors); leadership roles at Global Executive Learning and Wescott Financial Advisory Group, LLC; and former COO at Caliper Human Strategies

■ ■ ■

"The most dangerous leadership myth is that leaders are born—that there is a genetic factor to leadership. This myth asserts that people simply either have certain charismatic qualities or not. That's nonsense. In fact, the opposite is true.
Leaders are made rather than born."

— *Warren Bennis*

The skills of symphony orchestra musicians are typically evaluated in auditions, and after that, by orchestra leaders and other musicians on an ongoing basis. In this way, newly hired musicians' strengths can be leveraged, and areas in need of development can be addressed in a timely manner. While business leaders are often aware of the specific competencies required for key roles, without credible and reliable assessment tools, it's very difficult to judge capacity and focus development efforts to achieve the organization's strategy. Innovation competency models typically provide only enough detail to build the capacity to innovate. Why are competency models inadequate for these purposes?

Some of the competencies required for innovation are aspirational, so when employees look to leaders as exemplars, they see very little evidence of their organizations' desired competencies. Are organizations measuring the right competencies to align with their strategies for the marketplace and for enhanced leadership performance? To accurately assess what leadership competencies are in place and identify performance gaps, assessment tools must be well designed and validated. In this chapter, we interview Harold Weinstein, who holds a Ph.D. in Counseling Psychology from Michigan

State University and has over 35 years of business leadership, P&L management, and international consulting experience. While serving as the COO for Caliper Human Strategies, an international human resources assessment and consulting firm, Harold created the company's strategy and witnessed its growth from $5 million to $30 million in sales.

A recognized authority on the relationship between potential and performance, competency measurement, and talent management systems, Harold has conducted research, designed assessment and coaching tools, and implemented a variety of services and systems that integrate the measurements of human potential, behavior and organizational results. He has also spoken at regional and international conferences on such subjects as how to hire the best people, the differences between leaders and managers, and developing a winning team. Additionally, Harold has written about human resources issues, including a book published by McGraw-Hill entitled *How to Hire & Develop Your Next Top Performer*. He has also been frequently quoted by such publications as *Fortune Magazine*, *Business Week*, *The New York Times*, and the *Wall Street Journal*. Please join us as Harold describes how leadership assessment can be a key element in organizational and innovation success.

QUESTIONS AND ANSWERS

Would you please define "leadership assessment" operationally?

Leadership assessment is the quantification of individual and team capacity, illustrated by demonstrating, learning, and exhibiting a set of desired multi-dimensional behaviors.

How can formal assessments determine whether organizations have the necessary leadership skill sets and competencies in place to meet both current and future demands?

Leadership assessment can produce measures that are objective, reliable, and valid. This is important because leaders play a key role in realizing the organization's vision, mission, goals, and objectives. Assessments can also measure a leader's abilities to engender trust; inspire others to create; conceptualize and manage change processes; hold others accountable for a future state; marshal team problem solving, creative capacity, etc.

How can formal assessments identify leadership gaps?

One identifies leadership gaps in the same way that organizational gaps are identified during strategic planning efforts. An effective gap analysis typically starts with a future vision, evaluates current reality, and then identifies the "gap" between where things are and where they need to be. Leadership assessment must first start with a question of "What's important?" from the organization's perspective.

If the business leaders don't know what's important or where the organization is going, from a future state perspective, how will they know when it has arrived or why it hasn't arrived? The question of "What's important?" provides a context for leadership assessment and helps with the identification, cultivation and retention of the organization's talent. It's also critical for building capacity, sustainability, and for disciplines such as succession planning and brand building.

What should business leaders take into consideration when assessing leadership competencies?

Even when the question of "What's important?" has been asked and answered, there can be misalignment between values and culture. Company leaders often talk innovation, while the culture doesn't reflect it. Leadership assessment tools can spell out what's expected of leaders in clear behavioral terms, within the context of the organization's values and what's required for innovation. This can assist leaders in moving toward specific behaviors that drive cultural norms and strategic outcomes.

Can you think of organizations that exemplify how effective leadership facilitates innovation?

Some companies, such as GE, are known for their cultivation and growth of leaders, and have built brands around leadership development. These companies create a whole culture around the development of leaders, for good or bad. In GE's case, there has been a direct connection between its commitment to and use of assessment and the behavior shifts of its leaders. Because of this, a company that was once exclusively focused on execution is now also focused on innovation.

Please cite a specific example of how organizations move leaders toward desired behaviors.

A good example is SAB Miller Brewing Company (a large international brewing company that owns MillerCoors, Pilsner Urquell, Peroni, Fosters, and 800 other brands of beer). There, the process begins with desired competencies and behaviors and a definition, by the participants' supervisor, of the person's strengths, struggles, expectations for movement to the next level, the role that the participant is currently functioning in, and how that role supports future aspirations.

Then a 360 multi-rater feedback assessment and other personality and learning styles measurements are conducted with the participant, followed with coaching in connection with an action learning project, where leaders learn by doing. Development is focused on business and personal challenges in the work environment and in the participant's family. The process involves periodic meetings with the supervisor to support ongoing growth of the participant and to facilitate coaching around critical behaviors. At the close of the process, there is a debrief with the individual participant. Then there are subsequent meetings with the learning officer and manager around next steps for development. This brings transparency to the entire process.

In what ways does leadership assessment ultimately translate to individual results, organizational performance, and innovation?

I see this process as a series of connected events that begin with defining the competencies, as the SAB Miller Brewing Company did. Then it's important for managers to function as coaches and for leadership and development functions to create programs that support the individual's development. The last step of the process is measuring individual, team, and organizational performance on the basis of objective criteria such as performance appraisals, successful team results, new product or service introductions, enhanced internal or external processes, number of patents filed, etc.

What do you believe are the most critical leadership competencies and behaviors for innovation?

The most critical leadership competency for innovation is the ability to distinguish between a mindset of curiosity and learning versus a judgmental or hypercritical mindset. These differing mindsets drive different kinds of leadership behaviors. A mindset that favors curiosity drives behaviors such as meta-thinking on diverse topics (such as seeing the forest versus the trees). It also means seeking a breadth of interests, encouraging questions, and having the tenacity to challenge conventional thinking.

The judgmental mindset can drive decision making only on the basis of what one already knows or on inherent biases or fears. In today's world, much is unknown and needs to be created as one goes. In any trial-and-error process, mistakes will be made. Leaders must allow for experimentation that encourages the taking of calculated risks and values learning. It's also vitally important for innovation to be able to look outside of one's self or the entrenched team for answers, tapping sources of information and perspectives outside the usual places.

We know that a fear of failure can negatively impact innovation. What are some attributes of people who deal with it well? Can assessments identify these characteristics?

Yes, personality or behavioral assessments as well as 360-feedback assessments can identify these characteristics, which typically include learning to adapt, recovering from mistakes, putting failures in the past and moving on. That means not being crippled by failure and also having the ego strength to return to errors and learn from them.

What are some other leadership competencies that drive innovation?

It's important to find a good balance between analytical thinking and broad-brush thinking—to be able to zoom in on details and zoom out with a high-level perspective. Highly innovative leaders are also able to think both quickly and slowly, versus defaulting to thinking too quickly. They also typically demonstrate an ability to change behavior. To effectively innovate, leaders need to model strengths such as resilience, risk-taking, and learning from successes and failures.

In closing, what are some of the major factors that need to be considered when assessing leadership effectiveness?

Assessment factors typically include stakeholders such as the boss, peers, direct reports, customers, family and leaders themselves. Another important factor is the context in which assessment is occurring, specifically the organization's culture, the type of challenges the leader is facing, and the expectations of that particular leadership role. Finally, the tools that are used to measure both baseline behaviors and growth must be valid, reliable and rooted in the desired future state of the organization.

TAKEAWAYS

- The executive leadership team must first determine what is important for the future of the organization. Then executives must view leadership assessment as a strategy to achieve organizational goals and objectives.
- Leadership assessment should be used as a tool for evaluating both current and future leadership gaps as well as the best ways to narrow or close them.
- Desired competencies and behaviors must be identified, communicated, and modeled.
- Ongoing assessment is necessary for determining whether leaders are exhibiting behaviors that support or inhibit innovation. In addition, the leadership assessment process must have a valid and reliable measurement component so that development efforts can be assessed on a pre- and post-basis, measured over time, and ultimately tied to organizational performance.

TAKING STOCK

- How might we incorporate a 360 leadership assessment that highlights innovation competencies?
- Is the assessment connected to the strategic plan, the organizational vision and values, and to reward and development systems within the company?
- How are leaders involved in the leadership assessment process—with succession planning, coaching, giving feedback, and holding people accountable for behavioral changes?

■ ■ ■

To learn more about Harold Weinstein's work, go to www.tada-advisors.com. If you found this chapter helpful, also see *A Business Case for Coaching, Employee Engagement, Executive Development,* and *Leadership Development.*

Chapter 19

Leadership Development

An interview with Elena DePalma, Senior Director of Organizational Effectiveness at Yale University and former Vice President, Human Resources, Merrill Lynch Credit Corporation

■   ■   ■

".... the demands for organizational change will make up a new agenda, a need to move from one pattern of performance to another, from one kind of leadership to another."

— Nicholas Imperator & Oren Harrari

Creative talent and strong leadership are some of the most critical components in any innovation process. Consequently, orchestra leaders, professional jazz ensembles, and leaders in almost all organizations must develop talent on an ongoing and consistent basis if they're to remain viable. Leaders today are expected to produce innovative solutions to complex problems while encouraging their employees to do the same. A highly diverse, multigenerational workforce can make effective leadership even more challenging. And financial hurdles, too, can make the leadership component more difficult, as leaders are continually asked to do things faster and better with fewer resources. Sadly, many leaders aren't up to the task. Many put forth their best efforts, yet they fall short because they lack skills in planning, complex problem solving, and decision making.

Elena DePalma, Senior Director of Organizational Effectiveness at Yale University with responsibilities for university-wide leadership of talent management and succession planning, tells how leadership can help to close a skills gap. Elena brought to Yale 20 years of leadership experience in human resources, training, and organizational development. She served in roles at Pitney Bowes and Merrill Lynch as well as the Vice President of Human Resources at Merrill Lynch Credit Corporation when it won the Malcolm Baldrige National Quality Award. Elena has extensive experience designing, developing, and implementing adult learning programs. She coaches numerous professionals and consults with senior management on issues related to strategic planning, performance management, succession planning, change management, and team building. Elena earned her Master's Degree in Clinical Social Work from Florida State University and a Bachelor's Degree in Business from the Ancell School of Business at Western Connecticut State University.

In the following Q&A, Elena discusses how, during uncertain economic times, leadership becomes an increasingly difficult task and requires more developmental attention—particularly since leadership development is crucial to innovative thinking and new approaches.

QUESTIONS AND ANSWERS

First, how do you define "leadership development"?

Leadership development is an intentional effort on the part of an organization or institution that provides leaders with the opportunity to develop knowledge, skills and abilities that support the realization of the desired culture.

Why do you think most executives believe that leadership development is critical, particularly in today's competitive environments?

A commitment to leadership development can be a key differentiator for an organization and an important ingredient for enabling the creation of a higher performing organization. Leaders need the knowledge, skills and the ability to bring out the best in the people they manage. However, I'm not convinced that most executive leaders believe that leadership development is critical. The more sophisticated and forward-thinking ones do. It's important today because, especially during difficult times, organizations are in need of the very best leaders, those who are able to inspire and influence and motivate others. Great leaders drive the culture.

Few people would argue that the last few years have been economically challenging for most organizations. What would you say to executives who might be thinking about reducing costs in the area of leadership development?

By investing internally in the development of experienced leaders and emerging leaders, an organization ensures it has an internal pipeline to fill positions as they become open. Not only is this the right thing to do, but the alternative—recruiting externally on a regular basis—can be cost prohibitive.

When many people think of leadership development, they think purely in terms of training, but in truth, there are other important aspects. Can you describe other development initiatives that are equal to or more effective than formal training?

Although it has its place, training is one of the least effective methods of leadership development. The most effective way to develop leaders is on-the-job development that places leaders into experiences that help them grow their skills. This might take the form of participation on a project team or other work group or simply standing in for their supervisor at a meeting. Depending on the situation, other extremely valuable methods of development include the use of 360 feedback, coaching, and mentoring. Mentoring can be especially useful when a senior leader is paired with a more junior leader, and both individuals can learn from each other.

Participation on non-profit boards is another excellent opportunity to develop leadership skills. There is a dual benefit too. Not only does the individual develop leadership skills like strategic planning, building consensus and leading through influence, but the local community benefits from their expertise as well. Additionally, exposure to a variety of best practices can be leveraged in their own businesses and be applied innovatively. Depending upon the circumstances, other effective methods can include junior executive training programs, rotational assignments, and action learning.

Why is leadership development so important as an innovation enabler?

Leaders drive the culture, so a focus on leadership development is a prerequisite for creating a culture that values innovation. To create a leadership culture that values innovation, there must be a focus on diversity, managing change, communication, and development of self and others. Additionally, in order for innovation to be enabled, the environment must be open to empowerment. Leaders must empower rather than control, and must provide a safe environment for employees to make mistakes. Of course, this doesn't apply to jobs where high compliance is critical (e.g., nurses, pilots, air traffic controllers).

How can leadership development help companies achieve their overall goals?

Leadership can be a key differentiator for a company. It is an important ingredient for ensuring the organization's activity is based on formal planning efforts and that it possesses the leadership skills to be able to implement those plans.

How can leaders create a culture of innovation? And how can leadership development enable that?

Leadership development enables a culture of empowerment that makes the environment safe for innovation to occur. Innovation is less prevalent in organizations with low trust, so any activities and initiatives taken to address trust issues can lead to a culture that is more conducive to innovation. Too much control, criticism, and unproductive politics can make innovation more difficult. Systems of communication must be open, well used, and available to all.

Additionally, developing mindful leaders helps to create a culture of innovation. These are leaders who are present and who, in a non-judgmental way, intentionally pay attention to their thoughts and what is happening around them. This self-awareness allows for greater recognition of emerging insights and innovative ideas. Diversity of thought is also a critical element in innovation. Leaders need to recognize that multiple perspectives are important in problem solving and decision making, and they should actively encourage and seek multiple perspectives or styles.

What leadership competencies do you believe are most important for leaders to develop or improve, as a way of enabling innovation?

Competencies such as empowering people, fostering trust, influencing, coaching, and inspiration enhance and enable innovation. I think the most important of these is inspiration. This is achieved by modeling values and commitment and by leaders standing up for these through what they say and do.

How can leaders anticipate, minimize, and deal with innovation obstacles as they arise?

They can enlist the help of a team of diverse individuals, do contingency planning, and delegate the development of solutions to staff, which helps them develop at the same time.

What can be done to teach leaders how to reduce risk when attempting to create value through innovation?

They should form committees and task forces and require cost-benefit analyses of ideas before submitting ideas for review. They should also utilize stage-gate procedures that begin with a small investment. Then they should provide additional funding for the idea, if it appears to be viable, or quickly discontinue the idea or project if it appears early on that it's not going to deliver a return.

What are some specific ways that organizations can help leaders enhance the critical skills that contribute to a culture of innovation?

While providing resources like training and other tools will help, the most effective way to encourage the desired behaviors is to model and reinforce them at the top of the organization. Then implement programs and other forums, formal or informal that reinforce, recognize, and reward those who demonstrate and are successfully using the behaviors. What applies to leaders most is what Mahatma Gandhi said: "Be the change you wish to see in the world."

TAKEAWAYS

- Secure a leadership development sponsor in senior management who knows that effective leadership can be a key differentiator.
- Make sure that leadership development is a key component in the organization's culture.
- Ensure that development initiatives go beyond traditional training.
- Select leaders who are representative of the desired culture and encourage them to model desired behaviors.
- Measure progress of leadership development efforts and communicate results.

TAKING STOCK

- Is my organization providing the leadership development that's necessary to realize our strategic long-term goals?
- Are we relying too heavily on training? Or are we also providing action learning, coaching, rotational assignments, and other development initiatives?
- Are the leaders in my company cognizant of the role that they play in enabling innovation? Are they skilled in facilitating it? How could they be further helped to do this?
- Do our top leaders model the values, purpose and behaviors that inspire innovation?

■ ■ ■

If you found this chapter informative, please also see *Change Leadership, Executive Development, Leadership Assessment, and Vision and Values.*

Chapter 20

Meaning and Purpose

An interview with Ilene Wasserman, Ph.D., President, ICW Consulting Group, LLC; Senior Leadership Fellow at the Wharton School and Faculty at the Philadelphia College of Osteopathic Medicine

■ ■ ■

"Between stimulus and response, there is a space. In that space lies our freedom and our power to choose our response. In our response lies our growth and our happiness."

— Viktor Frankl

When symphony orchestra and jazz musicians know that they're bringing joy to an audience, they believe their work has meaning and purpose. How important might it also be for employees, other than musicians, to find meaning and purpose, particularly in day-to-day tasks? How might leaders in all environments help people find meaning and purpose in their work—and in their innovations? When asked to innovate, people need to perceive that the innovation itself has value. They also need to determine that they can bring it about in meaningful ways.

In his book entitled *Meaningful Work*, Dr. Michael Steger, a faculty member at Colorado State University, relays a story told by J. J. Ryan, author of the book *Humanistic Work: Its Philosophical and Cultural Implications*. Ryan describes an observer who is watching three men breaking boulders with iron hammers. When he asks what they're doing, each of the men answers this question very differently. One man says, "I'm turning big rocks into little rocks." Another says, "I'm working to feed my family." And still another, with great pride, says, "I'm building a cathedral!"

Although the second man might find meaning indirectly in providing for his family, Steger believes that the third man is one who views his work as maximally meaningful. Notice that we didn't say that man "does meaningful work," because, as this story suggests, meaning and purpose are highly subjective. With that in mind, how might leaders spur employees to innovate and sustain the innovation process despite obstacles, failures, and frustrations at each phase? In this chapter, Ilene Wasserman, Ph.D. assists us in answering these questions as well as understanding how successful leaders help employees find meaning in their work while also ensuring value for key stakeholders and achieving alignment between individual and organizational goals.

Ilene is a thought leader, "scholar-practitioner," college professor, and author of a number of book chapters and articles. Through her research and direct observation, she brings perspective regarding how leaders facilitate innovation. As the Founder of ICW Consulting Group and President of Innovative Communities at the Workplace, Ilene consults to organizations on executive leadership development, team development, and organization culture change. Her clients include major Health Care Systems and members of Businesses for Social Responsibility as well as universities and community organizations. Prior to starting her own practice, Ilene was Vice President and Principal at Kaleel Jamison Consulting Group, where she worked with educational institutions, public and private collaborations, and Fortune 50 and Fortune 100 companies. She holds a Ph.D. in Human & Organizational Development from Fielding Graduate University as well as a Masters of Social Work and a Masters of Education in Counseling from Washington University. Please join us and learn about her contribution to this important topic.

QUESTIONS AND ANSWERS

How do you define "purpose" and "meaning" with regard to work?

I think of them in two ways. At the organizational level, they usually center around the organization's mission, vision, and values. At the personal level, they're often defined by the tasks that people need to perform and by the values, concerns, and goals that individuals associate with those tasks. Individuals need to know that what they're being asked to do makes sense—that what they do is part of a bigger story that has value or provides some benefit of greater good. That can mean saving lives, protecting the environment, or simply providing products or services that improve the quality of life for their customers.

Why all the current focus on helping people find meaning and purpose in their work?

There are a number of different forces at play today. First, are the increased demands for meaning and purpose by knowledge workers. Second, are challenges brought about by the economy with regard to employees' limited mobility and employers' need to do more with less. Third, are the values of people in today's workforce who are best motivated by work that go beyond material gains. Meaning can vary for each individual and it can shift with external changes, but it's important to realize that it's also shaped by people's interactions with others. When organizations create working communities that align responsibilities with the mission, work takes on different meaning and people are likely to rise to a higher level of performance than when tasks are simply assigned.

How do individuals find meaning—or *make* meaning—from daily and often routine tasks?

It's important for people to have opportunities to articulate their own intrinsic connection to the work that they do as well as how they do it. Some jobs have inherent meaning and purpose—such as those of firefighters, law enforcement officers, healthcare workers, and others in the helping professions. However, like the story that opened this chapter, meaningful work can go beyond a specific task. This is even more likely when leaders can help people find meaning in their work by showing them how key stakeholders benefit from their efforts.

In what ways can leaders create organization cultures that help employees find meaning in what they do?

Author Neal E. Chalofsky, in his book *Meaningful Workplaces*, reminds us that work is made meaningful by the work itself as well as where and how it's done. With this in mind, many organizations today are exploring ways to create values-based cultures that encourage employees to engage in robust dialogue and to explore meaning and purpose in their work. Although dialogue is a good start—because it enables people to share their ideas when addressing key issues and decision making—it's critical that they also experience feelings of trust and of belonging. Some leaders have customers or end users talk with employees about the benefits they've enjoyed as a result of an innovation, product or service.

What can organizations and leaders do to align stakeholders around meaning and purpose?

Achieving alignment can be challenging because internal stakeholders, such as board members, employees, and leaders, will likely interpret meaning and purpose differently from external stakeholders. And because external stakeholders range from customers, clients, users, shareholders, to special interest groups, communities, regulators, legislators, and communities, they're likely to have competing goals and priorities. Aligning values with the mission can serve as good starting points, but leaders must also assure that meaning and purpose is articulated for each constituent. That means showing them how the work performed in an organization is connected—directly or indirectly—to the mission.

Leaders achieve ultimate success when they can help people see—through customer or client testimonials, endorsements, and success stories—how their efforts link to a product or service that makes life more meaningful and/or easier. Buy-in and sponsorship are key, so if leaders communicate the "why," people will often take on responsibility—and ownership. Then it's important to demonstrate how people's efforts are connected to the success of their departments, divisions, or units. Imagine leaders of a not-for-profit organization engaging employees in the conversation when there is a need for change, such as cost-cutting or streamlining services. Engagement, along with a reminder of the organization's mission and purpose can, even in challenging times, generate support.

How can leaders help people align their individual goals with organizational goals?

Successful leaders find out what's personally important to employees and then reinforce that through goal setting and recognition. Leaders usually share the big picture first, as opposed to simply communicating "the simple facts." However, meaning and purpose are subjective matters. They're not only realized when a goal is achieved or a certain result or solution is attained. Most people need to feel that they're making a difference at various phases of the process. That's why milestones and celebrations around success are so important. These celebrations are also an opportunity to invite people to tell stories that reinforce what's meaningful. This, and ongoing dialogue, are what lay the groundwork for shared visions and goals, that facilitate collaboration, and that foster a desire to work in sync.

How can organizations and leaders convey meaning and purpose for desired innovations?

Innovation success is mostly associated with the value proposition of a particular innovation initiative. Successful leaders know how to create meaning in the early phases of the process and sustain it even when facing obstacles in the later phases of the process. They convey an authentic presence thus not falling prey to a perception of "innovation for innovation's sake." Leaders must help people translate how meaning for the organization is consistent with their own personal values. That then can spur action at all stages of the innovation process. However, leaders also need to ask questions, listen, clarify, and resolve conflict when it inevitably arises.

What are the best ways to convey meaning and purpose in early phases of the innovation process?

The first phase of the innovation process—issue identification and clarification—requires that the issues under review create value for intended stakeholders. Customer and market insights provide context for a story that the project can "live within," and they also build momentum for idea generation. Idea generation, the second phase of the innovation process, is when it's critical to connect the innovation initiative with the core mission or purpose of the organization. This creates organizational alignment with the core purpose, which is necessary for the innovation to be successful.

This phase of the innovation process involves generating as many ideas as possible, without regard to whether they're viable. Having a way to dialogue and reach alignment around purpose and meaning is crucial. Learning helps to sustain and deepen meaning for everyone involved because it paints the full context of what it inspires. This is important for the next step in the innovation process—when ideas are evaluated, screened, or developed.

How can meaning and purpose be ensured when screening, developing, and implementing ideas?

In the screening and developing phase, leaders also play a pivotal role regarding how the intended innovation will meet the needs of either or both internal and external stakeholders. If leaders understand choices and explore opportunities early on—prior to investing a great deal of time and resources—they can ensure that resources are properly allocated or preserved. This means collecting, organizing, and making sense of the forces that will help shape the acceptance and practicality of new products, services, business models, distribution systems, etc. The activity in this phase then lays the groundwork for the final stage of the innovation process, where meaning and purpose must be clear at the forefront. Having meaning and purpose in the forefront helps to inspire people when they anticipate or encounter implementation obstacles.

In concluding, are there some tried-and-true methods for securing meaning and purpose?

People live in stories—those they tell about themselves, about others, and about relationships. Stories are a compelling way to convey that there's more to working than simply carrying out tasks. People create personal meaning from their observations. To me, the real essence of living a life with purpose and meaning is having it reflected in everything we do and make. That includes the relationships and stories we make as well as the work product. Organizations must continually manifest purpose and meaning—not only in stories—but also, in actions that speak their values. Their values are the compasses that provide direction and that keep people aligned and on course.

TAKEAWAYS

- Meaning and purpose are powerful drivers for individual and team performance as well as enablers for innovation at all phases of the process.
- To motivate people in today's workforce, leaders must learn about peoples' needs and help them create meaning in their work.
- By showing how peoples' actions meet stakeholder needs, leaders can paint a larger picture of the greater good and begin to lay the groundwork for alignment between personal and organizational goals.

- Most people will support an innovation if they perceive meaning and purpose behind it; if they feel they have a voice; and if they believe that they're capable of supporting the innovation in ways that make sense.
- To successfully innovate, leaders must listen, clarify, and resolve conflict when it arises.

TAKING STOCK

- How skilled are my organization's leaders at helping employees find meaning and purpose in their work?
- Are leaders able to help key stakeholders find meaning and purpose throughout the innovation process?
- Do executives encourage the collaboration that's necessary for aligning personal goals with organizational goals?

■ ■ ■

To learn more about the work that Ilene does, go to icwconsulting.com. If you found this chapter helpful, also see *Buy-in, Sponsorship, and Commitment, Competition and Collaboration, Employee Engagement, Shared Vision and Values,* and *Storytelling.*

Chapter 21

Personal Accountability

An interview with Paul B. Sniffin, Founder and Managing Partner, CPI/New Options Group and Partner of the Mid-Atlantic Region of Cornerstone International Group

■ ■ ■

"The ancient Romans had a tradition: whenever one of their engineers constructed an arch, as the capstone was hoisted into place, the engineer assumed accountability for his work in the most profound way possible: he stood under the arch."

— *Michael Armstrong*

In the same way that each musician is critical to the success of a musical performance, each person on almost any team is critical to achieving overall goals and objectives. Nowhere are individual roles in teams more critical, however, than in military missions. For example, people involved in helicopter medevac missions must work with others collectively to get the wounded out of life-and-death situations as expeditiously as possible. The two pilots, two gunners, crew chief, and medic on board these helicopters all play a critical part. If any one individual fails in these missions, everyone is in potential danger.

Taking into account today's constant change, stiff competition, and unexpected shifts in market demands, many leaders have had to challenge basic tenets of doing business. In certain situations, they've also needed to redefine long-standing concepts and practices related to planning, leadership, and experimentation. In this chapter, we'll explore the possible need to redefine traditional definitions of failure and personal accountability.

We chose Paul Sniffin for this chapter because of his experience in business environments as well as his leadership roles in high impact military operations. As a CEO of a boutique talent management consulting firm and former combat pilot, Paul has had experience with accountability from a variety of perspectives. Beginning his career as an officer in the U.S. Marine Corps, Paul also served as a combat helicopter pilot in Vietnam. Since that time, he has functioned in a variety of leadership roles with two global consulting organizations. He has more than 25 years of experience in the field of career and performance consulting and with building sales organizations and leadership teams. In addition to coaching and advising senior executives, Paul guides and develops high-potential leaders.

As a former chair of a global talent management consultancy, Paul grew the organization to more than 200 offices. Throughout his career, he has been at the forefront of change, most recently in helping to develop credentialing in executive coaching and career management practices. Paul currently oversees the strategic direction of CPI/New Options Group. He is certified in multiple diagnostic assessments, including 360° multi-rater leadership tools for assessing and developing executive teams. Paul has authored numerous articles and has lectured on leadership and career topics. Please join us as he shares a story about personal accountability that occurred during his military service in Vietnam and how he views personal accountability today.

QUESTIONS AND ANSWERS

How do you define "personal accountability" and the way it drives organizational accountability?

Team efforts usually drive how things get done in organizations of all kinds. Holding team members accountable for doing what they say they're going to do is a critical component of team effectiveness. However, it's been my experience that, all too often, team members find it difficult to confront individual members when they fail to fulfill their commitments. If each person pulls his/her weight and fulfills commitments, teams, in aggregate, are held accountable and well positioned to innovate. When teams are individually accountable on an enterprise-wide basis, it translates to organizational accountability. So in effect, personal accountability is a component, as well as the starting point, of organizational accountability.

Would you share a good example of personal accountability from your experience in the military?

When flying, pilots need to make constant adjustments in conjunction with wind direction and velocity, as well as weight, air temperature, altitude and humidity. Life requires similar adjustments and so do efforts to drive innovation. Much of what we encounter has to be dealt with conditionally. Yet, in the military—and particularly during combat—accountability isn't defined conditionally. Given the nature of the work, people are either accountable or they're not. The mission is always "number one," and each person has to rely on others to fulfill critical roles.

Here's an example of that: When picking up and transporting wounded Marines during one of my missions, my comrades and I found ourselves under intense enemy fire—and to everyone's surprise, one of our gunners wasn't returning fire. This placed the team in such a vulnerable position that the mission's crew chief found it necessary to throw the gunner on the floor of the aircraft, wrench away his gun, and begin opening fire himself. Bottom line: The whole team and the wounded Marines in the plane had been put in unnecessary danger that day because one person had fallen short of his responsibilities.

After my team and I completed the mission, I could tell that the gunner—a kid who was only about 18-years old—was devastated. After inviting him to tell me what had happened, I learned that this young man had lost all confidence in himself after freezing up and knowing that he'd let the team down. Realizing that it was important for him to learn from this experience, so he could be better prepared for the next mission, I asked what he might do differently the next time. I also reassured him that he wasn't the only person to react this way, and I explained how the stress of combat can cause people to react in ways that are contrary to their intentions.

So the lesson here is that falling short of expectations is not the same as lacking accountability?

I believe that when someone truly fails to be accountable, there's usually a question of intent or a conscious decision to not commit or follow through on something that was committed to previously. In this case, freezing out of fear wasn't a conscious decision to avoid responsibility. In fact, falling short of expectations is something that most of us do at some point in our careers and in our lives. Surely the gunner was trained for this type of mission, and he was most likely capable; however, judging from his age, he probably didn't have a wealth of experience. That mission might have even been his first. We know that in life-and-death situations, almost anyone can become paralyzed with fear. In this situation, the questions to be asked are these: Did the gunner have the confidence to do the job? And was he capable?

Does this example show how accountability needs to be defined in conjunction with capability and confidence?

Without personal accountability, individuals don't hold to their commitments. This can have a negative impact on the functioning of their teams and can ultimately affect an entire organization. Individuals need to ensure that they have the confidence and capability to fulfill their commitments, yet this is also something that leaders need to assess. In this way, everyone can ensure that expectations are communicated—and considered—before holding people accountable for tasks that might exceed their abilities.

What lessons can leaders and executive coaches like you apply from this story?

People often associate failure with a lack of accountability, but that's a judgmental way of looking at things. Many times, people have to be helped to reframe situations in which they've failed so they can stop blaming themselves. They must do this to restore their confidence and move on. Often peoples' mistakes are a result of blind spots, organizational politics, inadequate resources, or lack of skills. The list is actually quite long. At the same time, these factors shouldn't be used as excuses for mistakes or failures, but rather as opportunities to examine different or new strategies to deal with external challenges in successful and satisfying ways.

How might reframing "failure" relate to innovation?

When people feel they've failed, they lose confidence. This makes them reluctant to take the risks that are such an important element of innovation. When individuals are held accountable, the entire system is fueled by follow-through, support, and achievement. This is how trust is built. Without trust, there is little collaboration, and without collaboration, there is often a lack of alignment. All of these factors can negatively impact innovation.

So how can leaders drive innovation while still holding people accountable for their actions?

I believe the heart of innovation resides within leaders, yet before leaders can hold people accountable, they need to energize and motivate them. This is most often done by communicating compelling messages that move people to action. If we examine the lives of great men and women—people who were supreme in their calling—they used the power of words. Think of Winston Churchill, with his directive in the worst of times, "We will never, never give up." Another example is President John F. Kennedy's promise, "We will land a man on the moon in ten years." And one of the best examples of all is Martin Luther King's "I have a dream" speech. These people's words changed the course of history, and powerful messages such as theirs can be replicated in business.

How do organizations ensure team accountability?

Team goals are typically achieved through formal accountability mechanisms that are documented in strategic plans, such as goals, objectives, tasks for specific people, and timelines. But it's also critically important for teams to have role clarity, especially where there are overlapping responsibilities or accountabilities. Larger systems can be negatively impacted when even a few team members don't pull their share and aren't held accountable by the team. Like any other system, when one part isn't working, the entire system can be compromised.

Do you think that accountability mechanisms can inhibit or prevent innovation as well as enable it?

Many times people are rewarded for adhering to a rigid plan that's no longer relevant. Other times, they're rewarded for doing whatever it takes to "make their numbers." If people aren't held accountable for realistic goals, important tasks might not get done—or at least not on time or within established quality standards. On the other hand, if people are held too highly accountable (through overly rigid goals and objectives that don't flex with changing markets, customer demands, etc.) individuals, leaders, and teams will typically sacrifice innovation in favor of certainty. This is also true if recognition and reward systems reinforce irrelevant goals or if they reward people for fixing problems that don't require solutions.

In closing, what do you believe to be the single most important step that leaders need to take, regarding the kind of accountability that's such a critical enabler of innovation?

Leaders need to ensure that there's a clear mission, specific and achievable goals, and absolute individual commitment to agreed-upon objectives because those are the starting points for personal accountability.

TAKEAWAYS

- Accountability starts with individuals and teams and collectively becomes organizational accountability.
- To be accountable, people need to stay focused on the goals to be accomplished.
- Trust forms the foundation for accountability within organizations and also facilitates the risk taking that's needed for innovation.
- People shouldn't be labeled as "failures" or as "lacking accountability" when they've been given tasks that exceed their understanding or capability.
- Executives shouldn't expect that accountability systems can take the place of inspired leadership, compelling missions, visions, and value propositions. All are needed.

TAKING STOCK

- Have leaders in my organization defined accountability in ways that might inhibit innovation?
- Are leaders in my company actively inspiring people and coaching them to be maximally productive and innovative while also employing accountability systems to ensure results?
- Is there a high degree of trust in my organization? If not, are rigid accountability definitions and systems at the root of a lack of trust?

■ ■ ■

To learn more about CPI-New Options Group, go to www.cpi-newoptions.com. If you found this chapter useful, also see our chapters entitled A *Culture of Innovation, Courage, Execution, High Performing Teams,* and *Resilience.*

Chapter 22

Shared Vision and Values

An interview with Jim Kouzes, Dean's Executive Fellow of Leadership, Leavey School of Business at Santa Clara University and Co-Author of the Best-Selling Book, *The Leadership Challenge*

■ ■ ■

"Leadership is not an affair of the head. Leadership is an affair of the heart."

— *Jim Kouzes and Barry Posner*

For jazz musicians, distributed power and shared visions are givens. For symphony orchestra leaders, the issue is a bit more complex but they too can distribute power by inviting the input and ideas of musicians regarding music to be played and how it's to be played. When doing this, they lay the groundwork for individual visions of what a performance will be like and for how the audience will react. Then conductors must work at aligning individual visions to produce a shared vision. Clearly, a personal vision is the first critical step toward a shared vision, for a team in almost any organization.

However, before formulating a personal vision, leaders must examine their own personal values. And to enlist support, leaders must have intimate knowledge of their followers' personal aspirations, values, hopes, and dreams. If they don't already know this, they must ask questions and listen carefully. It's also important for leaders to be enthusiastic about their vision and to make it a cause for the commitment of others. In order to give the vision life, they must also instill hope and confidence—and they must speak from the heart. This chapter describes how a compelling vision can evoke excitement in others, how it becomes contagious, and how leaders can create a shared passion through inspiration.

We interviewed Jim Kouzes, co-author of the book, *The Leadership Challenge* and co-developer of *The Five Practices of Exemplary Leadership*® framework. *The Leadership Challenge,* now in its 5th edition, is a result of 30 years of extensive research. The *Wall Street Journal* has cited Jim Kouzes as one of the 12 most requested non-university executive education providers to U.S. companies. In 2010, he received the Thought Leadership Award from the Instructional Systems Association. In 2010-2013 he was listed as one of *HR Magazine's* Most Influential International Thinkers. He is the recipient of the American Society for Training and Development (ASTD) 2009 Distinguished Contribution to Workplace Learning and Performance Award, and was named one of the Top 100 Thought Leaders in Trustworthy Business Behavior by Trust Across America in 2010-2015 and honored a Lifetime Achievement recipient in 2015.

As an experienced executive, Jim directed the Executive Development Center (EDC) at Santa Clara University from 1981 through 1987. From 1988 to 2000, he also served as president and then CEO and chairman of the Tom Peters Company. Jim also founded the Joint Center for Human Services Development at San Jose State University, and prior to that, was on the staff of the University of Texas School of Social Work. Please join us as he describes the significance of vision and values, how to envision the future, and how to enlist others in supporting a vision.

QUESTIONS AND ANSWERS

How do you define "vision" and "values" and why you think they enable innovation?

My co-author Barry Posner and I define vision as an ideal and unique image of the future for the common good. We define values as the principles that guide everyday decisions and actions. Values are vital because, as our research clearly shows, personal values drive commitment. In our research, we also find that that the ability to look into the future is the quality that distinguishes leaders from others. Both values and vision serve to motivate and empower people, for the long term and the short term.

Innovation requires experimentation and risk taking—and typically results in failures. To persist in spite of potential failures, leaders must know the principles to which they are committed. It is similarly so with vision. Innovation requires a long-term view. It is about possibilities, not probabilities, and leaders are possibility thinkers. It requires thinking not only about today, but also tomorrow. It requires something different—something that hasn't been done before. And innovation also requires thinking about others. It requires thinking outside of yourself—about the organization you're a part of, the community you live in, and the planet you live on. Innovation requires seeing the possibility in your mind's eye. The vision conveys what leaders have in mind when they're thinking about a new idea, solution, or process—or about what success looks like to them.

Let's talk about an old model of leadership—the command-and-control style—and how that can create obstacles or resistance to innovation.

In order for people to do their best, they need to feel in control of their own lives. When they feel that others control them, they aren't as engaged in their work and they are much less likely to come up with new and creative solutions to difficult problems. Under conditions of oppressive control, people will want to rebel. You can't compel people to innovate. That drive comes from the inside, and it only thrives in environments of freedom and experimentation.

Based on what we've found, the old command-and-control style of leadership is outdated and ineffective because it doesn't encourage shared values or the serve-and-support leadership approach needed for innovation. It's important to remember that leaders can't command people to adopt their values or adhere to their vision of the future. People will only commit to *shared* values and vision—to principles and purposes that are intrinsically important to them.

Experimentation is at the heart of innovation. It's all about trying, failing, and trying again. If people think that they're going to get punished for doing something new and different, then they're not likely to experiment—and are, therefore, not likely to innovate. People must be assured that they won't be punished if, in the spirit of innovation and experimentation, they don't get things right the first time.

Can you contrast that with the model put forth in The Five Practices of Exemplary Leadership®?

In our research, we asked people to tell us about their Personal-Best Leadership Experiences. We gathered thousands of stories and were able to codify them into The Five Practices of Exemplary Leadership®. The first is "Model the Way." This means clarifying values and setting an example based on those values. The second is "Inspire a Shared Vision." It means envisioning the future and enlisting others in a shared vision. The third is "Challenge the Process." This means searching for opportunities to improve and experimenting, taking risks, and learning from inevitable mistakes. The fourth is "Enable Others to Act." This involves fostering collaboration and strengthening others' self-determination. And the fifth is "Encourage the Heart." This involves recognizing contributions of individuals and celebrating successes that they've had together. When leaders are performing at their best, they definitely don't try to control others. Rather, they create a climate in which people can become leaders themselves.

Would you explain how shared values form a critical foundation for shared visions?

People are more committed when they choose to follow, rather than when they're mandated to follow. People have to see the fit between their own values and the organization's values in order to willingly support something. When alignment is in question, leaders should ask themselves, "To what extent are employees clear about their own values and to what extent are they clear about the organization's values?"

As you would expect, the highest level of commitment to an organization is present when employees are clear about the organization's values *and* clear about their personal values. If employees are unclear about both, they'll have the second lowest level of commitment. The lowest level of commitment, surprisingly, is when employees are clear about the organization's values but not clear about their own. What's even more surprising to many people—and most instructive—is that the second highest level of commitment is where employees are very clear about their personal values but not clear about the organization's values. In other words, personal values drive commitment. If employees don't know what they personally stand for, then they're not likely to be committed to the company's values, even if the company were to give them a laminated card that spells them out.

Why is it important for leaders to reflect on the past when formulating a vision?

As I mentioned earlier, being forward-looking differentiates leaders from other people, and this is even more critical in senior-level positions. Vision provides us with a sense of where we're headed, which is especially important in volatile, adverse, and uncertain conditions. So, how do I, as a leader, come to see that future and understand it? It turns out that those leaders who look backward before looking forward actually look farther ahead! We can't make progress toward the future if we can't understand where we came from. History holds much of what's important to us—our values and what we stand for. It's the foundation that got us from where we were to where we are now. Think of it in terms of a career path.

When we do a "lifeline" exercise with leaders to examine the high points and the low points of their careers, we ask them, "What enables you to go from a low to a high?" What people most often talk about are the values in their lives that helped them to get reoriented and to move forward. This better focuses our attention on our destination. Reflecting on past events, which also involves examining our values, allows leaders to see further ahead and to do more and newer things because they're building upon strengths. It helps you to understand what's at your core and what's most important to you.

Would you show readers how a vision can stretch us to imagine breakthrough results?

No one has ever said to us, "I did my personal best by keeping everything the same." Doing our best as leaders is about stretching ourselves. Don Bennett told us what has become one of my favorite stories. He was the first amputee to climb Mt. Rainier. When I asked him, "How did you get to the top?" Don told me, "One hop at a time! I imagined myself at the top of that mountain 1,000 times in my mind every day. Once I started climbing, I looked down at my foot and I said, 'Anyone can hop from here to there, so I did.' I got to the top one hop at a time." Don was clear about his destination—the top of Mt. Rainier—and that clarity fueled his inner desire to keep on climbing despite the cold, the ice, falls, and the near blizzard conditions. Also, getting to the summit was really not his ultimate vision.

What Don saw was that his success could inspire other individuals with disabilities to see possibilities for themselves. That's why, after summiting Mt. Rainier he started the amputee soccer league and aspires to qualify it as a Paralympic sport.

How do leaders secure buy-in by helping people get in touch with their ideals?

Here's one exercise we use: We say to leaders, "The legacy you leave is the life you lead." Then we ask them to think of LIFE as an acronym for *Lessons, Ideals, Feelings,* and *Expressions.* We ask leaders to visualize 10 years out and imagine that they're receiving the Leader of the Year award. We say, "People are talking about the lessons they learned from you, the ideals you've stood for, the feelings they had when around you, and how you expressed your ideals in action. What would you want them to say? And, what can you do today to put those lessons, ideals, feelings, and expressions into practice?"

How do leaders create "dreams" that inspire?

In another exercise, I say just two words: "Paris, France," and I ask, "What comes to mind when I say those words?" People say, "The Eiffel Tower, the Louvre, the Arc de Triomphe, wine, good food, romance, love," and so on. All of these are tangible places, images, or personal feelings. Then I ask, "How many of you immediately thought of the square kilometers or the population of Paris?" No one has ever raised a hand in response. People don't think immediately in terms of statistics or numbers. They remember things in pictures, in feelings, in images that they have of places or people. Leaders must communicate vision in ways that will stick in our minds. They need to talk about vision in terms of real places, real people, and the experiences that people will have when they're in that future. That's how leaders breathe life into hopes, dreams and aspirations—and how they make the intangible tangible and the abstract real.

TAKEAWAYS

- Leaders must make innovation a choice by communicating a clear vision of the future.
- Meaningful work supports progress. It's vital for a leader to know the values that are most important to their teams.
- History holds much of what's important to leaders—their values and what they stand for. It is the foundation that gets them from past to present.
- To inspire others, leaders must evoke memorable images and breathe life into hopes, dreams, and aspirations. That means encouraging people to envision real experiences that they want to have in the future.

TAKING STOCK

- What do I want people to say about me ten years from now?
- What can leaders do today in my organization, to put into practice our ideals, aspirations, and feelings?
- How can we encourage others to share the company's vision and values?

■　■　■

To learn more about *The Leadership Challenge*, go to www.leadershipchallenge.com/WileyCDA. If you found this chapter helpful, be sure to also see the chapters entitled *A Culture of Innovation, Buy-in, Sponsorship, and Commitment,* and *Employee Engagement.*

Chapter 23

Storytelling

An interview with Jana Sue Memel, President of the Hollywood Way and Producer, Writer, Director of Award-Winning Movies and Television Shows

■　■　■

"You have to get people emotionally engaged. No one got up the courage to storm the Bastille after receiving a memo."

— John Kao

Jazz musicians tell a story whenever they perform. Unlike symphony orchestra leaders, they don't need to follow strict protocols or prescribed formats for presenting a composer's score. They compose as they go, making the performance a musical journey that has no clearly defined destination or route to get there. Today, some conductors add interest to their performances by providing a history about each piece and also about who composed it. By interacting directly with their audiences, these leaders form a bond—and in some cases, a strong emotional connection—with the audience and even the composer. Can stories (or "strategic narratives" as they're sometimes called in business settings) be used to inspire employees to take action? Can storytelling also be an effective way to support innovation?

In an online *Harvard Business Review* communication entitled, "Storytelling That Moves People," authors Robert McKee and Bronwyn Fryer say, "Persuasion is the centerpiece of business activity. Customers must be convinced to buy your company's products or services, employees and colleagues to go along with a new strategic plan or reorganization, investors to buy (or not to sell) your stock, and partners to sign the next deal." Today, business schools such as Harvard and Columbia, as well as design schools such as the University of Minnesota's School of Architecture, are offering courses in storytelling. The World Bank uses it for knowledge management. The National Institute for Occupational Safety and Health (NIOSH) employs storytelling for safety training. Blue Cross/ Blue Shield uses it for diversity training. Additionally, organizations such as Kaiser Permanente, Intel, Nestle, Lufthansa, and Samsung use storytelling for insights work, long-range planning, marketing, and product redesign.

What advantage does a story have over more formal communications methods? Stories can also help leaders manage change by clearly articulating shared visions and values. Yet specialists in the fields of neuroscience and psychology have also made amazing discoveries about how stories can also foster collaboration and how they can reinforce an organization's brand, both internally and externally. Writers and playwrights are experts at storytelling, and for this reason, we interviewed Jana Sue Memel. She understands storytelling and employs it in a most powerful way—through her production of movies, films, and TV series that have earned three Academy Awards, an Emmy Award, eight Oscar nominations, and numerous Emmy nominations.

Jana's work also earned awards from the Writer's and Director's Guild, a Humanitas Prize, two CableAce Awards, and 18 CableAce nominations, including nominations in the Best Series category for three consecutive years. In addition to producing, Jana wrote and directed "Champion," a feature length documentary based on the life of Evander Holyfield and adapted "Faultline" for ABC Family, "Ruby Fruit Jungle" for PRN Productions and "Life and Death At 17" for Hoggwood. She also worked on a pilot for Fox and on features at New Line, Warners, Disney, and Universal. Please join us as Jana shows how stories can enable innovation.

QUESTIONS AND ANSWERS

How do you define "storytelling"?

In a broad sense, storytelling is the process of taking a set of facts and wrapping them in emotion, to compel action. Stories help us interpret life events and give meaning to our life and work. Neuroscientists and psychologists tell us that whenever we seek to inform, teach, persuade, or compel people to take action, it's best done by igniting emotions. Persuading through emotion is what sets storytelling apart from the use of purely factual business communications.

Why are so many leaders in the C-suite looking to storytelling to inspire innovation?

Stories are the best vehicle to use when building or reinforcing a brand message and for communicating organizational mission, vision, values, and character. In today's competitive environment, successful CEOs and other leaders use stories to motivate their people to reach for ambitious goals and objectives. That often means taking on tasks that haven't been done before, that entail risk, that can have formidable obstacles, and that arouse fear. In the absence of an "official" story, employees often make up their own, and seldom do their stories accurately reflect a leader's thoughts and vision. When leaders seize the initiative and tell their own stories, they inspire people to action and move them to adopt desired behaviors and a shared vision of a positive future. Leaders today know that they need to persuade by building consensus and relationships. To do so, they must move beyond a dull rendition of facts, and breathe life into their messages by connecting with people's hearts and minds in ways that encourage them to take action and embrace innovation.

Why is it necessary to evoke emotion, and how can leaders do that effectively?

Neuroscience has proven that we are not persuaded to take action by reason alone. Emotions trump rational arguments nine times out of ten. Facts without context have no meaning. Context is the story of your facts. It gives them meaning and inspires action. When leaders default to conventional rhetoric—building business cases on an intellectual basis with details, quotes from authorities, and statistics—it is difficult to achieve lasting buy-in. To spur audiences to action, leaders need to ascertain needs and reassure people that those needs will be met when they buy into the leader's vision. Leaders also need to help their audience find the emotional meaning or context for what they're being asked to do. Data inspires thought. Emotion is the fuel that inspires action and meaning.

How can leaders use stories to encourage the behavioral changes that need to support innovation?

In a change or innovation situation, people want to know how they might be personally hurt or helped. Since its human nature to resist change, leaders need to re-channel fear of the unknown into a clear positive vision of the future. To accomplish that, leaders must encourage new beginnings and sometimes-painful endings. Leaders can encourage goal-oriented performance by packing emotional power into convincing stories that paint pictures of how the change or innovation will make people's lives better—not worse. Traditionally stories have been the societal vehicle for teaching and reinforcing values. Effective leaders have successfully used them to communicate performance expectations and to explain the behaviors required for change. They know that their stories must "engage," not "sell," and that, if they encourage people by making a change or innovation appear beneficial, people will most likely do what's asked of them. Leaders who describe challenges in the form of stories cause people to think differently, take action, and bravely change their behaviors.

Why are data-laden forms of business communication less effective in compelling action?

Speakers who present with text-filled PowerPoint slides invite people to read during their presentation. This causes two things to happen: First, people read faster than we can speak, so they finish reading our slides while we're halfway through talking about them. Once a slide has been read, people in the audience feel they've taken in the most important information and often tune out until the next slide appears. Second, the brain needs to break words down into images, in order to process them. Our brains can only perform one task at a time, as much as we'd all like to think we can multi-task. When people are reading a slide, they're literally not able to focus on what we're saying so, when speakers use bullet points, they're actually distracting the audience from what's being said—and making it more difficult for people to remember important messages. Compelling stories that are filled with descriptive visual imagery hold people's attention and keep them anchored in the moment.

If a leader's primary goal is innovation through action, why do messages need to be remembered?

Not all messages are immediately actionable. Some need time to incubate. Others require time for champions to assemble a critical mass of support. This consensus is all-important for decision making because, as we know, individuals make very few decisions anymore. Teams make most decisions, and usually, not all team members will have attended a presentation. If stories are told with enough emotional contexts, those who are in attendance will be able to remember the salient points and pass them on to those who weren't present. The same ability to remember salient detail does not exist when a leader presents a torrent of facts unaccompanied by emotional context. Since all long-term memory is tied to sensory input, when leaders use words that encourage people to actually see what they are describing, the audience easily remembers key messages and can pass them on. Additionally, stories provide concrete models of positive and negative behaviors that will inspire people to take the actions the leader desires.

When attempting to spark innovation, how can leaders best prepare compelling stories?

It sounds paradoxical but by intensely preparing to deliver your story, you are often able to be more spontaneous. Today, it's easy to learn about people online. We can combine our stories with information that we know—or can learn—about our audiences. This provides us with clues to develop a contextual frame for the story that will have meaning to the specific audience that we're addressing. Another vital component of preparation is the formulation of leading questions you can ask the audience, making your presentation interactive and the audience partial owners of the narrative.

Successful storytellers train themselves to listen to what underlies audience members' questions so that they can influence accordingly in their responses. Effective leaders define goals when constructing their presentations. They also design takeaways for their audiences, paint pictures with words, and end their stories with calls to action. However, calls to action aren't as effective when they're direct appeals. They're most effective when told as stories that excite, energize, and "invite" or "encourage" people to take action. Successful leaders know that the more stirring a story is, the better its chances are of being remembered, repeated, and acted upon.

Is storytelling an innate ability or a skill that can be learned and leveraged for innovation?

We've been telling stories since we learned to speak. It happens so spontaneously and so easily that many neuroscientists believe we're hard-wired to tell stories. Abstract language, by contrast, is usually more difficult for us. Experts believe we learn it as a "second language." Although some of us become proficient at this second language, it's not the "native language" that we speak when we're relaxing with friends and family—and exchanging stories. It's the sensory images we innately use when telling stories that produce the excitement, wonder, and action that spurs innovation.

Is there a particular formula for stories that compels people to action?

Stories are usually about a hero's journey. In a business environment, the story's hero might be the CEO or other leaders, employees, or even the organization's products and services. When heroes encounter obstacles and surmount them, the audience is inspired. And yes, there is a formula that many compelling stories follow. If you decide to use the formula, start your story by setting up the background or context within which the story is set and also the characters who will inhabit it. Then describe an inciting incident that sets the story in motion. Next there's a "rising action," the build-up to an obstacle, which prevents heroes from reaching their goals. Undaunted, the heroes strive to overcome their obstacles. On the verge of success there is often still another turn during which heroes lose something. Finally, there is resolution, where heroes either achieve their goals—or not—depending upon whether the story is a comedy or a tragedy. Leaders can use this same formula for building their business stories. Even if their heroes fail to win, the takeaways from the failure—the lessons learned from it—can inspire and make a compelling case for action or a decision.

How can we be certain that storytelling will prompt people to act?

MRIs actually show that stories activate parts of the brain that aren't activated by more traditional forms of communication. They also show that storyteller's frontal cortexes light up when they're telling a story—as do those of the people hearing a story. None of this occurs when people hear a data-laden presentation. If that's not convincing enough evidence that storytelling works, MRIs also show that motor skills are activated during storytelling—explaining in part, how charismatic leaders, employing properly emotive stories, can propel people to take swift action. They know that storytelling is about engaging, not direct selling.

TAKEAWAYS

- Stories provide meaning and can be used as tools to excite, energize, and motivate—and to make messages memorable, repeatable, and actionable.
- When introducing change or an innovation, it's important to remember that people want to know how they'll be affected—and want their expectations and fears addressed.
- In order to build stories that will move their audiences to action, leaders need to ascertain the audience's needs, define their own goals in making the presentations, and be clear about their intended outcomes.

TAKING STOCK

- Do we truly understand the needs of our audience and use them as starting points for important messages?
- Do our leaders use stories to build and strengthen relationships with key internal stakeholders to reinforce our brand?
- Are we encouraging leaders to evoke emotion and inspire action through stories?

■   ■   ■

To learn more about Jana Sue Memel's work, go to www.hollywoodway.net/jana-sue-memel. If you found this chapter useful, also see *Buy-in, Sponsorship, and Commitment, Change Leadership, Employee Engagement, Meaning and Purpose,* and *Shared Vision and Values.*

Closing Thoughts:
The Power of Thrill

An interview with Donna Sturgess, President and Cofounder of Buyology Inc.; Executive in Residence at Carnegie Mellon University; former Global Head of Innovation at GlaxoSmithKline and previously Vice President of Marketing & Strategy

Donna is a senior marketer and innovator who focuses on thought leadership to drive vibrant and viable business solutions. She has been recognized as one of the Top 15 Women in Business by Ernst & Young and is the recipient of the Quantum Leap Award by the Advertising Women of New York. At Buyology, Donna provides strategic consultation to a variety of Fortune 100 companies across industries that include financial services, consumer package goods, media and entertainment, and technology. She has a proven track record in growing and managing brand portfolios and bringing remarkable innovation to the marketplace. A popular speaker and writer, with articles appearing in many publications including Harvard Business Review, Forbes, Brandweek, Advertising Age and many others, Donna also co-authored *The Big Moo*, by the Group of 33, edited by Seth Godin. She is also the author of *Eyeballs Out: How to Step Into Another World, Discover New Ideas, and Make Your Business Thrive*, published in October of 2010.

■ ■ ■

The previous chapters built a case for shared visions and values; for leaders who model and reinforce courage; for meaning and purpose in work; and for buy-in and sponsorship, particularly during large-scale change initiatives. Thought leaders who contributed to this section in the book also elaborated on the ways in which leaders help employees deal with the obstacles that often inhibit or prevent innovation. In summary, what are some of the added challenges that leaders must deal with in today's competitive environments?

Today's shorter commercial life of ideas puts significant pressure on organizations—and their people—to repeatedly convert ideas into cash. However, when knowledge is continually accumulated and distributed, it enables companies to operate at a speed far greater than that of their competition. The result is increased speed to market and in-market advantages, but there must be a continuous stream of ideas to leverage the speed advantage. When a company's cultural code is continually rewritten and enhanced by new ideas, some employees feel excited and energized, while others are fearful of the change that comes with it. Unfortunately, most leaders don't realize how important it is to actively manage fear—or they don't know how. When people feel fear, leaders need to step up to balance that response.

Leaders who are able to re-channel fear into positive forces wield tremendous power because they've learned how to create the conditions for thrilling work and the innovative thinking that results from it. One of the most important aspects of their jobs as leaders is to build or assemble skill within the team and empower talented people to act. Fear is a product of risk and leaders can support people as they assess and manage accompanying risks. However, leaders' efforts can't end there. Those who are highly successful also carve out time for team reflection so that people can savor the joy of their successes and feel confident about taking on future challenges. Leaders who give people the freedom to do thrilling work engage employees in exciting and ongoing endeavors, continually capturing what's being learned and then leveraging it. Leaders like Ed Catmull at Pixar know how to do that and also how to keep fear at bay to stimulate thrill in the workplace that creates remarkable innovation.

What's ironic to me about the power of thrill, however, is that many leaders and CEOs believe their companies could perform at higher levels and innovate better if they only had "the right people." They cite examples of how top talent lines up to work for companies such as Virgin, Apple, Patagonia, Pixar, and other companies as though these companies have some sort of "magic potion" that their companies don't have. Yet it should be obvious these high-flying leading organizations have no special potion. They've simply learned how to create the conditions for emotional thrill and excitement about the work, which in turn, spurs innovation. If the thrill is gone in your team, you have a problem. The question you should ask yourself is, "How do I give team members the freedom they need to define the work and own the challenge?"

In the book entitled *Just Enough Anxiety: The Hidden Driver of Business Success*, author Dr. Robert Rosen shares examples of how the right amount of anxiety can create a form of energy that boosts confidence and drives innovation. He shows that, in the same way that successful athletes re-channel anxiety for optimal performance, businesses can leverage it to help people eagerly embrace challenges. However, Rosen underscores that the "right amount" of energy is vitally important. Too much and people can feel overwhelmed or debilitated. Too little and there can be stagnation, mediocre performance, and few reasons to challenge the status quo. When anxiety and thrill are in the right proportions, they create the favorable conditions necessary to produce a continuous stream of ideas—and innovation—that helps companies convert ideas into cash and keeps them ahead of the game.

How do leaders achieve and maintain these ingredients and provide an empowered culture? They know that there is great power in supporting people and encouraging them to get out of the office, talk with customers, take in new information, and see the world through different lenses. Leaders can then tap into fresh perspectives and ideas from their teams, to translate them into game-changing strategies. Leaders do this by clearly communicating that they want new ideas and by reminding people that even bad ideas can be built upon or expanded. Yet team members must believe that their leaders value new ideas and that their interest and support is authentic—meaning they will be there when the going gets tough.

In the first chapter of my book *Eyeballs Out*, I outlined five steps for creating and maintaining thrill in business environments. Leaders need to: (1) invite novelty, (2) leverage anxiety, (3) equate risk with challenges, (4) foster exhilaration through accomplishment, and (5) allow time for reflection and recalibration when performance meets or exceeds expectations. Novelty can be introduced through immersion, special projects, and certain combinations of people who work synergistically in teams. But innovation must go beyond novelty. Leaders play a critical role in establishing a safe environment for innovation and providing support that empowers people with the freedom necessary to stimulate thrill. Leaders must also mitigate the fear inherent in risk by taking the point of view that risk is something to manage and evaluate continuously through a process. Equally important, they must set realistic goals and celebrate goal achievement since success generates a feeling of exhilaration that, in turn, reinforces high performance.

What I find interesting about the power of thrill is its direct relationship to high performance. The problem most leaders have is they say they want people to do great work, but they don't want to turn over enough of the control to let them own their work and be accountable for outcomes. Sounds like a trust issue, doesn't it?

When leaders provide opportunities for people to participate in peak experiences, it means they have the courage to let go of the reins and unleash their top talent to perform. The best talent requires freedom and support to perform, and when that is not available people will go elsewhere. Leaders must be able to build and motivate high performing teams. If your organization wants to produce big, bold ideas, it will also have to hold leaders accountable for team building and for creating a culture that reinforces high performance.

It's also important to keep in mind that no one leader builds and perfects best practices. The team of people who want to be part of a legendary story most often does that. When these employees perceive that their work has meaning, purpose, and value, they're excited about doing it—and eager to see the results of their efforts. And when employees are committed and engaged, they bring everything they've got to their work. Then both the company and individual team members win. Of course, it should be no secret by now that if there is any "magic potion" to be had, it's the essence and power of doing work that products the heart-pounding emotion of thrill. That's the source of energy that exponentially drives the high performance and innovation to ensure competitive advantage.

■ ■ ■

To learn more about Buyology Inc. go to www.buyologyinc.com.

Subsection III.
Managing and Leveraging Innovation

Introduction by Marilyn Blocker

Y ou can probably guess why this subsection appears last. Managing and leveraging innovation is about execution—and the execution stage of the innovation process is where the proverbial "buck" stops. Most people agree that it's also the riskiest. In this section, subject matter experts describe how leaders manage and leverage innovation. As in other parts of this book, symphony orchestra and jazz metaphors compare effective leadership in the world of music to the world of business, to provide unique insights and perspectives.

The Ultimate Challenge

Henry Mintzberg, the internationally known author and educator at McGill University, warns about comparisons, however, when he says, "The great myth is the manager as orchestra conductor. It's this idea of standing on a pedestal, and you wave your baton and Accounting comes in, and you wave it somewhere else and Marketing chimes in with Accounting, and they all sound very glorious. But management is more like orchestra conducting during rehearsals when everything is going wrong."

Leading almost any organization during today's times of uncertainty and turmoil is more complicated and demanding than in years past. In this chapter, you'll learn how a highly innovative leader execut-ed a successful organizational turnaround despite significant obstacles, crushing disappointments, repeated rejection, and even public humiliation. From this leader's story, you'll see how people, part-nerships, and processes were leveraged to turn inevitable failure into unprecedented success, but first some context for the story.

A Troubled Industry

In a January 21, 2014 *Slate* CultureBox article ("Requiem: Classical Music in America is Dead"), author Mark Vanhoenacker describes the current state of symphony orchestras in the U.S. He writes, "Classical music has been circling the drain for years [and] [t]here's little doubt as to the causes." With that, he describes two: (a) its "fingernail grip of old music in a culture that venerates the new" and (b) "an audience that remains overwhelmingly old and white in an America that's increasingly neither."

Vanhoenacker supports his views by citing research conducted by the NEA (National Endowment for the Arts) and former Juilliard professor, now musician and writer Greg Sandow. Vanhoenacker tells how, in 1937, the median age of people attending U.S. symphony orchestra performances was 28, and that by 1982, it had increased to 40. By 2008, it had risen to 49, and today the majority of U.S. orchestras are supported almost entirely by people in their 60s and older.

What can we learn from this and from today's many failed companies, bankruptcies, mergers, and hostile takeovers? We can see that if leaders rely solely on old ways of operating, and coast on past successes, their organizations can sometimes very quickly become obsolete. Even though arts industry experts are divided about Vanhoenacker's view that classical music is dead, most agree that to survive in the long-term, symphony orchestra leaders—like their business counterparts—will need to continually challenge traditional business models. That's also why music and business leaders alike must employ advantage-seeking, exploitation strategies (which build on or enhance existing products and services) as well as opportunity-seeking, exploration strategies (which have the potential to disrupt the competition and even entire markets).

The Battle Against Obsolescence

It might be difficult to understand how most symphony orchestras, after surviving for several hundred years, still operate on deficit economic models, with ticket sales producing, on average, only 30-35% of their earned income. Without the benefit of government support that symphony orchestras receive in other parts of the world, those in the U.S. have been filling the gap between earned income and operating expenses with grants, corporate gifts, and donations from loyal patrons.

During the last 50 or so years, that gap has been widening, due to declining subscriptions, reduced ticket sales, and fixed payroll costs negotiated with unions. And the gap grew even wider during the 2008-2009 Great Recession, when municipal support, corporate gifts, and state funding for orchestras almost completely evaporated.

An important reminder, however, is that survival back in 2008 and 2009 wasn't only a challenge for leaders in the music industry. At that time, many businesses around the globe were affected by global competition and an aging global population that was causing shifts in demand. In 2008 and 2009, it mattered little whether organizations were in the not-for-profit, public, or private sector. Almost all were at risk.

The Innovation Challenge

In the chapter *Why This Book*? I describe how a symphony orchestra metaphor can be a powerful symbol for both innovation success and failure. That's because an orchestra's focus is on building on what has worked in the past and achieving excellence though the mastery of time-tested traditions. Today's hyper-competitive business environments require much more than that, which is why a jazz metaphor—with its emphasis on exploration and improvisation—is also necessary if we're to learn from the world of music. Like jazz musicians, who continually co-create and experiment with new themes and approaches, innovative orchestra leaders and their business counterparts continually create new "music" or take existing "music" in new directions.

Music directors of symphony orchestras in the U.S. today face unique challenges that have direct applications in the world of business. We can learn from them as well as from successful business leaders who are skilled at leveraging a wide range of innovation enablers. From the examples provided by over 40 subject matter experts in this book, we can gain a complete understanding of how leaders also achieve balance in their organizations by skillfully managing opposing forces. These tasks constitute the multi-faceted innovation challenge that most leaders grapple with today, so within this context, I'll now begin the previously referenced story.

Wrong Leader?

It surely seemed as if something had gone terribly wrong at the Baltimore Symphony Orchestra (BSO) when a front-page headline in the July 18, 2005 edition of the *Washington Post* newspaper read, "Musicians Balk at Appointment of Music Director." Did this reflect concerns about the newly appointed leader's competence? Certainly the BSO was in need of a capable music director. The orchestra hadn't made a recording in 10 years, had only 50-60% attendance at concerts, and was between $16 and $17 million in debt. But what could have caused an alleged 90% of the BSO's musicians to reject the BSO Management's appointee? And who was this controversial music director?

The leader in question was Marin Alsop, whose impressive credentials, significant leadership roles, and many distinguished awards hardly seemed indicative of a music director who was lacking in any way. Before beginning her career as a world-renowned conductor, Alsop earned a master's degree from the prestigious Juilliard School of Music. And in 2005, she had been chosen Artist of the Year by Britain's classical music magazine Gramophone. In that same year, she had been the only symphony orchestra leader to have participated in the World Economic Forum, where prime ministers, presidents, and CEOs from major corporations worldwide gather to discuss common challenges.

If Marin Alsop were to sign a contract with the BSO despite the musicians' objections, she would become the first woman music director in the U.S. at one of the top 20 major league orchestras. Ironically, she had already earned the "first woman" moniker twice before. In 1989, Alsop had been the first "maestra" to receive the Koussevitzky Conducting Prize from the Boston Symphony Orchestra's Tanglewood Music Center. And in 2002, she had become the first female music director of the Bournemouth Orchestra—the oldest symphony orchestra in the United Kingdom.

M.S. Mason, author of "Conducting Energy" in *The Christian Science Monitor's* April 2002 edition writes about how, years earlier, the Bournemouth Orchestra musicians had voted unanimously to hire Alsop, even though she was an American conductor. This contrasted sharply with the alleged 90% of BSO musicians who were opposing her appointment in 2005, but what was even more ironic was that Alsop had already led a successful turnaround effort of another well-known symphony orchestra. After joining the Colorado Symphony shortly after it had emerged from bankruptcy, she had spent 12 years helping the organization improve overall quality, grow its budget, attract loyal donors, and gain increased regional and national recognition.

Bad Chemistry?

Why would the BSO musicians strenuously oppose a star quality appointee with a reputation as an audience builder? Wouldn't she be eminently qualified to reverse their orchestra's downward spiral? In Norman Lebrecht's July 27, 2005 article, "The Loneliest Job on Earth," he says, "The [BSO] players … had nothing against Alsop as a woman.…" (See *The Lebrecht Weekly* at scena.org.) But Richard Dyer, from the Boston Globe, said no musicians were going to say they objected to Alsop because she was a woman, and "libel considerations would prevent their attacking her musicianship." (See the July 21, 2005 edition of the online *Boston Globe* article, "In Hiring Process: Orchestra's Conduct Flawed.")

Richard Morrison, the chief music critic of *The Times* of London, said about the BSO controversy, "Over here, people are absolutely amazed at the fuss they made in Baltimore," and to that he added. "If they have a question about musicianship, the Baltimore players either have a very elevated sense of their self-importance or haven't worked with her enough." But was there another possibility that could explain the musicians' displeasure?

Could bad chemistry have been at the root of the BSO musicians' objections? Not likely. In a January 1998 *Rocky Mountain News* article, "Conductor with a Common Touch," music critic Mark Shulgold says about Alsop, "She is down-to-earth, accessible, witty." Elaine F. Weiss, in her September 26,

2005 article, "Marin Alsop Breaks the Glass Baton," describes her as having "a winning combination of technical virtuosity, professional polish, and personal charisma."

Weiss adds, "She aspires to make symphony halls welcoming places, not austere temples of culture where only the cognoscenti [persons who have superior knowledge and understanding of a particular field] dare enter." Known for blending contemporary and classical music, Alsop had gained fame for her gospel-jazz adaptation of Handel's Messiah. Could this have been the real source of the BSO musicians' pushback? Had they wanted to preserve the symphony as a pure and elitist experience? And might Alsop's style been the real cause of their negative response?

In 2005, other publications hinted at long-standing problems between the BSO management and musicians. And tensions had clearly escalated when the BSO management team violated union contract provisions by not communicating with musicians before appointing Marin Alsop. In fact, Richard Dyer speculates that Alsop was simply "an innocent bystander/victim" in "an ugly management-versus-musician conflict." But could she safely assume that to be true? There was a lot at stake if the musicians' rejection were to be something personal.

The Heart of Successful Execution

Alsop knew that a strong partnership with the BSO's 100 or so musicians was critical for her success, and that she'd need to assess whether they had sincere doubts about her professionally. She saw only one reliable way to do that. When she learned that a colleague had been scheduled to guest conduct at the BSO, she asked for ten minutes of rehearsal time to speak with the musicians directly. After the conductor agreed, Alsop arrived unannounced, and in less than the allotted time, outlined her artistic agenda for the next few years as well as her plan to address the BSO's challenges.

Then summoning all her courage, and putting at risk her decades of preparation for this very prestigious role, she told the musicians, "I can help you with all these issues, but I … won't sign the contract until I know you're with me." Then Alsop suggested that they take time to discuss her proposal, but after turning to leave, she was called back and told she had their support. In his 2005 article, Norman Lebrecht said of Alsop's actions, "That's Marin Alsop through and through. Of all current conductors, she is probably the best facilitator, the one who gets things done."

Turnarounds

Few people would dispute that getting things done is at the heart of successful execution, but would Alsop's can-do attitude be enough to facilitate another successful turnaround? When public utilities are in trouble, they can sometimes raise rates. Other public sector organizations might apply for additional funding. Private sector organizations sometimes seek venture capital from angel investors to enhance research and development efforts, purchase new technologies, and acquire other organizations. And some companies only need to achieve operational efficiencies by streamlining cumbersome or out-of-date processes.

Like other not-for-profit organizations, the BSO had very few options for accomplishing a successful turnaround. That's because concert halls are fixed assets that require ongoing maintenance, and most performances demand a large number of paid musicians. Typically, orchestras can't save their way to success any more than most companies can. In fact, the majority of arts organizations survive primarily by generating income through ticket sales and donations from loyal patrons.

Against All Odds

So was Marin Alsop able to beat the odds and achieve a successful turnaround? She was, and despite her rough start with the BSO, she renewed her contract twice since 2005. In February of 2017, Alsop told an audience at Oxford University that she had the longest extended contract of any music director in the U.S. to date. (See the February 24, 2017 video "Leading by Example: My Path to the Podium," part of the 2016-2017 Women of Achievement Lecture Series at ox.ac.uk.) In addition to her success at the BSO, Alsop continued to receive prestigious awards and invitations.

Shortly after her 2005 BSO appointment, she was the only music director to receive the prestigious MacArthur Fellowship—otherwise known as "the genius" award. In 2013, and again in 2015, Alsop became the first female conductor to receive one of the highest honors in the world of the symphony orchestra: an invitation to host the last night of the prestigious BBC Proms. The MacArthur Foundation's website describes Alsop as someone who "defies stereotypes" by offering "a new model of leadership for orchestras in the U.S. and abroad."

And in *How Great Women Lead*, authors Bonnie St. John and Darcy Deane say about Alsop, "Perhaps her potent inspiration is why BSO attendance numbers are climbing, their donations never dipped during the recession, and classical music venues across the country are looking to Marin Alsop for answers on how to stay relevant and vital to a new generation." What exactly did Alsop do to warrant such praise? What professional and personal strengths enabled it? And can leaders in other venues replicate her success?

Alsop ensured the BSO's relevance in its local community while also extending its footprint internationally. She also helped reduce the BSO's debt while assisting in increasing its revenues. These are no small accomplishments for almost any leader, and like many others, Alsop was tasked with playing an increasingly greater role in securing and continually growing new business. With that, she faced a significant and unique barrier.

A New Model of Leadership

In several interviews, Alsop shares how important it is for leaders to know what's putting their industries in peril. Very early in her career, she'd seen how the symphony orchestra was gradually, yet significantly, moving away from being a vehicle by which people got together to play music and socialize. Alsop suspected that growing perceptions of the symphony orchestra as a purely elitist experience could someday be problematic, and in 2007, that potential was fast becoming a reality.

Few people realize that the work of most music directors goes far beyond that of brilliantly orchestrating on stage. In contrast to the symphony orchestra's executive director—whose responsibilities run parallel to chief operating officers in other organizations—music directors like Marin Alsop are typically their organizations' public faces. Unlike executive directors, who usually have responsibility for Operations, Facilities, and Finance, music directors' functions are similar to celebrity athletes, singers, and actors. They need to draw people to performances by communicating value. They do this by reaching out to community constituencies, ensuring media visibility, creating educational initiatives, and obtaining funding from loyal donors, grants, corporate gifts, and endowments—all this while carrying out basic leadership tasks such as motivating and retaining key talent.

M.S. Mason, of *The Christian Science Monitor*, says about Marin Alsop, "… she enjoys every aspect of conducting and directing an orchestra, including fund-raising." After officially taking the helm in 2007, Alsop secured substantial donations by going beyond traditional income-generating activities. Knowing that she had to gain support for her agenda quickly, she also generated early wins. Like any good change agent, she identified some low-hanging fruit, and after that, she worked diligently to maintain momentum despite the natural resistance that sometimes impedes change.

The MacArthur Foundation website describes three key strengths that Alsop has continually leveraged throughout her career. The first, and most obvious, is her "masterful conducting technique." The second is her "visionary artistic programming." And the third is the way that she's able to "demystify challenging music for a wide range of audiences." (See the MacArthur Fellows Program at macfound. org/fellows/749.) So what can leaders in other industries learn from Alsop's professional strengths? You might be surprised at the parallels to those of successful innovators almost everywhere.

Educating and Selling

In a December 14, 2005 article in *The Economist*, Alsop was quoted as saying, "Conducting is a metaphor for who you are, and if it's affected and insincere, it becomes trite and inauthentic." (See the article "The Baltimore Symphony Did Not Like it When Marin Alsop was Appointed Music Director, the First Woman to Run a Major American Orchestra. Can She Win it Over?") Like successful leaders in other venues, Alsop is a "masterful conductor" who has established credibility in both internal and external environments, achieving success both "on stage" and "off stage."

The MacArthur Foundation website says about Alsop's second major strength that she's "recognized throughout the world for her innovative approach to programming." In the world of music, innovative programming equates to the new or enhanced products and services of other organizations. So if Alsop needed to expand the BSO's local and international audiences, she would need to use innovative programming to reverse the perception of symphony orchestra performances as an elitist activity. She would also need to convince her local audience that the BSO could deliver value. To do that, she would have to make the symphony more affordable and accessible—and before doing that, she'd need to make classical music more understandable.

So how did Alsop leverage her third strength to demystify the work of classical composers? She took on what even the most highly skilled salespeople consider to be a significant challenge: She educated potential customers before selling to them, and in so doing, instilled a greater awareness and appreciation of the arts. That ultimately allowed her to firmly embed the BSO into the fabric of its local community. So exactly how did she accomplish a successful turnaround?

A New Game

Many of the experts featured in this book describe innovation as a critical competency that can ensure sustainability. Andrea Zintz writes about this in the *Leading Innovation* subsection of this book when she says, "The game has changed…. Old rules no longer apply [and] today's executives must think in new and creative ways if they're to keep their organizations economically viable." Given the important role that programming plays in a symphony orchestra's success, we should ask what made Alsop's brand so different—and then determine how that, and other innovation initiatives, changed the trajectory of the BSO. So what, exactly, distinguished her programming from others?

Unlike other orchestra leaders in 2007—who featured only Western European compositions—Alsop had been offering a broad range of programs throughout her career. By adapting the BSO's programming to the tastes of different generations of patrons, she helped the orchestra meet the needs of current patrons as well as those of potential future supporters. And by delivering music that matched younger enthusiasts' tastes, she began to lay the foundation that would ultimately replace aging patrons. Then Alsop further grew the BSO's local audience by providing more culturally relevant music to Baltimore's diverse population. But that wasn't all that she accomplished.

A History of Excellence

In 2007, Alsop and the BSO management team members hired after her appointment did something unimaginable: While other orchestras throughout the United States were either going bankrupt or significantly raising the price of ticket sales, this team *reduced* the cost of tickets. How did they make the BSO more accessible and affordable at a time when orchestras almost everywhere else were struggling? Did they employ gap analysis, SWOT analysis, or some other formal strategic planning tools? If so, did this mean they'd been successful in building on the BSO's strengths, overcoming its weaknesses, identifying opportunities, and minimizing threats?

Marin Alsop built on the BSO's strengths by leveraging its long history of excellence and its top talent. She also addressed its primary weakness: lack of visibility. In a 2007 interview with PBS NewsHour's Jeffrey Brown, she said one of her first tasks was to help the BSO musicians release their first recording in over eight years and ensure their presence on iTunes and XM Satellite Radio. (See the YouTube video "Marin Alsop on PBS' NewsHour with Jim Lehrer, October 17, 2007," uploaded on February 19, 2008.)

Like many successful business leaders, Alsop seized the opportunity to use technology to identify opportunities like these and to introduce her organization's products and services in other highly visible ways. She also leveraged technology to expand the BSO's previous focus on a single local market to a broader international one. But what did she do to address the BSO's greatest threat of obsolescence?

Programs for the "Young" and the "Rusty"

Drawing from her experience at the Colorado Symphony, Marin Alsop knew that when organizations weave their value propositions into the fabric of their local, regional, and global communities, they can build strong support systems that maximize success in both the short- and long-term. She also knew that the BSO's value proposition would need to be supported by different types of innovation, so her focus expanded to include robust delivery systems, an enhanced brand, and valuable partnerships. She also continually built and enhanced partnerships with internal and external stakeholders, namely the BSO musicians, the University of Maryland, and the many people who eventually participated in the "BSO Academy" programs that she helped to develop.

Even glancing quickly at the various programs described on Marin Alsop's website (marinalsop.com) today, one can see how her efforts helped to make the BSO a prominent force in its community. Consisting of four tracks, Academy Programs include Academy Week, Music Educators Academy, Academy Clinics, and Rusty Musicians (or "Rusties"). During Academy week, BSO musicians provide lessons and coaching to approximately 100 amateurs in an immersive summer camp experience. The

Music Educators Academy, in collaboration with the University of Maryland, awards credits to music teachers and those pursuing a career in music. And throughout the year, Academy Clinics provide private lessons to amateurs before they're given opportunities to rehearse with the full orchestra.

Alsop aimed the BSO Rusty Musicians' program (or Rusties) at professional musicians who hadn't played in years, as well as those who hadn't yet performed professionally. Although this program was initially created for Baltimore residents, it soon expanded to include musicians from all over the world. This produced international visibility for the BSO as well as ongoing revenue streams. What's more, the Rusties program, like other Academy programs, clearly demonstrated that the BSO was actively serving its community rather than expecting to *be served* by it. That said, the focus of these programs was on current patrons. To ensure both short- and long-term success, the BSO also needed programs for future patrons.

A "Present" for the Future

The famous French author, journalist, and philosopher Albert Camus once said, "Real generosity towards the future lies in giving all to the present." In addition to directing the BSO's musicians to develop younger members of the Baltimore community, Marin Alsop personally funded a program called "OrchKids" (an abbreviation for "Orchestra Kids"). Taking only enough money to buy a car from the $500,000 "genius award" that she received from the MacArthur Foundation, she donated the remainder to purchase musical instruments for disadvantaged Baltimore youths. Today the OrchKids program serves over 1,000 students from pre-kindergarten through tenth grade, and Alsop's goal is to expand it to ultimately reach 10,000 or more children.

Alsop's efforts to develop future generations of both musicians and patrons are consistent with her modus operandi. Describing it in an August 25, 2014 presentation at the George Washington University School of Business, she told students and Dean Doug Guthrie about how one of her life's philosophies had come about after she'd received her first break. She said, "I understood that any opportunity I had was not to be squandered in any way." Consequently, her advice to others is, "Every time you have a chance, don't just do the minimum. Do the maximum you can—and it always grows into something else." (See "Conversations on Creative Leadership: Marin Alsop," posted on YouTube. com by Doug Guthrie.)

Generativity

In the 1950's, a famous psychoanalyst named Erik Erickson coined the term "generativity" to describe "a concern for establishing and guiding the next generation." (See C.L. Slater's 2003 article, "Generativity Versus Stagnation: An Elaboration on Erickson's Adult Stage of Human Development" in the *Journal of Adult Development*.) Leaders who exhibit generosity of spirit—and generativity—see themselves as having a higher purpose. They want to make the world a better place for others. In 2014, when concluding her presentation to GWU students, Marin Alsop said of her life's goal that she wanted "to try to make a difference in terms of possibility" because that's what her parents had given her: "this idea of a world filled with possibility."

Leaders like Alsop believe they have a responsibility to make it easier for future generations, and they demonstrate that belief in a variety of ways. In addition to financially sponsoring and launching the OrchKids program, Alsop established two others in memory of her parents and how they supported her dream to become a conductor. The Alsop Foundation and the Alsop Entrepreneurship Award both encourage innovative projects in music entrepreneurship. Although innovation is an undeniable part of our human DNA, leaders must build and nurture an innovation mindset—in themselves and others. Only then can the enormous potential that resides around—and *inside*—them be fully realized. In addition to helping people recognize their strengths and inspiring them to act upon them, leaders often provide opportunities to *apply* skills and competencies.

Believing that it's also important to thank the people who contributed to her success, and at the same time, "pay it forward," Alsop created the Taki Concordia Conducting Fellowship. Named in honor of her first official sponsor, Mr. Tomio Taki, the fellowship has helped at least a dozen aspiring women orchestra conductors gain the necessary visibility to secure conducting roles in the U.S. and abroad.

Insights

Marin Alsop's accomplishments provide a number of valuable insights and takeaways. First, to ensure customer and talent retention, leaders must establish strong partnerships with both internal and external stakeholders. Second, they must stay abreast of changing demographics, new and converging trends, and the ever-evolving needs, tastes, and preferences of their "audiences"—whether they're purchasers, patrons, or patients.

Third, leaders must respond appropriately to changing, unmet, and unarticulated consumer needs. And fourth, they must continually "fine-tune" their organizations to ensure that their people and processes are keeping pace with market changes. This means periodically reviewing, and sometimes quickly revising, business models, strategies, goals, objectives, and innovation initiatives.

Market-Driven Leadership

The Alsop story is a difficult act to follow, but in California's Silicon Valley, which is practically synonymous with innovation, another symphony orchestra leader successfully challenged the status quo. In the early 2000s, Andrew Bales, President of Symphony Silicon Valley, focused on improving the traditional symphony orchestra financial model. By doing that, he was able to preserve musical talent in his region after the long-standing San Jose Symphony had permanently closed its doors in 2001-2002.

When speaking with Bales, I learned that his orchestra earns a remarkable 60% of its revenue each year through ticket sales. Compared to other symphony orchestras, which earn only 30-35% of their income in this way, 60% is an extraordinarily high proportion—especially for an organization the size of Symphony Silicon Valley. Even more amazing is that this orchestra has managed to maintain these income levels since 2003—even during the 2008-2009 recession. Does Bales' orchestra have a secret formula for success? It has a formula, but it's not a secret.

The symphony's website once described it as "an example of an innovative business model in the arts." Bales says the orchestra is "market-driven and financially conservative" with "low overhead and the flexibility to match programming to its support base." With only six employees, including Bales, Symphony Silicon Valley's low overhead is a key success factor but it's not the only one. As previously mentioned, symphony orchestras—like most organizations—usually can't survive merely by cutting costs or achieving cost efficiencies. This orchestra utilizes a flexible workforce and performs with only the number of musicians that each piece of music requires. In the absence of pay for guaranteed performances, musicians who perform with Symphony Silicon Valley are similar to employees in many business environments today. They operate as free agents who also work for other employers—or for themselves.

Although some private donations are still needed to fill the gap between ticket sales and operating expenses, changes from traditional business models have enabled Symphony Silicon Valley to continually operate in the black. With a market-driven strategy, the organization can tailor its programming to offer only what its audience wants and is willing to pay for—in the same ways that other organizations effectively customize their products and services to meet specific customer or client needs.

Responses to Shifts in Demand

In the book, *Ten Types of Innovation*, authors Larry Keeley, Ryan Pikkel, Brian Quinn, and Helen Walters indicate that highly successful innovators employ five or more different types of innovation, whereas the majority of organizations utilize only one or two. Consequently, these authors urge leaders to move beyond product or service innovation to leverage innovation enablers such as their organization's brand, networks, structures, internal and external processes, product performance, product systems, delivery channels, and customer engagement.

Successful music leaders and those in the public, not-for-profit, and private sectors all know that they shouldn't rely solely on their "audiences" to tell them what they want, so they work diligently to identify current and potential future trends, shifts in demand, and changing demographics. But can business leaders also learn from the ways in which some arts organizations have responded to market changes?

Author, consultant, "turnaround king," and former President of the John F. Kennedy Center for the Performing Arts, Michael Kaiser writes about them in his 2015 book *Curtains? The Future of the Arts in America.* Kaiser says some audiences want technology-enabled multi-dimensional experiences, while others want more convenient times for performances or performances that are shorter. In response to changing needs like these, some arts leaders have reduced the number of performances in a calendar year and others have offered flexible purchase plans instead of season tickets. It should come as no surprise that the most successful leaders in the worlds of music and business continue to challenge traditional financial and operating models by exploring different ways of innovating, but is there something unique about what music leaders do?

Beyond Bounded Income

Michael Kaiser describes some other ways of innovating when he illustrates how some symphony orchestra leaders have moved beyond what was previously considered their "bounded income." A good example is the way in which a few well-known orchestras have made the finite number of seats in a concert hall almost irrelevant by delivering to virtual audiences. Broadcasting live performances in remote locations such as movie theaters, they're using an alternative distribution channel to sell many more tickets than if they'd been limited to a single location.

If you're a business leader or consultant, how might the size of an "audience" be increased through different types of innovation? And how might existing or new products and services be delivered to virtual audiences? Successful innovators aren't afraid to modify their business models as circumstances change, but the next topic in this chapter describes the critical behaviors that they must also possess.

Innovation Success Factors

In the Prelude of this book, I write about how inspiration sometimes manifests as a desire to give something back to the world after years of hard-earned life lessons and accumulated wisdom. I also describe how musicians, composers, and various other artists sometimes get their inspiration from dreams. At other times, inspiration may simply be a response to innovation challenges—complex problems that require both individual creativity as well as the different views and perspectives that come from diverse teams.

What are some of the key factors that are needed for sustainable innovation? And how do successful leaders develop critical innovation behaviors in themselves and others? What follows are six brief descriptions of innovation success factors, drivers, and enablers, as illustrated in the Marin Alsop success story and other parts of this book.

Inspiration

Born to professional musicians who played with the orchestra of the New York City Ballet, Marin Alsop undoubtedly inherited some of her musical ability. In addition to being encouraged by her parents, she was also influenced and supported by others. In her February 2017 lecture at the University of Oxford, Alsop tells how she was inspired to conduct when she was only nine years old. It happened when her father had taken her to a young people's concert at the New York Philharmonic and she'd personally witnessed a highly regarded maestro breaking with tradition.

After seeing this conductor smile and laugh, literally dance on stage, and even speak directly to audience members, Alsop turned to her father and announced her intent to become a conductor. Years later, in an interview with Jeffrey Brown of the PBS NewsHour, Alsop referred to this conductor as the force that had also continued to propel her dream. (See "Marin Alsop on PBS' NewsHour with Jim Lehrer," October 17, 2007, uploaded to YouTube on February 19, 2008.)

However, Alsop's story also includes an excellent example of how people can sometimes unwittingly sabotage inspiration. Excited about discovering her life's purpose at a young age, Alsop once again announced her intent to become a conductor—that time to her violin teacher at Juillard's pre-college program. Shocked at first by the teacher's response—"You know girls can't do that!"—Alsop was later disheartened. After seeking comfort from her mother, however, she was quickly reassured that she could do, and be, anything she wanted.

This story illustrates how the initial spark of innovation can be extinguished very quickly if it isn't protected and nurtured. Fortunately, Ruth Alsop knew what damage could be done if her daughter were to allow her dream to be sabotaged—intentionally or not. (See the video interview at makers.com/marin-alsop on the website of Makers, an initiative supported by PBS and AOL that features the largest video collection of women's stories.)

Motivation

The encouragement that Marin Alsop received didn't end with reassurance from her mother. In many interviews, Alsop tells how, when she arrived at breakfast the next morning, she saw a long wooden box—which she says she still has today. In her "Commemorative Video for Ruth and Lamar Alsop" (at www.marinalsop.com), she describes how it was filled with orchestra batons that her father had purchased. And in this video, Alsop says, "That was his way of saying, 'I believe in you. I'm here for you.'" Referring to this in her August 2014 presentation to GWU students, she said, "It was this kind of encouragement that was so incredible for me to have."

When some leaders think about what it takes to motivate people to innovate, they sometimes envision wildly charismatic leaders who generate a high degree of excitement. However, when considering Lamar Alsop's batons, we see that motivation can also manifest in other, more subtle actions. Elaine F. Weiss quotes Alsop as saying, "Each of us has the ability and capacity to impact other people's lives. Actions as simple as offering advice … or just being present to listen can have a dramatic effect." Of course, when people feel burdened by competing goals or ambitious agendas, they can sometimes lose sight of other important priorities such as the need to motivate. In these circumstances, they can easily forget that they're immeasurably powerful in their ability to influence and support others—often with little effort.

Unfortunately, not all leaders fully appreciate that innovation requires inspiration, motivation, and support. Those who undervalue these critical enablers, or don't make time for them, pay a price—as do their organizations. When leaders fail to ignite innovation through inspiration, they also miss opportunities to develop other essential qualities in their employees. With this in mind, here are two important questions for your consideration: What heights might someone in your sphere of influence reach because of your mentoring—or perhaps only a few words of encouragement? And conversely, what future maestro or "maestra" might you unknowingly *fail to inspire*?

Determination

People encourage innovation when they set a positive example and model the behaviors that support it. Marin Alsop frequently tells audiences how her parents constantly persevered in the face of obstacles. She says, "This is how they led their lives and this is what they expected of me." (See the video "Commemorative Video for Ruth and Lamar Alsop" on the Media page at marinalsop.com.) There are countless examples of potential innovators like Alsop who begin their journeys with powerful, yet seemingly unattainable, visions and dreams of what might be. The most supportive leaders encourage people like these to act on them, despite how unrealistic they might seem to be at the time.

Qualities such as determination can be a surprisingly powerful force that motivates—even when people don't have continued support. In many interviews, Alsop recounts the times that she'd been rejected for Julliard's conducting program and her many rejected applications for a conducting fellowship at the Boston Symphony Orchestra's Tanglewood Music Center. Fortunately, continued rejection didn't stop her from pursuing her goal. Instead, she began to build her career by freelancing as a violinist while also rounding up a group of friends from Juilliard to start her own ten-piece swing band, "String Fever."

Alsop's stated hope when creating her own enterprise was that she could enhance her conducting skills by surrounding herself with people who would help her learn by being honest with her. Decades later, in her presentation to GWU students, she smiled triumphantly while giving the following advice: "Just don't give up. You can stand there at the front door—you can bang, bang, bang and nobody will let you in—well, just go around the side and climb in the window while nobody's looking."

Collaboration

Despite all the valuable support that Alsop received from her parents and from the musicians in her string ensemble, she knew she'd need to achieve scale if she were to attain her dream of making a living as an orchestra conductor. That would mean finding someone willing to partner with her and support her orchestra financially. On a long shot, she approached a Japanese business executive and customer who had once paid for her orchestra's services in cash. With all the exuberance, daring, and determination of youth, Alsop asked Tomio Taki for his help.

Authors St. John and Deane quote Alsop's version of the request: "I said to him, 'Look, you don't know me at all and I don't really know you either, but I need help. I want to be a conductor. I want to start an orchestra…. it's the only thing in life I want. Would you help me?'" Unknown to Alsop at the time was that Tomio Taki owned the Anne Klein clothing company. However, even considering that fact, Mr. Taki's response of "Absolutely, I'll help you," could have been a spontaneous reaction that he might want to retract later—but he didn't.

In 1984, Tomio Taki collaborated with Marin Alsop to start their own chamber orchestra called "Concordia," which performed at the Lincoln Center in New York City. For the next 18 years, Taki continued to finance the orchestra and Alsop learned how to build and manage a board of directors, market Concordia, and assume the many responsibilities associated with a small enterprise. Their collaboration surely paid off for Alsop, yet other factors also drove her success.

Expectation

Marin Alsop tells how, despite opposition on her path to realizing her dream, she never wavered from her absolute certainty that a conductor was what she needed to be. Continually driven by her memory of the maestro at the New York Philharmonic who had inspired her decades earlier, Alsop pushed through many obstacles before eventually obtaining her first big break. With the experience she'd gained from conducting Concordia, she applied again for The Tanglewood Music Center fellowship. After four previous rejections, Alsop was surprised to learn that this application had been accepted, but she was also shocked to learn that she'd be performing with the iconic Leonard Bernstein—the very conductor who had inspired her when she was nine years of age!

Perhaps equally shocking was when Alsop won Tanglewood's prestigious Leonard Bernstein Conducting Fellowship for 1988-89, and the legendary maestro saw her potential and decided to mentor her. Recalling that experience, Alsop told GWU students, "It was incredible! He took me under his wing … We became very close, and I worked with him until he died three years later … It was amazing for me to … not only meet a hero but to have a hero exceed my expectations."

Clearly, Leonard Bernstein, Tomio Taki, and Marin Alsop's parents inspired, encouraged, and motivated her, but there was another factor that led to her success, and it went far beyond any support that she received from others. Alsop was driven by an expectation that her efforts to achieve the lofty goal she had set for herself would ultimately pay off. A distinguishing factor for most successful entrepreneurs and innovators like her is their firm conviction that, with effort and determination, they'll eventually succeed. Knowing that success might not be immediate, they're nonetheless convinced it will ultimately manifest—if not as a reward for their perseverance, then from what they might learn from their successes and failures.

Differentiation

People who anticipate positive outcomes have a particular brand of confidence that distinguishes them from others. When leaders provide meaningful feedback and support to employees who possess this quality, they build and reinforce the courage needed for authenticity. Then employees like these can differentiate themselves, and together with their leaders, model innovative behaviors that often inspire and motivate others. When this informal process continues as a ripple effect, it can help people advance even the most ambitious agendas.

Propelled by goals that distinguish her from other music directors, Marin Alsop has made the symphony a more meaningful experience for a broad range of audiences. By replicating Bernstein's strategies for connecting with people, she describes themes and motifs while also reviewing short passages before and after her performances. Elaine F. Weiss says Alsop has "fashioned herself into a musical ambassador…. Her own signature style is to climb down from the podium after a concert, pull up a chair, and answer questions from the audience….Elitists may be appalled, but audiences adore her."

Without a doubt, this practice differentiates Alsop from other conductors. She says about it, "Everything in life is about personal relationships—including the way one feels about music. I want to create as many opportunities for people to have that 'aha' moment—[to] give people the chance to really connect with the composers." What are some ways in which leaders in other organizations might leverage the relationships that they have with critical stakeholders?

The Case for Innovation

Jim Amos, one of this book's endorsers, has decades of experience forming and maintaining relationships with critical stakeholders—on teams, on boards that he chairs, and in a variety of environments that range from the military to retail management. Amos formed his beliefs about innovation from leadership roles on numerous boards, including the franchise initiative board that he currently chairs at Proctor & Gamble. His views on innovation and reinvention also stem from first-hand experience as former Chairman of the Board for two successful franchise operations (Tasti-D-lite and Planet Smoothie), and as former CEO and Chairman Emeritus of Mailboxes, etc. (currently the UPS Store).

At Mailboxes, etc., Amos and his senior leadership team executed a highly successful turnaround effort by introducing a broad range of innovation initiatives that put him in a strong position to make a case for innovation. About this subject, he says, "… leaders, organizations—and even entire countries—risk obsolescence, and even future collapse, if they fail to reinvent and innovate." Most people would agree with his views about innovation, but they might also ask, "If innovation is so critical for sustainability, why do so many other senior leaders have difficulty moving beyond mere rhetoric?" Equally perplexing is the question of why so many people resist innovation even when they accept that it's needed.

The well-known thought leader Gary Hamel addressed these seemingly contradictory behaviors when he said, "Despite all the pro-innovation rhetoric that one encounters in annual reports and CEO speeches, most still hold the view that innovation is a rather dangerous diversion from the real work of wringing the last ounce of efficiency out of core business processes." And Hamel added, "Innovation is fine so long as it does not disrupt a company's finely-honed operating model." When learning about the many leading organizations that have achieved both short- and long-term success through innovation, we can see how this powerful force can—and must—do more than simply disrupt.

A Dangerous Diversion?

Today, regardless of whether leaders are in health care or high tech, communications or consumer products, financial services or forensics, most have something in common: They might not like either the risk or the disruption that comes with innovation, but they know they must befriend both. That's because today, maintaining the status quo—in almost any sector or industry—can be one of the riskiest strategies of all.

Although many organizations succeed at innovation, many also fail, and this can happen despite the best of intentions and the strongest efforts. Sometimes it's because potential innovations aren't adequately supported. Other times, initiatives can stall or fail even when they're fully funded. And sadly, these aren't the only causes of innovation failure. It can also occur when innovation happens only in pockets of an organization; when it's carried out in a random manner; or when leaders default to command-and-control styles that restrict and inhibit it. Innovation failure also occurs when leaders coast on past successes, fail to effectively manage change, and continue to operate under outdated business models or insufficient infrastructures.

And innovation failure is a natural outcome when leaders: (a) place too much emphasis on operational excellence; (b) try to innovate without a formal plan; (c) give insufficient thought to the link between their business models and their innovation strategies; or (d) force a one-size-fits-all innovation strategy onto their organizations.

And of course, failure at innovation is almost guaranteed when leaders become victims of "innovation myopia." This kind of nearsightedness can occur when organizations rely solely on product or process innovation, as opposed to utilizing different types of innovation. So is there a common denominator among almost all innovation failures? Yes. It's simply the difficulty that most leaders encounter when they attempt to look beyond the short term to attempt business as UN-usual.

Large-Scale Change

When organizations are in decline, as the BSO was when Alsop first took the helm in 2007, their course of action and the timing of their actions are often predetermined. In these situations, leaders must use their organizations' impending failures as catalysts for change. Then they must quickly mobilize whatever forces are within their control. However, even in scenarios other than turnaround, leaders can fail if they're not mindful of the "tempo"—the speed—at which they introduce new or enhanced products, services, or different ways of operating.

That's because too much innovation, too fast, or too disruptive, can translate to unnecessary risk. Of course, the reverse can also cause innovation failure. If organizations rely solely on marginal or incremental improvements, innovation might be too slow. Then the result might be limited growth, which can ultimately compromise an organization's sustainability.

In her chapter *Leading Innovation*, Andrea Zintz says, "Times of uncertainty, radical change, and opportunity elevate the importance of leadership." Needless to say, when change is mismanaged, it can negatively impact both individual and organizational performance. Unfortunately, few leaders are sufficiently skilled at managing large-scale change. Those who are successful know that human beings usually perceive uncertainty as a threat. They also know that even though change might not necessarily be a detrimental force in itself, it can become destructive when it exacerbates normal fear responses and creates excessive turmoil—and even panic.

Change Management

When executing change, successful leaders consider factors such as the nature of the change to be made and the maturity level of the employees who will be impacted by it. They also determine the degree to which change has been introduced in the past as well as the timing and results of the most recent changes. These leaders know that if people are convinced of the need for new products, services, or processes, they'll be more likely to view them favorably and support them. Consequently, successful leaders communicate the "why" behind the innovations that they introduce, and whenever possible, plant the seeds for change *before* initiating it.

Successful change agents also appreciate that new systems, business models, and enhanced processes and procedures can be very stressful for employees, so they actively solicit people's input about how best to implement change. Effective leaders of innovation often assemble project teams or task forces with the goal of inviting recommendations for both strategy formulation *and* execution. They also know that people are more apt to accept change when they're involved and empowered. Equally important, these leaders have reasonable expectations of people who will be affected by it.

The Execution Challenge

When helping clients manage large-scale change, I've often cited the survival-of-the-fittest concept. Why? Because the "fittest" species aren't necessarily the strongest and healthiest—they're the most *adaptable*. The same applies to people. Although some adapt quickly to changes in their environment, others are inclined to become fossils. If leaders can empathize with employees in the "fossil" category, rather than harshly judging their delayed actions—or inaction—there's a two-fold benefit. One is that employees who are fearful of change are usually less anxious when they sense that managers have realistic expectations of their change capacity. And two, leaders feel less frustrated if they accept that current challenges might be exceeding certain employees' change capabilities.

How else do successful innovators move beyond resistance and encourage people to take the necessary risks associated with innovation? In the *Inspiring and Encouraging Innovation* chapter of this book, Megan Mitchell illustrates the importance of the creative process and the need to create a culture that supports innovation. She describes a basic innovation model that consists of four stages. To summarize here, people at the first stage are concerned with identifying issues and clarifying problems or "innovation challenges."

At the second stage, they explore and discuss ideas by engaging in brainstorming and other idea generation activities. At the third stage, once ideas have been generated, people vet and develop them, based on cost, viability, and organizational fit. And, as indicated at the beginning of this chapter, the "innovation buck" stops at the fourth and final stage of the innovation process. That's where ideas are translated into strategies and executed. Unfortunately, it's also the stage at which innovation initiatives are most likely to fail. That's because leaders who execute are often tasked with doing "double duty." They must maintain operational excellence while also implementing innovation initiatives. Sometimes leaders fail in these dual roles because they don't have the skills needed to achieve the delicate balance that's required. And other times they lack the perseverance, stamina, and raw courage that innovation often demands.

Crime and Punishment

Courage is a must have for many leaders who execute innovation initiatives because they're often blamed when projects don't take off as planned; when new processes inhibit what they're supposed to support; and when investments don't yield expected returns. Knowing this, we can understand why people in organizations that blame and punish employees often view innovation as the equivalent of a high-wire act without a net. If we accept that failure, by its traditional definition, is still a punishable offense in many organizations, it's also easy to understand why leaders have difficulty introducing methods that require experimentation.

With all this in mind, we can also gain insight into why some employees in these organizations work under enormous pressure to succeed at innovation. And we can appreciate why others go to great lengths to avoid innovation or simply procrastinate. However, blame and punishment aren't universal phenomena. Organizations that are known for innovation typically view "failures" as mere steps in trial-and-error learning processes. Most important, leaders in these organizations don't blame people if favorable results aren't achieved on the first try—or even after multiple attempts.

Balance and Opposing Forces

Like symphony orchestra leaders and jazz musicians, successful innovators appreciate the need for balance. Effective leaders continually improvise as they play with and integrate various opposites. Skilled at dealing with many invisible forces, they know how harmony and balance can either positively or negatively impact performance and innovation. However, music leaders, in particular, are experts at balancing opposing forces, and they're acutely aware of the polarities that create the tension required for creative thinking and problem solving.

In this chapter, I describe ten critical pairs of opposing forces and factors that leaders in almost every venue must continually balance to ensure top performance and sustainable innovation. Let's start with how these leaders know when to orchestrate and when to improvise.

Orchestration and Improvisation

I previously described the way in which music leaders balance these two activities when I introduced the symphony orchestra metaphor as an innovation enabler as well as a symbol of obsolescence. To briefly reiterate, this icon shows how successful leaders achieve mastery and preserve harmony by building on past successes, lessons learned, and time-honored traditions. At the same time, the symphony orchestra metaphor can spell disaster if it symbolizes failure to keep pace with change. As an effective complement, a jazz metaphor illustrates how leaders must continually explore new horizons and engage in ongoing disciplined experimentation, often by teaming up and co-creating with others.

By now, you might guess that most successful leaders are innately skilled at improvising, and you would be right. As humans, we're fundamentally built to survive, and we often do it through improvisation. However, leaders need to be mindful that improvising can be a two-edged sword if they improvise when they should orchestrate or when they employ improvisation primarily to put out daily fires.

Orchestration is very important at the execution stage of the innovation process, where balance is most critical. However, few of us are born with natural proficiencies at orchestrating innovation, so this unique enabler often requires new or different skills—and a different kind of focus. Consequently, most of us need to learn how to orchestrate from others who have that expertise.

Idea Generation and Execution

Jazz musicians often talk about finding the sweet spot between opposite forces. This concept can be applied effectively to yet another pair of opposites: the "front end" and "back end" of the innovation process. The front end of innovation, where ideas are generated, can be a particularly exciting stage, yet sometimes it's unwittingly abbreviated. This happens when people settle for only a few good ideas instead of the many that are usually required to successfully execute.

Even though people can sometimes short shrift activities on the front end of innovation, this stage usually receives far more attention than the back end. For many people, the final stage of the innovation process—where ideas are translated into actionable strategies and carried out—is the less exciting and more grueling stage. And as previously mentioned, it's also the stage where the greatest risk for punishable failure resides.

Despite all its challenges, the execution stage can be both challenging and rewarding. By continually taking in and evaluating information before acting on it, leaders at this juncture engage in a repeating cycle in which they vet, test, and iterate ideas before implementing them. Leaders who undertake these vital activities make innovation happen while also maintaining the strategic focus that keeps innovation projects on course and within budget.

Action and Strategy

Henry Mintzberg once said, "Management is about helping organizations and units to get things done, which means action." Although this statement is true, successful innovators know that action alone isn't enough to effectively launch innovation initiatives, and it's certainly not enough to sustain them. Action and strategy *together* are what's needed, and like other factors, they require balance and good timing.

Throughout the innovation process, action and strategy usually compete for the lead position. At the first stage, when people engage in problem identification and the hunt for "big ideas," action typically takes the lead—as it should. However, when leaders begin to screen ideas for viability, strategy should edge forward and remain in the lead.

In less-than-ideal situations, when action occurs in place of strategy—or precedes it—execution is invariably unfocused and chaotic. Under these circumstances, leaders can waste valuable resources, so they must ensure that strategy remains at the forefront as ideas progress. Then finally, at the execution stage, strategy and action must dance together in a delicate balance as ideas are continually enhanced and implemented.

Value Creation and Value Preservation

Successful leaders know that, like other opposing forces, value creation and value preservation must be carefully balanced. Consequently, they best manage and leverage innovation when they engage in activities that both *create* and *preserve* value. To create value, leaders typically work at bringing in new business. Other times, they might build on existing business or on new or previous innovations. In today's competitive environments, the most successful innovators create value by looking to many different sources for ideas.

Gone are the days when organizations focused only on employees in functions traditionally associated with innovation, such as Marketing or R&D. In fact, many now use idea management technologies on an enterprise-wide basis, to tap into people's creativity, knowledge, and skill sets. Other organizations preserve value, and conserve assets and resources, by identifying areas of inefficiency and replacing outdated, labor-intensive processes. This can also mean the purchase of sophisticated technologies and systems that will ultimately save costs through efficiencies. As previously mentioned, however, most organizations can't "save" their way to success, so they must also protect their brands, proprietary software, lean processes, and intellectual property rights, through copyrights, patents, and trademarks.

People and Processes

In the chapter *Inspiring and Encouraging Innovation*, Megan Mitchell writes, "For musicians and other artists, creativity is a given, yet very few business leaders appreciate its value as a raw ingredient for innovation." With that, she describes how innovation must begin with creativity. However, even when leaders receive formal training in innovation—and leave the classroom knowledgeable in the science of it—they aren't nearly as adept at the artistry that's also needed.

As you might guess, an imbalance can manifest between people and processes when leaders focus too intently on the process side (the science) of innovation and underestimate the "people side" (that is, the artistry). Imbalance—and innovation failure—can also occur when there's too much focus on people and a lack of attention on processes. Another endorser of this book, Dr. Robin Karol, author of *Product Development for Dummies* and former innovation leader at DuPont, continually underscores how innovation is a delicate balancing act between people and the processes that support them.

Freedom and Alignment

In his book, *Inside Conducting*, Christopher Seaman, Conductor Laureate for Life at the Rochester Philharmonic Orchestra, cites a quote by Zubin Mehta, the Israel Philharmonic Orchestra's Music Director for Life. Coming from a slightly different perspective, Mehta once said, "The balancing act between yielding and leading is an art that a conductor simply has to master." And Seaman adds, "Conducting an orchestra is two-way traffic: A conductor is taking in as well as giving out."

To further illustrate, Seaman tells us that maestros often use their batons to achieve a good balance between freedom and alignment. By "beating out time," they keep members of their orchestras in synch. However, they must do this carefully so that people "play in harmony" without being forced to adhere to a "mindless rhythm that leaves little room for creativity." With that, Seaman suggests that people's creativity and artistry "should be recognized, not controlled out of existence."

When business leaders co-create with their employees, they afford them freedom of expression while simultaneously securing buy-in. However, to fully enable innovation, they must do more than free people from excessive control. To skillfully align personal and organizational agendas, and balance individual freedom with organizational alignment, leaders also need to empower employees by providing space to develop and share their ideas. They must also work diligently to anticipate potential impediments and remove them so that employees can more easily execute ideas and strategies. Of course, they must also hold people accountable through well-designed performance scorecards and effective performance management systems.

Knowing that some people function best without structure, while others require a great deal of it, Seaman illustrates how savvy leaders vary their style based on their followers' experience and maturity. With this, he cites another quote from the famous conductor Richard Strauss, who said, "What may seem pedantic and fussy with one orchestra might well be absolutely necessary to keep a less experienced group together." Of course, the same is true of almost any team.

Disciplined Experimentation and Failure

Leaders who know how to encourage and support experimentation are as critical for mature and well-established organizations as they are for entrepreneurial start-ups. These leaders possess a different mindset about failure. Thomas Edison described it when he said, "I haven't failed. I've simply found 10,000 ways that do not work." What other organizations might call "failure," Edison and his team viewed as a fundamental factor that allowed certain options or strategies to be ruled out. The process of elimination also proved useful when Edison's inventors realized, often after the fact, that had their "failures" succeeded, products might have been too costly to commercialize.

Today, many organizations use "disciplined experimentation" and the scientific method to test hypotheses, fine-tune their efforts, and manage risk. They also construct guardrails and risk parameters that allow people to "fail fast" or learn from their mistakes while simultaneously preventing unnecessary failures. With these constructs in place, employees are empowered to experiment until they ultimately succeed—or until they hit guardrails that prevent catastrophic or irreversible failures.

New Ways and Business as Usual

Most leaders know that few organizations grow—or even survive—by looking backward. However, middle managers can easily get caught between the proverbial "rock and a hard spot" when they receive mixed messages from executives who only hype innovation. Sometimes these middle managers are told to explore new opportunities, while at the same time, they receive unstated messages, nonverbal cues, and actions from senior leaders that dictate business as usual. In other words, while executives sometimes actively promote innovation, their actions communicate a different message. Inwardly, they might only want employees to do what has worked for their organizations in the past, even if they know that sustainable innovation requires a continual search for new or more effective ways of operating.

As previously mentioned in *Why This Book?*, IBM Fellow Emeritus and former EVP Innovation and Technology, Nick Donofrio, says success in any field or industry requires "actively seeking out change and embracing it." And he adds, "Successful leaders in today's world know that change is always coming, so they don't wait for it. They look for it and capitalize on it."

Incremental and Disruptive Innovation

In some cases, when leaders are faced with apparent contradictions between innovating and conducting business as usual, they take a middle-ground position and choose to innovate only incrementally. It's important to utilize advantage-seeking, exploitation strategies (for incremental innovation) as well as opportunity-seeking, exploration strategies (for innovation that can disrupt competitors and even entire markets). Exploitation strategies can provide steady improvements, whereas exploration strategies allow organizations to compete in new and uncontested space—at least until others respond with equally impactful and disruptive innovations.

A good example of the need for exploration strategies can be found in Thomas Edison's philosophies. Long recognized for innovation, his General Electric Company (now GE) achieved growth through new products that dated as far back as its founding in 1892. Although the term "disruptive innovation" didn't exist during his time, Edison and his partners—as well as innovative leaders at competing organizations such as Philips—believed that a continuing stream of new technologies and innovations would be needed for their organizations to prosper.

Leaders in these organizations knew that when they deployed innovations as powerful weapons, competitors would respond accordingly—particularly if their innovations had the potential to substantially change market conditions or upset entire industries. As in years past, successful leaders today continually prepare for the impactful innovations of others by ensuring that their organizations are able to respond quickly to both threats and opportunities.

Structure and Flexibility

Most, if not all, organizations need some degree of structure. The question is how much and what kind. Many leaders view their organizations' structures as static and fixed when it would be better to think of them as flexible and resilient. My work with organizations at all stages of their lifecycles has revealed that it matters little whether they're highly structured or minimally structured. What does matter is whether they're designed to flex with the volatility of their particular markets as well as the changing needs of internal and external stakeholders.

What also matters is how well leaders achieve the right balance between structure and flexibility. For example, many employees find it difficult to innovate when inhibited by duplicative, conflicting, or labor-intensive processes. At the same time, they're equally challenged in environments where chaos and inefficiency prevail. Consequently, organizational structures need to provide enough support so that people are free to perform and innovate, yet not so much that they feel unduly restrained. To find the right balance between structure and flexibility, leaders must continually evaluate their organizations and reconfigure their structures to meet ongoing changes.

People, Partnerships, and Processes

By now you've seen how leaders can either support or inhibit innovation by how they maintain balance and manage change. To further describe the kinds of leaders that achieve sustainable innovation, consider what Christopher Seaman says about the variety of ways in which people lead. He says some are tolerant of "different ways of playing as long as they all fit with the bigger picture," while "others think there's only one 'right' way to play every note."

Seaman adds that leaders in the second category are powered by a very clear vision that "includes the integrity of the details." He says about the musicians who play for these leaders, " [They] complain that they can't play a single note without referring to their conductor … "They feel micromanaged and musically choked." And he adds, "A conductor who works in this way is taking a risk: [He's] reducing everything to his own size only rather than to the combined size of everybody present." Seaman believes that when conductors over manage, they're not only "infantilizing the musicians," but also "reducing their responsibility."

From this, it should be obvious that innovation isn't only enabled by creative people, but also by people who are sufficiently empowered to apply their creativity. However, that isn't enough to effectively drive and sustain innovation. Organizations also need effective and efficient processes. And what I haven't described yet are the strong partnerships that are also fundamental to high levels of performance and sustainable innovation. Whether organizations compete for funding, customers, or clients, people and partnerships play critical roles in meeting the needs of various audiences.

■ ■ ■

1. Innovation through People

For leaders in contemporary times, knowing when to "direct" and when to "allow" is sometimes difficult. Without a doubt, managing people was simpler in the days of Arturo Toscanini, Fritz Reiner, Herbert von Karajan, and other world-renowned maestros of the distant past. These commanding leaders were revered by audiences and feared by their musicians. Today, leadership skills, competencies, and personal attributes play a fundamental role in organizational success. What's more, people who lead today deal with challenges that were virtually unknown to leaders even decades ago. At a minimum, today's leaders must be skilled at managing employees in remote locations and also at motivating today's diverse, multicultural, multigenerational workforces.

With Millennials now comprising approximately 50-75 percent of today's global workforce, leaders must consider their unique needs and values and be adept at meeting those needs. In addition, they must understand what motivates people in all the generations that are represented in today's work environments. With that in mind, what should leaders know about the unique attributes of each? And how can the strengths of each generation of employees be leveraged to drive and sustain innovation?

Generational Differences

Managing today's knowledge workers isn't a whole lot different from managing creative talent—something for which music leaders have had decades of experience. Like symphony orchestra musicians and jazz professionals, today's knowledge workers—particularly Millennials—appreciate having avenues through which they can express their creativity. And like their musician counterparts, most employees today prefer to be led over being told what to do.

Baby Boomers, as well as Generation X employees, are capable of functioning at very high levels of autonomy, so they usually require only minimal supervision, but there's something else that leaders should keep in mind about Baby Boomers: Many have delayed retirement because they want to keep contributing. Knowing that, today's most effective leaders provide learning opportunities for these employees while simultaneously availing themselves of their many years of experience.

Alan Murray, editor of Fortune.com, described still another group of significant contributors in today's workforce in his October 2015 Editor's Desk article entitled "4 things I learned from our 40 under 40." Murray says about these employees, "It's not just the exuberance of this youth that makes this group so compelling. It is the message they send about their generation and our future. They see no obstacle too big to overcome, no challenge that can't be met…. [They] "bet big, have a purpose, and believe that failure is a good teacher."

So is any one generation better equipped to innovate than others? Many studies find that human beings are hardwired for innovation regardless of age. This is manifested in people's innate curiosity and ongoing desire to learn as well as their continual search for better and quicker ways to carry out tasks. In fact, ever since early human beings invented basic tools, they've been innovating—either as individuals or as members of communities. From this, we can safely assume that people, by nature, are motivated to innovate, but people can become demotivated if other factors aren't present.

Job Satisfaction

Researchers who study motivation tell us that the most satisfied and productive employees are highly engaged and excited about the work they do. Certainly it would seem as if symphony orchestra musicians would be among them, but this isn't necessarily true. Harvard researcher Richard Hackman discovered that despite their love of music, musicians in one of his studies ranked among the lowest in job satisfaction. In fact, Hackman found that their job satisfaction scores ranked slightly lower than the federal correctional officers who he also surveyed. (See Greg Sandow's *artsjournal.com* article "Not So Satisfied.")

Why were the symphony orchestra musicians in Hackman's study so unhappy about their work? Marin Alsop addressed this question in her 2014 presentation at the George Washington University (GWU) School of Business when she said, "They have been groomed from a young age to be the center, and then they have to let go and sublimate their ego to the greater good...." How might this apply in other settings? We shouldn't be surprised that most successful business leaders would strongly object to any activity that could cause their most brilliant and dedicated innovators to be sublimated—even if those employees tend to be a bit eccentric. Leaders like these *value*, rather than merely *tolerate*, different types.

Certainly there are instances in which leaders must help employees temper individual agendas to ensure positive outcomes of high performing teams, but they first attempt scenarios that integrate personal needs with organizational priorities. These leaders identify people whose creativity and innovation styles are best suited for each stage of the innovation process, so they can fully leverage individual and team strengths.

Teamwork

History is replete with examples of innovative geniuses, dating back to Copernicus, Leonardo DaVinci, and more recently Albert Einstein, Bill Gates, Steve Jobs, and others. Among these, Thomas Edison stands out once again as an excellent example—not only as a brilliant inventor, but also as a highly effective leader of innovation. In the book, *Innovative Intelligence: The Art and Practice of Leading Sustainable Innovation in Your Organization,* authors David S. Weiss and Claude P. Legrand assert that there are "innovative leaders" and "leaders of innovation." Edison was both.

As a leader of innovation, Edison knew that the real power of creativity didn't come solely from brilliant inventors engaged in individual pursuits. It came from teams of people who achieved synergy by building on one another's ideas and approaches. As previously mentioned, some of today's technologies form a strong foundation for teamwork and expand it to an enterprise-wide level through software platforms that support idea management and virtual collaboration.

When people are enabled by these technologies, they can very quickly solve problems, generate solutions, and produce results that often exceed what any one individual might accomplish independently. However, to work effectively in teams, people must first be engaged and motivated on a personal level. Effective leaders know this, so in addition to building cultures that encourage and support collaboration and teamwork, they also ensure that individuals are well-matched to the work they do. And of course they also recognize and reward them for the ways in which they contribute to their organizations' overall success.

Rewards and Recognition

Sometimes leaders inhibit or prevent innovation by inadequately reinforcing the efforts of aspiring innovators. Often this is unintentional. It's simply because the traditional metrics used to measure outcomes usually aren't relevant for innovation projects. Although some organizations today are attempting to capture value in new and better ways, their efforts to apply big data and analytics to potential innovations are still in their infancy.

Two aspects of recognition and rewards that require equal attention today are "on-stage" and "off-stage" talent. For example, music leaders know that if one section of a symphony orchestra is allowed to overpower others—in speed, volume, or perceived importance—the result will be unsatisfactory. If we think of the "on-stage" talent in an orchestra or jazz ensemble as the musicians who bring the music alive, we might appreciate the parallels in business environments.

Technology geniuses, rainmakers, charismatic leaders, and people with highly specialized skills and competencies can also be viewed as "on-stage" talent. However, "off-stage" talent, in both orchestras and business organizations, typically have essential "shows to run" as well. Unfortunately, because off-stage employees are nearly invisible, they often go unrecognized and insufficiently rewarded. To inspire both "on-stage" and "off-stage" employees, leaders must reward people equitably. However, that doesn't mean compensating everyone in the same way.

The value in pay-for-performance systems is the ability to differentiate between high-performing employees and those who simply show up. However, this type of compensation system can only provide tangible rewards, and that can lead to still another way in which leaders err. By overestimating the power of financial compensation and tangible rewards, leaders can underestimate the effect that non-financial rewards have on motivating people to perform at their highest levels. Successful leaders reward and recognize people both tangibly and intangibly, while ensuring that rewards are correlated with performance. However, this is only one of many leadership practices that motivate and engage people.

Engagement

When Marin Alsop was invited to participate in the World Economic Forum in 2005, the topic of her panel discussion was non-financial incentives for employees—an area often overlooked by leaders who believe that employees are only interested in tangible incentives and rewards. In a variety of interviews, Alsop indicates that communication is such a critical factor for keeping people motivated and engaged, leaders must continually strive to be transparent.

Certainly effective communication is a motivating force, but it's not the only way by which leaders like Alsop ensure that people stay engaged once the initial thrill of an innovation is gone. There's another factor that plays a significant role in employee engagement, yet it's not often written about. In her article "Conducting Energy," M.S. Mason says about Marin Alsop, "Her energy, love for music, and business drive … make her a force to be reckoned with."

If you've already read the chapter *Inspiring and Encouraging Innovation*, you know that a passion for innovation can be highly contagious. You can probably also guess that unleashing people's passions isn't always enough to fully engage them—and keep them engaged. To accomplish that, leaders must model the energy, enthusiasm, and risk-taking abilities required for innovation. That usually means they, themselves, must be engaged and personally motivated. Leaders must also communicate, either directly or indirectly, that what they're doing—and what they're asking others to do—has meaning and purpose. With that in mind, let's look at how leaders excel at relationships with their employees.

Volunteers, Not Hostages

In the introduction to this book's innovation success stories, Jim Amos says "… many leaders don't think of their employees as people with whom they have relationships. They think of them more as 'hostages' or simply as 'workers' who are paid to do certain jobs." Amos warns, "No matter how much we might pay them, employees—and leaders—are free to leave at any time. And many do—when organizations function poorly and leaders fail to inspire and connect." He adds, "The most innovative and highest-performing employees are propelled by a higher purpose that goes beyond pay." Consequently, Amos' advice is to view these employees, and *all* employees for that matter, as "volunteers."

Many of the innovation experts featured in this book would agree. They believe that people innovate best when leaders enlist both minds and souls. With that, let's consider what Marshall Goldsmith, one of two Thinkers50 thought leaders featured in this book, says about job satisfaction. He says, "When we do what we *have* to do we are compliant. When we do what we *choose* to do we are committed." Successful innovators know that the latter is what enables the buy-in that's crucial for sustainable innovation.

■ ■ ■

2. Innovation through Partnerships

In the last decade or so, leaders who innovated through traditional product and service categories have increasingly shifted their focus to new business models as well as expanded value chains and enhanced internal and external processes. Partnerships, too, have played a significant role in this shift—as both catalysts and outcomes.

When we think of the kind of partnerships that facilitate innovation, we typically envision those with vendors, suppliers, and even competitors. However, most successful innovators also partner with consumers, customers, clients, and employees, even though they might not think of these relationships as partnerships. To better understand the role that partnering plays in innovation, let's get acquainted with three primary categories of partnerships that enable it.

Strategic Partnerships

Some organizations achieve scale through mergers while others create economies of scale by joining forces with similar institutions. Joint ventures can either be permanent (such as merged back-office costs) or temporary (as in collaborations on particular projects or coordinated marketing efforts). Through strategic alliances such as these, organizations can penetrate new markets, increase market share, and enhance their brands. Many also combine or share complementary technologies and talent that can help accelerate commercialization of new products or services. Partnering can also help many organizations produce potentially disruptive innovations because, by joining forces with others, leaders are often able to spread costs as well as risk.

Large companies often partner with small organizations to infuse new thinking, experiment off-site with new products or services, and quickly purchase intellectual capital rather than having to develop it themselves. The advantages of small organizations partnering with large companies might seem obvious, but sometimes they only want to become suppliers. In other situations, they look to large companies for venture capital or to benefit from corporate incubation programs. For small organizations, partnering can also be a way to gain market knowledge as well as access to large customer bases, distribution networks, and experts with specialized skills.

From these examples, we can see how partnering can bring advantages as well as disadvantages. For example, when the fit between partners turns out to be less than ideal, differences in thinking and approaches can cause conflicts that negatively impact innovation. As a result, it's important for leaders to evaluate potential partners for compatible values and for their ability to deal with inevitable conflicts. When leaders can skillfully negotiate shared responsibilities, work through competing priorities, and commit to resolving differences, the benefits of partnerships more than offset the effort they require. And even in the most challenging scenarios, strategic partners might only need to reconcile some misunderstandings or misperceptions.

Employee Partnerships

To achieve and sustain innovation success, leaders must build relationships with both external and internal customers—in other words, their employees. Equitable compensation and consistent application of human resources policies are two of several basic factors that contribute to strong employee-employer partnerships. However, many employees today also want to have a voice in how business is conducted, particularly in their respective work areas. Effective leaders are well aware of this, and so they actively solicit and honor input and feedback from employees.

These leaders know that to earn and maintain the level of trust needed to partner for innovation, they must build systematic and systemic innovation capabilities rather than relying on a random collection of initiatives. They also know that they must communicate frequently with employees to show how senior executives are responding to new and converging trends. With that, successful leaders regularly send the message that their organizations are keeping pace with competitors by producing meaningful outcomes to innovation challenges.

Regardless of whether organizations partner with internal or external stakeholders, or both, a high degree of trust is required. Most often trust is built incrementally over time, but sometimes the good will that forms the foundation for it can occur with a single act. Think back to how Marin Alsop accomplished that with the BSO musicians when, in reference to her contract, she said, "I won't sign unless you're with me."

Consumer and Community Partnerships

As we saw in the Marin Alsop story, community partnerships can be important drivers of innovation for some organizations. In a 2013 *Business Insider* article entitled "How to Stay in Business for 100 Years," author Alexandra Levit writes about centenarian organizations. She says, "Among the traits that these successful organizations have in common are a laser-sharp customer focus, a willingness to chart new territory, and a close relationship within the communities in which they operate." Levit also tells us, "Customer focus applies just as much to nonprofits as it does to Fortune 500 entities."

Knowing this, effective orchestra leaders cater to their audiences. They select music in response to changing preferences in the same way that their business counterparts introduce new or enhanced products and services. Business leaders listen to the voices of consumers while also observing their buying behaviors. By engaging in consumer insights work—and allowing people's needs, preferences, and actions to drive their organizations' goals and strategies—leaders can exponentially increase the likelihood of innovation that's sustainable.

■   ■   ■

3. Innovation through Processes

Despite how excited people might be about new ideas and different ways of operating, innovation initiatives can get stalled or permanently thwarted by outdated, cumbersome, or inefficient processes and procedures. As a result, successful innovators ensure that robust infrastructures are in place rather than tolerating those that are insufficient, piecemeal, or chaotic.

You'll learn from the experts in this subsection about formal processes that create and preserve value. They describe how they're fundamental to building innovation capability as well as constructing effective risk management programs. These contributors also describe how critical processes can either drive or inhibit innovation, depending upon how well they're integrated with other key innovation drivers and enablers. Our contributors also describe how innovation is dependent on a variety of processes, both traditional and non-traditional.

Repeatable and Predictable Processes

Vijay Govindarajan and Chris Trimble, two of many best-selling authors featured in this book, tell us that organizations historically competed by making the majority of their processes repeatable and predictable. These authors also say that when leaders try to innovate in the same way, they most often fail. That's because, for the most part, innovation is neither predictable nor repeatable. Does this mean that these processes are innovation barriers, rather than enablers? We might view them that way if we're unaware of how organizations have also benefited from them.

By doing more than simply enabling efficiency through specialization and the division of labor, repeatable and predictable processes laid the foundation decades ago, for centers of excellence, metrics and benchmarking, performance standards and scorecards, and others. These processes also support performance management systems by enabling leaders to reward high-performing individuals and teams while also taking action when performance targets have been missed. Repeatable and predictable processes also play critical roles in supporting process optimization, strategic and operations planning, and risk management. Now let's get acquainted with some other key processes that support innovation.

Open Innovation

Digitization has enabled many organizations to transcend old research and development models by accessing a "global laboratory" of virtual networks that crisscross the globe. The process by which people utilize this virtually unlimited lab is called "open innovation." Hila Lifshitz-Assaf, an assistant professor at New York University's Stern School, described this form of "external innovation" as a question in a paper that she presented at Harvard Business School in 2013. (See "The Lab is My World or the World is My Lab: Boundary and Professional Role Identity Work of R&D Organizational Members Encountering Open Innovation," presented at Harvard Business School Organization Science Winter Conference 2013.)

Lifshitz-Assaf asserts that open innovation isn't an either-or proposition, meaning it can be combined with in-house efforts to innovate. Through open innovation, organizations have formed relationships with academic institutions, suppliers, labs, think tanks, customers, and even competitors. In addition to facilitating a blend of ideas from both internal and external perspectives, open innovation has helped leaders create avenues for informal or strategic partnerships of both local and virtual varieties. However, this is only one of the many ways in which leaders today achieve sustainable innovation, so let's now look at some of the other repeatable processes that successful innovators employ.

Process Optimization

Many leaders view innovation as a core competency and a sustainable differentiator, but what happens when some people believe that the processes associated with it are nothing more than necessary evils? At a minimum, ideas for improving both internal and external processes can fail to become executable solutions, resulting in lost opportunities.

We've probably all seen how inefficient or ineffective systems and processes can negatively impact optimal performance. They can also do this by not allowing enough time for people to devise more effective and efficient ways of operating. By devoting sufficient resources to periodically and formally assess key processes, leaders can determine how well they're supporting performance as well as innovation goals and initiatives.

Strategic and Operations Planning

If leaders frequently find themselves blindsided by new or unanticipated discoveries, it usually means they need to be more alert to what's going on in both their internal and external environments. Planning, as a forced discipline, can help. It can also produce secondary benefits. First, the planning process can provide opportunities for ongoing fine-tuning and course correction. Second, it can enable necessary breaks for reflection. Third, it can foster collaboration. And fourth, it can be a way to challenge long-held assumptions.

Leonard Bernstein once said, "To achieve great things, two things are needed: a plan, and not quite enough time." Like other critical processes, planning requires careful balance. Unfortunately, in many organizations, it's often synonymous with "too little too late." Sometimes there's also "too much planning and not enough doing," and other times, "too much doing and not enough planning." When done correctly, planning can save time and other valuable resources because it can help leaders reflect on the past, evaluate the present, and envision the future. And when leaders take time out for reflection, they often find themselves with greater insight, enhanced abilities to learn from past successes and failures, and more white space from which to bring forth new options.

Most important, the contributors to this subsection tell us that strategic and operations planning can only bring full and lasting value if the processes that provide meaningful information are ongoing and dynamic. Then decision makers can stay abreast of both internal and external changes and respond accordingly. Although the primary value of planning lies in its ability to help people transform broad strategies into specific initiatives, the real magic occurs when leaders involve people at various organizational levels in both strategy formulation and implementation. By sharing goals and objectives, leaders can bring plans alive in much the same way that symphony orchestra leaders bring life to their musical scores.

Organizational Risk and Portfolio Management

As previously mentioned, leaders must create value through continual innovation and preserve that value by carefully managing risk. Contributors to this section tell us that sometimes people refuse to take preliminary actions as a way to avoid or minimize risk. By contrast, successful innovators *manage* risk—and help others manage it—by establishing formal risk management systems that protect assets and minimize liabilities.

This often means anticipating potential problems with specific strategies, weighing their advantages and disadvantages, and then taking calculated risks. A good example of this is the way leaders construct innovation project portfolios. Rather than gambling on a single potential game-changing strategy, they manage innovation as they do other investments, diversifying on the basis of risk profiles, projected timeframes, and required resources.

Successful innovators employ a variety of risk management strategies throughout the innovation process. Good examples are the risk parameters that leaders create in advance of initiatives and the ways in which they secure agreement on projects before they're implemented. Another is how they consider thresholds when deciding whether or not to authorize additional investments. These leaders also employ methods such as scenario planning, which help them identify numerous options and enable them to assess the likelihood that certain conditions—good and bad—will manifest.

Rapid prototyping is another way in which successful leaders manage risk. They construct models of products to be developed and then continually enhance them. Leaders sometimes also establish beta sites, where experimentation can occur on a small scale and be expanded if potential innovations appear to be viable. Still another way in which leaders manage risk is "in stages." The practice of stage-gating enables informed decision making as more information becomes available and as better decision-making tools can be used. However, the concept of "pay-as-you-go" funding is best illustrated through the use of an "innovation funnel."

Envision a transparent funnel filled to its widest part (the top) with many potential innovations and early stage projects. As ideas and projects move through the innovation process from idea generating to vetting, their progress is reflected visually. As the funnel narrows and only those ideas that show promise are advanced, leaders can set appropriate guidelines for new product and service innovations and make informed decisions about additional funding.

Personal Risk Management

Equally important to managing organizational risk is knowing—and accepting—that risk also occurs at the personal level. One way in which leaders help to reduce individuals' fears about risk is to use the innovation funnel as a feedback loop. In this way, discussions can be initiated and the funnel can serve as a highly effective instructional tool for assessing why some projects fail to advance beyond early stages.

As a final word on personal risk, leaders can help people reduce their fears by continually sharing their organizations' risk management strategies. When communicating in this way, they send a message that sound risk and portfolio management call for disciplined experimentation, as opposed to random, hit-or-miss approaches. Leaders can also reduce fear about risk by making their organizations' commitments to new ways of doing business highly visible.

■ ■ ■

Exemplary Leadership

To reinforce the innovation concepts highlighted in their respective sections, Andrea Zintz and Megan Mitchell end their chapters with personal stories about successful innovations that were powered by exemplary leaders. The short story that follows describes my experience as one of the founding officers of a start-up banking subsidiary of John Hancock Financial Services, now a subsidiary of the Canadian insurance company Manulife Financial.

First Signature Bank & Trust (FSB&T) began as a small enterprise, and only 4 years after its inception, became the 12th largest VISA gold card issuer in the United States. How was a fledgling organization with limited resources able to compete with some of the largest and longest-standing U.S. financial institutions? Much of First Signature's success could be attributed to its innovative culture. For example, when the Bank was in its infancy, its CEO, Jim McLaughlin, exemplified a "learning leader" by actively seeking out senior leaders at successful companies to replicate their best practices. He also enabled FSB&T to play a pioneering role in the use of technologies and processes that transcended traditional brick-and-mortar business models.

Team-Based Leadership

Additionally, McLaughlin brought out the best in people by insisting on very high-quality standards while also displaying an infectious sense of humor that stimulated creativity and alleviated the stress of a start-up operation. He also valued diversity and demonstrated that by selecting senior leaders who had experience outside of the financial services industry. What's more, McLaughlin continually encouraged these leaders to replicate successful practices and processes from their previous organizations while ensuring that their work was supported by strong infrastructures.

Jim McLaughlin also had an innovation mindset that enabled him to foster "learn-as-you-go" processes that supported the disciplined experimentation that's so critical to start-ups and mature organizations alike. He also galvanized a senior leadership team that rarely succumbed to politics and turf issues—in part because he leveraged each leader's strengths and complemented weaknesses with strong teamwork.

When senior executives at the parent company decided to focus on their core businesses and sell their banking subsidiary, they shared in FSB&T's success by providing generous severance packages and career transition programs to those who had built the enterprise from scratch. This enabled several of us to replicate the Bank's successful strategies at other organizations. With that, I also want to recognize two other leaders of innovation: Dave Bjornson, retired CEO of the Southwest Washington Service Area of Providence Health and Services and Keith Flagler, former General Manager at the Philips Silicon Valley Center.

Dave Bjornson was a master at creating a culture of innovation and Keith Flagler skillfully oversaw a shared services function at a high-tech incubator of Royal Philips, a company over 120 years old, ranked by FastCompany in 2014 as one of the 50 most innovative companies in the world. The experience that I gained at a globally recognized innovator—and the ways in which I was inspired by these three leaders—are what drove me to produce the basic outline for this book.

Concluding Thoughts

For many people, unleashing another's potential fulfills a higher purpose. Some might even view it as a way to achieve immortality. One of my hopes is that, veteran or novice, you'll be among the many possibility thinkers who value innovation and nurture it in others. I also hope that this book will help you realize your greatest innovation potential.

If you're the kind of person who wants to make a difference, you might have already identified some challenges in need of innovative solutions. If that's the case, I encourage you to apply what you've learned by teaming up with like-minded people, sharing your passions, and championing other innovators. For now, my thanks go to the leaders, practitioners, authors, and educators who generously shared winning strategies and best practices so that we might all succeed in our respective innovation journeys.

■ ■ ■

Marilyn Blocker
Managing Principal
Innovation Outcomes
www.innovationoutcomes.com
info@innovationoutcomes.com
www.linkedin.com/in/marilynjblocker

Chapter 24

A Business Case for Strategic Partnerships and Alliances

An interview with Cheryl Perkins, CEO and President of Innovationedge and former Senior Vice President and Chief Innovation Officer at Kimberly-Clark

■ ■ ■

"The corporation as we know it is unlikely to survive the next 25 years. Legally and financially, yes. But not structurally and economically."

— *Peter Drucker*

Nowhere is an effective partnership more evident than in the interactions of members of jazz ensembles, where players listen carefully, take turns with solo performances, and provide support by building on each other's ideas. However, times have changed. Co-creation is also evident in today's symphony orchestras, wherein some orchestra leaders collaborate with musicians on the type of music to be played and even how it's to be played. Also evident is how some orchestra leaders today are surviving difficult economic times by forging strong partnerships—not only with musicians, but also recording artists, audiences, and entire communities, both local and virtual.

For most conductors in times past, the concert hall was home, and few strayed from it except to perform as guest conductors. Successful conductors back then functioned as soloists; whereas today, they function as ambassadors and partners. The concept of partnerships—with audiences, other orchestras, and musicians—would likely have been inconceivable to the highly acclaimed greats such as Sir Thomas Beecham, Toscanini, and Von Karajan.

Today, leaders in all sectors strive to make their organizations leaner. With this, it can be challenging to allocate the time, talent, and resources needed for continual and rapid innovation. External partnerships and alliances can often provide opportunities to drive innovation and growth while simultaneously reducing risk and costs through resource combinations and economies of scale. Developments in the areas of information and communication technologies also create options for increasing capability and capacity—and often without adding fixed costs. Consequently, many leaders today are exploring technology combinations through strategic partnerships and alliances. Additionally, leaders have formed partnerships for the purpose of outsourcing. This is only one model, however, and not necessarily the most effective choice.

Partnerships and alliances can also enable extended value chains, entrance into new markets, and expansion of existing distribution channels. However, in the same way that partnerships and alliances can bring advantages, there can also be disadvantages. To explore the pros and cons of partnerships and alliances, we interviewed Cheryl Perkins, whose three decades of expertise and new-to-the-world innovations have been recognized by *Consumer Goods Technology* (as a "Top Executive Driving Vision" in the consumer goods industry). She was also recognized by *The Asia Pacific Congress* (through its "Excellence in Innovation Award") and by the Dow Jones Sustainability Indexes, which recognized Cheryl for her exceptional sustainability strategies. In 2006, *BusinessWeek* named her one of the Top 25 Champions of Innovation in the World.

As a global innovation thought leader and holder of ten U.S. Patents, Cheryl is a sought after keynote speaker worldwide. She is also a co-author of the book *Innovation Fatigue: Overcoming the Barriers to Personal and Corporate Success*. As the founder and president of Innovationedge, Cheryl works closely with C-level executives and leaders across many industries to help build sustainable innovation capabilities and define growth opportunities through brand-building initiatives, game-changing business plans and strategies, and strategic alliances and partnerships. She also helps inventors and entrepreneurs commercialize their inventions and "create an edge" through winning business plans and alignment with strategic corporate partners. Please join us as Cheryl describes the strategies and due diligence processes that can enable successful partnerships as well as inhibitors that can prevent or derail them.

QUESTIONS AND ANSWERS

First, would you define "strategic partnerships" and "alliances" and how they can enable innovation?

Leaders can facilitate differentiated and meaningful innovation by forming strategic partnerships and alliances with inventors and other entrepreneurs, suppliers, vendors, academic institutions, and other organizations—including competitors. Although it isn't always easy to find and successfully engage the right partners, they can help organizations create more innovative cultures from the "outside in."

Would you elaborate with some specific examples of how partnerships can create more innovative cultures?

Time and time again we see the benefits of encouraging and soliciting ideas from outside organizations and of those people who reach out to create collaborative relationships. Benefits can be in the form of reduced costs, lower risk levels, and the freeing up of internal resources for conducting strategic experiments for other potential innovations. While simultaneously reducing risk, companies can extend capabilities into new-to-the-company or new-to-the-world areas by defining marketplace gaps or opportunities in unserved—or underserved—segments and by expanding geographies, markets, channels, and categories with new technologies, products, and services. Experience has shown when leaders successfully collaborate with complementary and compatible partners, they can also improve business processes and increase speed to market.

In what ways might leaders effectively vet potential partners?

A good first step is to assess the internal competencies required to deliver on current or anticipated future objectives and goals. By defining their current tangible and intangible transactions, leaders can determine what their companies can—and cannot—do internally. And by examining the current ecosystem and defining current and future needs, they can create competency grids that identify gaps and help determine how potential partners might close those gaps.

How can leaders ensure that potential partners have the required competencies?

Leaders can construct competency grids in ways that their criteria spans a wide range of behavioral and leadership competencies to specific technical competencies, often within a variety of disciplines. Comprehensive grids allow senior leaders to evaluate individual and organizational performance from multiple perspectives, including performance related to specific programs, projects, or products. Once leaders have created competency grids for their own organizations, they should provide the same template to potential partners, asking them to construct competency grids, as well. Then each should review, discuss, and share examples and references that can validate the specific competencies identified.

As a final way of ensuring that potential partners have the required competencies, leaders must then do effective due diligence, to determine whether potential partners are a good fit. If partnerships demand cultural compatibility, leaders should determine the degree and nature of the differences and decide whether culture change needs to be driven in one or both organizations. On a final note, leaders can prevent or mitigate problems with "partners of partners" if they perform the same due diligence on partners' networks that they've done for the partners themselves—including competency grids and validation from specific examples and references.

What are some key challenges or pitfalls in forming partnerships?

One major challenge can arise when leaders select initiatives without having clearly defined business needs or business propositions. Another can occur when leaders view potential partnerships from a pure technology perspective. Although many partnerships are based on technology that can be leveraged, it's important to look at the opportunity from a much broader business perspective.

Another obvious challenge or pitfall can be encountered when leaders rely on unproven partners, or if they focus only on high-risk ventures. Pitfalls can also occur when leaders in one or both companies err on delivering in accordance with mutually agreed-upon objectives or when they fail to structure partnership models or arrangements in ways that match the risk tolerance of both parties. And finally, problems can also occur if either party isn't able to manage required culture change or lacks the ability to manage relationships.

How can organizations work with a high degree of transparency and still protect intellectual property?

Sometimes organizations attempt to protect their intellectual property by keeping partners at arm's length. This lack of engagement usually stalls relationships from developing and ultimately produces trust issues. Even in a best-case scenario, these behaviors can prevent deliverables from being realized or realized within desired timelines. The best ways to protect IP are when both parties define what they need to own prior to engaging in the relationship. Leaders shouldn't have the expectation that any one partner will meet all needs; often market access is enough to ensure commercial success. During initial collaborations, however, it's important that both parties define what IP is currently owned, what needs to be owned by each, and what will be jointly owned in the future.

What organizational changes might be needed to successfully partner with others?

Specific types of partnerships and desired outcomes determine changes that might be needed in organizational structures, processes, and practices. Often leaders choose to hire Alliance Managers with excellent decision-making abilities to manage complex relationships and to drive organizational change. These individuals have a critical role of ensuring that results are delivered within agreed-upon timelines and budgets, and that the relationship and desired behaviors remain intact over time.

How might Alliance Managers help to effectively drive change?

They can often raise awareness about events, systems, and attitudes that can shut down innovation. Skepticism, distrust, and a lack of sharing are silent killers of innovation. Silent, because in these situations, people often go through the motions—appearing to be onboard and driving innovation—when, in fact, they have, not bought in and might be undetectably disinterested or intimidated. In some cases, people might hold back or save their best ideas for other "safer" opportunities or for those aligned with political agendas. While innovation might remain the mantra in these circumstances, people might only welcome familiar kinds of innovation from insiders or trusted allies. The "not-invented-here" (NIH) syndrome is one of the most common barriers facing innovators, and it can occur at many levels.

Although NIH often manifests as an organizational or process issue—or as poor corporate strategies—it's actually more often a matter of politics or unhealthy human pride. However, NIH syndrome doesn't have to be a terminal condition. Effective Alliance Managers—and skilled leaders—can overcome or offset it by demonstrating the ability of partnerships to ease workloads or enrich organizations by providing diverse ideas and perspectives. Additionally, when leaders recognize and reward individuals and teams for soliciting and adopting external perspectives, fear and resistance are often mitigated.

What must leaders do, to nurture and sustain mutually beneficial partnerships?

Assuming they've done their due diligence by identifying competencies and structuring partnership or co-development arrangements to match their own particular risk tolerance, leaders need to manage portfolios appropriately with balanced risks. When culture change is required, it's critically important to deploy effective change management strategies that secure buy-in and sponsorship. However, the most important factors in sustaining mutually beneficial partnerships are communicating extensively and transparently—and ensuring that each partner can rely on others to consistently deliver quality results on time and within budget.

TAKEAWAYS

- Leaders can deliver differentiated and meaningful innovation through strategic partnerships and alliances that can leverage unique capabilities and competencies.
- Partnering can extend reach and capability by enabling businesses to experiment with lower risk and fewer internal resources. By sharing risk, leaders can often redeploy current resources for other possible innovations.

- Leaders must invest time up front to select partners that meet defined criteria for certain expertise, risk tolerance, presence in certain markets, etc.
- Due diligence is critical, and when culture compatibility is important, leaders need to drive culture change.
- Alliance Managers can be used to manage complex relationships and to drive organizational change.

TAKING STOCK

- Does my company have the required competencies to deliver on current and future goals?
- Do we have the capability to effectively manage partnerships and alliances?
- How might we find complementary partners, in terms of competencies, risk tolerance, and culture compatibility?

■ ■ ■

To learn more about the work done by Innovationedge, see www.innovationedge.com. If you found this chapter helpful, be sure to also see our chapters entitled *A Culture of Innovation, Business Model Innovation, Open Innovation,* and *Shared Visions and Values.*

Chapter 25

A Path to Innovation Excellence

An interview with Rowan Gibson, Internationally Best-Selling Author, Top Keynote Speaker, and Advisor to the *Fortune 500* on Strategic Innovation

■ ■ ■

"It is best to do things systematically."

— *Hesiod*

Successful leaders, like experienced jazz musicians, continually introduce new ways of thinking and new approaches. In the same way that leaders in private, public, and not-for-profit sectors must innovate through new products and services, so must leaders of symphony orchestras—or they run the risk of obsolescence. The challenge for many orchestra leaders, however, is that they must remain state-of-the-art in terms of artistic ability while also running the equivalent of a small business. This means securing funding and earning income from concerts, community events, and recordings. It also means forging strong relationships with patrons, donors, and key stakeholders in their communities.

Given that innovation is critical to organizations entering new markets as well as those capturing new growth opportunities and transforming their industries, why do so many people struggle to make innovation work? Although some organizations seem capable of successful innovation in the short term, few have the systems and processes required to support innovation in ways that are sustainable in the long term. For example, how many leaders have actually built a highly distributed, "all-the-time-and-everywhere" capability for innovation that is systemic and deeply embedded in their organizational DNA? How many senior leadership teams have committed to the comprehensive and ongoing journey of reinvention and transformation? And how many have set out and made progress on the all-important path to innovation excellence?

Rowan Gibson is the internationally best-selling author of *Rethinking the Future* (Nicholas Brealey Publishing), *Innovation to the Core* (Harvard Business Press), and *The 4 Lenses of Innovation* (Wiley). In addition to his books, which are published in a total of 25 languages, he has also authored numerous business articles, blog posts, and columns about innovation. Frequently interviewed on television, radio, online, and in business documentaries, Rowan's media appearances include Forbes, CNN, BusinessWeek, Harvard Business Review, and BBC World Service. As one of the most in-demand public speakers and experts on innovation, he has shared the stage with notable figures such as Bill Clinton, John Naisbitt, and Jim Collins.

Rowan manages a global innovation management consulting firm and functions as a strategic advisor, management educator, and innovation consultant, working with clients in 61 countries, including Accenture, Bayer, British Telecom, Coca-Cola, Dow Chemicals, Haier, Heinz, IBM, Mars, Microsoft, Philips, P & G, Roche, Siemens, and Steelcase. He is also a co-founder of innovationexcellence.com, the world's most popular innovation website, boasting tens of thousands of community members from over 170 countries. Please join us as Rowan describes how companies can achieve growth and continuous reinvention through a systemic and sustainable capability for innovation.

QUESTIONS AND ANSWERS

Why is it so important to develop an organization-wide capability for continuous innovation?

First, because innovation drives growth. After Apple re-focused its efforts on disruptive innovation back in the late 1990s, it was able to introduce a series of breakthroughs that took the company from a footnote in the history books to the global powerhouse it is today. Second, innovation drives renewal. In a world of hyper-accelerating change, hyper-competition, rapid commoditization, and unprecedented customer primacy, success can only be sustained through continuous innovation at the level of the core business model. Successful leaders know that innovation is too important to leave to chance so they aggressively create, nurture, and maintain their organization's innovation capability.

What makes it so difficult for organizations to move from innovation "rhetoric" to "reality"?

Most organizations have not yet developed a clear model of innovation as a highly distributed, "all-the-time-everywhere" capability. Their leaders still tend to think of this capability as a department or a specialized function, such as R &D, that involves a few experts—as opposed to something that engages everyone in their organization, as well as constituencies beyond their organization. The quality movement some 30 or 40 years ago went through a similar evolution. It was only when responsibility for quality was spread beyond quality departments that it became a part of everyone's job.

How can organizational leaders create the preconditions for innovation?

One thing's for sure—it doesn't happen by chance. It requires intervention and commitment from executives, who need to drive and support innovation in the same way that they support other critical enterprise capabilities. For a start, they can begin to create the preconditions for innovation by giving their people time and space for discovery, ideation, and experimentation; by maximizing the diversity of thinking in their innovation teams; and by fostering the kind of internal and external connection and conversation that can serve as a breeding ground for breakthrough ideas.

Is there a way for companies to approach ideation more systematically and more strategically?

Essentially, innovators look at the world from certain perspectives, or view it through different "lenses," to discover opportunities that others can't see. In fact, four particular perspectives, or "lenses," seem to be the source of most successful innovations. The first enables innovators to challenge orthodoxies and question deeply held dogmas about what drives success. The second lens is about spotting and harnessing trends that have the power to revolutionize an industry. The third enables innovators to view their organization as a collection of core competencies and strategic assets that can be leveraged or recombined to create new value. And the fourth allows employees in their organizations to see things through customers' eyes, understanding their unarticulated needs, and addressing them in innovative ways. By using these four lenses, organizations can empower people with the thinking tools of radical innovators.

How should companies actually define what innovation means to them?

Most companies' leaders define innovation too narrowly, limiting their innovation efforts to the search for new product ideas or disruptive new technologies. To overcome this "innovation myopia," it's important to look for opportunities across the entire business spectrum—to widen the front end of the innovation pipeline by innovating in services, processes, cost structures, marketing strategies, management systems, organizational functions, and across every component of a business model.

How exactly does business model innovation work, and why is it so important?

It's important because products and services can be quickly replicated and commoditized, but disruptive business models are much more difficult to replicate. Innovators can create impact across an entire business model by asking: "Who do we serve?" "What do we provide?" "How do we provide it?" "How do we make money?" and, "How do we differentiate and sustain an advantage?" Then, by viewing each component through the "four lenses" previously mentioned, they can ask: "What are the orthodoxies that need to be challenged?" "What can we learn and apply from new trends and discontinuities?" "Which core competencies and strategic assets could be recombined to create new value?" and "How might we recalibrate each component of the business model based on current or future customer needs?"

What questions should be asked to effectively evaluate ideas?

Business innovators need to look for ideas that can have the most potential "impact." Here are three helpful evaluation questions: "Could this idea dramatically reset customer expectations and behaviors?" "Does it have the potential to change the basis for competitive advantage?" And, "Could it change industry economics?" There are also other good questions that organizational leaders can ask: "If we succeeded at this idea, how many people would actually care?" "How might people's lives be changed or improved as a result?" "How much productive change could it bring to the industry as we know it today?" and, "How much would company and/or industry economics change as a result?"

How can innovators find ways of achieving focus in their innovation efforts?

By framing strategic themes such as corporate challenges, customer problems, or industry issues, organizations can focus on "aiming points," such as GE's focus on ecological energy, Apple's focus on personal media, and McDonald's focus on getting into coffee and localizing its menus around the world. What I do with organizations is help them create a strategic architecture with the three or four big strategic themes that will define and focus their innovation efforts.

In what ways can leaders create, multiply, and manage the resources needed for innovation?

They can use existing budgeting processes, budget set-asides, and central pools of money to fund internal or external ideas for game-changing innovation. Others look to skunkworks, incubators, grassroots funding models, or the ways that Silicon Valley companies obtain capital and talent. Equally important, leaders need to know that it's possible to "innovate on the cheap," by tapping into the latent brainpower of "ordinary" employees as an organization-wide source of extraordinary innovation.

What are the best ways to manage innovation investment risk—and even de-risk innovation?

First, leaders must define potential opportunities as "sprints" or "marathons" in terms of development time, investment pace and scale, and market penetration. In other words, should the opportunity be scaled up quickly, or does it require a more patient, long-term investment plan? It's also important to try to diminish risk by designing low-cost experiments to first validate the critical assumptions on which an idea is based, rather than rushing to develop and market an idea that might be an expensive disaster. My advice is to not bet everything on a single idea, but to hedge one's bets by constructing and managing a portfolio of strategic experiments or sharing the risk with partners.

How can organizations achieve a dynamic balance between the supply and demand aspects of innovation?

First, "innovation supply" refers to the volume of new ideas and opportunities coming from inside and outside an organization. "Innovation demand" refers to the ability of decision makers to respond to, nurture, and act upon potential game-changing opportunities by providing the necessary vision, support and resources. Critical supply-side enablers include an IT infrastructure for innovation, and open innovation infrastructures and processes for connecting with external constituencies, as well as broad-based training, coaching and mentoring, and rewards and recognition that foster employee engagement. Demand-side enablers include making leaders accountable for achieving bold stretch goals. When organizational leaders carefully orchestrate these enablers and drivers, and continually monitor and adjust them, they can ensure an effective balance of supply-and-demand.

What elements are critical in building a systemic innovation capability and institutionalizing it?

Four interdependent and mutually reinforcing components must come together to build and institutionalize innovation: leadership commitment and organization structure, systematic processes and enabling tools, the right people and the right skills, and a pro-innovation culture aligned around the appropriate values. By properly addressing and integrating these four mutually reinforcing components over time, organizations can achieve and sustain innovation excellence.

It's also important to identify impediments to innovation, such as competing values, skill deficits, restrictive organizational or political structures, or certain traditional management processes, such as strategic planning and compensation structures. Then, it's important to frequently audit innovation performance and manage the tensions that are inherent to innovation. It must be unbounded yet focused; radical yet prudent; committed, yet tentative; creative, yet systematic; impatient yet persistent. Leaders must constantly monitor these polarities to ensure balance. This isn't something that's learned by reading a book. It can only be learned by doing, gaining experience, and by continually fine-tuning. These are the hallmarks of organizations that are truly achieving and sustaining innovation excellence.

TAKEAWAYS

- Innovation excellence doesn't happen by chance. Leaders must continually nurture innovation capability and continually monitor to ensure that it's systemic and sustainable.
- Leaders must create time and space for ideation and experimentation, maximize diversity of thinking, and enable connection and conversation.
- Innovation should be approached systematically by challenging orthodoxies, harnessing trends, leveraging resources in new ways, and understanding unmet customer needs.
- Innovators need to look for ways to innovate in every part of their organizations' business models, while managing risk through disciplined experiments, learning, and pacing.

TAKING STOCK

- Is my organization building a systemic, systematic, and sustainable innovation capability?
- Does our innovation process produce radical ideas that could potentially disrupt our industry, or at least have a significant impact on it?
- Are we doing everything possible to achieve innovation excellence in our organization?

■ ■ ■

To learn more about Rowan's work, go to www.rowangibson.com. If you found this chapter useful, also see our chapters entitled *A Culture of Innovation, Benchmarking and Metrics, Business Model Innovation,* and *Risk/Portfolio Management.*

Chapter 26

Benchmarking and Metrics

An interview with Andria Long, Vice President of Innovation & Insights at Johnsonville Sausage; former Vice President of Innovation & Strategy at Sara Lee; author; and innovation speaker

■　■　■

"One accurate measurement is worth a thousand opinions."

— Admiral Grace Hopper

We might think that the success of most jazz ensembles and symphony orchestras is subjective, but it can also be measured with traditional metrics. Since as much as 60-70% of an orchestra's operating expenses are covered by donations, orchestras must have strong development initiatives for the long term. When there is a decline in attendance, ticket sales, or membership subscriptions, an orchestra's revenue is negatively impacted. It can also be adversely affected when orchestras don't make enough recordings or when the sale of recordings doesn't match what was projected. Ticket sales, level of debt, and income from products, programs, and performances are all factors in making basic comparisons such as forecasts versus actuals. Comparisons like these are important for orchestras and businesses alike, but can benchmarking and metrics have other uses?

Benchmarking and metrics can also help leaders align on organizational goals and ensure that actions are consistent with stated goals and strategies. In addition, they can enable more accurate methods of planning, forecasting and identifying opportunities. In time, they can also yield meaningful data for informed decision making, personal and organizational accountability, and performance management. Benchmarking and metrics can also provide early warning signals that enable course corrections or a complete change in direction. These signals are especially useful when innovation initiatives are ambiguous or in need of adjustments to respond to changing market conditions.

We interviewed Andria Long for this chapter because of her expertise in innovation and strategy and her particular focus on benchmarking and metrics. In her former vice president role at Sara Lee, Andria consistently facilitated transformational revenue growth. She also worked on some of the most recognized and valuable brands in the consumer products industry, which include Cheez-It, Huggies, St. Ives, Jimmy Dean, Hillshire Farm, Johnsonville, and Ball Park. Also drawing from her experience at other top-tier companies such as Kimberly Clark and Kellogg, Andria developed a unique insights-based approach that yielded dramatic new product successes. This approach was used in the launch of seven IRI (Information Resources Incorporated) Pacesetter awards and 15 products with more than 5 years' successful sales growth that generated over $500MM and pipeline revenue of $2.5B.

When speaking about innovation, Andria provides guidance on how to achieve innovation success based on firsthand experience with leading innovators. She is a requested guest lecturer and speaker at professional association conferences and for MBA students at the Kellogg School at Northwestern, Chicago Booth, Michigan State, and the University of Florida. Andria holds an MBA in Marketing and Finance and a Bachelor of Science in Marketing from the University of Florida. Please join us as she describes how benchmarking and metrics can identify opportunities for innovation.

QUESTIONS AND ANSWERS

Would you please define both "benchmarking" and "metrics"?

Benchmarking is a process that provides fact-based information for both internal and external comparisons. When done externally and based on critical success factors and key performance indicators, benchmarking can inform leaders about how their companies are doing in relation to peers, competitors, and best-practice organizations. Internally, it can be used to compare the performance of departments, divisions, or product lines, to determine why some might be performing better (or worse) than others. Most importantly, benchmarking and metrics can provide fact-based criteria as alternatives to emotional "gut-based" decisions or those made in conjunction with pet projects or political considerations. Metrics are the measurements used to enable benchmarking.

How might benchmarking facilitate innovation?

When used for external comparisons, benchmarking enables leaders to determine whether their organizations are holding even, lagging behind, or moving ahead. In this way, benchmarking can also produce information that facilitates innovation and keeps an organization relevant and focused on staying ahead of the competition. In the same way that benchmarking can be used for external comparisons, it can also be used internally to help leaders set goals, make decisions, and set realistic expectations for both individual and organizational performance. At the same time, benchmarking can enable businesses to identify potential opportunities to innovate. It can also determine the size and scale of innovations and help leaders anticipate potential innovation hurdles.

Why are metrics important for measuring organizational performance and for enabling innovation?

The former GE CEO Jack Welch was famous for his use of the expression "What gets measured gets done." Welch knew that benchmarking and metrics could provide an objective basis for specific accountabilities, performance management systems, and business scorecards. He also knew that metrics could be useful in aligning department or operating unit goals with broader organizational goals and for assigning rewards. Metrics can signal an organization's commitment to innovation and validate that it's critical for success. They can also help companies assess whether internal and external processes are supporting versus inhibiting innovation. Additionally, metrics can aid in constructing defined processes to objectively evaluate potential breakthrough innovations, line extensions, and new uses for products and services.

How are metrics also useful for other purposes?

When used as tools for risk management, metrics can provide a basis for a portfolio management approach to innovation. They can help decision makers assess the relative risk of breakthrough and incremental investments and define an appropriate mix of risk. Additionally, metrics can help companies determine the kind of product mix that's required by providing the basis for current and historical pipeline analysis and consumer performance, product performance, and advertising performance. And finally, metrics can be used for quality improvement purposes, helping leaders to determine which areas need improvement and how they might be improved. An example of this could be both the "hard" and "soft" metrics used to evaluate the processes and performance of key functional areas such as R&D and Operations as well as enabling functions such as Information Technology, Accounting and Finance, Human Resources, and Customer Service.

How can benchmarking and metrics support new product development and risk management?

Within marketing functions, internal metrics measure the success of products and services, which typically include portfolio management, pipeline performance, and pipeline valuation. Portfolio management metrics profile the product mix and determine the types of innovation and investment needed for each type of project or innovation. Metrics balance risk by ensuring that products earn anticipated revenue and profit and enable projects to be prioritized. This is accomplished by using specific metrics for each one—such as net dollar sales volume, profit, probability of success, capital investment, and consumer metrics. Pipeline performance is evaluated on current versus historical performance.

And pipeline valuation is based on the total value of products or services in the pipeline. Since a failure is more likely early in the new product development process, metrics reflect not only the total number of products in each stage, but also discounted product performance based on the percentage of failure projected for each product in each stage. Other critical metrics for products evaluate speed to market and total time from concept to launch, as well as how much time each product is spending in each stage.

What external and internal data should be measured to assess new product launches?

External data should measure actual market performance. These metrics usually include post launch analysis, which is critical for the cycle of learning needed for innovation. External metrics can also measure how quickly the product is distributed. Velocity is another critical metric, in that it measures how fast the product is selling. Spending metrics—usually in the form of consumer and customer support—show spending that was originally forecasted versus what is actually being spent. And finally, there are metrics that measure sales volume and profit by comparing actuals to what was forecasted.

What are typical problems with benchmarking and metrics?

Incorrect benchmarking or metrics can cause decision makers to overreact to perceived versus actual threats—and can also mislead by providing false assurances that show the company to be performing better than it is in reality. Problems with benchmarking and metrics generally fall into five categories: the type of data that's used, the source of the data, how data is gathered, its accuracy, and how it's used. Internal data—particularly historical data—might reside in several locations, with multiple owners, and within a number of different systems. Since data is often not maintained in standard or consistent formats, there's a potential risk in making "apples-to-oranges" comparisons. There can be problems with external data as well. It might not be shared publicly, and even when it is, accuracy can be problematic because most businesses want to position themselves favorably. Inaccuracies in either internal or external data can create the potential for leaders to take the wrong course or continue on their current course when they should be changing direction.

How might these problems negatively impact performance or inhibit innovation?

One of the most common problems is when leaders begin the benchmarking process with unreasonable goals. This can demotivate and potentially set people up for failure. Another way that benchmarking and metrics can be problematic is when they're used only for getting an initial snapshot of what competitors are doing. Benchmarking and metrics are of limited use if they aren't providing a constant check on programs, product or service launches—or for continuous improvements to internal and external processes. By contrast, when benchmarking is done on an ongoing basis, it can provide cycles of learning that are useful for improving performance and for identifying opportunities to innovate.

Can metrics be used to evaluate both soft (intangible) and hard (tangible) data?

There are many critical enablers of innovation, so when people in organizations benchmark their practices against those of leading innovators, soft data, which is anecdotal and usually gathered in informal communications, can be a good way to identify where change or culture transformation is needed. Although soft metrics are often a subjective call, they can help decision makers understand why their businesses might not be meeting goals. Soft data can provide information that hard data, such as statistical measures, can't. Benchmarking and metrics can help organizations measure both "the soft stuff" and "the hard stuff," since each is needed for successful innovation.

How can benchmarking and metrics set the right level and type of innovation for an organization?

Innovation is definitely not a one-size-fits-all proposition. By utilizing objective tools and processes—such as benchmarking and metrics, leaders can more accurately determine what their organizations need. Metrics vary by industry and are also different for companies in the public and private sectors. In the private sector, benchmarking and metrics can help leaders determine whether top-line and bottom-line growth can be achieved through various innovations—and even show which innovations hold the greatest promise. By using objective tools and processes, leaders can ensure that their companies stay relevant within their particular categories and with respect to their competitors. Additionally, when utilizing benchmarking and metrics, leaders can determine the right frequency (i.e., the number of initiatives) and the right amount of money invested in potential innovations. While many people associate innovation primarily with the front end of the process—where ideas are produced, discussed, screened or built upon—benchmarking and metrics are what help leaders determine whether innovation is being implemented and whether it's consistent with their organizations' goals and strategies.

TAKEAWAYS

- In addition to providing performance comparisons, benchmarking and metrics can provide useful information for goal setting, alignment, and accountability.
- Benchmarking and metrics can also guide risk management strategies by enabling leaders to assess innovation opportunities and define appropriate mixes of risk.
- Metrics can be used for evaluating both "soft" and "hard" data.

- When benchmarking and metrics are used incorrectly or used improperly, they can produce overreactions to perceived threats and also mislead with false assurances.
- When done early and on a continuing basis, they can establish meaningful baselines for measurement and allow leaders to maintain a pulse on both internal and external environments.

TAKING STOCK

- Does my organization typically benchmark early enough in our processes?
- Do we continually benchmark ourselves against our competition, course-correct, and change direction when needed?
- How might we apply metrics to the "people side" of our business so that we're inspiring and rewarding people for innovating?

■ ■ ■

To learn how benchmarking and metrics are related to other innovation enablers, see our chapters on *Business Model Innovation, Personal Accountability, Risk/Portfolio Management,* and *Scorecards and Performance Management.*

Chapter 27

Business Model Innovation

An interview with Lisa Love, Ph.D., Director, Guest Research & Insights, Alaska Airlines and former Vice President at GfK; Senior Manager at Amazon; and Global Business Manager at 3M

■ ■ ■

"A dearth of good ideas is rarely the core problem in a company that struggles to launch exciting new-growth businesses. The problem is in the shaping process."

— *Clayton Christensen and Michael Raynor*

Orchestra leaders must effectively run businesses in the same way that other leaders do. When existing models don't produce enough revenue, maestros and maestras must change their fundamental business models accordingly. This might include enhanced efforts to promote the orchestra—both nationally and internationally—as well as producing more recordings and creating programs that generate income from other sources. In other settings, business model innovation can help organizations achieve growth by entering emerging markets, introducing products into different tiers of the pyramid, deflecting lower-tier competitors, and incenting customers to participate in the market when previous offerings were complicated or expensive.

Business model innovation can also be an effective response to changes in market dynamics such as share loss, commoditization, or new products and services introduced by competitors. Under stable conditions, incremental adjustments can be successful, but when there is extensive change, organizations must often disrupt or be disrupted. Most organizational leaders know this intuitively, but risk is difficult for many of those who fear that there is a lot at stake. That said, it's helpful when leaders can distinguish between perceived risk and actual risk.

Additionally, to achieve a good balance between risk and growth, it's important that leaders be able to accept that growth, by definition, involves uncertainty and thus risk. Leaders also must understand that the time and other resources required to reduce risk to near zero significantly impacts the business opportunity and ability to achieve game-changing innovation. One way to achieve this is by gaining a thorough understanding of their industries and competitive environments before introducing new business models.

For this chapter, we interview Lisa Love, who has a strong track record throughout her career for setting strategic direction for emerging and transformational new businesses. Before joining Alaska Airlines and Gfk, Lisa led a team at Amazon of category buyers for small appliances, dinnerware, flatware, stemware, and event and party supplies in the Kitchen & Dining business. And before Amazon, she led several strategic growth initiatives at 3M, a company known for 100 years of innovation and for thousands of products in addition to its Post-It® notes and Scotch® tape. Working with various divisions and teams at 3M, she helped to transform growth trajectories that include initiatives for new growth ventures, value creation, and business model innovation.

Prior to her work at 3M, Lisa was a market research consultant to corporate and public sector clients, including McDonald's, Target, Frito-Lay, and the United States Postal Service. She has a Ph.D. in Communications Research from the University of Illinois at Urbana-Champaign and MS and BS degrees from Texas A&M University. Please join us as Lisa describes how business model innovation can be a key enabler and how the perceived and actual risks associated with it can be minimized through effective risk management processes.

QUESTIONS AND ANSWERS

Would you please define what "business model innovation" is and how it can enable growth through innovation?

Unlike new product development efforts, where companies typically launch a new product or service offering—or enhancements to existing products or services—business model innovation actually refers to the transformation of a business or the creation of an entirely new business within a company that has its own budget, profit formula, and processes. Successful business model innovation almost always involves diversification of revenue streams in ways that create sustainable, profitable growth. This is evident in the results of a study conducted over a 10-year period by Doblin, a consulting firm that's part of the global strategy firm Monitor. Doblin's findings revealed that less than two percent of innovations produced more than 90% of new value for organizations, driven largely by innovations in business models and networking.

This growth can be accomplished in a number of ways, including movement into near adjacencies through value chain expansion or partnering with other organizations. Other forms of business model innovation might involve enriching customer service, expanding channels of distribution, or even evolving products into components, semi-finished goods, or finished goods. Taken a step further, some new business models incorporate products into existing systems or comprehensive turnkey solutions.

Clearly new business models can enable innovation, but how might they also inhibit it?

Business model innovation is most successful when leaders make it such an integral part of strategy, that, after a few successes, they can't envision their businesses without it. However, in the same way that business model innovation requires investments, innovators also must protect and defend existing business through consistent funding. If they allow new efforts to divert resources from core activities, it can undermine the existing strengths that are necessary for funding future innovations.

What happens when executive leadership is risk averse about potential game-changing opportunities?

It's often difficult for leaders to initiate broad-based business model innovation because there can be much to lose. However, change is sometimes fueled by necessity, and this can happen when competitors—often smaller, more nimble companies—spot gaps in the market and successfully seize opportunities. What's certain is that the marketplace can move quickly, making even the strongest incumbent obsolete, so market leaders are often forced to play defense. But proactive business model innovation is usually a better option.

How can leaders achieve a delicate balance between risk and growth with new business models?

They can conduct value chain analysis to identify major players and their relative power (i.e., market size, share, and profitability) at each stage in the value chain. Another effective way of making the unknown explicit is described in two articles entitled "Discovery-Driven Planning," by McGrath and MacMillan, in a 1995 edition of *Harvard Business Review*, and in "Strategic Assumptions Prioritization," from the Corporate Strategy Board, 2003.

These articles describe how risk can be effectively managed by defining success and assumptions early and answering the biggest, most impactful questions first. Specific activities include creating a reverse P&L to define financial success three to five years out, identifying assumptions, and prioritizing assumptions that can most significantly impact the success of the project. However, another way of balancing risk and growth is to separate growth funds from operating budget. This ensures that new business models are designed to limit sunk costs and minimize fixed or recurring costs. This approach enables leaders to make the best data-driven business decisions without pressure to deliver more immediate return on investments. It also allows leaders to walk away when thresholds are exceeded, instead of trying to redeem opportunities by throwing good money after bad.

What can leaders do to maximize the success of business model innovation?

Leaders must keep in mind that new business models are most often successful when they're customer-driven or focused on clearly identified market spaces or adjacencies with strong strategic fit. Equally important—for breakthrough innovation—is that the idea be big enough, or that the new products and services are fundamentally different from those currently offered. A large, attractive or high-growth market opportunity can be a powerful motivator that mitigates fears about risk and helps growth teams and senior leaders persist when things don't go as planned. Another way to maximize success is to enlist the help of people who have experience with business model innovation and a proven track record for *creating* businesses—not simply *managing* them.

How can special project or innovation teams best manage risk and maximize success?

Helping teams re-frame failing as a means of innovation is one strategy that can improve the odds of success. Another option is to minimize the risk of ultimate failure by using rules of engagement to outline expectations in advance, to clarify questions about strategic direction, and to specify how decisions will be made and by whom. These rules can also link milestones and the resources associated with each assumption so that there are alignment checkpoints. Teams can then plan in advance for situations that might require additional resources, deeper cross-functional engagement, or accelerated timelines. Another way to improve the odds of success is to encourage teams to test multiple business models early in the process, rather than optimizing too soon.

Conducting post mortems on unsuccessful efforts can facilitate, and in some cases, accelerate learning. Then business models can be adapted in real time, and models can be hybridized based on actual data. Growth programs are also best managed with milestones and metrics that operationalize how assumptions will be tested and by aligning resources to test the highest risk assumptions. By testing assumptions and exploring unknowns early, resources can be invested at a pace that mitigates risk. War-gaming exercises can also be useful in simulating likely competitive responses to proposed new business models and then developing counterstrategies.

What are typical barriers that must be anticipated when launching new business models?

External barriers can occur if organizations misjudge the value proposition of an innovation, sell in inconvenient channels, or sell at the wrong price. More difficult to address are changes in customers' organizations or the market, preemptive moves by competitors, and underestimation of time and effort needed to work with external partners. However, more formidable than external barriers are internal barriers. These are often created by an absence of dedicated funding, executive commitment, or passionate project leadership that perseveres in the face of change resistance. If these elements are missing—if leaders and employees are risk averse or the organization's culture isn't receptive to change—ideas will likely go underground to survive. This risk adversity can delay badly-needed adaptation or result in employees clinging to outdated infrastructures to meet the needs of new business models.

How can leaders reduce internal barriers to business model innovation?

If resistance is due to previous change that had superficial support, or was undermined by little or no resourcing, then change will be an uphill battle. Yet even when change is perceived positively, it can be difficult to guide new business models through organizational and infrastructural barriers that were designed for existing businesses. To achieve early wins and ensure ultimate success of new business models, leaders need to communicate that growth is a priority and also that it's safe to fail. Additionally, because new business models frequently differ from existing models, it's important to create a common language, establish new success metrics, and encourage conversations around change and risk.

Leaders might also want to highlight best practices for growth programs that illustrate how innovation success is often the result of trial-and-error processes and new behaviors—and then articulate desired behaviors. To help people navigate the change process, it's also important for the finance organization, HR function, and strategic planning experts to provide real-time, hands-on support. It is critical that leaders maintain an unwavering financial commitment to business model innovation, continuing to sponsor it through difficult quarters or periods of financial constraint.

In closing, how can new business models be successfully defined and measured?

The most obvious success comes from business model disruptions that generate high returns and are difficult for competitors to copy. However, success typically goes beyond these obvious benefits when organization leaders gain a deeper understanding of industry needs and when they gain access to significant new opportunities. That might mean higher-value relationships with customers, but it can also mean sustainable advantages over the competition that not only produce gains in sales and profitability, but also provide funding for subsequent innovation. All this said, one of the most important outcomes of business model innovation is when leaders see that a growth mindset and receptivity to change is valuable—and that they can pay dividends in both the short and long term.

TAKEAWAYS

- New business models can help achieve growth or offset loss, commoditization, or unfavorable market conditions, enabling organizations to bring about game-changing innovation.
- Leaders and project teams can employ a variety of strategies to anticipate and manage the risk that's often associated with business model innovation.
- When introducing new business models, leaders must anticipate and deal with potential internal and external barriers.

TAKING STOCK

- Is my organization engaging in business model innovation, and if so, are we effectively anticipating and managing the risk associated with this change?
- Is my organization safeguarding itself against disruptive innovation by competitors?
- How can we change our organizational culture, to make it safer for people to take calculated risks?

■　■　■

If you found this chapter useful, also see our chapters entitled *A Culture of Innovation, Change Leadership, Risk and Portfolio Management,* and *Shared Vision and Values.*

Chapter 28

Consumer Insights

An interview with Regina Lewis, Ph.D., Associate Professor at the University of Alabama and former Vice President at InterContinental Hotels Group and Dunkin' Brands, Inc.

■ ■ ■

"Innovation vanguard companies set different priorities. Instead of focusing on their competition, they focus on their customers, their needs today and unarticulated needs, wants and desires they can satisfy tomorrow. Instead of focusing on shareholder value, they focus on creating exciting, unique customer value, believing that if customers are served, shareholders will be ultimately rewarded."

— Robert B. Tucker

The world has changed a great deal since Henry Ford told his customers that they could choose whatever color they wanted for their car as long as it was black. Customers today have greater access to information and are therefore savvier and more demanding. Another difference today is the way in which customers' needs and preferences can rapidly change. Still another difference is the speed at which new information about buying trends and changes in demographics becomes available. Jazz musicians and symphony orchestra leaders are well aware of how people's tastes in music can change over time. In the same way that audiences want to hear new music or new renditions of their favorite music from the past, customers want to see new or enhanced products and services.

Compounding this challenge for business leaders is that today's consumers have greater access to information and are therefore savvier and more demanding. Successful leaders are those who make it a priority to know how customers behave and what they want, as well as what they might want in the future. Data analytics enable greater insights than what were possible in the past. However, to fully succeed at driving innovation, leaders, insights professionals, and employees with direct exposure to customers need to also know what consumers are thinking and feeling. This means having the ability to interpret emotions and mood states through an understanding of physiology, psychology, and other disciplines.

We selected Regina Lewis to interview for this chapter because of her 20+ years of insights and strategy experience in leading retail, hospitality, packaged goods, and high-tech companies. Regina has a proven track record of building departments, motivating teams and students, and conducting insights work that utilizes myriad methodologies and drives business success. Currently an Associate Professor at The University of Alabama, Regina draws from corporate experience in customer and consumer insights as the former VP of Global Insights at Intercontinental Hotels Group and former VP, Consumer and Brand Insights at Dunkin' Brands Inc.

Prior to those roles, Regina was the Director of Research at women.com/Hearst, where she built a research revenue stream that approached $2 million by developing, pitching and implementing pioneering research programs for clients including P&G, Toyota, Union Bank, and Jenny Craig. She also served as the Director of Research for Miller/Huber Relationship Marketing, where she developed, managed, and presented customer-centric research learning and database analyses for Levi's, Oracle, Cisco, and Robert Mondavi. Regina holds an MBA from Columbia Business School and a Ph.D. in Communications Research from The University of North Carolina at Chapel Hill. Please join us as she describes the importance of insights work.

QUESTIONS AND ANSWERS

First, we'd like to know how you define "customer and consumer insights."

Customer insights and consumer insights are one and the same, but I prefer to use the term "consumer insights," as all customers are consumers. That said, I view a consumer insight as any meaningful piece of information about an audience that can be used to improve a business. Sometimes, it's new data or information that we might not have known or attached value to before, and other times it's a deeper truth or an "aha" about a consumer. One example of uncovering insights is how Dunkin' Donuts conducted extensive one-on-one interviews using a psychologist to understand patrons' responses when asked to compare us to our competitors. The "ahas" that emerged in this work about competitive brands and their consumers allowed us to build a phenomenal brand through positioning based on psychographic insights.

How do consumer insights enable companies to differentiate and innovate?

Customer insights shed light upon how consumers view specific products and services. It's important to distinguish insights from traditional market research, which focuses on conducting studies, facilitating focus groups, and analyzing the results. Insights work goes beyond that and is part of a bigger strategic picture. Firstly, insights work focuses on actual customer behavior as well as their likes and dislikes. Equally important, it helps marketing professionals identify unmet needs and make recommendations for how articulated and unarticulated consumer needs can best be met—in the present and in the future. This is how insights professionals and insights teams help organizations differentiate and gain or maintain competitive advantage.

If an organization isn't investing in efforts to address customers' unmet needs or anticipated future needs, then we have to ask, "For whom is the organization innovating?" A lot of effort goes into innovation, and doing that without consumer insights is like working in the dark. Without insights into the hearts and minds of consumers, organizations can't serve them well. That's because they are either innovating purely for the sake of innovation, or they are innovating for themselves—not their customers. A great example of this was when a decision was made at Dunkin' Donuts to launch a crème brulee holiday flavor. When the insights team took a step back and asked our consumer panel their thoughts about this, they didn't even know what the flavor was. Another great example at Dunkin' Donuts was when a group came to me and said, "We need you to figure out what our in-store merchandise should be, like t-shirts and mugs." A bigger question should have been, "Why are we offering in-store merchandise?" For example, "Is it to increase sales or to enhance the brand?" Another bigger question is, "Do consumers really want this merchandise?"

What factors do you consider when making decisions about the best ways to gather insights?

Some insight-seeking questions require exploratory insights work; others require quantitative work. For example, if a question can only be answered by a personal, emotional response on the part of the consumer, then a face-to-face, one-on-one interview will yield the greatest depth of learning. If a question requires that the answers obtained be generalizable across a large population—for example, if a company is seeking likelihood-to-purchase information for a product in final stages of development—then a large-scale survey will be in order.

How have you helped organizations predict demand for new or enhanced products and services?

I've used various methodologies over the years, from innovative qualitative work that asked consumers to "diary" their thoughts in new ways to leading-edge quantitative work that informed companies about the ROI of dozens of possible hotel design changes. I've overseen "shop-alongs," where an insights professional went through Dunkin' drive-throughs with moms to gauge their potential purchase of new products, and I've orchestrated global brand health and demand tracking that resulted in real-time actions. All of this work was important for innovation because it drove the right innovation, which is innovation based on insight. Without insights work, it's very difficult for companies to invest effectively in the newest concepts and the most profitable ideas.

How can new technologies improve data gathering or data utilization to meet customer needs?

Technologies are opening up additional avenues for better data collection, analysis, structure, storage, and lightning-quick corporate response to findings than could possibly be discussed here. There are numerous online qualitative and quantitative tools, and these tools are continuing to evolve. There are endless opportunities to collect data in real time via social media and web behavior. In the hotel business, instant feedback mechanisms allow issues that impact the customer experience to be immediately addressed rather than three months down the road. At InterContinental Hotels Group, for example, technology allowed us to examine the complete experience of travelling, and understand consumer mindsets throughout that whole experience. After learning that one of customers' greatest anxieties was whether they actually would be able to check into their rooms upon arrival, we began sending them texts assuring them that their rooms would be ready and waiting for them. This is only one example of how new technologies allow deep insights and turnkey innovation to meet important consumer needs.

Should consumer insights be a continual and ongoing process?

The gathering of consumer insights is a never-ending process for any brand. It exists long before any product or service is even a "twinkle in a company's eye" and continues into a product or service's "cash cow" days. Insights efforts should end only when a brand takes its last gasp—and not until that time. Why? Because the world is always changing. A good example is when McDonalds announced it was launching premium coffee, and Dunkin' Donuts had to intensify its consumer insights activity to maintain its competitive position. Another example of the ongoing need for good insights work goes back to the recession in 2007. When many consumers, almost overnight, started carpooling and using mass transit in response to high gasoline prices, roadside Dunkin' Donuts locations were quickly, and negatively, impacted. It became instantly important to understand how consumers' buying habits were changing, so we brought in consumers and spoke with them about whether they might get their coffee at different locations, buy it from competitors, or even start making it at home. In response to our learnings, we quickly installed flexible kiosks in strategic areas to serve our customers' changing needs and keep our business healthy.

What role do organizational leaders play in utilizing insights?

In my view, the very best way to ensure ongoing consumer insight work is to hire leaders who understand its critical value and who support creative ways of uncovering insights. A great example is when Dunkin' Donuts hired Jon Luther as CEO. Jon believed that intelligence in business should work the same way as in the military, in that there should be no barriers between the information gathered and the "generals." He created my VP of Insights position, which reported directly into the C-suite, to send the message that as the eyes and ears of the consumer, insights professionals needed to be included in strategic development at all levels in the company. Jon's actions showed beyond doubt that insights can only succeed to the extent that a leader understands his or her need to know.

Jon knew that insights specialists could help leaders like himself ask and respond to vital questions such as these: "What consumer desires are being met and not met?" "How well are we anticipating future needs of consumers?" "How are we perceived by consumers and non-consumers?" "Where can we grow or extend our brands?" "How are our competitors viewed by consumers?" "Which consumers are most likely to recommend our products and services to others?" "In which medium is our voice most powerful?" and "Are we limiting innovation to our current resources and capabilities, or are we allowing consumers to drive our efforts—and then building capabilities and allocating resources as consumer needs evolve and change?"

Do you have any final words about the value of insights?

In order to evaluate and improve upon any organization's capacity to meet current or anticipated consumer needs, insights work is mandatory. People's relationships with your offerings, your processes, your technologies and much more must be identified and understood through insights work. Additionally, there must be a focus on developing strategies related to customer service, pricing, product and service functionality, and new offerings or enhancements. In the absence of insights, there can be no such strategies. It's important that insights experts and teams have input at all levels of decision making, because consumer insights as a discipline plays a major role in brand stewardship. Finally, it is important to keep in mind that the primary role of insights professionals isn't simply to validate ideas that people have already come up with, but rather to lead organizations and assist them in constructing innovative strategies that address an ever-changing terrain.

TAKEAWAYS

- Insights drive the development of products and services that are relevant to the consumer.
- Organizational leaders must effectively communicate that consumers drive the business and that it's incumbent on all employees to continually identify and meet consumer needs.
- Insights teams must understand that every consumer's voice matters, be open to hearing many points of view, and creatively use new techniques and breakthrough technologies.
- Insights team members should have input and provide assistance in formulating all strategies and actions related to consumers.

TAKING STOCK

- Does my company have ways of gathering consumer insights and asking the right questions to effectively innovate by offering new or enhanced products and services?
- Do our insights-gathering methods provide the best information possible about the hearts and minds of our consumers?
- Are we utilizing our insights professionals at all levels of strategic development and decision making?

■　■　■

If you found this chapter useful, also see *A Design Mindset, A Path to Innovation Excellence, Business Model Innovation,* and *Peripheral Vision.*

Chapter 29

Execution

An interview with Chris Trimble, Researcher, Best-Selling Author, and Faculty at the Tuck School of Business at Dartmouth and The Dartmouth Center for Health Care Delivery Science

■ ■ ■

"The challenge for the leader is to run the operational world, designed to maintain business performance as it is today, and to allow people to move into the innovation world as well, so they can operate flexibly and step outside of today's rules and structures in order to develop new ways of thinking."

— Jonne Cesarani

To survive, symphony orchestras rely on donations, membership subscriptions, and income from concerts, special events, and recordings. In addition to paying the salaries of conductors, musicians, and staff, these income-generating activities enable orchestras to pay for marketing, concert halls that are rented or owned, and expenses that keep concert halls heated, cooled, and in good repair. Certainly all organizations need to generate sufficient income to cover basic operating expenses and to ensure strong overall performance, but times have changed dramatically regarding the ways that organizations do this.

Years ago, generating income was primarily a matter of maintaining market share and keeping operations stable and profitable by achieving efficiencies. Most organizations responded to business challenges by employing defensive strategies that enabled them to carve out and defend their strong market positions through entry barriers. In the book *The Other Side of Innovation*, Chris Trimble and his co-author, Vijay Govindarajan, show most companies' ongoing operations evolved into what they call "Performance Engines." Although these engines are still the backbones of most successful organizations, they're no longer a single determinant of success in today's competitive environments. In fact, Govindarajan and Trimble view performance engines as the "antithesis of innovation."

In this chapter, Chris Trimble draws upon more than a decade of research on how the best-managed organizations effectively execute innovation initiatives. One of Chris's latest books, co-authored with Vijay Govindarajan and titled *Reverse Innovation* helps companies achieve growth in emerging markets. Their first book, *Ten Rules for Strategic Innovators*, was published in 2005, and less than six months later, was listed on the Wall Street Journal's Top Ten Recommended Reading list and recognized by *Strategy & Business* magazine as the best strategy book in 2006. In 2013, Chris and Vijay also wrote a parable entitled *When Stella Saved the Farm: A Tale About Making Innovation Happen*.

Chris is a keynote speaker who, in addition to writing best-selling books, has published in Harvard Business Review, MIT Sloan Management Review, California Management Review, BusinessWeek, Forbes, Fast Company, and The Financial Times. His career combines rigorous academic research with practical experience gained as a submarine officer in the U.S. Navy. Chris holds an MBA degree with distinction from the Tuck School and a Bachelor of Science degree with highest distinction from the University of Virginia. Please join us as he describes how "the reflexes of efficiency can be augmented with the muscles of innovation."

QUESTIONS AND ANSWERS

How do you define "execution" as it applies to innovation?

It is what comes after the commitment to a good idea. It is the blocking and tackling of getting the innovation work done.

Why do so many organizations have difficulty in executing innovation initiatives?

Their focus is typically not on innovation—it's on day-to-day operations—on their Performance Engines, which are designed to be efficient, on time, and on spec. Well-managed Performance Engines are a good thing—and all great companies have them—however, they're most often incompatible with innovation because of their focus on repeatable and predictable processes. Innovation is, by nature, exactly the opposite: non-routine and uncertain. It goes hand-in-hand with uncertainty and risk. Yet, the Performance Engine is what 97% of companies focus on and the reason why CEOs can stand in front of Wall Street with forecasts that are realistic and reliable.

How can organizations best execute innovation initiatives?

Organizations execute in one of three different ways: Model 1, making innovation everyone's job every single day; Model 2, making innovation a process; and Model 3, creating special teams and special plans. The first model—making innovation everyone's job—is a powerful approach, but people are usually so busy that almost all their time is taken up by daily operations (by the Performance Engine). Any project that's bigger than what a handful of people can do with slack time poses a problem for Model 1. This model is more powerful in releasing creative energies, but has limitations with the execution side of innovation.

The second model—about making innovation a process—calls for mapping it out stepwise and having people specialize at their particular pieces of the puzzle. This most often means making innovation repeatable, yet when organizations try to make innovation repeatable, they typically succeed only at incremental innovation. Creating fundamental redesign or entrance into new markets usually happens best with Model 3.

The third model—which creates special teams and special plans—is the least familiar of the three models and also the most difficult. It's also the most robust. To effectively use it, organizations must attack the fundamental incompatibilities of repeatability and predictability of the Performance Engine by creating special teams and special plans.

So tell us what you mean by "special teams."

Special teams consist of two key elements: (a) dedicated teams and (b) shared staff. Dedicated teams work on specific innovation initiatives. Shared staff ensures the success of the Performance Engine while also supporting dedicated teams (hence the word "shared"). Dedicated teams utilize disciplined experiments, typically employing a scientific method of formulating hypotheses, verifying results, revising hypotheses, and updating special plans. Dedicated teams also assist organizations in decisions to: (a) fail fast (by terminating projects that are unable to demonstrate potential ROI in a certain period in time), or (b) to appropriate additional resources for potential breakthrough products and services. Most importantly, dedicated teams, in partnership with shared staff, ensure that good ideas get executed.

Would you further describe the differences between special teams, shared teams, and dedicated teams, and elaborate on their respective challenges?

A special team, as we define it, is not one group of people but a partnership between a dedicated team and shared staff. Shared teams execute and sustain excellence in ongoing operations, but since they support—and are a part of—the Performance Engine, they can typically only entertain small changes. Although people on shared teams tend to keep their same roles, structures, and responsibilities over time, once innovation becomes a focal area, they're typically challenged with more work. In the past, shared staff only needed to be concerned about ongoing operations but in most organizations today, they're required to take on new projects—and in some, also supporting dedicated teams.

Dedicated teams are typically assembled for disciplined experiments, and each team dedicates focus to only one innovation initiative at a time. Although shared staff is rarely challenged, in terms of assumptions about roles, titles, authority, power and responsibilities, dedicated teams need to be frequently assessed. Dedicated team initiatives—or projects—should be built as new organizations, establishing baselines at zero and building from the ground up. The most challenging aspect in creating the right dedicated team is ensuring that people will be able to work together effectively. If dedicated teams are formed with people who have worked together before, it's easier, but then team members tend to behave in the same ways they did when they were totally focused on the Performance Engine. To be truly innovative, dedicated teams usually require outsiders.

How do companies typically get dedicated teams and shared staff to work together effectively?

It's not easy to get these teams to partner because it's not a natural partnership. It's like asking Mars and Earth to play well together. Team leaders often need help from senior executives, and senior executives must sometimes go deep and dirty to adjudicate the difficulties with teams that have competing priorities. When senior leaders are not actively in the mix, ongoing operations usually win and innovation suffers.

You believe that organizations need to view every innovation initiative as an experiment and then learn from experimentation. Could you elaborate on that?

Organizations can't be flexible and adaptive if they're not learning, but the key objective is to test critical assumptions first and then learn fast. That means key outcomes need to have custom plans drawn from blank pages and experiments need to be formalized. That's difficult for most organizations, but for those who experiment in this way, the learning is invaluable. In fact, we believe that learning needs to become the number one priority and profit the number two priority. Know, however, that we're not talking about the amorphous "feel good" notion of learning. We're talking about a very specific form of learning that quickly and inexpensively converts assumptions into knowledge. It's learning that's based on accurate predictions, because accurate predictions lead to better decisions. This ultimately leads to better results.

What happens when businesses focus exclusively on profits and not on learning?

When the focus is too much on profits, innovation leaders are typically asked, "Did you meet the numbers in the plan?" Some companies are maniacal about this, with initiatives that can make or break careers. This is deadly for innovation initiatives because most of these types of plans are overly optimistic. As soon as innovation leaders experience failure, they can get defensive. Then learning stops, good conversations about assumptions stop, and promising initiatives may get dropped or stalled.

How can organizations help special teams succeed at execution—and innovation?

First, organizations need to be careful about ensuring that shared staff has the resources needed to do two jobs at once (i.e., to continually support the Performance Engine and also support dedicated teams). Second, when building dedicated teams, leaders should identify the required skills sets and ensure that teams are built with these skill sets in mind. Too often leaders choose people for their teams who they know, like, or with whom they feel comfortable. To be successful, organizations and leaders need to shift prevailing mindsets and ensure more objective selection processes.

How do leaders in successful organizations ensure accountability while encouraging learning?

Successful leaders realize that there is more than one form of accountability. There are actually three. The first one is accountability for results—delivering as expected. The second is accountability for actions—working hard and staying engaged. The third is accountability for learning—running disciplined experiments and learning from them. Readers will probably know that it's rare for companies to systematize this kind of evaluation, but as predictions become more accurate, they should be viewed as direct evidence of learning. For companies to fully leverage innovation for competitive advantage, learning and experimentation need to be added to traditional scorecards.

TAKEAWAYS

To create a special team:

- Leaders need to build teams as if they're building a new company "from scratch."
- Organizations must expect a certain degree of discomfort with this new model.
- Leaders need to anticipate conflict, act in advance, and get help from other senior executives.

To create a special plan:

- Organizations need to formalize experiments.
- Leaders need to break down hypotheses into cause and effect assumptions.
- Teams need to seek the truth by eliminating biases in interpretation of results.

TAKING STOCK

- Does my organization innovate as well as manage our Performance Engine?
- Would it be useful for us to create special teams for innovation initiatives?
- How can we best equip leaders to execute ideas?

▧ ▧ ▧

To learn more about the work of Chris Trimble, see www.chris-trimble.com. If you found this chapter helpful, be sure to also see chapters entitled *A Culture of Innovation, A Path to Innovation Excellence, Business Model Innovation, Employee Engagement,* and *High Performing Teams.*

Chapter 30

Product and Process
Lifecycle Management

An interview with Marianne Lambertson, Vice President, Corporate Communications at Verastem; former Vice President, Strategic Development at Pernix Therapeutic, Inc.; and former Vice President at Bayer Healthcare Pharmaceuticals

■　■　■

"Innovation has nothing to do with how many R&D dollars you have. When Apple came up with the Mac, IBM was spending at least 100 times more on R&D. It's not about money. It's about the people you have, how you're led, and how much you get it."

— Steve Jobs

Successful musicians and leaders operate with transparency and engage in ongoing communication and collaboration, but much more is needed to achieve excellence. To effectively "orchestrate" innovation, jazz ensembles, symphony orchestras, and organizations in all sectors must have the right individuals, systems, and processes in place. Only then can achieve greatness in a variety of venues and survive today's many economic challenges. A good example of this from the private sector was the way in which American Motors Corporation (AMC) became the industry's lowest-cost automobile manufacturer in the mid-1980s, prior to being acquired by the Chrysler Corporation.

How did AMC achieve that distinction? As is the case with many innovations, the organization's efforts began with a challenge. Aspiring to compete more effectively against larger competitors, AMC's leaders found a way to speed up the company's product development process. When the Chrysler Corporation purchased AMC, leaders took product lifecycle management (PLM) to the next level by expanding the company's existing product data management system throughout the entire enterprise. As an early adopter of PLM technology, AMC recorded development costs that were half the industry average. Subsequent to that time, product lifecycle management has moved from heavy automobile manufacturing to other industries, including consumer products, pharmaceutical, and biotech. So what exactly is PLM and how might organizations replicate the success that AMC and Chrysler's had with it?

For this chapter, we interviewed Marianne Lambertson, who defined PLM and showed how it can be used to powerfully support innovation. Bringing over 25 years of healthcare experience and 20 years of operational experience in the global bio-pharmaceutical industry, her expertise in both domestic and global commercial operations ranges from early-stage to end of lifecycle. Marianne's experience also includes strategic marketing and new product planning, in-line marketing, and tactical planning as well as lifecycle management, medical affairs, product valuations, and due diligence.

Marianne has led all communication efforts, both internal and external, as well as Public Policy, Medical affairs and Product Life-Cycle Management. She has also collaborated as an independent consultant with organizations in the pharmaceutical, biotech, and healthcare industries, helping them improve and extend their commercial capabilities. In Marianne's former Vice President role at Bayer Healthcare, she was responsible for the integration of a newly created business unit that became the highest revenue producing business unit at Bayer Healthcare Pharmaceuticals in the US. Prior to Bayer, she held numerous commercial roles escalating in responsibility with Altana Pharma, Elan Pharmaceuticals, Schering-Plough Corp. (now Merck & Co.), and Solvay. Marianne completed graduate studies at the City University of London, England and earned a Bachelor's degree from Auburn University. An avid life-long learner and guest lecturer, she has mentored students at universities across the United States. Please join us as Marianne describes how product and process lifecycle management drives innovation by integrating people, processes, and systems.

QUESTIONS AND ANSWERS

First, how is "product lifecycle management (PLM)" different from "product *and* process lifecycle management (PPLM)"?

PLM, in its initial form, used to mean simply getting the most from a product in the outer years. Used primarily as a conceptual roadmap of a product's costs and sales measures, its main focus was on sales milestones and events. In time, however, PLM evolved into a more robust approach, eventually enabling companies to manage the commercialization of their products' entire lifecycles, from inception to design, manufacture, service, and even disposal.

PPLM used to be an obscure specialty, practiced mainly in the engineering functions of manufacturing companies. Today it encompasses the development and manufacturing aspects of a product as well as its commercialization. PPLM is useful in helping leaders manage the descriptions and properties of a product throughout its development and useful life. The various aspects of PPLM include resource management, change control, holistic financial management, and risk management.

How, exactly, does PPLM add value by achieving process excellence?

Today, forward-thinking business leaders in many sectors and industries see PPLM as an essential discipline that powers growth and helps to manage costs, improve pricing, and drive innovation. How does PPLM do that? Because of its broad scope, PPLM deals with cross-functional business activities and is typically utilized to solve some of the negative effects that can occur within traditional functionally oriented organizational structures.

In the past, both product and project-specific data were managed separately through different systems that were not interlinked. This used to inhibit informed decision making by preventing a free flow of information at the right time, in the right format, and to the right people. PPLM's benefits include its ability to provide leaders and decision makers with a "big picture" view of the total environment in which a product resides. Because PPLM involves a variety of different processes, it takes into account the company's organizational structures, its information technology systems, and the various people and partners who are involved in key processes. By integrating all functional areas, PPLM can bring focus to a product's holistic lifecycle.

With product and project lifecycle management now integrated within PPLM, various data elements can be converted into valuable information at critical decision points, and at any juncture along the continuum. When project data is combined with relevant product data, the calculated lifecycle cost can be more realistic, and PLM can enable critical stakeholders to make better decisions. This has the potential to improve profitability across even the broadest global product portfolios, while simultaneously accelerating innovation. In this way, PPLM can also help organizations cope with the increasing complexity and challenges of developing new products for global competitive markets.

How can PLM and PPLM also enable innovation?

Today, few companies rely on breakthrough innovations; instead they fill their innovation pipelines with potential product extensions or enhancements. They also expect lower margins for existing products, and so many organizations today are looking for ways to improve their development processes. In addition to soliciting consumer insights, company leaders are strongly focused on bringing products to market faster and on optimizing the value of those products from the day of launch to the very last day of market demand. Through efficient management of information and processes, PPLM can enable them to make better business decisions while aggressively protecting and leveraging their intellectual property.

Sometimes product lifecycles are difficult to control because of siloed information systems that provide little or no visibility into R&D work, safety and compliance risks, and labeling or packaging activities. PLM and PPLM can accelerate innovation of the "right" products without compromising quality or requiring additional resources because it compresses development time, and involves all stakeholders early on. When there's a "single version of the truth," key stakeholders can be appropriately informed in real time and processes can be streamlined accordingly. By providing information to all key stakeholders, PLM and PPLM can enable R&D, legal, marketing, and sales functions to spend less time on information transfer or "getting up to speed."

By bringing together folks in R&D and marketing as well as designers, PPLM enables them to simultaneously reduce costs, mitigate risk, accelerate time to market, and improve worker productivity—all the while boosting bottom-line contributions. Another good example of how PPLM can improve overall performance is through increased throughput from R&D functions that can, in turn, create more commercially-minded research and development teams. Product development and marketing functions are then able to join together in collaborative ventures. This, of course, represents a huge step forward—and away from the traditional butting of heads.

In what ways might PLM and PPLM inhibit as well as support innovation?

Surely any kind of process or formal structure has the potential to inhibit innovation. The only drawback that I can see with PPLM, however, is the tendency of marketers to focus on what's next instead of on what their companies can sell at present. While the next generation of new products is almost always most appealing to commercial teams, it is essential to make the most out of currently marketed products—and find innovative ways to do things outside of R&D labs. In my experience, involving many stakeholders and gaining input from a variety of functions in addition to R&D and Marketing are useful ways to create comprehensive marketing strategies. Ironically, what truly drives innovation is what's often regarded as "naïve" thinking on the part of non-marketing and non-R&D types. Can PPLM inhibit innovation? Yes, if its processes don't include people who are outside of the functional areas that are traditionally associated with a particular innovation. That said, leaders should involve all critical stakeholders in PPLM processes and encourage them to participate in marketing strategy formulation and implementation.

What key elements are needed to manage product and process lifecycles effectively?

In my opinion, three important elements must be in place. The first is a leadership mind-set of curiosity and transparency. This is manifested when it's normative in an organization to place a high value on the strategic hiring of people who can work efficiently on their own—essentially as entrepreneurs—while also working in matrix-like teams of other internal entrepreneurs.

The second element is the practice of hiring individuals who can see *both* the forest *and* the trees—and who can respond to change proactively as well as reactively. The third important element encompasses the systems, processes, and people that foster and enable collaboration, a vital ingredient for innovation. Although there are many examples of how innovation can thrust an organization to the next level, it's important to keep in mind that it rarely happens by accident. Most times innovation requires attention—and *intention*.

What obstacles are typically encountered when introducing new products?

A common obstacle is an unexpected post-launch crisis. I once launched a pharmaceutical product that had an incredible efficacy, safety, and tolerability profile. Yet only months after launch—and after nearly a decade of trials with thousands of patients across the globe—a rare but fatal side effect was discovered when this product was used in conjunction with another product. In clinical trials, one can't test for every possible combination, yet in most industries there are obstacles to commercialization that go beyond post-launch surprises. To prepare for, or mitigate implementation obstacles, most organizations incorporate commercial thinking into early-stage development planning. Today, when evaluating the commercial market potential of a new product, crucial business decisions need to be made regarding ultimate sales, profitability, and product outcomes, projecting years—and even decades—ahead.

What are the potential challenges for managing products and processes during their entire lifecycles?

Many companies that utilize the principles of PPLM still do not fully apply them as integrated and corporate standards. Another challenge is the differing regulatory hurdles that people encounter, when attempting to serve global markets. A significant obstacle is the growing use of software and systems throughout the lifecycle that are incompatible with each other or that are simply not shared by various functions. In addition to these challenges is the demand for sustainability. With today's fast pace, there seem to be two to three more products that offer even greater benefits than the last innovation. It's much tougher now, for senior executives to plan for growth through innovation. That's, in part, because it's become increasingly more difficult to hit narrower market windows and to launch products with the right balance of cost and quality that generates success in new markets.

What role does risk management play in managing a product or process's lifecycle?

Although many companies might have the information they need to predict and prevent risks, they typically capture information poorly. Even if they effectively predict and prevent risks, their information often resides in a number of different areas within an organization. This makes information difficult to locate when needed, and can also produce inconsistencies in format that can make it almost impossible to reuse. Lifecycle risk management is a key aspect of collaboration that enables decision makers to identify risks, and in some industries, take into account safety measures as well. Lifecycle risk management allows leaders to follow-up on known or unknown risks while developing pre- and post-marketing vigilance plans, and in some industries, safety measures as well. By incorporating risk management into an overall PPLM plan, organizational knowledge is improved. In addition, the right resources can get pulled in when most needed and lessons learned can be applied to both current and future products.

What advice would you give to leaders who want to perfect their PLM and PPLM processes?

I'm not sure that there is a "perfect" PLM or PPLM process. However, I can tell you that, in my experience, when leaders have the optimal mindset, create cultural norms of collaboration and transparency—and have in place the right individuals, systems, and processes—they're much more likely to make the most of their products and able to launch new products at greater speed and for less cost. Those factors, in themselves, are important drivers of both incremental and breakthrough innovation.

TAKEAWAYS

- Development of any product is a complex process that requires collaboration among multidisciplinary teams.
- The hallmarks of successful product development usually include careful coordination of processes, prudent allocation of resources, and effective utilization of appropriate methods and tools.
- The development and management of any product must take into consideration how three different domains—product, project and organization—can be best interlinked.
- PLM and PPLM can ensure superior product quality and increase speed to market.
- These approaches can also yield significant reductions in risk and in the total cost of products.

TAKING STOCK

- How might my organization better measure the profitability of a product in terms of R&D spending?
- Do we have the infrastructure to support our current global innovation goals and product development needs as well as anticipated future needs?
- Who currently owns PPLM in my company—and should another function own it instead?

■ ■ ■

If you found this chapter helpful, also see *A Culture of Innovation*, *A Path to Innovation Excellence*, and *Business Model Innovation*.

Chapter 31

Open Innovation

An interview with Victor Welch, Marketing and Innovation Strategy Manager at Huntsman Corporation, former Director, Marketing & Customer Insight at GE Global Research, and former Marketing and Business Development leader at 3M

■ ■ ■

"Because not all the smart people work for you."

— Bill Joy

When we think about jazz, we might associate it with an unspoken mandate to continually push beyond current boundaries to integrate new thinking and ideas. That is, after all, what the essence of jazz is all about. So how do leaders of orchestras and other organizations accomplish that? Music leaders today collaborate with creative directors, musicians, and sometimes even board members when deciding on programming and selecting scores. What is it called when people reach outside their organizations to collectively produce new ideas, new approaches, and new technologies? Some call it "open innovation." Can leaders in all settings benefit by sharing what's worked and what hasn't in the same way that they share new ideas and approaches? How can executives mitigate the risk that "not all the smart people in the world" work for them? The answer to these question is simple: Leaders can open their minds and doors to embrace smart people everywhere—through open innovation.

Looking back to the invention of the light bulb, it might seem impossible to envision that Edison would have ever sought help from someone outside of GE for a critical component—the filament. In his day, company executives diligently protected and maximized breakthrough ideas. Today, knowledge is distributed, competition is greater, and in many industries, entry barriers are lower. All this creates tremendous commercial pressure to find the next good idea or innovation. As people in organizations increase their efforts to partner with labs, academic institutions, suppliers, customers—and even competitors—they can increase their options exponentially. This enables ideas to be generated internally and externally, reinforcing the concept of open innovation—which is certainly preferable to relying exclusively on internal perspectives and large, internal research labs.

For this chapter, we interviewed Victor Welch because of his work with two leading innovators, GE and 3M—companies with rich histories and more than a century of success with innovation. Vic's experience with open innovation was gained primarily through his work at GE Global Research, an outgrowth of Thomas Edison's original central laboratory. While at GE, Vic analyzed the commercial and business impact of technology trends and programs to provide an analytical framework and data that helped GE leaders assess the potential impact of technology projects and suitable alternatives.

Vic's work at 3M was primarily focused on marketing and business development, where he functioned as a Marketing Manager in the U.S. and a Business Development Manager in the U.K. Vic earned a BSC with honors in Metallurgy and Microstructural Engineering from Sheffield Hallam University and a DBA in Business Administration from Cardiff University. Please join us as he describes various approaches to open innovation and illustrates how it can add value.

QUESTIONS AND ANSWERS

How is "open innovation" typically defined?

Those who are familiar with open innovation often think of the competitive challenges put forth by companies such as Innocentive or the educational non-profit organization, XPRIZE—which funds radical breakthrough innovations for humanity. However, I believe open innovation can simply be having an open mind and realizing that someone else might have a new and innovative solution to my problem. I also think of open innovation as covering a whole spectrum of approaches that include challenges, platform development, outbound innovation, technology scouting, and strategic partnerships and alliances, to name a few.

What are the implications of open innovation for large corporate R&D functions?

Some people in large R&D labs fear that open innovation will render their jobs unnecessary. They actively resist it, engage in denial, or hope that it's a fad that will eventually go away. To them I would say, "Open innovation is the new reality, and it's here to stay. It's far better to cover all the bases and look both inside and outside for good ideas." Intel CEO Andy Grove's book, *Only the Paranoid Survive*, gives us all food for thought. People in R&D have the potential to actually increase the value of their functions if they innovate externally as well as internally. I think that Hila Lifshitz-Assaf sums up the issue succinctly in the question put forth in a paper at Harvard Business School entitled, "The lab is my world or the world is my lab?"

How do you define open innovation challenges, and do they actually enable innovation?

Innovation challenges are often contests that incent people to compete by providing financial rewards or other forms of recognition. GE has run several open innovation challenges over the years, most notably the Ecomagination challenge, which represents the company's commitment to imagine and build innovative solutions to today's environmental challenges. Themes include low carbon, powering the grid, and powering the home. Now allow me to also define "grand challenges" with an example. The largest prize in history for an open innovation challenge was awarded by the XPRIZE Foundation for SpaceShipOne, the Ansari commercial flight into space. Grand challenges are often identified when participants spend far more in solving problems than the actual value of the prizes they receive. The purpose of these challenges is primarily to accelerate innovation for participants who see commercial opportunities beyond the challenge itself.

To answer whether these challenges actually enable innovation, I say, "While high profile innovation challenges are great publicity for a company, the question I continually ask is, 'Do they provide a good rate of return?'" In my opinion, the jury is still out on that one. In fact, I personally believe that the more day-to-day challenges, such as those addressed by P&G's Connect + Develop model, are more effective paths to open innovation. A good example of these are the challenges that NASA has issued, though its Innovation Pavilion—a web challenge platform that is used both internally and externally. Clearly NASA is a leading innovator with regard to these types of web challenge platforms, yet they're becoming increasingly more common in a variety of organizations and industries.

Please define platform development and show how it supports open innovation.

Much has been written about the value of a platform in dominating a market space. Think Microsoft Windows, Google Android or Apple's iTunes. Using a platform for open innovation is also a way of building in longevity, particularly in software. We see this in the way that the SAP users group (a volunteer organization) has built a community of developers—and in the way that Mozilla develops its Firefox browser. Both are reliant on open innovation, and interestingly, both are non-profit organizations. SAP founded its user group in 1990 and Wikipedia has been around since 2001, validating that this kind of open innovation and collaboration can be extremely sustainable.

We're also interested in what you can tell us about outbound innovation.

Amazing as it might seem, some organizations would rather let their ideas gather dust—and even maintain IP protection for them while they're gathering dust—as opposed to seeking better homes for them. However, this is rapidly changing through outbound innovation, when organizations recognize that opportunities exist. In this way, they look externally for solutions when they're unsure about how to capitalize on them internally. I can think of four scenarios for outbound innovation, and I'll describe the first one in this way: "We like the idea but it's just too risky for us at the moment, so let's find a partner to share the risk and if it works out, share the rewards too."

The second scenario is this: "We're interested in the technology but we can't get scale, so why not partner with an enterprise in a non-competing market segment, to get the scale for our operations?" A third is: "We're not sure we want the technology, but if we can grow it with a partner, we can agree to terms that allow us to bring it back into the enterprise sometime in the future." And the fourth scenario: "Although we have no interest in the intellectual property, we can sell or license the idea for a one off payment and/or royalties."

So moving on to some of the other approaches to innovation, what about technology scouting?

In their attempts to acquire or form alliances with others, people in some organizations utilize a network of "scouts" who have a feel for what's going on in a particular geography, market, or technology space. A great example of this was when a GE talent scout discovered Check-Cap, a start-up company that was making an ingestible disposable imaging capsule, designed to help detect colorectal cancer. We can think of these scouts as being the connectors between companies' R&D centers and the outside world because as they search out opportunities, they bridge the worlds of "open" and "closed" innovation.

So that leaves us with customer/supplier cooperation as the last of the five approaches you've cited. Could you tell us how organizations typically partner and form strategic alliances?

Working with key suppliers and customers as partners can be a valuable way to gather new ideas and hear about new problems from a variety of different perspectives. The first advantage is that it's generally a low cost method for open innovation. Second, it can strengthen the relationships between companies and suppliers, and also companies and customers. And third, it doesn't require an extensive vetting process, where each partner needs to invest time assessing each other's competencies and abilities to effectively partner. However, many companies also utilize universities and government labs, web-based talent markets, and even competitors as sources for new ideas. Competing companies—in the same industry—can achieve economies of scale or leverage opportunities to share risk by negotiating agreements and abiding by the terms.

In addition, there is still another source of ideas in what Professor Eric von Hippel calls "lead users" in his book *Democratizing Innovation*. Lead users are the free spirits who solve problems, often without the knowledge of companies that had offered the original products or services. Even though the efforts of end users can enhance or create in ways that result in commercial value, the only reward that they typically seek is to know that they've solved a complex problem or made things better or easier for others. To summarize, almost all markets and technologies have lead users who apply their skill sets within a whole range of possibilities. If people in organizations seek them out and get inside their minds, they might just find that some current—and even future—problems have already been solved!

TAKEAWAYS

- Open innovation is here to stay. It is economical, broad-based, and virtually limitless.
- As with any tool, people can choose to employ it or not.
- Different approaches to open innovation include innovation challenges, platform development, outbound innovation, technology scouting, and strategic partnerships and alliances.
- Customers, suppliers, and even competitors can partner to enable and leverage open innovation, provided appropriate agreements with competitors are negotiated and honored.
- People should not ignore or discount the efforts of lead users—those who have little interest in financial gains and only want to solve complex problems or make a difference.

TAKING STOCK

- Is my organization innovating both internally and externally?
- Are we actively managing the fears of people who might be resisting open innovation because of concerns about job security?
- Could we be doing more to encourage open innovation by creating contests, partnering with others, or encouraging and conversing with lead users?

■ ■ ■

If you found this chapter useful, also see *A Business Case for Strategic Partnerships and Alliances, A Culture of Innovation, Business Model Innovation,* and *Idea Management and Virtual Collaboration.*

Chapter 32

Peripheral Vision

An interview with Paul J. H. Schoemaker, Ph.D., Founder and former Chair and CEO of Decision Strategies International; former Research Director of the Mack Institute for Innovation Management at the Wharton School; and Best-Selling Author

■　■　■

"When spring comes, snow melts first at the periphery because that is where it is most exposed."

— Andy Grove

In the same way that directors of symphony orchestras must be mindful of changing demographics and the current tastes of their audiences, business leaders need to constantly be aware of forces that could affect their organizations' success. Today—more than ever—success is determined by an ability to differentiate and deliver value. In the private sector, that typically means enhancing new products or services or introducing new offerings. In the public and not-for-profit sectors, it means offering new or improved services to advance the mission and secure or increase funding. However, there is a common denominator for success—even survival—among most organizations, and it's called "vigilance."

For some organizations, the need for vigilance might be more evident than others. For example, the U.S. Federal Bureau of Investigation (FBI) has perfected scanning through a method described in this chapter called "spatter vision," which is commonly used for identifying would-be assassins. However, from prehistoric times to the present, there has been a need for all living things to scan for the weak signals that can help to anticipate, avoid, or mitigate the consequences of being blindsided. Although each organization's challenges are unique, all must employ both "focal" and "peripheral" vision to detect, interpret, and act upon changes in political landscapes, markets, and in the unarticulated needs of customers, clients, or end users.

In this chapter, we interview Paul Schoemaker, a leading scholar, author, and entrepreneur in business and philanthropy. Paul has advised leaders at the largest corporations worldwide and at many Fortune 100 companies. Some of his notable efforts include his helping newspaper leaders understand how the internet would impact their industry and his advice to the Chief of the Cherokee Nation about approaches for retaining traditions and cultural identity. Paul has shared stage billings with Bill Clinton, Warren Buffet, Rudolph Giuliani, and Jack Welch and has published many books and articles that have appeared in *Harvard Business Review*, the *Journal of Mathematical Psychology*, *Management Science*, *Brain and Behavioral Sciences*, and *The Journal of Economic Literature*.

Ranked by the Institute for Scientific Information (i.e., the ISI index) as one of the top one percent of scholars worldwide in business and economics, his deep insights and experience are evident in his most recent book, *Winning the Long Game: How Strategic Leaders Shape the Future*, written with Steve Krupp; in *Brilliant Mistakes: Finding Opportunity in Failure*; and in his book co-authored with George S. Day entitled *Peripheral Vision*, upon which this chapter is based. Paul holds a Ph.D. in Decision Sciences from the Wharton School, University of Pennsylvania and BS in physics. Please join us as he shares how organizations can improve their peripheral vision.

QUESTIONS AND ANSWERS

First, how do you define "peripheral vision"?

We can think of peripheral vision as being the opposite of central or "focal" vision, which is named after the part of our eyes called the fovea. Focal vision offers the highest resolution and therefore the sharpest sight, but it is also the narrowest view of the world. By contrast, peripheral vision—with its lower resolution and fuzzy vision—provides the widest view of the world. In prehistoric times, peripheral vision is what allowed humans to detect potential threats (such as the mountain lion about to spring) as well as potential opportunities (such as the deer in the woods that might provide dinner).

How do you think peripheral vision might lay the foundation for growth and innovation?

Peripheral vision plays the same role today that it did in prehistoric times. In organizations, it helps us know where to pick up signals, how to look for them, and what the signals mean. The data that's continuously examined by decision makers (and what gets reported to investors) is usually secured through focal vision and is easy to gather. By contrast are the weak signals that appear on the edge of vision. Peripheral signals are sometimes difficult to detect because they're almost always weak and ambiguous. Nonetheless, when leveraged, they can be the basis for organizational growth and innovation. If ignored, they can be problematic. Through periodic "eye exams," organizations can diagnose and treat poor peripheral vision, because when "treated," images on the periphery can allow organizations to quickly seize opportunities or deal with threats that can inhibit growth, innovation, or survival.

In what ways do organizations pay a price for poor peripheral vision?

Organizations that don't have good peripheral vision don't have early warning systems. Consequently, they're unable to prevent surprises that can emerge as undetected threats or missed opportunities. In either of these scenarios, organizations without good peripheral vision are unable to respond to changing situations or trends. For organizations in the public and not-for-profit sectors, it can result in a lack of funding. For those in the private sector, it can mean an inability to effectively compete.

Of course, in the same way that organizations are vulnerable, when their peripheral vision is impaired or ignored, CEOs are also vulnerable, if they miss opportunities or threats. In a study conducted by a training company called Leadership IQ, directors who had fired CEOs were asked about the circumstances that had led to the terminations. Fully 31 percent said the CEOs had mismanaged change; 28 percent said they had ignored customers; 27 percent said they had tolerated low performers; and 23 percent said they were terminated for "denying reality." Clearly, problems with peripheral vision can manifest in many different ways—with all having negative ramifications for innovation and growth.

Can organizations "treat" poor peripheral vision, and if so, how is that done?

Like athletes, organizations have certain inherent strengths and weaknesses that can be overcome or mitigated, depending upon their history and constitution. However, organizations can train and enhance peripheral vision more easily than athletes can, because they're more malleable than human bodies. In my book *Peripheral Vision: Detecting the Weak Signals That Will Make or Break Your Company*, George Day and I devote a chapter to each of the seven stages for improving vision on the periphery. The first stage is scoping—knowing where to look for weak signals. The second is scanning—knowing how to look for signals. The third is about interpreting signals. The fourth is about probing to more closely explore weak signals. The fifth stage involves acting upon weak signals. The sixth is about learning and adjusting in response to them. And the seventh is about leading and taking action accordingly.

What are some ways that organizational leaders can determine where to look for weak signals?

Organizational leaders can employ a combination of directed and undirected searches in the same way that the FBI does, when training agents to find would-be assassins in a crowd through "splatter vision." This approach involves purposely looking through the crowd without focus into the far distance (in undirected search mode). This lack of focus helps agents better detect changes that can quickly be brought into sharp focus through a direct search. Organizational leaders can replicate this approach by conducting undirected searches to determine where relevant threats and opportunities might lie. Also, they should ask questions such as, "What have been our blind spots in the past?" and "What might we want to replicate from other organizations or industries?"

Organizational leaders can also decide how wide their lenses (or their scope) need to be, based on their unique internal and external environments. Decisions regarding scope width should be determined by factors such as stability or volatility as well as the speed at which an organization needs to react. Decisions should also be made on the basis of market conditions, technology perspectives, economic and political issues, legal and environmental concerns, and so on. Indeed, I recommend that organizations even compile data points that go beyond their optimal scope, as a way of validating scoping boundaries and adjusting as new information is acquired. After all, peripheral vision is about detecting weak signals amid white noise, and when too many signals are missed, a wider scanning domain is advisable.

In what ways can executives know how to look as well as where to look?

Before constructing a portfolio of appropriate scanning methods, leaders must determine whether their strategies will be that of "exploitation" (searching within well-defined and reasonably familiar domains) or of "exploration" (searching unfamiliar domains). Exploratory scans can be active or passive, with passive scanning simply requiring that people keep antennae up and wait to receive outside signals—usually from familiar sources. However, this type of scanning tends to reinforce prevailing beliefs rather than challenging them. By contrast, active scanning is usually hypothesis-driven, and based upon specific questions that need to be answered by "search parties" of both outsiders and insiders. Scanning needs to take in diverse sources, but at minimum, should include customers and channels, competitors and "complementors," and technologies. This kind of scanning continually challenges the status quo—and is made possible by special teams, new data sources, frequent strategy meetings, and focus groups.

How can organizational leaders effectively interpret weak or ambiguous signals?

When interpreting data, it's important that people avoid, or at least minimize, cognitive or emotional biases that can lead to groupthink. That means seeing through the eyes of competitors as well as customers. One of the most significant impediments to accurate interpretations of the periphery is the urge to impose too much order on an inherently ambiguous or "fuzzy" picture. It's important not to lock in prematurely on initial images. The key to interpreting the periphery is in suspending judgment and "triangulating," which means looking—or scanning—from different vantage points.

In what ways can leaders probe to explore weak signals more closely?

In contrast to simply watching and waiting, organizations can use the scientific method to formulate and test hypotheses, design experiments, and explore various options. This means less sense-making at first and more time spent on generating competing hypotheses to explain the ambiguous data. This discipline provides a framework that can mitigate the temptation to prematurely act upon ambiguous data from the periphery. However, to utilize different methods of probing and exploring, organizations also need to develop capabilities for flexible responses—particularly if they're contemplating bold and potentially disruptive innovations.

How should executives decide what to do with insights gained from probing?

It's vitally important to know whether to learn or leap. When organizations need to act fast and with flexibility, several different approaches need to be used. These typically include a "sense-and-respond" management style as well an ability to de-risk through prototyping—which allows organizations to succeed or to fail fast. Different approaches can also involve networking, conducting small experiments, and adopting an "options perspective" that facilitates agility by having a previously agreed-upon portfolio of options. This is preferable to placing one big bet or employing fixed styles of decision making.

What can leaders do to learn and adjust?

Peripheral vision entails lateral thinking in addition to the well-defined, linear problem solving and decision making that most organizations employ. Lateral thinking requires that people look at data through multiple lenses, ask disconfirming questions, and rely on intuition as well as analysis. Most important for fast learning and adjusting, are the ongoing and iterative processes of scoping, scanning, interpreting, and acting. Equally important are issues-oriented discussions and flexible strategies, inquisitive cultures, knowledge systems, and advanced analytics that can eliminate and overcome organizational silos.

How do successful executives create agendas for action?

Our book, *Peripheral Vision*, easily sums that up in Six Lessons from the Periphery. Lesson 1: Peripheral vision is more about anticipation and alertness than prediction. Lesson 2: The problem is not a lack of data but of good questions. Lesson 3: Scan actively but with an open mind because the periphery won't always come to you. Lesson 4: Use triangulation to better understand the periphery. Lesson 5: When catching glimpses from the periphery, it is wise to probe before jumping. And Lesson 6: Balancing peripheral vision and focal vision is a central leadership challenge.

TAKEAWAYS

- Periodic "eye exams" can help detect poor peripheral vision and enable treatment.
- Leaders must know *where* and *how* to look for ambiguous or weak signals.
- Once peripheral signals are identified, executives should explore.
- Exploration and probing can enable accurate interpretation, determine relevance, and assist organizations in exploring various options.
- Once options are identified, leaders need to take action.

TAKING STOCK

- Is my organization flexible and inquisitive enough to continually scan for weak signals?
- Do we have systems in place for sharing and properly evaluating information, so that we know what to do about weak signals that could potentially disrupt?
- Have we constructed strategy portfolios that can prepare us to respond quickly?

■   ■   ■

To see subjects related to peripheral vision view our chapters entitled *A Culture of Innovation, A Path to Innovation Excellence, Consumer Insights,* and *Execution.*

Chapter 33

Planning

An interview with Joan M. Coffman, FACHE, President and Chief Executive Officer at HSHS St. Mary's Hospital, Decatur, IL, Hospital Sisters Health System (HSHS); former President and CEO at HSHS St. Joseph's Hospital, Chippewa Falls, WI

■ ■ ■

"Today, change is frequently discontinuous and unpredictable … innovation refers less to a plan or procedure than to the organization's ability to capitalize on constant turbulence."

— Nicholas Imparato and Oren Harrari

Most successful orchestra leaders would say that planning is critical to successful performances. However, they might define planning in a variety of ways. One might be the way in which contemporary music leaders solicit input from musicians regarding programming; another might be the way that a musical score should be executed. Successful leaders in almost all settings rely on planning to set direction and monitor efforts to get to their respective destinations. Effective planning can also provide ways to build on previous successes as well as back-up plans that enable changes in direction. Many of us have heard the saying, "Failing to plan is planning to fail." Earl Nightingale took a slightly different approach when he said, "All you need is the plan, the road map, and the courage to press on to your destination."

Inspiring as Nightingale's quote might be, the changing landscapes in today's world often render yesterday's road maps irrelevant. Planning today must be a dynamic, real-time, continual process that enables leaders to anticipate and quickly adapt. Leading innovators know that planning can also be a useful tool for ensuring future success by enabling innovation. That's because planning provides a bridge from an organization's current state to where it needs to be in the future. In other chapters of this book, we've described how organizations can become irrelevant if they fail to react to changes in their internal and external environments. In order to rapidly adapt to change or shift to a new direction, leaders must often invest time and effort in formulating a variety of scenarios including multiple contingency plans and entire portfolios of potential strategies.

For this chapter we interview Joan Coffman, a healthcare leader in an industry that has witnessed a sea change ever since the advent of managed care in the early 1990s. As CEO of various local hospitals, Joan conducts planning with local board members, physicians, and leaders. At HSHS, a multi-institutional healthcare system that encompasses 14 hospitals, she also interacts with people at local, divisional, and system levels. A fellow of the American College of Healthcare Executives (ACHE), she served on the board of ACHE's Wisconsin Chapter as well as local boards that include the Greater Chippewa Valley United Way, the Chippewa Falls Family Support Center, and the Chippewa Valley Technical College Foundation. Joan is also a member of the Rural Hospital Issues Group of the Federal Office of Rural Health Policy and serves on the Governing Council of the American Hospital Association (AHA) Section for Small or Rural Hospitals.

Joan was elected to the Wisconsin Hospital Association (WHA) Board of Directors; functioned as President of the WHA's West Central Region; and was a member of the WHA's Council on Public Policy. She also received the 2014 Partners of WHA's "Best of the Best" Administrative Award and the 2015 Wisconsin ACHE Regent Senior Executive Award. Joan holds a Master's degree in Business Administration from the University of New Orleans. Please join us as Joan describes how planning can play a pivotal role in helping leaders recognize opportunities, minimize or avoid failures, and facilitate the information sharing, transparency, and collaboration that enables focus, buy-in, and alignment.

QUESTIONS AND ANSWERS

How do you define "planning," and how can it be an enabler of innovation?

As we look through a lens toward tomorrow, we need to be both strategic and operational, so planning should embrace both strategic and operations planning. Planning can be an enabler for innovation through the dialogue and creativity of the persons involved in the planning process. That's why it's important to decide who should participate and to ensure that all relevant functions are represented.

Why is planning critical to innovation and what happens when organizations don't plan effectively?

Planning is inspirational so it can foster growth—both individually and collectively. Effective planning fosters teamwork and maximizes collaboration and commitment. Planning also ensures focus on mission, vision, and strategy and represents a unified voice that's instrumental in building solidarity. Organizations that fail to plan run the risk of failure because the status quo will not sustain them in today's fast-paced environment. By sitting still, organizations essentially ignore the freight train that's coming at them at 500 mph, and in doing so, risk mergers, acquisitions, or closures. Through planning, leaders can listen to others' ideas and align interests, based on what they know today and what they can forecast for tomorrow. Once solid foundationally, leaders are better prepared to make shifts as challenges are presented.

What do you think are important elements in strategic plans today?

Strategic planning must provide a temporary roadmap based on history, current SWOT analyses, market demands, community needs, and high level visions and goals. People in all functional areas need to understand the vision and goals in order to collaboratively implement with all constituents. Therefore, mission and vision statements are important because they define why organizations exist—both internally and externally. Value propositions are important elements as well because they set companies apart from their competitors and illustrate the value that they provide to various stakeholders inside and outside the company. Guiding principles, too, are important because they define desired behaviors, particularly when people are faced with challenges—or opportunities. Goals are also critical elements, in that they identify where businesses want and need to go. Lastly, areas of focus and strategies are important because they define how organizations will get to where they need to go within specified time frames.

What are important elements in today's operating plans?

Operational planning has to follow strategic planning to provide boots on the ground and specific ways in which strategic plans will be implemented. In many of today's environments, however, operations planning can get bogged down if leaders focus too intently on what's worked well in the past and if they fail to plan for the future. For this reason, operating plans should include contingency and scenario planning, because, although strategic plans might contain great strategies, there have to be ways to deal with competitors' responses to those strategies.

Role clarity and goal congruence are also critically important for effective operating plans. Other important elements include well-defined action plans with corresponding leads for each of the actions identified. Communication plans (both internal and external), are also important elements, as are back-up plans. In smaller organizations, Plan Bs can be somewhat simple because it's easier to change direction than in larger organizations. When organizations are larger, more people are involved in decision making and there are multiple layers of communication. Yet in both large and small corporations, plans might need to address cultural change as well, if new and broad-reaching initiatives are being introduced. Those are much more complex scenarios than a simple change in tactics, since culture change calls for marketplace intelligence and a compelling argument for different approaches.

Do you think that strategic plans should contain talent management and succession plans as well as specific strategies that call for innovation?

It's essential for companies to attract and retain the talent necessary to carry out strategic plans, yet succession planning isn't generally thought of until critical positions are suddenly vacant. Although potential replacements can't be expected to know everything—or be able to fully turn the key if a critical position is vacated—there should be at least three to five people who could continue day-to-day operations in a cohesive fashion until a replacement can be found. Emergency succession plans and talent management plans should be a part of any strategic planning effort since the process can identify gaps that, when closed, create talent pipelines for future needs. With regard to innovation, it needs to be an inherent, built-in characteristic of both strategic and operating plans, as opposed to a stand-alone philosophy. Innovation also needs to be viewed as part of everyone's job description as well as a necessary component of all C-suite positions.

In your experience with various planning processes, what's worked well and not so well?

Successful leaders realize that, as issues become more complex, cross-functional depth and breadth might need to be added to the planning bench. It also goes without saying that all dialogue must remain within the four walls until plans can be formally communicated. The process breaks down when the right people aren't present during planning, when information is leaked, or when one or more members of the team aren't aligned with the plan. All of this can reduce the chances of a unified voice, alignment with a common direction, and skilled execution. Personalization or emotional attachment can also seriously detract from the planning process. Skilled facilitators can enhance planning efforts by bringing objectivity to the process and by sharing their knowledge of the marketplace and competition.

What are the best ways for leaders to ensure that plans are flexible and adaptable?

Leaders have to pay attention to the marketplace and stay engaged. That means reading publications and keeping abreast of what's going on—at Capitol Hill and with their competition. There's so much change in traditional healthcare environments today, and generally in the healthcare industry, yet it's important that all organizations today be extremely nimble. Leaders have to respond to change as quickly as the competition responds—and this is true in all industries.

Are there ways in which planning can inhibit or stifle innovation as well as enable it?

Planning can inhibit or stifle innovation if the right people and decision-makers aren't included in the process; if contingency planning and scenario planning aren't happening; and so on. However, planning can also be an inhibitor of innovation if people rigidly adhere to plans, as opposed to responding flexibly to unanticipated change or challenges. Another way that planning can inhibit is if it's not a real-time process. We're often reminded that planning needs to be an ongoing process as opposed to a one-time or quarterly event.

Do you also see value in linking planning with team development?

There is great value in crucial conversations that lead to the building of trust among team members and to building teams that are highly collaborative. If skilled facilitators are used, teams can be assessed and taught to observe what they do well and not so well. Facilitators can also provide helpful feedback for beginning difficult discussions about current and future states.

How have you prevented or minimized potential implementation barriers?

First, let's talk about typical barriers. People who are unable to make decisions or who hold to a course that's no longer tenable can create major implementation barriers. Other barriers can be a lack of role clarity, communication, or focus. As mentioned before, planning needs to start with the right people at the table so they have a unified voice and a shared vision. For this, trust is needed, but to build trust, planners need to accept that people grasp concepts at different rates and respond to change in a variety of ways. To ensure alignment, leaders must speak with some people one-on-one to deal with individual fears and other sources of resistance.

How have I personally minimized implementation barriers? Communication, communication, communication—especially the kind that includes active listening! As with any other process, effective planning requires leaders to tease out what people might not be able to voluntarily or directly communicate. This requires leaders to ask questions so that potential resistance can be identified and addressed in a timely manner. If we accept that planning is most effective when it's an ongoing process, then two-way communication needs to be an ongoing process as well.

TAKEAWAYS

- Leaders need to pay close attention to the marketplace and adapt plans accordingly.
- Planners should identify key stakeholders, involve them at the beginning of the planning process, and ensure that they stay engaged.

- Timelines must be defined and communicated along the way.
- Collective decisions need to be made with all key functional partners.
- Leaders must actively listen and identify potential implementation barriers to address them reactively and proactively.

TAKING STOCK

- Are all key functions appropriately represented in our planning process?
- Are our plans fluid and able to adapt to changes, including competitors' responses to our strategies?
- Do we have contingency plans? Are they up to date?
- Have we considered scenario planning?

■ ■ ■

If you found this chapter useful, also see our chapters entitled *Benchmarking and Metrics, Business Model Innovation, Buy-in, Sponsorship, and Commitment, Competition and Collaboration,* and *Execution.*

Chapter 34

Process Redesign and Optimization

An interview with Michael J. Bear, Associate Professor at New York University; Member of Cabots Point Partners; and former Chief Operating Officer/Chief Financial Officer of Private Banking at U.S. Trust

■　■　■

"A company's capacity to consider ideas is limited only by the robustness and flexibility of its processes."

— John Kao

Jazz ensembles, symphony orchestras, and organizations in all sectors must have the capability to consistently deliver products or services in ways that inspire audiences and customers. And all must provide compelling reasons for consumers and recipients to "repurchase" and also recommend products and services to others. To accomplish this, orchestra leaders must inspire musicians, and business leaders must inspire internal and external customers. However, having the right idea or "the better mousetrap" isn't always sufficient. Leaders must be skilled at motivating people to perform while also providing supporting infrastructures and effective and efficient processes that maximize innovation capability.

In the private sector, ineffective or inefficient processes can hurt a company's cost position and ultimately hinder its efforts to compete. If there are too many handoffs or if processes are redundant, cumbersome, or costly, they can significantly impact organizational performance. And in all sectors, weak or ineffective processes have the potential to negatively affect customer and client relationships, even causing permanent damage to an organization's reputation. To avoid this kind of scenario, leaders must be visibly committed to continuous process improvement through ongoing evaluation of both internal and external processes. In time, most discover that the best processes are those which provide enough structure to be effective, efficient, and repeatable, while still allowing for some flexibility and occasional exceptions.

For this chapter, we interviewed Michael Bear, a senior leader with expertise in strategy, international operations, finance, infrastructure, performance improvement, and turnaround management. Mike's direct line experience includes assignments as a CEO, President, Chief Operating Officer and Chief Financial Officer with P&L responsibility in financial services, technology, and manufacturing companies of varying sizes. He began his career designing advanced aircraft engines at GE, held various consulting roles at Mars & Co and Coopers & Lybrand, and served internationally as an executive with Citibank.

Mike holds a Masters in Business Administration from Harvard Business School, a Master of Science in Mechanical Engineering from MIT, and a Bachelor of Science in Mechanical Engineering and Applied Mechanics, cum laude, from the University of Pennsylvania. In his current roles, Mike provides management advisory and operations consulting services to financial services, manufacturing, private equity, and venture capital firms. He also teaches courses in global leadership strategy and performance effectiveness at New York University (NYU). Please join Mike as he describes how process redesign and optimization can enable innovation while improving individual, team, and organizational performance.

QUESTIONS AND ANSWERS

Would you please define and contrast "process redesign" and "process optimization"?

First, let me underscore the importance of defining the concept of "process." If we view it as a set of tasks and activities that produce inputs and outputs, then process design (or redesign) is a response to the question, "What does the process do?" By contrast, process optimization is an answer to the question, "How well does the process do what it's intended to do?"

What are some of the characteristics of good process design?

Good process design is grounded in both measurement and facts. The ability to compare and contrast different approaches and make fact-based decisions is extremely useful in optimizing design. Process design and process optimization are often associated with frameworks, methods, and tools such as Six Sigma, process mapping, root cause analysis, gap identification, customer value assessment, and even brainstorming and change management techniques.

Other important aspects of design have to do with flexibility and trade-offs. Flexibility considers whether a process can facilitate doing many things at once (such as producing multiple products) or whether it can be easily adapted to respond quickly to changes in business conditions. Trade-offs balance the characteristics of the process, which are typically related to cycle time, cost, and quality. For example, when people try to achieve faster cycle times or decreased costs, the trade-off will likely be a lower quality standard.

How do process redesign and optimization add value and enable innovation?

First, value must be determined from the perspective of consumers, which means asking what they want and what they might not be getting. With products, value often translates to additional features, increased functionality, or entirely new products. Yet classic marketing approaches and simple extensions of existing products can sometimes miss opportunities to add value. That's because people are sometimes so intent on producing a disruptive innovation that they can overlook the obvious. It's critical to keep in mind that innovation doesn't always need to be radically new and different.

Some of the best examples of process innovation occur when teams find something that works well in one situation and then adapt it to a completely different situation. A good example of this might be if one office were to outperform other offices with regard to acquiring new customers. When the leader of the top performing office shares its methods of delivering to customers, or how it functions internally, it can lead to improved processes for all offices. In fact, when best practices are standardized and universalized, it can often translate to better results for entire organizations.

In what ways might process improvement and optimization inhibit as well as support innovation?

If we evaluate process optimization from a tactical perspective, we gain an understanding of the tasks required for a successful result. Innovation can be inhibited if roles aren't clearly defined—or assigned—or if resources aren't appropriately managed. Innovation can also be negatively impacted if people don't create sufficiently detailed schedules or if they fail to monitor activities on the critical path. Another way that innovation can be negatively impacted is if leaders overwhelm their organizations with too much change at once.

Other ways that process redesign and process optimization can inhibit innovation is if they're not aimed at opportunities that can truly leverage it and if critical tasks aren't done by the right people. For example, when reviewing our processes at Citibank, we typically tried to answer two key questions. The first question was, "Is the process aligned with the business strategy?" If it wasn't, the second question was, "Who should lead a redesign effort?" Often those who excel at process redesign and process optimization efforts aren't the right people to ensure successful implementations. If leaders don't have an appreciation for the unique skill sets required to deal with complex implementations, they also won't know how to play to people's strengths. Then time, effort, and valuable resources can be misdirected or wasted—and innovation is often inhibited or completely prevented. This can also be the result if leaders don't commit to process redesign and process improvement—or if they don't allocate the required resources.

Yet even when leaders fully commit to process optimization and have the best of intentions, they can unknowingly inhibit innovation. How can that happen? Many leaders tout the merits of collaboration, but too much collaboration can lead to groupthink, a formidable enemy of successful implementation and innovation. However, a single technique can help. When design teams invite senior leaders to challenge their ideas and solutions in a structured way, they can receive valuable feedback as well as helpful input for the next design cycle. This also creates high-level sponsorship for other changes that might be critical for successful implementation.

How should project managers and leaders go about optimizing a process?

There are many ways to approach process optimization. Most of them can be addressed by answering the following questions: "What is the purpose of the process?" "How does one tell if it's successful?" "What are the key measures of that success and what are the thresholds for each measurement?" "What are the trade-offs between the various measures as they relate to quality, cost, service, and cycle time?" "What tests can be used to verify that the changes will work?" "What would be useful ways to mitigate risks?" "Are the end outputs likely to vary or will they remain similar?" And, "What are the best ways to prepare for implementation?"

Seasoned project managers stay on top of current activities, planning ahead for weeks, and sometimes months. They also actively seek out people in the organization who will support the implementation and encourage them to participate in various change initiatives. As a way to enhance an organization's innovation capability, project managers and leaders also anticipate roadblocks, make mid-course corrections, and develop mitigation strategies for risks. Project managers and leaders also consider creative alternatives or reasons for approved exceptions in advance of major initiatives. In addition, they typically establish performance metrics that can measure, track, and reward progress and strategies. Project managers and leaders might also decide to conduct a demonstration pilot, or a series of pilots, to validate new concepts. This usually allays concerns while allowing people to establish successful track records. This, in turn, helps mid-level managers gain the confidence and trust of executive leaders.

Would you comment on how technology can enable, enhance, or inhibit process optimization?

Technology can play multiple roles in enabling and enhancing process optimization. On the project management side, technology tools can assist teams track ideas, plan activities, monitor progress, and manage project resources. On the project content side, they can help people conduct cost-benefit analysis while also facilitating process mapping, simulating process flows, identifying bottlenecks, and optimizing efficiencies.

Technology is also useful when automating (or semi-automating) labor-intensive processes. This can significantly reduce cycle time and cost while still producing consistent quality and repeatable precision. All told, technology has the potential to improve design and speed implementation, sometimes saving teams a considerable amount of time and effort. However, I once had a mentor who expressed caution when he said, "Beware of relying too heavily on technology." The danger is that businesses can lose flexibility because of limitations in the technology of the time—and even with what might be introduced with future technology releases. If business conditions change substantially, and technology doesn't keep pace, organizations can have difficulty responding to changing consumer needs that can lead to increased opportunities in the marketplace.

What advice would you give to leaders who are about to launch major process improvement and process optimization initiatives?

It's imperative to prepare for and understand the nature of change and resistance to it. An important perspective to keep in mind is that process redesign and optimization concepts originated in manufacturing environments. When adopting the terminology and concepts of process design and optimization in non-manufacturing settings, leaders are likely to encounter resistance to change. Ironically, people often know that there are better ways of doing things but they simply don't have the experience or comfort level to communicate their desire for change. In these scenarios, fear can prevent people from taking risks and even from doing the same things in new or unfamiliar ways.

I believe there is no better use of a leader's time than to help an organization prepare for change. To do this effectively, however, they need to communicate clearly the purpose of the change and also provide the necessary resources to facilitate it. Employees will generally listen, but they'll also take cues from the nonverbal actions of their leaders. Consequently, leaders need to "walk the talk" through active engagement and by explicitly linking performance objectives to the successful implementation of various changes. It also means assigning the best people to various initiatives and becoming actively involved in steering teams and in ongoing communication of plans, goals, and progress. That's an important part of the innovation recipe—and it's also what truly builds innovation capability.

TAKEAWAYS

- Good process design can deliver intended outputs in an efficient, effective, and flexible manner.
- Process optimization requires an understanding of what customers value as well as trade-offs.
- Several tools and techniques can enhance success, including clear communication, effective risk management, performance metrics, demonstration pilots, and proofs of concept.
- Resistance to change is the number one obstacle to new processes, making senior management's involvement crucial for success.

TAKING STOCK

- Are my organization's current processes doing what they're intended to do? Are they doing it well?
- In what areas are our competitors doing better than we are and why?
- Do we have a fact-based method for consistently ensuring the quality of our products and services?

■ ■ ■

If you found this chapter helpful, also see *A Path to Innovation Excellence, Benchmarking and Metrics, Change Leadership,* and *Consumer Insights.*

Chapter 35

Risk/Portfolio Management

An interview with Kaye O'Leary, Principal at Tevera Consulting and former Chief Financial Officer at Caribou Coffee

■ ■ ■

"The ability to innovate is only as good as how one can accept changes and take risks."

— Franco Paolo Liu Eisma

One of the orchestra leaders featured in this book—Joann Falletta, Music Director of the Buffalo Philharmonic Orchestra and the Virginia Symphony Orchestra—tells us what can happen when leaders are inexperienced or ineffective at managing risk. In the United States, where orchestras aren't publicly funded, they face many of the same challenges as do business leaders today. Consequently, the focus of almost any current leader needs to be on sustainability—and on the many risks that can potentially threaten it. This means that leaders must keep risk at the forefront of their day-to-day activities and decisions. Risk for both orchestra leaders and business leaders is a two-edged sword. Without it, there is little or no progress, yet poor risk taking can deplete valuable resources, including time.

Innovation risk can be viewed from both personal and organizational perspectives, and both require courage. For example, new ideas aren't often received enthusiastically. People who try to introduce them can sometimes even cause credibility problems, yet it has been argued that there are risks that one must take, risks that one cannot afford to take, and risks that one cannot afford *not* to take. Certainly this is true of organizational leaders who have fiduciary responsibilities. However, when evaluating risk, leaders almost everywhere must take into consideration the needs of both internal and external stakeholders. With this in mind, many organizations maintain "innovation portfolios" that, like financial portfolios, represent a range of risk from low to high. Low risk portfolios often contain incremental innovation initiatives, and high risk portfolios contain initiatives for radical or disruptive innovation. What are some effective principles of risk taking and risk management that can be applied to innovation risk?

We interviewed Kaye O'Leary for this chapter because of her strong background and current focus on value creation through corporate strategy and governance. Kaye draws from experience gained while holding finance positions at Caribou Coffee, Bucca di Beppo (BUCA Inc.), Navitaire (an Accenture subsidiary), Pepsico, Dun & Bradstreet, Dannon, and A. H. Belo, where she had first-hand knowledge of risk from both personal and organizational perspectives. At BUCA Inc., Kaye was instrumental in re-capitalizing the company, in avoiding NASDAQ delisting, and in settling its Department of Justice and SEC investigations without financial penalty.

At Navitaire, Kaye was responsible for developing the company's growth strategy through acquisitions and the establishment of domestic and international offices. At Carlson Companies, she gained valuable experience as the Vice President of Business Planning. Kaye holds an MBA in Finance from Pace University and a Bachelor of Science in Management from Rensselaer Polytechnic Institute. She currently serves on the Board of Directors for Western National Insurance Group, on the Board of Regents for St. Mary's University in Minnesota, and on the Board of Directors for Food for Hungry Minds. She is a past Board Chair for the Girl Scout Council of Greater Minneapolis.

QUESTIONS AND ANSWERS

First, would you please share your thoughts on the subjects of "risk" and "portfolio management"?

Risk and portfolio management concepts are standard tools in corporate finance to evaluate capital investments and potential M&A opportunities. A corporation's cost of capital is dependent on its risk profile and its risk profile is dependent on its portfolio of businesses. In general, corporations use one cost of capital to evaluate all future potential investments, including innovation, be it through M&A or internal development.

What do you believe are important considerations in managing innovation portfolios, when assessing and ensuring balance between evolutionary and revolutionary initiatives/projects?

By definition, one of the benefits of portfolio management is that it allows and supports organizations to take some big/risky (revolutionary) ideas and some moderate (evolutionary) risk projects. If organizations are using risk profile portfolio management as an excuse to not invest in revolutionary ideas, they're not embracing or effectively executing the concept of portfolio management. Over time, if an organization only invests in moderate/low risk projects, it will "dumb down" its portfolio and lower its risk, thereby also lowering its potential rate of return for investors.

How have you typically made decisions about risk decision-making criteria and dimensions, such as potential ROI, resource requirements, strategic fit, stretch, and timeframes?

Pure or academic implementation of financial investment principles would argue that firms should take on projects that provide the greatest rate of return (which incorporates risk), regardless of the length of time of the project, the resource requirements, etc. In practice, I believe organizations do—and should—consider many different factors in the evaluation of new projects, such as: strategic fit, length of time, organizational impact, government regulations, and community impact.

With regard to product innovation, capital investment and or M&A opportunities, it's certainly easiest to implement risk management in large, stable organizations that have the required human and financial resources. They can operationalize the concept of balancing different risk profiles to take into account different innovation project maturities; for example, those that require immediate and/or sustained investments.

In addition to safe bets (i.e., incremental innovation) and stretch bets (i.e., breakthrough innovation), do you think that an innovation portfolio should also include a variety of specific challenges related to marketing, service, technology, and process or performance improvement?

I believe that depends on the nature of the business and the lifecycle stage of the business. For more mature, large conglomerates, definitely "yes." For start-up, smaller organizations, it might not make sense.

Tom Peters once said, ""The three keys to business success: "Test fast. Fail fast. Adjust fast." Do you agree with this? If so, what are the best ways to do that?

I believe the applicability of this concept depends on the nature, size, resources and maturity of the business. While this concept is a great aspirational saying for new product innovation, it's not always "real world," particularly in industries like pharmaceuticals or med-tech. The word "fast" takes on an entirely different definition in different industries.

How do you think leaders can encourage people to take risks that are necessary for innovation—particularly radical or breakthrough innovation?

I believe it's largely driven by a culture that embraces new ideas, creativity, and speaking up. It's important to not penalize failure. I'm reminded of a story told to me by Ken Melrose, the former CEO of The Toro Corporation. Toro prides itself on its ability to bring innovative products to the outdoor power equipment industry and on how it encourages product engineers to develop new equipment.

After many years of investing both financial and human capital in the development and commercialization of a new product, Toro finally decided to pull the plug on the project. The project's lead product development engineer was dejected and fearful that it would reflect poorly on his capabilities.

Shortly after the decision to cancel the project, the product development engineer arrived at work to find a note summoning him immediately to the CEO's office. Certain that he was going to be reprimanded or terminated, the engineer timidly made his way to the CEO's office and found CEO Ken Melrose sitting outside the closed door that led to his office. Ken asked the engineer to join him inside his office and when Ken opened the door, the engineer was greeted by the whole senior leadership team with balloons and cake. All were celebrating what was learned from the organization's mistakes.

Upon returning to his work station, the engineer was immediately surrounded by the other project engineers. When they learned that their co-worker had not only kept his job, and that his efforts had been supported and celebrated, the entire group was energized and innovation soared. I think this is a powerful example of an organization that understands how successful innovation isn't dependent upon having the best stage-gate process or the most creative new product team. Innovation thrives in organizations that encourage trial-end-error and that understand how failure is an integral part of learning.

Do you believe that employees (and leaders) should be rewarded for taking risks, even when that might not have produced a positive result? If so, why?

Yes, I definitely agree with this. Leaders who don't embrace failure and learn from it will either continue to make the same mistakes or, worse yet, will begin to shy away from taking risks and will sink to mediocrity. I also firmly believe that post-mortem reviews of all projects, investments, M&A activities, etc. should encourage learning.

What is a good way to determine whether a company's risk management practices are enabling or inhibiting innovation?

Overzealous or misguided executives could take the approach that, in order to improve success, the company should lower risk. In this scenario, organizations run the risk that I've spoken of earlier, when I talked about them taking on only low risk projects and over time, sinking to mediocrity. I believe organizations can monitor this by running effective post-mortem processes that not only evaluate the outcomes of projects against financial return but also against the strategic plan and strategic risk profile of the organization. If projects are consistently under-delivering against the organization's strategic goals, then the "risk" component of project evaluation might be set too high or be given too much importance.

What might be the best way to reward leaders for taking calculated risks and for managing risk effectively?

I'm not sure there is one best way, but I do think that all individuals want to feel supported and secure in their work environment. Developing a culture that supports and is consistent with the risk profile of the organization is the most critical component. Other critical components include celebrating new ideas and encouraging people from all functions and levels of the organization. I believe organizations must then set up processes and organizational designs that allow their desired innovation profiles to flourish. Finally, I think the traditional reward mechanisms such as compensation and promotion are valuable in reinforcing experimentation.

TAKEAWAYS

- People must understand the strategic goals of the organization and how risk fits with the strategy and vision of the organization.
- Leaders must develop a culture and processes that are consistent with the risk and innovation profiles needed to achieve the organization's strategic plan.
- It's important to celebrate success, embrace disappointments, and learn from mistakes.
- When evaluating the potential investment in new projects (e.g. new products, capital expenditures, M&A) it's important to understand all of the decision-making criteria (e.g. financial, organizational, cultural) and evaluate the potential projects against all relevant criteria.
- Executives should conduct post-mortem analysis of all projects, asking, "What worked?" "What didn't work?" "Why?" "How do we change?" etc.

TAKING STOCK

- Is my organization's risk management strategy flexible enough to allow for radical or disruptive innovation?
- Have we recently examined how well our risk management strategy fits with our current vision and strategies?
- Have we created a culture that embraces failure and learning from mistakes?

■ ■ ■

If you found this chapter useful, also see our chapters entitled *A Culture of Innovation, A Path to Innovation Excellence, Benchmarking and Metrics,* and *Courage.*

Chapter 36

Scorecards and Performance Management

An interview with Renée DeFranco, Chief People Officer at NicePak/PDI; former Head of People & Organizational Capability at Novartis; and former leadership roles at Hewlett-Packard, Allied Signal, and Chemical Bank

■　■　■

"The greater danger for most of us lies not in setting our aim too high and falling short, but in setting our aim too low, and achieving our mark."

— Michelangelo

Leaders of symphony orchestras and business leaders alike must have winning strategies for mobilizing and aligning their people resources. In business environments, it's also critical to use measures and systems for both strategy execution and innovation. The foundational principles for business scorecards and performance systems used today actually had their origins over a century ago in the highly structured and operationally oriented manufacturing organizations of the industrial revolution.

As a way of increasing efficiency, Frederick Taylor—educator, consultant, and the "father of scientific management"—would break jobs into specific "motions" and analyze them to see which were essential. Then he used a stopwatch to determine how long it took for workers to do the job most efficiently. Taylor's work in time and motion studies linked rewards and incentives to employees who turned out certain quantities of work (i.e., "piecework") while still meeting established quality standards. Standards in Taylor's day had little variance. They were primarily based on line-of-sight perspectives and carried out by managerial directives that communicated, "Do what you're told."

So what are more effective ways of measuring performance today, for work done by service organizations and knowledge workers? Scorecards and performance management systems can still be effective vehicles for evaluating and rewarding performance in that they optimize role clarity and alignment and provide an objective basis for performance feedback—to individuals, teams, and organizations. However, today's diverse environments call for an entire continuum of measures and rewards that are tailored to the needs of employees, as well as specific work environments.

For this chapter, we interviewed Renée De Franco because of her expertise with individual, team, and organizational performance scorecards. Renée has senior leadership experience with world-class organizations that include Hewlett-Packard, AlliedSignal, and Novartis. Bringing perspectives as a human resources business partner and leader in industries that include pharmaceutical, biotech, technology, and financial services, Renée's particular strength has been in meeting business challenges with both innovative and practical people-related solutions. Her areas of expertise include performance management, based on both short- and long-term business strategy and goals as well as areas such as organizational restructuring, outsourcing, talent development, and workforce and succession planning. Renée holds a bachelor's degree and an MBA from Fairleigh Dickinson University and has published two Thomson Reuters articles: "Inside the Minds—HR Leadership Strategies" in 2011 and in 2012, "HR Communication Strategies: Helping Employees Understand What Health Care Reform Means for Them." Please join us as Renée shares her expertise regarding scorecards and performance management.

QUESTIONS AND ANSWERS

How do you define "scorecards" and "performance management"?

Let me start with the premise that a "scorecard" is a performance management framework that has been widely adopted by industry and is now seen as the critical foundation in a holistic strategy execution process. In addition to helping organizations articulate strategy in actionable terms, scorecards can provide a roadmap for strategy execution and for mobilizing and aligning people resources. Scorecards provide feedback around both the internal business processes and external outcomes in order to continuously improve strategy, performance, and results. When fully deployed, they transform strategic planning from an academic exercise into critical action items.

Have scorecards and performance management (PM) systems changed enough over the years to accommodate new ways of operating?

Scorecards have evolved from their early use as a simple performance measurement framework to being part of strategic planning and management systems. The "new" scorecard transforms an organization's strategic plan from a passive document into daily "marching orders." As part of a management system (rather than only a measurement framework), they enable organizations to clarify their vision and strategy and translate them into action. Although changed, today's scorecards still retain traditional financial measures, and these measures can only tell stories about past events. They're inadequate for guiding and evaluating the journey that today's organizations must make to create future value through investment in customers, suppliers, employees, processes, technology, and innovation.

How can scorecards and PM enable innovation?

When leaders are strategic about innovation, they fully integrate it into their organization's planning and management processes. Because scorecards require documentation of goals and objectives, as well as individual responsibilities and accountabilities, they can bring value in three ways. First, they can be excellent tools for setting goals and for ensuring role clarity and alignment. Second, scorecards can assist in measuring progress against stated goals and objectives. And third, they can provide an objective basis for recognition and rewards. Because this structure enables the passage from strategy to action, it also forms the foundation for a performance management system that outlines specific individual responsibilities and accountabilities.

What are some advantages of using a balanced scorecard?

The first advantage of using the balanced scorecard method is that by looking at four aspects of a company's performance (i.e., Financial, Processes, Customers, and Learning), leaders can get a more complete view of company performance. Unlike traditional methods of tracking only the financial health of a business, the balanced scorecard gives leaders a full picture as to whether the company is meeting objectives in all critical areas. While it may seem as if a company is doing well financially, if customer satisfaction is down, if employee training is inadequate, or if processes are outdated, the organization can be vulnerable. Balanced scorecards can allow stakeholders to determine the health of short-, medium-, and long-term objectives at a glance. Finally, balanced scorecards can ensure that strategic actions match the desired outcomes as articulated in the organization's business strategies.

Can scorecards and PM systems also hinder innovation?

Poorly designed scorecards can restrict innovation if performance goals and objectives are set too high or too low. They can also limit and prevent it if they're focused on the wrong priorities or if they're not aligned to the organization's overall strategy. Additionally, they can restrict innovation if results can't be measured objectively or if achievements aren't recognized and rewarded. Today's knowledge workers face difficult challenges when dealing with many fluid situations. As a result, most leaders today need to continually "adjust the reins" of their performance systems. Fear, however, often causes leaders to do just the opposite: continually tighten the reins as pressures build.

Performance management systems can inhibit innovation if organizational goals aren't translated and cascaded into more refined goals and expectations at the unit, team, and individual levels. Compounding this are the times that leaders request HR departments to respond to individual performance problems with rigid policies, practices, or tools. Scorecards weren't intended to take the place of effective leadership practices, such as providing performance feedback in a timely manner and developing people in conjunction with new or challenging tasks. When leaders don't address problem performance—or it's not addressed effectively—innovation can suffer. Of course, performance also suffers if Band-Aids are applied since they don't fix inherent or underlying problems.

How can PM systems best measure and optimize individual performance?

Well-structured and well-implemented performance management systems align people with organizational goals. They also optimize objective performance appraisal processes by clearly spelling out goals and individual accountabilities as well as the required competencies and desired behaviors around how goals are to be achieved. One approach to ensure alignment and focus is to define and communicate a number of "strategic themes" pulled from the organization's business strategy. Typically these themes relate to internal business processes and act as pillars that support the over-arching business strategy. This approach allows for continued communication throughout the organization so that performance can be evaluated on all levels—individual, business unit, and organizational.

How can scorecards and performance management systems be best used to ensure individual and organizational accountability?

The most effective practice is to establish a hierarchy of goals where each level supports goals directly relevant to the next level, ultimately working toward the organization's strategic direction and critical priorities. In order to ensure individual and organizational accountability, it's important that scorecards be cascaded down, first to the business-unit level, where corporate goals are translated into business-unit goals, and from there to personal performance objectives.

This approach provides employees the ability to develop performance objectives based on a clear understanding of corporate and business-unit objectives. Also important are frequent reviews that incorporate changes in the organization's internal or external environments and that assess progress (or lack of progress). Constructive and specific feedback about expectations, milestones, and reassessment of goals and objectives are all important factors. In cases where individuals aren't performing according to expectations, leaders should construct and communicate written performance improvement plans.

In your opinion, what is the single most important element in attempting to maximize performance?

The single most important element in maximizing both organizational and individual performance is to ensure alignment of goals and objectives from top to bottom. The complex process of understanding the business model and identifying both performance drivers and appropriate measures can often generate confusion regarding the causal relationships between drivers of performance and performance measures.

To be predictive, rather than simply backward looking, the balanced scorecard approach should also focus on those activities and processes that an organization needs to get right to ensure performance against strategy. This task is critical because the lack of a cause and effect relationship between drivers of performance and indicators—perhaps from invalid assumptions about the business model—will lead to adverse organizational behavior and performance. For this reason, each performance measure must be clearly communicated, as well as what the key performance indicators are, and how each is achieved.

What are the best ways to leverage scorecards and performance management systems?

As with any other key business process, scorecards and performance management systems should call for formal and periodic review, since as operating conditions change, so must business strategies. Successful balanced scorecards can integrate the management of tactics and strategy into a seamless ongoing process with periodic meetings to review results and facilitate wider involvement. The balanced scorecard must be based on linkages between individual, departmental, and business-unit actions to make strategy a continual learning process. In this way, scorecards can help leaders monitor and measure actions and their impact, thereby helping them allocate and manage resources to deliver maximum stakeholder value.

TAKEAWAYS

- Scorecards are typically used to evaluate new or enhanced products, services, processes, or initiatives.
- Performance management systems and scorecards can be effective tools and processes for ensuring alignment and clarity around goals and objectives as well as business models and strategies.
- Scorecards and performance management systems are most effective when goals and objectives are tied to measurable, quantifiable results.
- Qualitative goals can be objectively measured if they're based on internal or external customer surveys, completed projects, or successful initiatives.

TAKING STOCK

- Do we have formal scorecards to measure individual, team, and organizational performance?
- Does our performance review process allow enough flexibility for new and better products, services, and processes? How might we allow more room for innovation?
- How can we best incentivize people to remain open to new opportunities and take necessary risks?

■ ■ ■

If you found this chapter informative, see our other enabling chapters entitled *Benchmarking and Metrics, Execution, Human Resources as a Strategic Partner, Personal Accountability,* and *Planning.*

III. Denouement and the Art of Improvisation

Section III. Denouement and the Art of Improvisation

Marilyn Blocker

You might remember from the chapter *Why This Book?* that the denouement in classical music and in literature signals an ending. From a business perspective, it sometimes signals an end to the way that organizations have traditionally done business, and in other situations, it simply signals "the end"—period.

This final chapter is a signal that the end of our innovation journey together is near. Along the way, we've seen how a symphony orchestra metaphor illustrates how successful organizations build on time-tested strategies and long-established structures and disciplines. We've also seen how a jazz metaphor describes the ways in which successful leaders meet today's innovation challenges: through co-creation, improvisation, disciplined experimentation, and a general openness to new ideas and approaches.

Given the volatile nature of today's current markets, what else might make a jazz metaphor an important factor in successful innovation? In Pamela Meyer's book *Quantum Creativity: Nine Principles to Transform the Way you Work*, we learn that the concept of "Yes, and" (mentioned in other parts of this book) is one of the first concepts that jazz musician novices put into practice. This concept is also one of the most important elements in the teamwork that's necessary for innovation. That's because "Yes, and" thinking—as opposed to "Yes, but" thinking—encourages discovery and enables action to unfold as people build on one another's ideas.

Keith Johnstone, an improvisation teacher and author of the book *Impro: Improvisation and the Theatre*, says about this important principle, "There are people who prefer to say 'Yes', and there are people who prefer to say 'No'. Those who say 'Yes' are rewarded by the adventures they have, and those who say 'No' are rewarded by the safety they attain. There are far more 'No' sayers than 'Yes' sayers, but you can train one type to behave like the other." Knowing that innovation requires creating value and protecting value, we can see how both "yes thinking" and "no thinking" are needed.

When drawing other parallels between the worlds of music and business, we can see how both orchestral and jazz metaphors can be helpful. We can also appreciate how improvisation and the "Yes, and" approach are compelling mandates for leaders who must continually recreate their organizations and flex with new challenges. In this chapter, you'll see how these approaches and others can also reduce some of the stress that comes with unrelenting change.

The Discipline of Jazz

Today, many leading universities, including Harvard and Stanford, offer improvisation courses in their business curricula. And companies such as American Express, DuPont, Ford, PepsiCo, and Proctor & Gamble retain professional musicians and other artists to teach their leaders how to effectively improvise. That's because they view improvisation as something that can help them respond better to increased competition and other organizational challenges. However, jazz didn't always enjoy a valued place—or even a *legitimate* place—in the world of music, let alone the world of business.

According to John Kao, in his book *Jamming: The Art and Discipline of Business Creativity*, jazz was once considered to be "marginal," "licentious," and even "subversive." Kao, a former Harvard and Stanford professor of innovation, tells us that jazz was also viewed as "freedom run amok" and that it initially had very few enthusiasts. Over the years, however, it persisted as it spread around the world and morphed into as many as 20 different styles, based on local, regional, and national cultures. Of the two forms of music referenced throughout this book—classical music and jazz—the latter seems to have fared better over time. Why is that? The strength of symphony orchestras is reliant on the past, and jazz, at its very roots, is about the future. So what might we learn from the wisdom of famous jazz musicians and soloists?

Relentless Change

Even from quotes that date back to the 1920s, we can see how the concepts that are fundamental to jazz can effectively bridge to the realities of today's business challenges. Nowhere is this more evident than the ways in which leaders today must deal with ongoing change. Some leaders outside of jazz venues enthusiastically embrace it, but most others fear it. So let's hear what some jazz greats of the past have to say about change—and how it might be reframed for organizational success.

The famous trombonist, J. J. Johnson said, "Jazz is restless. It won't stay put and it never will." The legendary bandleader, composer, and pianist Duke Ellington said that jazz is constantly morphing—and bringing new challenges in much the same way that doing business is. Jazz cornetist, pianist, and composer Bix Beiderbecke once said, "One thing I like about jazz, kid, is that I don't know what's going to happen next." Clearly, jazz musicians find change exciting, so they not only initiate and leverage it—they embrace it with enthusiasm.

How might leaders and other people in business environments view change as an exciting challenge, rather than a threat? Neuroscience research reveals that, in the face of uncertainty, we almost universally experience a threat response that causes us to resist or deny change. However, this same research provides evidence that change can be viewed as enjoyable when people feel empowered and confident about their ability to deal with it. What then, could help leaders deal with the unexpected and unplanned? And how might that counter our genetically imbedded threat responses? If change could be reframed for organizational leaders, might it become the same stimulating and driving force as it is for jazz musicians?

All Play and No Work?

The American singer, actress, and dancer, Lena Horne, once said this about the burdens that occur during times of change: "It's not the load that breaks you down. It's the way you carry it." If leaders could share their challenges—with other leaders and also with their employees—might that be a good way to lighten their loads? If so, how would leaders do that?

When jazz musicians "jam," they share what some people might regard as a burden by making their tasks fun. They do this by playing intuitively and listening intently to one another for opportunities during which each can temporarily "carry the load." What else can be learned about jamming that might help organizational leaders? When playing together informally, one musician might solo while others "comp"—which means they provide "acCOMPaniment." Once a player finishes soloing, another builds on whatever was last played. In this way, all musicians have opportunities to individually shine.

When a jazz musician makes mistakes while jamming, others often play on those mistakes, taking the music in another direction. Yet even when mistakes don't occur, jazz musicians continually experiment with different combinations and sometimes even engage in some healthy competition. Jamming introduces new themes and new ideas simply because it's a more creative and collaborative way of approaching work. And if practice makes perfect, we might also think of jamming in organizational settings as the ideal way for teams of people to try something on for size, play with it a while, and determine its viability before committing serious dollars.

Certainly we can see how the most successful innovators engage in a form of jamming when teams employ trial-and-error methods and participate in disciplined experimentation. Could the same force that empowers jazz musicians and fuels jam sessions enable people in business environments to "play as they go," collaborating on an ever-changing series of "notes"?

The Ultimate Team Sport?

If leaders could become expert at improvisation through jamming, might they react more confidently to day-to-day business challenges during both good times and bad? Improvisation is what leaders almost everywhere do during times of trouble—such as when they fail to keep up with rapid changes in the market and need to quickly mobilize and redirect their efforts. But why not also improvise in good times?

In a world where organizations must maintain operational excellence while also encouraging creativity and innovation, leaders often need to lighten their loads by partnering with others. When they formally and informally come together to discuss business challenges, or share potential strategies and best practices, it can alleviate some of the isolation that they feel today. Unfortunately, the majority of people intuitively resist partnering in this way, and only a few business leaders would likely put any credence in a process that's similar to jamming. In part, it's because many people have a fundamental misperception about jazz.

In his book *Jamming*, John Kao writes, "They don't appreciate the training, the practice, and especially the structure and disciplined study that typically precede mastery in jazz. They know even less about its most important ingredient: improvisation." Kao tells us that although improvisation might appear to some people as simply "play," that kind of play is usually only possible after many years of experience and hard work. Unfortunately, most people also aren't aware of the value that jazz can offer as a metaphor, so they can't draw from it as a valuable resource or a model for solving business and innovation challenges—but you can.

Polarities for Creative Tension

Skillful orchestration and jazz are both about achieving a balance between apparently opposing forces. We see how this occurs in business venues when leaders balance the status quo with something new. In other words, when they build on traditional ways or current successes while also exploring new products or services, different processes, and unconventional means of expanding markets. Skilled musicians, orchestra leaders, and business leaders alike have learned how to continually balance history and tradition with innovation and reinvention.

Although balancing polarities can present challenges, it can also generate the creative tension that almost any artist and leader needs to produce valuable outcomes. In sharp contrast to symphony orchestra leaders, jazz musicians don't attempt to resolve the tensions that result from polarities. Instead, they work with the tensions—and even "play" with them—to bring about something better or different. If you're an educator, how might you describe this concept to students? If you're a student, how can this expand your views about innovation? And if you're a leader, practitioner, or consultant, how might you replicate this concept in your organization or in your client organizations?

The Beauty of Improvisation

In the same way that skilled jazz musicians work at reconciling individuals' needs for self-expression with their responsibility to others on their teams, so must leaders in almost any environment. It's also important to keep in mind that improvisation is more than merely preparing for surprises and adapting or responding skillfully and quickly. In some ways it's similar to the music of a symphony orchestra, in the way that it transcends words. Unlike classical music, however, improvisation takes on a life of its own and goes where it needs to go. When this happens, jazz musicians willingly surrender and "go with the flow," remaining open to whatever might emerge.

In business, improvisation manifests when people who are tasked with producing new ideas and approaches gather together to engage in brainstorming and other forms of idea generation. To some, the process of free association might appear counterintuitive, but it can actually provide viable outcomes. Ideation and improvisation can generate ideas that lead directly to value-generating inventions and innovative approaches because these activities bypass traditional ways of thinking—or they expand them. During the brainstorming process, as in jamming sessions, people build on one another's ideas, exemplifying how the whole is often greater than the sum of its parts.

Although jazz musicians must rely on one another to perfect a distinctive style, they do this in a different way from their symphony orchestra counterparts. For example, the goal of most symphony orchestra musicians is to achieve mastery by following a score; whereas, in jazz, the goal is to produce an entirely new melody or theme. In business, the goal that most closely corresponds to that of jazz is the introduction of new or enhanced products or services, streamlined processes, or paradigm shifts. Any of these outcomes might be enabled by an entirely different business model, by entering new markets, or by expanding globally. With that, there's a great deal that we can learn from jazz musicians, but first a story about a highly skilled jazz great whose legacy illustrates the critically important innovation enablers of inspiration, talent, and perseverance.

▨ ▨ ▨

In the 1920s, Louis Armstrong, often described as the "father of jazz," was a popular character who dazzled crowds—both onstage and offstage. Armstrong was described as "gregarious," "lovable," and "charismatic." Blessed with a stage presence unlike any other performer in his time, he played at a very young age in many major cities throughout the United States and Europe. Most significant about Armstrong's success, however, was the way in which his personality, artistry, and accomplishments allowed him to access the upper echelons of American society. This meant frequenting restaurants and hotels that predominantly catered to Whites, and at a time when people of color had difficulty penetrating even the most basic racial barriers.

Coming into prominence in the "Roaring 20's" as an innovative and inventive musician, Armstrong was a foundational influence for jazz, and ultimately, for rock and roll as well. His prominence is evident by his induction into the Rock and Roll Hall of Fame and by his posthumous lifetime Grammy Lifetime Achievement Award in 1972 from the Academy of Recording Arts and Sciences. The famous singer and actor Bing Crosby once said about Armstrong, "He is the beginning and the end of music in America." And the jazz great, Duke Ellington, said, "If anyone was a master, it was Louis Armstrong."

Differentiation

Although Armstrong's career began with mastery of the cornet, he also had an extraordinary talent for improvisation as a virtuoso trumpet player. In fact, he was among the first musicians to enable the trumpet to emerge as a solo instrument in jazz. Armstrong's innovations raised the bar in many other ways, but what is most remarkable about his success is that, as the grandson of African slaves, he had to overcome the formidable challenge of growing up in abject poverty.

Abandoned by his father as an infant, Armstrong grew up in a rough section of New Orleans and at a very young age, began selling newspapers by day, and hauling coal at night, to keep his mother from a life of prostitution. Although this gave him a difficult start, it also played a key role in his becoming a very talented musician. That's because, by delivering coal to the brothels and dance halls in New Orleans' red-light district, he was exposed to the bands that jammed there.

Louis Armstrong also found inspiration when working for a family called the Karnofskys, a Lithuanian-Jewish immigrant family that owned a junk yard. Knowing that Armstrong had no father to guide him, the Karnofskys took him under their wing, feeding and nurturing him as they would a member of their own family. Amazed that they would do this—especially since they were subjected to the same kind of discrimination that he was—Armstrong wore a Star of David pendant during his entire adult life. In this way, he honored the Karnofskys for their inspiration, generosity, and love.

An Unlikely Start

Although Armstrong was initially inspired by the Karnofskys and the jazz greats of the red-light district, it was the New Orleans Home for Colored Waifs that created the tangible platform for his career in music. Having been sent to the home numerous times for delinquency, Armstrong frequently came in contact with the administrator, Professor Peter Davis, who eventually made him leader of the school's band. At only 13 years of age, Louis Armstrong began to draw attention by the way he played music.

After being released from the Home for Colored Waifs, he got his first job as a musician—at 14 years of age. Learning from older musicians whenever he had the opportunity, Armstrong eventually won the support of Joe "King" Oliver, who acted as a mentor and father figure in much the same way that the administrator for the New Orleans Home for Colored Waifs had. After "going to the University," which is what Louis Armstrong called traveling with and learning from Joe Oliver, he eventually replaced Oliver as the band's leader.

At age 20, Armstrong had already begun to establish himself as an innovator. He did this by visibly distinguishing himself from other musicians with a style that was difficult to imitate. In 1922, he took a calculated risk, as many innovators do, by joining the many musicians who were moving to Chicago. However, Armstrong left Chicago a few years later to accept an invitation to play with an established orchestra in New York City, where he could seek more prominent billing while continuing to grow professionally.

When working in New York, Armstrong switched from cornet to trumpet, and even experimented with the trombone, as a way of blending in better with other musicians. However, when he ultimately found the tightly controlled style of the orchestra leader too restrictive, he returned to Chicago, which had become the center of the jazz universe. As one of the first jazz musicians to inject his style and personality into solos, Armstrong was finally able to make a sufficient living without his day jobs. Timing also worked in his favor, with the Roaring 20s being part of a boom that encouraged people to spend money on entertainment.

Reinvention

Unfortunately, Armstrong's connections with members of Al Capone's famous Chicago gangs threatened to hold him hostage to a lifestyle and a musical style that he would eventually need to reject. And when the Great Depression of the 1930s virtually closed down Chicago's jazz scene, Armstrong looked for a way to respond to the challenge and to simultaneously escape Capone's gang. After moving to Los Angeles in search of new opportunities, he appeared in his first movie, *Ex-Flame*, which helped him become known as both a musician and singer.

Once again, Armstrong distinguished himself as a true innovator by bending original melodies and the lyrics of existing songs. He also became the ultimate improviser—in both film and song. For example, when his sheet music once fell to the floor during one of his performances, he shouted, "I done forgot the words," and began to "scat sing." By using sounds and syllables in place of actual lyrics, Armstrong, without any conscious intent, popularized a new art form.

In 1931, when swing bands became the rage in Chicago, Louis Armstrong played in ensembles that were similar to the style of Guy Lombardo. However, his desire to experiment with something new didn't sit well with Chicago's mob leaders, who finally insisted that he get out of town. Armstrong's creative response was a cross-country tour of the United States, but after being shadowed the entire time by the mob, he ultimately escaped to Europe. Interesting to note is that, despite his travels within the U.S. and abroad, Armstrong never forgot his roots. Throughout his professional career, he corresponded by mail with old friends in New Orleans while also incorporating nostalgic tales of these characters into his music routines.

An Incremental and Disruptive Innovator

As an innovator who engaged in continuous process improvement, Armstrong was one of the first artists who improved his performances by listening to his music on reel-to-reel tapes. Taking them with him as he traveled to and from various gigs, and learning about music that ranged from blues, swing, and jazz, to classical symphonies and opera, he exemplified great breadth and depth as a musician. With an appreciation of other musical forms, Armstrong also recomposed the music of his time. In this respect, he incrementally improved on something already in existence while also employing what we would call "disruptive strategies" today.

Neither Armstrong's incremental innovations nor his disruptive innovations were a guarantee of continued success, however. When his unorthodox methods of playing caused problems with both his fingers and lips, he found it necessary to improvise once again. Returning to the United States, he reinvented himself, appearing once again in movies and even attempting his first theatrical appearance. Armstrong's continual efforts to improve and experiment eventually resulted in his being chosen as a substitute for the widely acclaimed bandleader Rudy Vallee. This opportunity enabled Armstrong to become the first African-American to host a national broadcast on the CBS radio network.

In the mid-1960s, Louis Armstrong gave up traveling to settle permanently in New York. However, his idea of "settling" didn't mean settling in the usual sense. In 1964, he recorded his biggest-selling record, "Hello, Dolly!" which lasted 22 weeks on the Hot 100 list and quickly went to No. 1 on the pop chart. Proof of his being loved by both young and old was when, at 62 years of age, Louis Armstrong dislodged The Beatles from the Number 1 position that they'd held for 14 consecutive weeks. After that, he continued to live out a favorite expression: "Musicians don't retire; they stop when there's no more music in them." In the last few years of his career, Armstrong's failing health restricted his schedule, but he continued to play until one month before his 70th birthday, at which point he died in his sleep, leaving behind a legacy that can't be overstated.

■　■　■

Why profile Louis Armstrong in this chapter? Two reasons. First, although we might think of him as a highly successful performer, Armstrong was also an exemplary leader. A banjo player named Johnny

Saint Cyr once said about his band leading style that he was "very broad-minded" and that "he always did his best to feature each individual." These are common traits of leaders who know how to inspire and sustain innovation.

The second reason for profiling Louis Armstrong is that he exemplifies the kind of innovator who continually rises above adversity by improving on winning strategies from the past while also experimenting and reinventing. What can we learn from Armstrong's professional success and his wisdom? And what might we learn from other jazz musicians that came after him? Armstrong's life story, and the many quotes from other jazz greats, can provide food for thought as well as inspiration.

In keeping with the theme of this chapter, the pearls of wisdom that follow—known metaphorically in the world of jazz world as "riffs"—succinctly describe the parallels between successful jazz musicians and successful innovators. These pearls also illustrate how jazz can be an instructive medium. If you don't know what riffs are, don't worry. They're simply "interpretations," "variations," or "translations" of themes. They're also short musical motifs that are typically used as introductions or refrains.

Structure versus Freeform Approaches

In *Jamming*, Kao defines a riff as something capable of standing on its own. By using a riff as a metaphor, we can describe how people function individually and in teams. When working effectively in teams, they synchronize their efforts, taking turns at solving challenges and then deciding how best to implement ideas. But almost any team effort has individual performance at its root, so in John Kao's words, individual performance is, "always enabled by—and never detached from—the team that facilitates [individual performance]."

The way in which jazz can solve challenges makes it both unpredictable and exciting. It's also what enables jazz musicians to change with the times in the same ways by which successful leaders and organizations change with new demographics and ever-evolving consumer needs. But does everyone appreciate jazz? People unfamiliar with it often believe that this form of music is nothing more than a series of random tunes without discipline, structure, or process.

The foundational characteristics of jazz aren't often obvious to an uninformed audience, in the same way that an organization's infrastructure isn't usually evident to customers or key stakeholders. So most people don't know that it's the structure in jazz that actually enables freedom and free-form expression. Of course, the same can be true in business environments. Bobby Hutcherson, one of the greatest jazz vibraphonists, captured the essence of what structure is to jazz when he said, "The whole thing of being in music is not to control it but to be swept away by it. If you're swept away by it, you can't wait to do it again, and the same magical moments always come."

We've seen throughout this book how innovation must begin with inspiration and freedom of expression. In the first subsection, we learn that successful leaders of innovation provide structure for new ideas by fostering conditions that facilitate "creative collision." In these environments, employees are able to "collide" with one another, either physically or virtually, to share and build on ideas.

When people are able to translate their ideas into actions, they complete the innovation cycle. They can then, in Bobby Hutcherson's words, get "swept away" by the passion that surrounds new ideas. When this happens, employees remain actively engaged and supportive of their organizations' missions and goals. This active support is an essential part of innovation in that it underscores the connection between creativity and innovation at the same time that it fuels existing talent and attracts new talent.

Individual and Team Creativity

Nancy Wilson, an American singer of blues, jazz, cabaret, and pop once said, "Even though there are really no original themes or stories to tell, it's about the way you tell the story." She should know, after having produced more than 70 albums and receiving 3 Grammy Awards. But there's still another important comparison to be made between successful jazz musicians and leaders of innovation: It's their respect for simplicity.

Charles Mingus, a highly influential jazz double bassist, composer, and bandleader once said: "Making the simple complicated is commonplace; making the complicated simple, awesomely simple, that's creativity." Because jazz can be at once simple, yet complex, it mirrors some of the basic principles of good design and good leadership in the way that it brings creativity alive. Still another distinguishing feature of jazz is its distributed power. This is often what makes some people think that it's without structure.

In business environments, this sharing of control is what leaders and employees who want to make a difference often find inspiring and liberating. So how exactly does distributed power work in jazz? When jazz musicians jam, they formulate loose strategies for deciding who will do what, yet always with the idea that they'll revise decisions if situations dictate the need for other approaches. And so jazz is about synchronous and asynchronous connections.

Jazz is also about each player's engagement in a give-and-take relationship. This is evident when jazz musicians provide the accompaniment that allows each player opportunities to shine through solos. And this loosely defined approach is also similar to the strategies employed by start-up and other organizations that must achieve and maintain speed through flexibility. Their leaders typically formulate entire portfolios of strategies in advance and retain them for future reference, with the intention of drawing on them whenever real-time challenges or opportunities present themselves.

Democracy in Action

The saxophonist Stan Getz, best known for his worldwide hit single *The Girl from Ipanema*, says about creativity and jazz, "A good quartet is like a good conversation among friends." In his article, "All About Jazz," Greg Thomas, an astute advocate and also a critic of jazz, says, "Jazz is improvisation and syncopation, with resilience and flow, with earthy elegance, nuance, and subtlety, with the integrity of individual expression within (usually) a group context, with true democracy in action."

Why is a democracy so important in jazz and in today's work settings? It's what can motivate and retain top talent, particularly Millennials. And this talent is most often a driving force that can help organizations in all sectors enhance overall effectiveness and facilitate competitive advantage in the private sector.

Diversity

As mentioned in the introduction to this chapter and in other parts of this book, jazz musicians continually build on one another's ideas. For this reason, the phrase "Yes-but" is discouraged in jazz and also in most organizations' brainstorming sessions. That's because "but" is a word that can inhibit the creative process. By contrast, the phrase "Yes, and" can help teams produce high-quality ideas that can lead to elegant solutions. That's because the concept of "Yes, and" encourages and supports diverse perspectives and approaches. It also acknowledges an individual's ability—and responsibility—to accept someone else's idea or piece and add to it or take it somewhere else, even if there's a mistake in it. Then the next person passes it on to others for further additions or changes.

People in technology professions call this process "remix." Sometimes it's employed to change something completely, and at other times, simply to build on something already in existence. Professional facilitators sometimes use remix to reframe current assumptions and methods. With this approach, no idea is bad because people can transform almost anything into something that's viable, relevant, and timely.

Sonny Chriss, an alto saxophonist who was prominent during the bebop era of jazz, described the remix process when he said, "Everybody takes from everybody else and adds their own thing and goes on from there." The legendary jazz vocalist and Tony Award and Daytime Grammy Award winner Pearl Bailey captured the essence of what diversity brings to the creative process when she said, "Never, never rest contented with any circle of ideas but always be certain that a wider one is still possible."

How easy is this? It's not. In fact, there is typically more friction within heterogeneous groups than in homogeneous groups. However, if team members of diverse groups accept early on that conflict is inevitable, they're more inclined to value their differences than feel a need to eliminate or invalidate them. When people see the results of diverse perspectives, innovation truly becomes a team sport for employees and a sustainable differentiator for their organizations.

Listening and Learning

Sun Ra (born Herman Poole Blount) was a prolific jazz composer, bandleader, synthesizer, and piano player as well as a poet and philosopher known for his "cosmic philosophy." On one occasion, his comments seemed like antecedents to today's current rap music. Humorously capturing the concept of listening and learning in one of his compositions, he said in rap style, "You made a mistake. You did something wrong. Make another mistake, and do something right!"

Sun Ra's quotes are a reminder that in order to communicate—and innovate—effectively, leaders must be proficient with a variety of different media, both oral and written. That often means sharing a compelling vision through storytelling, which has the power to motivate people to take action. The kind of communication that supports creativity and innovation also demands that people communicate freely, openly, and—in today's fast-paced environments—*instantly*.

Inherent in our current electronic communication, however, also lies a new challenge: lost meaning and misinterpreted messages. Benny Goodman, a clarinetist, and bandleader, known as the "king of swing" during the 1930s era, shared some wisdom that we can easily apply today. He said, "Sometimes when you start losing detail, whether it's in music or in life, something as small as failing to be polite, and you start to lose substance."

From this, we know that in organizational settings, and particularly when leaders speak, people hear more than words. Tone, pacing, body language, and eye contact all send messages. Often leaders overlook the fact that the most effective communication is usually a two-way process. And they can only successfully innovate if they practice active listening, which requires interpreting cues correctly. To build a culture that fosters innovation and experimentation, leaders must actively listen to their employees and to one another.

Experimentation and Learning

To successfully innovate, leaders must also engage in learning through experimentation, which usually involves a good balance between "learning" and "unlearning." In high performing teams, as in jazz ensembles, people listen and follow cues—both verbal and nonverbal— to learn what each player is saying and thinking. When doing this, jazz musicians (and individuals in business settings) know when it's their turn to play and when they need to allow others to play.

Successful leaders are attuned to the nonverbal and verbal cues that can guide them in deciding when to lead and when to inspire others. Listening and learning means taking lessons from failures as well as successes. Those who excel at innovation persevere if they believe an idea has merit. They also continue to experiment after something fails on the first, second, or third try. They know that innovation is, above all, a numbers game, and that it's also about creating something of value for consumers or organizations, regardless of how many attempts that might require. However, successful innovators also know when and where to draw the line so that resources can be allocated to innovations that show more promise.

Count Basie, the famous jazz pianist, organist, and composer described this idea with a riff when he said, "If you play a tune, and a person don't tap their feet, don't play the tune." Surely Count Basie earned the right to give that advice. Formally recognized for his many innovations in music, he led a band for almost 50 years, and had 4 records inducted into the Grammy Hall of Fame. To what did Count Basie attribute his success? A good deal of experimentation and learning.

Successful innovators know that it's critically important to discover why customers, clients, or constituents are "tapping their feet"—or not. In fact, these concepts are basic to effective design thinking and consumer insights work, in which the behaviors and attitudes of consumers are formally observed and analyzed. Insights professionals keep the cycle of innovation going—from experimenting with ideas to experimenting with implementation. Then they continue to try out different designs or solutions, based on what consumers continue to buy—or don't buy.

Forgetting and Unlearning

Dianne Reeves, a contemporary jazz singer, once said about her creative efforts in cooking and in music, "[When creating jazz] I work with my ear to try to make it feel right." And about cooking, she said, "I just keep changing it until I like the way it tastes." Jazz saxophonist and composer Charlie Parker once said, "You've got to learn your instrument. Then you practice, practice, practice. And then, when you finally get up there on the bandstand, forget all that and just wail."

Practicing is what skilled musicians do—as well as learning, letting go, and trusting that their talents and hard work will serve them well. Most leaders would agree that, when experimenting and improvising, the ultimate challenge lies in developing skills to deal with uncertainty. Jazz players call their response to uncertainty "making it up as one goes along." Although Charlie Parker might believe that success is about "forgetting" and "just wailing," the legendary trumpeter, bandleader, and composer Miles Davis describes it as "mastering the art of un-learning."

In the same way that explorers, bushwhackers, or cross-country skiers expend tremendous energy, perseverance, and courage when they cut new paths, so do business leaders when they attempt to "unlearn" what is no longer ensuring their organizations' success. Learning and unlearning can occur in a variety of ways. For example, after jazz performances, musicians typically discuss what worked, what didn't work, and what might be done differently next time. Military organizations also do this as an effective way to learn and "unlearn," calling it "after-event analysis" or "post-mortem evaluation."

Although many organizations outside the military also use this tool, it still tends to be vastly under-used, given its potential value. This is unfortunate because when people take time out to reflect, they can significantly enhance their organizations' success. We can see how forgetting and unlearning are vital activities for organizations that wish to develop products or provide services for people in both developed and developing countries.

However, many organizations—especially those that are only doing business in the developed world—give in to the natural tendency to build on previous successes. This is true even when the act of producing something new could result in a more valuable or cost-effective strategy. Vijay Govindarajan, featured in a chapter at the beginning of this book, says that to innovate successfully in developing markets, leaders must "forget" about what made them successful in established markets, and instead, create from scratch.

A Balance Between Old and New

Stan Kenton, a pianist, arranger, and composer who led the 39-piece "Innovations in Modern Music Orchestra" once said, "I don't think you can replace great themes. But I think people do want to hear fresh arrangements of them. They don't want to hear them played the same way all the time." How might this relate to the world of business?

To protect the success of a brand, leaders must know how to preserve it. Although they need to build on the foundation of their brand to satisfy current needs, they must also keep in mind that consumers are almost always hungry for something new. The late Warren Bennis, Professor of Management at the University of California, wasn't a musician but he captured an important task for leaders who see value in learning from people in the music world. Bennis said, "Leaders must encourage their organizations to dance to forms of music yet to be heard."

Miles Davis said something similar when he told his musicians, "Don't play what's there; play what's not there." What did Davis mean by that? No one knows for sure, but it was probably his way of encouraging people to reach for higher goals—or to play their own music rather than copying others. It might have also been his way of telling his musicians to look beyond the obvious. Jazz musicians do this when they draw from an ever growing "portfolio" of skill sets and experience, giving themselves license to depart at times from strategies based on the loose agreements that they constructed during jamming sessions.

We can learn a great deal from jazz, but one of the most important learnings is that musicians—and innovators—need to be agile, dynamic, and responsive to one another. This is especially true if a mistake requires a corresponding strategy or when people need to quickly implement a new strategy for other reasons. A jazz ensemble also exemplifies the ultimate in team performance: a democracy and meritocracy in action. What can business leaders learn from this? In addition to exploring ways to satisfy external customer needs, organizations need to meet the requirements of internal customers (i.e., employees).

One way to do this is to select and develop top talent with a focus on responsiveness and resiliency. By knowing what constitutes good jazz, and having the ability to improvise, successful business leaders can ask questions during employment interviews that assess flexibility and agility. Once the right talent is in place, these leaders also ask questions such as: "How can I ensure bench strength?" "How can I inspire the team to reach new heights?" And, "How might I shake things up enough so that tethers to the past can fall away?"

Execution

The famous musician Clark Terry was still an expert innovator at 93 years of age. With over 900 recordings and a career in jazz that spanned more than 70 years, he performed for 8 U.S. presidents and served as Jazz Ambassador for many State Department tours in the Middle East and Africa. At the time of his death, Clark had been featured in more than 50 jazz festivals on all 7 continents. His advice about how to stay current is remarkably simple: "Imitate, assimilate, and innovate."

Many people believe there are no original ideas—only dots that creative people connect and then use as road maps for new or enhanced products, services, processes, or paradigm shifts. Jazz pianist and instructor, Benny Green recognized this when he said, "A jazz musician is a juggler who uses harmonies instead of oranges." Successful leaders of innovation imitate jugglers when they balance their energies to meet day-to-day operational demands while simultaneously preparing for more balls to be thrown at them.

John Kao says, "Jazz—like business—implies a series of balancing acts." And although not all innovation is deliberate and planned, Kao tells us, "It must always be disciplined—but never driven—by formulas, agendas, sheet music. It must always be pushing outward, forward, upward—and therefore, inevitably, against complacency."

Failure and Other Enablers

Ironically, innovation is often the result of fortuitous mistakes. Cole Hawkins once said, "If you don't make mistakes, you aren't really trying." Ornette Coleman said, "It was when I found out I could make mistakes that I knew I was on to something." And Miles Davis said, "Do not fear mistakes. There are none." Successful innovation leaders allow room for error. Some even encourage it, knowing that it's a necessary element in experimenting and learning.

This is not to imply that leaders should tolerate shoddy workmanship, uncompleted tasks, or mistakes in areas where a lack of compliance or failure to meet high quality standards could result in dire consequences. But people need to accept that innovation is a trial-and-error process in which errors are often ways of eliminating options and learning about what doesn't work as well as what does. Jazz musician Dave Brubeck said about making mistakes, "There's a way of playing safe, there's a way of using tricks, and there's the way I like to play, which is dangerously—where you're going to take a chance on making mistakes in order to create something you haven't created before."

Frank Barrett, a jazz musician and professor of management at the Naval Postgraduate School in Monterey, California, wrote about mistakes in his book *Yes to the Mess: Surprising Leadership Lessons from Jazz*. In a 2012 interview with *Forbes*, Barrett said, "Endemic to jazz, errors push musicians to reach beyond their comfort zones.... Jazz musicians assume that you can take any bad situation and make it into a good situation." Obviously, this is a good lesson for most business leaders.

Faith in the Process

One cannot underestimate the value of an organizational culture that produces the right conditions for generating and executing ideas. We've seen many examples of how a compelling vision can overcome fear and uncertainty by keeping people focused on what's possible. Grammy Award winner Sarah Vaughan once said, "When I sing, trouble can sit right on my shoulder, and I don't even notice." Fats Waller once said, "So easy, when you know how." For others, however, neither music nor leadership is easy. The famous trumpet player and composer Dizzy Gillespie said, "It's taken me all my life to learn what not to play." And Miles Davis said, "You have to play a long time to be able to play like yourself."

In *Yes to the Mess*, Frank Barrett describes a concept he calls "radical receptivity." By that, he means having faith in one's self and others to generate ideas and bring them to fruition. Faith is critical to innovation because producing and implementing new ideas is sometimes a lengthy process that requires a great deal of patience and perseverance. Sometimes when people use trial-and-error strategies to learn what works—and what doesn't—they can get discouraged. The most famous jazz singer in the 1920s and 1930s, Bessie Smith, implied that faith was needed for the journey when she said,

"It's a long old road, but I know I'm gonna find the end." Not everyone is hardwired for faith, however, so leaders must be able to connect on all levels, with a variety of different strategies and leadership styles, if they're to provide the necessary inspiration, guidance, and support for innovation.

Leading not Dictating

In the *Leading Innovation* section, we learn that the leadership models of the 1970s and 1980s made sharp distinctions between leaders and managers. There was a perception of leaders as those who are capable of working within boundary-less structures because they rely on their personal power. By contrast, managers were viewed as needing position power to control, monitor, and ensure conformity and compliance through their place on an organizational hierarchy. Managers were also expected to make sure that everyone "sang" or "played" like everyone else.

The legendary singer and songwriter, Billie Holiday, described the leadership model of the 1970s and 1980s when she said, "If I'm going to sing like someone else, then I don't need to sing at all." When considering the needs of a new generation of employees, today's leaders and music directors must *lead* rather than *dictate*. Unlike a marching band where people are expected to follow a beat and comply with a leader who insists on uniformity, consistency, and predictability, the power that fuels jazz—and that motivates and inspires today's top talent —is decentralized and distributed.

Head and Heart Leadership

JoAnn Falletta, Music Director and conductor of the Buffalo Philharmonic Orchestra and the Virginia Symphony Orchestra, says this about leadership on her website: "In this time of rapid and unpredictable change in the arts, it is no surprise that the music director entering the 21st century bears markedly different responsibilities than did his 19th century predecessor … Added requirements are broad … vision, a clear understanding of the … objectives of the organization and the courage to explore new possibilities and options coupled with the wisdom to preserve the best of tradition." Falletta's observations of effective leadership also include leading with both head and heart, for which she herself is known.

Jazz vocalist and Rock and Roll Hall of Fame inductee Dinah Washington described the value in leading from the heart when she said, "I lead with my heart all the time." Ella Fitzgerald, the legendary jazz singer often referred to as the "queen of jazz," once said, "Just don't give up trying to do what you really want to do. Where there is love and inspiration, I don't think you can go wrong." In truth, leaders must know when to lead from the heart and when it's appropriate to operate from the head. Operating from the head keeps efforts aligned with the organization's mission, strategies, and needs of consumers. Leading from the heart inspires courage and helps people manage change, take the necessary risks to innovate, and perform at their best.

A Few Last Riffs

This chapter would be incomplete without some riffs from unexpected sources. The Greek philosopher Plato once said, "Music gives a soul to the universe, wings to the mind, flight to the imagination, and life to everything." *And Albert Einstein once said, "Logic will get you from A to B. Imagination will take you everywhere."*

Whether you're a leader, consultant, practitioner, educator, or student, it's our hope that this book has stirred your imagination and empowered you. After learning about the many best practices, strategies, and success stories within it, you undoubtedly feel more confident about innovating in a world of continuing complexity and challenge.

You've no doubt learned from our many experts that innovation today must go beyond solitary endeavors. The "Yes, and" approach that's basic to jazz is needed for effective teamwork and collaboration, and can be applied almost anywhere. What's more, this approach can make innovation a thrilling adventure to be enthusiastically celebrated.

With that, here is my wish for you: May you learn from symphony orchestra musicians who are driven by a passionate desire for mastery and excellence. May you also "play" at your work, as jazz musicians do—with total abandon and sheer joy. And when you're innovating, may your diligence and imagination merge together in a genuine labor of love!

Marilyn Blocker
Managing Principal
www.innovationoutcomes.com
info@innovationoutcomes.com
www.linkedin.com/in/marilynjblocker

IV. Acknowledgments

Andrea Zintz, Megan Mitchell, and I thank all of the contributors who made this book possible. We also thank our clients and the organizations that inspired much of the material in this book, including those organizations that allowed their leaders and practitioners to participate in this work. We extend a special appreciation to Frans van Houten for his introduction and to Jim Amos, Nick Donofrio, and Robin Karol, who each took time to review and endorse this book. Additionally, we individually acknowledge all those who personally inspired and supported us, as follows:

- *A big thanks to my mother, who reinforced creativity in my earliest years. Thanks also to the many friends and colleagues who continually encouraged me to write. I also want to thank the special leaders for whom I've worked and who encouraged me to innovate, specifically Jim McLaughlin, Dave Bjornson, and Keith Flagler. And a huge thanks goes to Andrea and Megan for all their hard work, stamina, and optimism. These talented professionals brought unique skill sets and experience, enhancing the book in their own ways as described in the Prelude and in the Why This Book? chapters. Finally, I'd like to thank my husband, soul mate, and best friend, Ed Blocker, whose joie de vivre and ongoing support continually excite and inspire me.* — Marilyn Blocker, Managing Principal of Innovation Outcomes

- *I'd like to thank my parents, Paul and Lucille, my many friends, family, and colleagues for all their love, encouragement and inspiration in writing this book. In particular I would like to thank Siamak, Merilee, Tom, Johanna, Marci, Karen, Lee-Anne, Homer, Heidi, Gillian, Kristen, and Peter for being both sounding boards and cheerleaders. Thanks to Bill and Erni who kept me fed and watered. I would also like to thank Marilyn and Andrea for their support, professionalism, expertise, and gentle coercion to get this book ready to share with the world. From all, I have appreciated your support more than you can know.* — Megan Mitchell, Principal, Megan Mitchell Consulting & Program Director, Centre for Excellence in Applied Innovation Management, Schulich Executive Education Centre, Schulich School of Business, York University

- *The collaboration with Marilyn and Megan has been fun and enlightening, and I thank them both for their support and understanding through all the zigs and zags of life during interviews and book-writing. Thanks to the members of Strategic Leadership Resources, Margherita and Kelly, whose support allowed me to attend to my writing. Thanks also to my husband and best friend, David Bernstein, who supports me in all my efforts with love and understanding, and to my children, Ali and Jessie—who inspire me to stay creative.* — Andrea Zintz, Ph.D., President of Strategic Leadership Resources LLC

V. Author Biographies

Marilyn Blocker

As Managing Principal for Innovation Outcomes, Marilyn Blocker draws on a 30-year background that includes multi-industry leadership and consulting experience. She has met challenges at all stages of the organizational life cycle, in both start-up and mature organizations, and at corporate, division, and business unit levels.

While serving on a variety of senior leadership teams, Marilyn contributed to strategic planning and operational decision making, most recently as Vice President at a Silicon Valley-based high tech incubator site of Royal Philips (formerly Philips Electronics North America Corporation). She functioned previously as one of the founding leaders of a John Hancock Financial Services subsidiary and had also held leadership roles at Providence Health and Services, Verizon Communications (formerly GTE), and The Coca-Cola Company. At Providence Health and Services, she led a successful culture transformation effort and at John Hancock (now Manulife), she helped its First Signature Bank & Trust (FSB&T), a start-up banking subsidiary become the 12th largest VISA gold card distributor in the U.S. only five years after inception.

Marilyn's blend of experience in quality management, organizational development, and human resources management has enabled her to continually focus on the people, partnerships, and processes that support successful business transformations and sustainable innovation. Her key practice areas include individual and team coaching, leadership development, and change management. She has provided both internal and external consulting services in the public and not-for-profit sectors as well as Fortune 100 and global leaders in technology, healthcare, financial services, consumer products, telecommunications, and manufacturing.

Marilyn graduated with honors from the University of Maryland, where she earned an MBA and an MSM (Master of Science in Management). She also holds a certificate in Executive Management from Cornell University and is a certified Senior Professional in Human Resources (SPHR) through the Human Resources Certification Institute (HRCI). She has written for BusinessWeek and the University of Wisconsin, served on executive committees of various not-for-profit and municipal boards, and has spoken at professional association meetings and conferences. Marilyn has also functioned as a guest lecturer, graduate school advisor, and adjunct professor at New York University (NYU), teaching creativity and innovation. To learn more about her leadership and consulting experience, go to www.innovationoutcomes.com and https://www.linkedin.com/in/marilynjblocker

Megan Mitchell

Megan is an accomplished speaker, collaborator, facilitator, and educator with 25 years of experience in innovation, leadership development, and change management. She is the Principal of Megan Mitchell Consulting and the Program Director for the Centre of Excellence in Applied Innovation Management at Schulich Executive Education Centre, Schulich School of Business at York University, one of the world's leading business schools.

Megan's sales, marketing, and leadership roles in Fortune 100 companies have given her a strategic lens and a practical edge when consulting, facilitating, training, and providing team and one-on-one coaching. Prior to starting her own firm, she was the Director of Innovation and Leadership Development with Johnson & Johnson Inc. and Pfizer Consumer Healthcare. In one of her corporate roles, Megan designed strategies for building a culture of innovation, delivered training, and led transformational projects for innovation teams tasked with critical business opportunities. In particular, she helped one team win the Canadian National Quality Institute Award for a Healthy Workplace and another save over $2 million in the project's first year. In recognition of her leadership, she received the prestigious W.E. Upjohn award for Innovation.

Megan currently assists individuals, executive management teams, and cross-functional groups to maximize productivity and successfully develop creative and innovative solutions for today's business challenges. For her, leadership is all about building capacity and managing one's own creative resources to foster supportive environments. Passionate about facilitating effective change in a positive and energetic way, she also enjoys working with leaders and teams to establish vision; identify ways to build a climate that brings out the best in people; and achieve team alignment at cascading levels of organizations.

Megan has been a frequent leader at the World Future Society, Mindcamp Creativity Conference, and the annual conference for the Creative Problem Solving Institute. She holds a Master's Certificate in Innovation Management from the Schulich Executive Education Centre (York) and earned a B.A. in Honors Business Administration (HBA) from the Ivey School of Business from the University of Western Ontario, Canada. A lifelong learner, she recently completed a Certificate in Positive Psychology from the Wholebeing Institute.

Megan holds certifications in various assessments including DISC and FourSight, and is a Professional Learning Executive with certifications in Learning Strategy, Needs Analysis, Design and Instructional Tools and Techniques. For more information about Megan's background and experience, please visit www.meganmitchell.ca and https://www.linkedin.com/in/mitchellmegan.

Andrea C. Zintz, Ph.D.

Andrea Zintz is President of Strategic Leadership Resources LLC (SLR), specializing in executive and high potential leadership strategy, succession and development. She has over 40 years of experience in leadership development, change management, Human Resources development, and training. Acting as a consultant, strategist, team facilitator, executive coach, and trainer, Andrea helps organizations undergoing restructurings, mergers, acquisitions, and changes in management and key processes.

Andrea works primarily with senior and high-potential leaders in business units of Fortune 500 corporations and mid-sized companies in a variety of business sectors. She has provided consulting services to companies in consumer products, pharmaceuticals, electronics, consumer health care, commercial real estate, energy, advertising, medical device, defense, manufacturing and financial services. Andrea's strategic focus is the development of a strong leadership pipeline. She has deep expertise in raising self-awareness and in training sales and line leaders to create high performance teams through coaching, teaching, and mentoring. She is currently co-authoring a book with Jane Firth entitled *Grit, Grace and Gravitas: Demystifying Executive Presence*.

Prior to starting her consulting practice, Andrea was vice president of Hudson Talent Management, and President of Andrea Zintz and Associates LLC, a leadership and organization development consultancy. She was also the co-founder of the Center for Inquiring Leadership, a training company for leadership effectiveness. In these roles she designed and executed landmark work in the development of internal coaches within major companies. As Vice President of Human Resources and Management Board member of the Johnson & Johnson subsidiary, Ortho Biotech, Inc., Andrea helped lead the growth of the company from $40 million to $500 million in a 6-year period, and launched 2 breakthrough biotech products that lead the market today. She also led executive leadership development for North America from J&J Corporate.

During her tenure at J&J, Andrea was highly awarded for her work in organization culture transformation, Human Resources, and leadership development, where her special interests included executive women advancement, diversity, and mentoring. She was trained as a Black Belt as part of the J&J Process Excellence effort and as an examiner and team leader for the Competitive Assessment Process at J&J. Andrea received her M.A. and Ph.D. in Human and Organization Systems from Fielding Graduate University, is a member of the National OD Network, and serves on the board of Dress for Success Mercer County. She is also a recipient of the YWCA Tribute to Women in Industry Award. To learn more about Andrea's background and work, go to www.strategicleadershipresources.com and www.linkedin.com/in/andrea-zintz.

VI. Contributors

VI. Contributors

VII. Index

VII. Index

Made in the USA
Columbia, SC
29 May 2018